JUDICIAL REVIEW AND BUREAUCRATIC IMPACT

International and Interdisciplinary Perspectives

How effective are the courts in controlling bureaucracies? What impact does judicial review have on the agencies which are targeted by its rulings? For the first time, a collection of essays brings together the insights of two intellectual disciplines which have hitherto explored these questions separately: political science and law/socio-legal studies. Leading international scholars from both fields present new research which focuses on the relationship between judicial review and bureaucratic behaviour. Individual chapters discuss fundamental conceptual and methodological issues, in addition to presenting a number of empirical case studies from various parts of the world: the United States, Canada, Australia, Israel and the United Kingdom. This volume constitutes a landmark text offering an international, interdisciplinary and empirical perspective on judicial review's impact on bureaucracies. It will significantly advance the research agenda concerning judicial review and its relationship to social change.

DR MARC HERTOGH is Associate Professor of Socio-Legal Studies at the Faculty of Law, Tilburg University, The Netherlands.

DR SIMON HALLIDAY is Nicholas de B. Katzenbach Research Fellow at the Centre for Socio-Legal Studies at the University of Oxford.

CAMBRIDGE STUDIES IN LAW AND SOCIETY

Cambridge Studies in Law and Society aims to publish the best scholarly work on legal discourse and practice in its social and institutional contexts, combining theoretical insights and empirical research.

The fields that it covers are studies of law in action; the sociology of law; the anthropology of law; cultural studies of law, including the role of legal discourses in social formations; law and economics; law and politics; and studies of governance. The books consider all forms of legal discourse across societies, rather than being limited to lawyers' discourses alone.

The series editors come from a range of disciplines: academic law; socio-legal studies; sociology; and anthropology. All have been actively involved in teaching and writing about law in context.

Series Editors

Chris Arup
Victoria University, Melbourne
Martin Chanock
La Trobe University, Melbourne
Pat O'Malley
Carleton University, Ottawa
Sally Engle Merry
Wellesley College, Massachusetts
Susan Silbey
Massachusetts Institute of Technology

Books in the Series

The Politics of Truth and Reconciliation in South Africa
Legitimizing the Post-Apartheid State
Richard A. Wilson
0 521 80219 9 hardback
0 521 00194 3 paperback

Modernism and the Grounds of Law
Peter Fitzpatrick
0 521 80222 9 hardback
0 521 00253 2 paperback

Unemployment and Government
Genealogies of the Social
William Walters
0 521 64333 3 hardback

Autonomy and Ethnicity
Negotiating Competing Claims in Multi–Ethnic States
Yash Ghai
0 521 78112 4 hardback
0 521 78642 8 paperback

Constituting Democracy
Law, Globalism and South Africa's Political Reconstruction
Heinz Klug
0 521 78113 2 hardback
0 521 78643 6 paperback

The New World Trade Organization Agreements
Globalizing Law through Services and Intellectual Property
Christopher Arup
0 521 77355 5 hardback

The Ritual of Rights in Japan
Law, Society, and Health Policy
Eric A. Feldman
0 521 77040 8 hardback
0 521 77964 2 paperback

The Invention of the Passport
Surveillance, Citizenship and the State
John Torpey
0 521 63249 8 hardback
0 521 63493 8 paperback

Governing Morals
A Social History of Moral Regulation
Alan Hunt
0 521 64071 7 hardback
0 521 64689 8 paperback

The Colonies of Law
Colonialism, Zionism and Law in Early Mandate Palestine
Ronen Shamir
0 521 63183 1 hardback

Social Citizenship and Workfare in the United States and
Western Europe
The Paradox of Inclusion
Joel F. Handler
0 521 83370 1 hardback
0 521 54153 0 paperback

Law, Anthropology and the Constitution of the Social
Making Persons and Things
Edited by Alain Pottage and Martha Mundy
0 521 83178 4 hardback
0 521 53945 5 paperback

JUDICIAL REVIEW AND BUREAUCRATIC IMPACT

International and Interdisciplinary
Perspectives

Edited by Marc Hertogh and Simon Halliday

CAMBRIDGE
UNIVERSITY PRESS

PUBLISHED BY THE PRESS SYNDICATE OF THE UNIVERSITY OF CAMBRIDGE
The Pitt Building, Trumpington Street, Cambridge, United Kingdom

CAMBRIDGE UNIVERSITY PRESS
The Edinburgh Building, Cambridge, CB2 2RU, UK
40 West 20th Street, New York, NY 10011–4211, USA
477 Williamstown Road, Port Melbourne, VIC 3207, Australia
Ruiz de Alarcón 13, 28014 Madrid, Spain
Dock House, The Waterfront, Cape Town 8001, South Africa

http://www.cambridge.org

First published 2004

Printed in the United Kingdom at the University Press, Cambridge

Typeface Goudy 11/13 pt.   *System* LaTeX 2$_\varepsilon$ [TB]

A catalogue record for this book is available from the British Library

Library of Congress Cataloguing in Publication data
Judicial review and bureaucratic impact : international and interdisciplinary dimensions /
edited by Marc Hertogh and Simon Halliday.
     p.   cm. – (Cambridge studies in law and society)
Includes bibliographical references and index.
ISBN 0 521 83918 1 (hardback) – ISBN 0 521 54786 5 (paperback)
1. Judicial review of administrative acts.   2. Judicial review.   3. Bureaucracy.
I. Hertogh, M. L. M., 1968–   II. Halliday, Simon.   III. Series.
K3175.J827   2004
374′.012 – dc22   2004040794

ISBN 0 521 83918 1 hardback
ISBN 0 521 54786 5 paperback

CONTENTS

ACKNOWLEDGMENTS

The idea for this volume first took shape on the steps of the Central European University in Budapest, Hungary, during a joint meeting in 2001 of the Law and Society Association and the Research Committee on the Sociology of Law. During a rainy lunch break, in between conference sessions, we discussed the fact that, despite the growing importance of judicial review worldwide, there were still very few empirical studies available about its actual effects on government bureaucracies. Moreover, there was no single publication that combined studies from different countries and different academic disciplines. This led to the idea to publish such a much needed collection of essays ourselves. In November 2002 we organised a very stimulating and enjoyable two-day workshop on 'Judicial Review and Bureaucratic Impact' at Tilburg University, the Netherlands, with a group of leading international scholars. The results are published in this book.

For their support and assistance we would like to thank a number of people and institutions in particular. The generous financial support provided by the Netherlands Organization for Scientific Research (NWO) enabled us to invite all contributors to this volume to attend the workshop. We are also very grateful for the sponsorship of Tilburg University (Department of Jurisprudence and Legal History), the Centre for Socio-Legal Studies, University of Oxford, and Cambridge University Press. Thanks are also due to Vina Wijkhuijs who assisted in the running of the workshop and to Vidya Kumar who helped us prepare the manuscript for publication. In addition, of course, we would like to thank the authors in this volume who – with no exception – reacted very positively to our first invitation to join this project. Their constructive and cooperative attitude has been a great stimulus for us to go ahead with our plans and bring it to a close. Finally, we are much indebted to Finola O'Sullivan of Cambridge University Press who was supportive of this project right from the start and who was very helpful throughout the publication process.

Marc Hertogh and Simon Halliday
Tilburg and Oxford
October 2003

NOTES ON THE CONTRIBUTORS

Peter Cane   Professor of Law, Research School of Social Sciences, Australian National University, Australia

Bradley C. Canon   Professor of Political Science, University of Kentucky, USA

Robin Creyke   Alumni Professor of Administrative Law, Australian National University, Australia

Yoav Dotan   Associate Professor, Faculty of Law, Hebrew University, Jerusalem, Israel

Malcolm M. Feeley   Professor of Law, University of California at Berkeley, USA

Simon Halliday   Nicholas de B. Katzenbach Research Fellow, Centre for Socio-Legal Studies, University of Oxford, UK

Marc Hertogh   Associate Professor of Socio-Legal Studies, Faculty of Law, Tilburg University, the Netherlands

John McMillan   Commonwealth Ombudsman and Professor of Administrative Law (on leave), Australian National University, Australia

Genevra Richardson   Professor of Public Law, Queen Mary, University of London, UK

Martin Shapiro   James W. and Isabel Coffroth Professor of Law, University of California at Berkeley, USA

Lorne Sossin   Associate Professor, Faculty of Law, University of Toronto, Canada

Maurice Sunkin   Professor of Law, University of Essex, UK

INTRODUCTION

MARC HERTOGH AND SIMON HALLIDAY

INTRODUCTION

This collection of essays concerns the relationship between judicial and bureaucratic decision-making. It considers the impact of the courts on bureaucracy. Its focus, then, is on a particular aspect of a broader field of enquiry which is often called 'judicial impact studies' – the social scientific exploration of the significance of the courts to social change.

The impact of court decisions has to date been the focus of two intellectual traditions, each with its own specific characteristics and perspectives. The first tradition is within political science (largely in the United States), within the law and courts sub-field. The second tradition is somewhat younger and has grown out of (largely Commonwealth and European) socio-legal studies generally and administrative law in particular. Political scientists have been concerned broadly with the significance of courts to social and political change in society. For socio-legal studies/administrative law, the concern has been to test the efficacy of the court's supervision of executive action, or (relatedly) its power to protect the rights of citizens as the subjects of the state. Whereas the political science project has been concerned with social change and the dynamics of power within the polity, the socio-legal/administrative law project has been more specifically focused on testing the widespread assumption within the legal academy and doctrine that law has power over government. While political science has been concerned very generally with court decisions of any type (so long as they required or suggested social change), the socio-legal/administrative law project has been concerned quite specifically with the judicial review of administrative action. Whereas political science has generally considered major policy shifts at quite a macro level, the socio-legal/administrative law project has focused more on micro social change in relation to small and particular aspects of public law. Finally, whereas studies in political science usually have taken a 'top-down' strategy, focusing on the impact of a particular decision, the socio-legal approach usually employs a 'bottom-up' perspective, focusing on how public officials and the general public interact with the law.

Thus far, both projects have developed separately. This collection, however, aims to combine both approaches for the first time. Despite their many differences, both approaches share a deep concern with *bureaucracy*. Bureaucracies are an important vehicle by which the policy choices of the courts are translated into social change on the ground, regardless of whether one takes a macro or micro perspective. Whether the bureaucracies be schools, prisons, workplaces, health authorities, tribunals, welfare agencies or the centralised civil service, a common and vital concern for the two projects is how bureaucratic decisions are socially produced and the significance of law to these processes. This collection of essays uses the study of judicial review's impact on bureaucracies to bring the two projects together, to take stock of the different disciplinary insights, and to put forward a research agenda which benefits from this synergy.

A shortcoming of much of the early judicial impact research, that is also reflected in many contemporary analyses, is its strong local or national focus. Traditionally, most studies focused exclusively on the United States with little reference to the situation in other jurisdictions. More recent studies elsewhere have been similarly introspective in thinking about judicial review and bureaucratic impact. It is interesting to note, however, that many impact scholars make the point that, within their respective jurisdictions, there is a substantial lack of empirical data concerning judicial review's impact on bureaucracies. Although it has become almost trite to complain that there is only a small amount of empirical evidence concerning this issue (at least in most jurisdictions), the claim is probably still a powerful one in general. This problem can be alleviated to an extent by drawing on research from different parts of the world, and it is in this vein that the research for this volume of essays has been collected. Although judicial review's impact should be researched in a context-specific and jurisdictionally sensitive way,[1] there is still much to be gained by looking at other countries and their research traditions, particularly, as Richardson observes in Chapter 4, in relation to front-line bureaucratic decision-making. Comparative insights can shed some light on the research gaps in relation to one's home country and inspire hypotheses to be tested in comparative perspective. It is hoped that this collection of essays can begin the process of gathering pertinent material from different countries and encourage this approach to the overall research project of studying judicial impact.

OVERVIEW OF THE BOOK

The book has been divided into three parts. Part 1 considers conceptual and methodological issues pertaining to the study of judicial impact and bureaucracies. Part 2 presents empirical research from a number of different countries. Part 3 considers the future of judicial review and bureaucratic impact.

Part 1: conceptual and methodological issues

The first part of this volume of essays takes a conceptual approach to the question of judicial review and bureaucratic impact. Indeed, one of the main aims here is to unpack exactly what is meant by 'judicial impact'. The chapters in this part of the book engage with a number of the important and preliminary questions which must be considered in orienting one's enquiry into the relationship between judicial decisions and bureaucratic behaviour. In addition (and connected) to such conceptual issues, the question of methods is also focused on, both in terms of basic methodological approaches, and in more specific terms of which research techniques are appropriate for particular questions of impact.

Peter Cane addresses two principal questions in the opening chapter: (1) what is judicial review? and (2) why should we be interested in its impact? The link between the two questions is that both raise the issue of what judicial review is for. Cane sets out the argument that the task of researching judicial review's impact must be driven by a contextualised understanding of judicial review's function in society. He demonstrates the contingency of judicial review's function by reference to a sample of constitutional contexts – England, the United States,

[1] See the essay by Cane in Chapter 1 of this volume.

Australia and India. He sets out four corresponding models of judicial review, each with its own set of assumptions and ambitions: a rule of law model (England); an institutional design model (United States); a hybrid model combining the features of the previous two models (Australia); and a social justice model (India). Additionally, Cane suggests that the enterprise of researching judicial review's impact sits most comfortably within an instrumentalist view of law – the view that law and legal institutions should be understood and assessed by reference to their (likely) effects on human behaviour. Provocatively (at least for a volume such as this), he questions whether judicial impact scholars will ever be able to collect sufficient empirical data to be able to think comprehensively about judicial review and bureaucratic impact, or to make instrumentally based policy choices. In light of this scepticism, he suggests that we might pay more attention to the non-instrumentalist or 'expressive' functions of judicial review.

Maurice Sunkin in his chapter surveys some of the main conceptual issues raised when seeking to identify what research into judicial review and bureaucratic impact might be about. He considers two main sets of conceptual issues. The first concerns what might be described as issues of territory: what ground is to be covered in research on the impact of judicial review and bureaucracy? This involves identifying the terrain to be explored in the research and the principal features of the landscape. In this context, the two basic questions are: (a) the impact of what? and (b) the impact on what? In relation to the 'of what?' question, he notes that judicial review may be regarded as a process of litigation, as judgments of the court, and as a set of legal norms, values and principles. In relation to the 'on what?' question, he observes that there are a number of further questions to be answered in thinking about the impact of judicial review in research terms: what bureaucratic sectors? which organisational context? and what kinds of impact? Sunkin's careful mapping of the conceptual terrain of judicial impact research is illustrated (and so made more accessible) by drawing from his own research on the impact of judicial review on social welfare administration in the United Kingdom. The second part of his essay is concerned with what he describes as 'evaluative and analytical' issues. He looks at the different methodological approaches of positivism and interpretivism and considers the implications for the framing of research questions and the design of research strategies. In this section, he also looks closely at the problems associated with the meaning of 'impacts' in this context and the related issue of causation.

In his chapter, Bradley Canon draws on a relatively long history of judicial impact studies in the United States (including his own research) to develop a conceptual model of agency reactions to judicial decisions. His model is designed to guide research into the bureaucratic implementation of judicial policies. He focuses on agencies which are hostile or indifferent to judicial decisions and sets out an analysis of the three steps undertaken by agencies when considering how to implement a judicially mandated change. Step 1 is called 'interpretation'. Here the agency interprets how a court decision applies to its own actions. Canon demonstrates that this is not always as straightforward as it might at first appear. Interpretations may be coloured by the agency's attitude to the court and the decision, and what the court proclaims may not be the same as what the agency understands. Step 2 involves the agency searching for a behavioural response. The agency search can be influenced by a number of factors, including the presumed reactions of agency clients and funders, and agency resources. Canon suggests that most agencies engage in a rough cost–benefit analysis, though he notes that this must also consider what he terms 'psychic costs' – for example, the effect of agency responses on its commitment to law-abidingness. Step 3 is called 'implementation of behavioural response'. This can range from full compliance to doing nothing at all. Again, Canon sets out a variety of factors which influence this process. These include the attitude of the agency to the expertise of the courts, the closeness of the relationship between the court and the agency, the impact of compliance on resources, threats of sanctions and so forth. Canon concludes his chapter with a discussion of the methodological tradition of US judicial impact studies and a survey of the research techniques which have been used.

Part 2: international case studies

The second part of the book contains chapters from a number of authors who, while recognising the complexity of the enterprise, have conducted research which aims to understand the significance of judicial review to bureaucratic practices. These case studies come from a number of different countries: the United Kingdom, Canada, Australia, Israel and the United States. The aim here is to offer a brief (and inevitably limited) snapshot of the research that is being conducted in different jurisdictions concerning judicial review and bureaucratic impact. In addition to presenting substantive empirical data, the authors also helpfully situate their work within the research traditions of their own countries and thereby point readers to other research which should be of interest.

Genevra Richardson in her chapter considers UK socio-legal research which has explored the impact of judicial review on bureaucracies. Most of the work in the United Kingdom has been undertaken by administrative law scholars and has considered the influence of judicial review on government agency decision-making practices. It should be noted, however, that this is different from its US administrative law counterpart. As Shapiro explains in Chapter 9, judicial review in the United Kingdom has focused much less on rule-making practices and much more on substantive ground-level decision-making. The focus in the UK research on the judicial review of administrative action, then, means also that it generally has a narrower focus than US judicial impact studies. Nevertheless, as Cane points out in Chapter 1, the UK 'administrative law' project may be regarded as one element of the wider enterprise exemplified currently by US political science. Richardson sets the scene by giving a précis of existing work in the United Kingdom, and usefully draws out some common themes. First, she notes that judicial review should be seen as a series of steps and not as a discrete event. Secondly, she describes the common scepticism about the ability of judicial review to positively influence government bureaucracies. Thirdly, she observes that a number of the studies describe the potentially negative effects of judicial review. Richardson also presents data from her own study (with Machin) concerning the impact of judicial review on tribunal decision-making. This research exemplifies the micro-sociological approach which much of the recent UK socio-legal research has adopted in approaching the question of judicial review's impact. Her findings cast doubt on a presumption of some of the literature that juridical process values have a greater chance of penetrating non-legal systems than do other types of legal norm. Richardson's study concerned a decision-making environment where a very strong competing value system existed – medicine. The tribunal under study was the Mental Health Review Tribunal which makes decision about the detention of patients in hospital for medical reasons. Her case study, then, presents a particularly stark – perhaps extreme – example of the common situation where competing value systems co-exist in the administrative arena, requiring law to compete with other systems for attention and influence.

Lorne Sossin's chapter focuses on Canada, and explores the hitherto neglected topic of 'soft law'. By 'soft law', Sossin refers principally (at least for his case studies) to the range of non-legislative guide-lines, rules and administrative policies used to guide administrative decision-making practices. He observes insightfully that soft law con-stitutes a particularly significant window into the relationship between judicial review and bureaucratic decision-making. Soft law is the prin-cipal means by which judicial standards and requirements are commu-nicated to front-line decision-makers. It constitutes, then, a conduit for communication between the judicial and executive branches of govern-ment in which both legal and administrative influences on discretionary authority may be articulated. As such it suggests itself as an obvious and rich site of enquiry for our understanding of the impact of judicial review on bureaucracies. However, as Sossin notes, soft law is also a means by which the judiciary may receive messages about the admin-istrative context in which legal standards are operationalised. Soft law, then, closes the 'feedback loop' and re-focuses our attention on how the courts use and respond to administrative reactions to judicial man-dates. Sossin presents three case studies of the recent use of soft law in response to important Canadian appellate court decisions and thereby illustrates the importance of soft law to our understanding of judicial impact, and also the potential of soft law for improving the dialogue between the courts and the executive. Sossin's chapter is also signifi-cant because it makes an important link between what we might call the political science and the administrative law projects concerning the impact of judicial review. He notes that, in Canada, scholarship has been dominated by the impact of the courts on the policy-making and legislative processes. He cautions against the enquiry stopping there, however, refuting the presumption that 'the court's decision is the end of the story of a legal challenge to government action, rather than the beginning of a complex new chapter'.

Robin Creyke and John McMillan report some findings of their research in Australia which was the first of its kind in that jurisdic-tion. Creyke and McMillan set out to test two (related) forms of popular scepticism within administrative law scholarship: first, that government agencies use the ability to remake a decision according to law simply to reproduce the same negative decision but within a judge-proof form – a kind of administrative law 'creative compliance';[2] and, secondly, that experiences of judicial review have little or no impact on future policy

<hr />

[2] D. McBarnet and C. Whelan, 'The Elusive Spirit of the Law: Formalism and the Struggle for Legal Control' (1991) 54 *Modern Law Review* 848–73.

and routine work. They present the findings of survey research which sought data about the resolution of citizen–government disputes in the aftermath of judicial review decisions. The research is significant in that it covered a ten-year period of judicial review litigation and received a very high response rate. As such it represents an unusually authoritative picture of governmental reaction to judicial review. The survey asked three basic questions which are explored in the chapter: (1) was the citizen's case reconsidered in accordance with the order of the court? (2) If so, what was the final outcome? (3) Was there any change in the law or in the agency's practice that flowed from the decision? The data from the survey disturbs the popular scepticism mentioned above. Decisions were reconsidered in accordance with judicial rulings in virtually all cases. More significantly, however, these reconsiderations resulted in a favourable outcome for the citizen in approximately 60 per cent of cases. Further, the data in response to the third question suggests that experiences of judicial review had longer-term effects on administrative practices in approximately one-third of cases. Creyke and McMillan also provide a profile of the cases in the sample which reveals important data about the nature of litigants, the nature of disputes and the grounds used to challenge government decisions.

Yoav Dotan focuses on Israel and investigates the impact of the court in relation to one of its most important functions – the protection of core human rights. He examines the responses of the Israeli Supreme Court to the use of torture against suspected terrorists during interrogations by the Israeli security services. As such, Dotan's focus spans the interests of some other chapters in Part 2: on the plight of the individual litigant, as per Creyke and McMillan's chapter; and on the values of decision-makers, as per, for example, Richardson. Dotan charts the approach of the Israeli Supreme Court to torture cases over a period of over thirty years (1970–2001). He divides this period into three eras of judicial attitudes: first, the court avoided looking at the matter in any depth; secondly, the court ostensibly sought to regulate the use of torture; and, thirdly, the court banned it completely. Dotan's study is revealing in demonstrating how the procedural realities of judicial review can undermine the ability of the courts to control the bureaucracy. He shows that during the 'regulation' era, the litigants had already been tortured by the time the matter could be heard by the court. In some cases, the courts were satisfied with the government's assurances that it was no longer using physical pressure in interrogation. In others, injunctions were granted, but only after the government was invited to respond, by which time it was too late. This gives a particularly clear illustration of the need to look beyond pyrrhic victories in the courtroom to the social realities on the ground in thinking about the significance of judicial review. Following the outright banning of torture, however, the practice ceased immediately, and Dotan sets out his explanatory hypothesis – that the terms of the court's decision were unequivocal and left no room for legal or procedural manoeuvring on the government's part, and that the political climate precluded senior government officials from turning a blind eye to illegal practices. Dotan's chapter is important in exploring the issue of impact over time, picking up this theme of Sunkin's chapter in Part 1. It is also a significant study by virtue of the importance of the function ascribed to the court and the extreme circumstances in which the question of impact is being tested.

Malcolm Feeley focuses on the United States in his chapter. He reverses the flow of much of the judicial impact studies by exploring (like Dotan, in part) stories of success rather than failure. By narrating the history of prison reform in three case studies, Feeley demonstrates how judges transformed themselves into administrative agencies, developing, overseeing and implementing structural reform. In each of the case studies – Arkansas, Texas and Santa Clara County, California – the judges appointed a special master to play the role of a multifaceted executive assistant. Feeley draws out from the case studies common functions played by the special masters which ensured the relative success of the judges' reform programmes. They acted as the eyes and ears of the court, provided corrections expertise, floated trial balloons and took the heat for the judges. Feeley stops short of trying to assess the 'impact' of the court in any specific sense. However, his case studies demonstrate clearly that the courts, through their special masters, were highly significant actors in lengthy and complex periods of prison reform. His chapter is important because it focuses our attention on the judge as administrator as well as policy maker, and because success stories such as these provide important sites of comparison in relation to much of the impact literature which stresses the limits of the courts' influence on bureaucracy.

Part 3: the future of judicial review and bureaucratic impact
The final part of the book explores the future of judicial review and bureaucratic impact. The aim here is to consider both the direction

which future research might take, and also the way in which it might be carried out.

Martin Shapiro considers the history of the development of US administrative law in order to reflect on the future of administrative law in the European Union. He sets out an argument that the regulatory politics of the EU will provoke the development of an EU administrative law of rule-making. The rise of the EU as a regulatory authority, he suggests, will push regulatory politics in Europe towards a legalism associated with the United States (when traditionally the European regulatory style was one of negotiated compliance). As the regulated population becomes less willing or able to rely on concessions at the national implementation stage (because implementation is varied across different national contexts in a single market), it will become more interested in shaping the content of the rules themselves. In parallel, pro-regulatory forces facing corporatist national implementation of EU rules will be inclined to seek tougher EU rules and to become participants in the administrative rule-making process. This alliance will push for an administrative law that ensures their participation. Unless the European Court of Justice defers to the technocratic expertise of those engaged in the comitology process (which he argues will not happen), then European administrative law will move in the same direction which US administrative law moved in the 1960s. However, having set out this prediction for European administrative law, Shapiro considers the implications for judicial review and bureaucratic impact. Here the comparative history of the US experience provides something of a paradox. On the one hand, the impact of judicial review on bureaucratic agency behaviour in the rule-making process was massive, obvious and uncontested – such that empirical investigation was not necessary. On the other hand, the attempts of the Supreme Court to rein in the excessive activism of the lower courts presented much more intractable questions of impact. The problem (discussed in a number of the chapters) of how to isolate the influence of the court amidst a complicated picture of social action re-emerges. Indeed, he suggests that in relation to the EU, although his prediction is that there will be an increase in agency behaviour towards greater transparency and participation, it will be similarly difficult to separate out the influence of the courts from the influence of the Parliament, the Council or the Commission.

Marc Hertogh and Simon Halliday conclude the collection by reflecting on the chapters, drawing out some themes and suggesting a research agenda for the study of judicial review and bureaucratic impact.

We begin by taking up the challenge posed by 'impact agnosticism' – the view that we may never be able to collect sufficient data to be able to talk comprehensively in terms of the impact of judicial review – and defend the enterprise of judicial impact studies. In the rest of our concluding chapter we set out three important concerns for continuing judicial impact studies. First, we argue that future enquiry should benefit from interdisciplinarity and methodological pluralism. We problematise the concept of 'impact' itself and try to unsettle some of the existing dichotomies which are used to categorise different approaches to judicial impact research. Secondly, we describe the awkward position of judicial review, set as it is between high expectations and sometimes disappointing realities. Here we summarise some of the themes from the collection which highlight the barriers which lie between judicial rulings and bureaucratic behaviour. We explore the importance of the changing nature of government to judicial impact studies, as well as highlighting the competition of different normative systems within the decision-making environment. Additionally, we focus on the issue of communication, both between courts and bureaucracies, and within bureaucracies themselves. Thirdly, and finally, we argue for an integrative approach to the study of judicial impact, whereby judicial impact studies can be situated within broader law and society research, and benefit from the insights produced by this wider scholarship.

PART ONE

CONCEPTUAL AND
METHODOLOGICAL ISSUES

CHAPTER ONE

UNDERSTANDING JUDICIAL REVIEW AND ITS IMPACT

PETER CANE

INTRODUCTION

The project of studying the impact of judicial review raises many questions. For instance, what do we mean by 'judicial review' and by 'impact'? Are we interested in impact on the behaviour of individuals, or on larger social structures, or on something else? Are we concerned with immediate or longer-term impacts? What is the relationship between the functions, purposes and objectives of judicial review and its impact? And, most fundamentally of all, *why* are we interested in the impact of judicial review? In the first section of this paper, I will suggest that, although various common-law jurisdictions share a basic concept of judicial review, when we look more closely – and I will be focusing on England, and the United States, Australia and India (all at the federal level) – we can identify various models of judicial review, each based on a different set of ideas about its functions and objectives. For this reason, I would argue, the impact of judicial review needs to be studied in a contextualised way by reference to judicial review's objectives and functions. Also, it should not be assumed that, when we discuss the impact of *judicial review*, we are all talking about the impact of the same thing or, at least, of a single institution with a single set of objectives and functions.

The second section of the paper addresses the question of why we are interested in the impact of judicial review. Here I want to argue that concern with the impact of judicial review finds its most comfortable home within an instrumentalist approach to law in general, and judicial review in particular. By instrumentalism I mean the view that law and legal institutions should be understood and assessed by reference to their (likely) effects on human behaviour. For the instrumentalist, the chief value and importance of legal rights and powers, duties and obligations, is as means to ends. Non-instrumentalism, by contrast, rests on the view that law and legal institutions should be understood and assessed in terms of concepts of interpersonal, social and political justice. For non-instrumentalists, the value of and justification for law depends not on its effects on human behaviour but rather on whether it embodies and expresses the right values concerning the way people ought to behave towards one another. The basic instrumentalist idea that judicial review should be understood as means to ends underlines the point that impact can be understood only in relation to objectives. Until we are clear about objectives, we are not in a position to engage in meaningful study of the relationship of means to ends. The link between the questions addressed in the first two sections of the paper is that both raise the issue of what judicial review is *for*. The third section ponders on the practical significance of ignorance and uncertainty about the impact of law in general and of judicial review in particular. In this section I want to suggest that we need to take seriously the possibility that we may never know enough about the impact of judicial review to enable us to make properly informed, instrumentally based policy choices about the desirability of, or how best to design, judicial review institutions.

WHAT IS JUDICIAL REVIEW?

In one sense, judicial review refers to 'the invalidation of laws enacted by the normal or regular legislative process, because they are in conflict with some superior law, typically a constitution or treaty' – 'higher law judicial review' as Martin Shapiro calls it.[1] This is not the topic of this paper. Here I am concerned with judicial review defined as scrutiny by the judicial branch of government of decisions and actions of the executive branch to police compliance with rules and principles of 'public law' (including, but not limited to, 'higher law').[2] Judicial

---

[1] M. Shapiro, 'The European Court of Justice' in P. Craig and G. de Búrca (eds.), *The Evolution of EU Law* (Oxford, Oxford University Press, 1999), pp. 321–48, at p. 321.

[2] For present purposes, it is not necessary to explore the reach of judicial review beyond the institutions of government to all those sites where 'public power' – 'governance' in modern jargon – is exercised.

review, understood in this sense is the subject of several of the essays in this volume (those by Sunkin, Richardson, Dotan, Sossin and Creyke and McMillan). The essays by Feeley and Canon, by contrast, are located within a wider political-science tradition of interest in the impact of courts generally on the formulation and implementation of public policy. From this perspective, the essays in the former category can be seen as contributing case studies to this larger political-science project.

Even in terms of the relatively narrow definition adopted in this essay, the constitutional and institutional environment in which judicial review operates and, hence, the objectives and functions that are ascribed to it, differ from one jurisdiction to another. These differences are suggestive of different 'models' of judicial review. Models are interpretations of complex social phenomena. I do not suggest that the models I propose provide the only, or even the best, possible interpretation of the institutions of judicial review in the various jurisdictions. Nor do I want to argue that there is a simple or one-to-one relationship between the various models and the institutions of judicial review in any particular jurisdiction. Reference to particular jurisdictions is intended only to provide concrete illustrations of the models.

An English, rights-based, rule-of-law model

At a theoretical level, judicial review in England is most commonly understood in terms of the concept of the rule of law.[3] According to this approach, the prime function of judicial review is to police the legal boundaries of executive power, whether laid down by Parliament in statutes (either directly by imposing limitations on the scope of powers, or indirectly by importing limitations on power imposed by EC law or the European Court of Human Rights (ECHR), or by the

---

[3] Ever since Dicey conceived the rule of law in terms of the rule of 'the ordinary courts', there has been a debate about the question 'whose law is to rule?'. This debate has recently attracted far more attention than it deserves (the question, 'what law is to rule?', is more important). Many of the most significant contributions can be found in C. F. Forsyth (ed.), *Judicial Review and the Constitution* (Oxford, Hart, 2000). An analogous debate in Australia is about whether judicial review (in federal law) is grounded in the common law or the Australian Constitution. See e.g. S. Gageler, 'The Underpinnings of Judicial Review of Administrative Action: Common Law or Constitution' (2000) 28 *Federal Law Review* 303. This debate has more point in Australia than in England because, under the Australian Constitution, the High Court has entrenched judicial review jurisdiction.

courts in the 'grounds' of judicial review. This emphasis on the rule of *law* is important for defining not only what, positively, judicial review is for, but also, negatively, what it is not for. For instance, judicial review does not police compliance by the executive with *political* (as opposed to legal) principles of right conduct – this is primarily a task for Parliament via the various accountability mechanisms by which it performs the function of scrutinising the conduct of executive government. Nor is judicial review primarily concerned with establishing and policing bureaucratic (as opposed to legal) principles of 'good administration'. To the extent that this task is undertaken outside the executive itself,[4] ombudsmen are prominent amongst the monitors. Judicial review, then, is only one of various accountability mechanisms that constitute a dense network of systems of 'audit, grievance-handling, standard-setting, inspection and evaluation'.[5]

Equally importantly, judicial review is not the only, or perhaps even the most important, mechanism of legal accountability. What are loosely called 'tribunals' play a central role in handling complaints against government of non-compliance with legal rules and standards. Tribunals process vastly more individual grievances about government decisions and actions than does the Administrative Court. In relation to such cases of what we might call 'bureaucratic judicial review' (i.e. review of 'street-level' bureaucratic decisions), it may be doubted that the Administrative Court has any advantage over a specialist tribunal. Where the Administrative Court comes into its own is in relation to what we might call 'high-profile judicial review'. Here I am thinking of cases such as *M. v. Home Office*[6] and the *Fire Brigades Union*[7] and *Pergau Dam*[8]. Such cases are high-profile in the sense that they concern issues of wide public interest that may be politically controversial; they often involve decisions taken personally by (or close to) high-ranking elected members of the executive government; and they are brought by 'public interest organisations' in pursuit of a political agenda

---

[4] Concerning mechanisms of intra-executive accountability, see C. Hood, C. Scott, O. James. G. Jones and T. Travers, *Regulation Inside Government: Waste-Watchers, Quality Police and Sleaze-Busters* (Oxford, Oxford University Press, 1999).
[5] *Ibid*, p. 4.   [6] [1994] 1 AC 377.
[7] *R. v. Secretary of State for the Home Department, ex parte Fire Brigades Union* [1995] 2 AC 513.
[8] *R. v. Secretary of State for Foreign and Commonwealth Affairs, ex parte World Development Movement* [1995] 1 WLR 115.

rather than by individuals acting on their own behalf and in their own interests.

High-profile judicial review is – like bureaucratic judicial review – concerned with establishing and policing a legal framework for the conduct of government. But in terms of their subject matter and their political context and significance, the two types of litigation are quite different. Whereas bureaucratic judicial review is concerned with the protection of the rights and interests of individuals (or, through the medium of representative standing, of groups of individuals) against government illegality, high-profile judicial review is typically concerned with challenging government illegality as such 'in the public interest'. The advantage that the Administrative Court has in such cases derives from its being part of the High Court and being staffed by holders of high judicial office. It is certainly arguable that the status of the Administrative Court is critical to its ability to entertain complaints against the political executive of central government in the reasonable expectation that any finding against the government will be taken seriously.

A US separation-of-powers-based, institutional-design, model

The development of judicial review in the United States is inextricably linked with the history of the independent regulatory agency. The first of such agencies – the Interstate Commerce Commission – was established in 1887, and Roosevelt's New Deal saw the creation of a large number of agencies in the 1930s. The last wave of new regulatory activity rose in the 1960s and 1970s, with a focus on consumer protection, health and safety and the environment.

From the start, multifunctional regulatory agencies (performing legislative and adjudicatory as well as executive (enforcement) functions) were seen as problematic in terms of constitutional separation of powers, representing, it was thought, a 'fourth branch of government'.[9] However, such objections became muted in the face of post-Depression

---

[9] J. O. Freedman, *Crisis and Legitimacy: The Administrative Process and American Government* (Cambridge, Cambridge University Press, 1978), Chapter 2; and S. Breyer, R. B. Stewart, C. R. Sunstein and M. L. Spitzer, *Administrative Law and Regulatory Policy: Problems, Texts, and Cases* (4th edn, New York, Aspen Publishers, 1999), Chapter 2. A recent Supreme Court pronouncement on this issue is *American Trucking Association* v. *Environmental Protection Agency*, 121 S. Ct 903 (2001), discussed in 'Leading Cases' (2001) 115 *Harvard Law Review* 518.

political reality, and the focus of legal concern about regulation shifted to questions of process – as manifested in the enactment of the Administrative Procedure Act (APA) in 1946. The APA represented a compromise between the supporters and the opponents of multifunctional regulatory agencies: procedural control was the price for acceptance of departures from formal separation-of-powers principles.[10] In the United States, judicial review (or, at least, scholarship about judicial review) is overwhelmingly preoccupied with controlling the activities of independent regulatory agencies.

The APA established a distinction between adjudication and rule-making. In the early years after its enactment, adjudication was the preferred regulatory standard-setting procedure. In the 1960s and 1970s, however, agencies increasingly turned to rule-making. The response of the courts to this development[11] was to develop an 'interest-representation model' of judicial review, the rationale of which was the subjection of administrative rule-making to pluralistic pressures, similar to those that the legislature experienced, by giving interested parties standing to challenge administrative rules (as opposed to the application of such rules in individual cases) in the courts. At the same time, in order to facilitate judicial review of the substance of administrative rule-making under the so-called 'hard-look' doctrine, agencies were required to develop rule-making 'records'. Hard-look judicial review is designed to ensure that agencies not only allow interests to participate in the rule-making process, but also that the agency listens to what they say. The intrusiveness of these developments was to some extent counterbalanced by the decisions in the *Vermont Yankee* case[12] (limiting the courts' power to impose procedural requirements on agencies) and the *Chevron* case[13] (which established the principle of judicial deference to agencies' interpretations of their empowering statutes).

---

[10] See generally M. Shapiro, *Who Guards the Guardians: Judicial Control of Administration* (Athens, GA, University of Georgia Press, 1988), Chapter 2.

[11] Most famously described by R. Stewart, 'The Reformation of American Administrative Law' (1975) 88 *Harvard Law Review* 1669.

[12] *Vermont Yankee Nuclear Power Corporation v. Natural Resources Defense Council Inc.*, 435 US 519 (1978).

[13] *Chevron USA Inc. v. Natural Resources Defense Council Inc.*, 467 US 837 (1984). Another view is that it represents an attempt by the Supreme Court to prevent the various inferior federal courts putting different interpretations on one and the same statutory provision.

Comparison of the English and US models

In England, regulatory agencies have, of course, been targets of judicial review, and more so in recent years as the number of regulators has grown, especially in the wake of the privatisation of public utilities. But the law and practice of judicial review in England is certainly not focused on such agencies in the way it is in the United States. This is partly because, by comparison with the powers of US independent agencies – which have been dubbed 'governments in miniature' – those of British agencies, particularly to make rules and enforce compliance – have historically been modest. By comparison with judicial review in the United States, English judicial review has been – and still is – more concerned with the 'core' of government than with independent agencies, and more with government as provider than with government as regulator. This is reflected in the fact that some of the hottest topics of debate amongst British administrative lawyers in the past decade have concerned the contracting-out of the provision of public services, joint public/private funding of infrastructural ventures, the creation of quasi-autonomous agencies for the delivery of public services, and the contractualisation of relationships between units of executive government.[14] The implications of such developments for the rule of law, and for judicial review as a technique for upholding it, have figured prominently in such debates.

The different theoretical underpinnings of judicial review in England and the United States respectively can be illustrated by reference to the *Chevron* case.[15] As already noted, this decision established a general principle of judicial deference to agencies' interpretations of statutes. Coupled with the doctrine of 'hard-look' review of the substance of administrative rules, it produces a doctrinal position that is precisely the converse of that in England, where the courts claim monopoly power to decide what statutes mean, but have traditionally been extremely unwilling to entertain challenges to the substance of secondary legislation. The English position makes sense in terms of a rule-of-law foundation for judicial review: the substance of administrative rules is seen as a matter of policy, not law. Some people think that the US position is simply anomalous,[16] but it can perhaps be supported on the basis

---

[14] See e.g. M. Taggart (ed.), *The Province of Administrative Law* (Oxford, Hart, 1997).

[15] *Chevron USA Inc. v. Natural Resources Defense Council Inc.*, 467 US 837 (1984).

[16] S. Breyer, 'Judicial Review of Questions of Law and Policy' (1986) 38 *Administrative Law Review* 363.

that agencies are better equipped than courts to choose between competing interpretations of their empowering statutes.[17] However, this argument might be thought inconsistent with the willingness of the courts to engage in hard-look review. The resulting tension can perhaps be resolved by explaining hard-look review in pluralistic terms, and *Chevron* deference in terms of relative institutional competence, provided both of these explanations are conceived as being based on separation-of-powers principles.

The preoccupation of US judicial review[18] with administrative rule-making, as opposed to administrative adjudication (i.e. the resolution of disputes between individuals and government), is, of course, in stark contrast to the position in England, where non-parliamentary rule-making has predominantly been the province of the elected executive rather than appointed officials or government agencies. As a result, in England the focus is on parliamentary scrutiny of the substance of executive rule-making rather than on judicial review of the rule-making process. And, whereas, in the US, judicial control of administrative rule-making procedure is understood primarily in terms of constraining agency power, in England, judicial control of administrative adjudication (through the medium of the rules of natural justice, which do not apply to rule-making) is understood primarily in terms of protecting the rights and interests of individuals. This point can be made more generally: judicial review in the United States is fundamentally concerned with issues of institutional design and the allocation of power, whereas, in England, it is primarily concerned with striking a balance between the rights of the governed and the powers of the governors.

History may help to explain this difference of approach. The main institutions of US federal government were consciously conceived and created at a particular 'historical moment' as an integrated and internally balanced whole, amidst vigorous and quite sophisticated debate about fundamental questions of institutional design. By contrast, evolution has played a much more significant role than revolution in the development of British government. A central theme of British constitutional history is the relationship between the monarch and the people, the Crown and its subjects, the government and its citizens

---

[17] Breyer, Stewart, Sunstein and Spitzer, *Administrative Law and Regulatory Policy*, p. 260.

[18] Or, at least, of US administrative law scholarship.

(or, in the neo-liberal world of the late twentieth and early twenty-first centuries, its 'clients' or 'customers'). It is for this reason, I would suggest, that the language of 'rule of law' has a more prominent place than that of formal 'separation of powers' in British political and legal thought.

Over the past thirty years, constitution-building has played an unprecedented role in the British polity. Membership of the European Union, devolution, implementation of the Human Rights Act 1998, and other developments (such as 'the hollowing-out of the state'), have transformed the constitutional and legal landscape. The scene is now filled with interacting and competing legislative and administrative institutions that are arranged in complex horizontal patterns and vertical hierarchies. Such changes have greatly enhanced the constitutional power and importance of courts,[19] and they pose deep questions about the interaction between a new constitutional legalism and the traditional predominance in the constitution of political institutions oriented primarily to the people. The new arrangements afford to individuals – especially corporations – and groups rich and varied opportunities to play institutions off against one another in the courts to their own advantage. Institutional complexity of this sort is a strong catalyst for – even if not a precondition of – litigation strategies based on issues of institutional design. There is, therefore, a very good chance that, in years to come, the English law of judicial review will focus more on institutional design – and be less preoccupied with individual rights – than in the past.[20]

A hybrid Australian model

Australia has a Westminster-style political system, but a US-style written constitution. It has inherited the rights-focused, rule-of-law tradition of English judicial review, but judicial review is embedded in a constitutional structure based on formal, triadic, separation of powers. The prime use of judicial review in Australia is redress of individual grievances rather than interest-based regulation of administrative

---

[19] Dicey understood the link between legalism and institutional complexity. Federalism, he said, 'means legalism': A. V. Dicey, *An Introduction to the Study of the Law of the Constitution* (10th edn, New York, St Martin's Press, 1959), p. 175.

[20] The rapidly developing case law on Article 6 of the European Convention of Human Rights as it applies to administrative processes is an early sign of this development.

decision-making. At the same time, the influence of the Constitution is clear on every page of the document that can fairly lay claim to mark the beginning of the modern history of administrative law in Australia, the Report of the Commonwealth Administrative Review Committee (the Kerr Committee).[21] The chief credit for the establishment of the Kerr Committee must be given to Lionel Bowen, the Commonwealth Attorney-General at the time, and Sir Anthony Mason, the Solicitor-General of the Commonwealth, and later Justice and Chief Justice of the High Court of Australia.[22] Their view was that the available machinery for the redress of citizens' grievances against the government was woefully inadequate. Judicial review was riddled with archaic technicalities, and anyway could not get to the merits of bureaucratic decisions. Judicial review needed to be renovated. This was done in the Administrative Decisions (Judicial Review) Act 1976. More importantly, the Kerr Committee recommended a new system of 'merits review' of administrative decision-making.

The form that the new system of merits review was to take was dictated by the Kerr Committee's view about the implications of the separation of powers entrenched in the Constitution. Under Chapter III of the Constitution, the 'judicial power of the Commonwealth' is vested in the High Court and other federal courts. The Constitution has also been interpreted as forbidding the conferral of non-judicial power on such 'Chapter III courts', which are staffed by judges with security of tenure. According to the Kerr Committee, the power to review administrative decisions on the merits is not part of the judicial power of the Commonwealth, but rather belongs to the executive power. Therefore, it cannot be conferred on a Chapter III court.[23] The power of merits review therefore has to be vested in 'tribunals' which exercise executive power, and in which the judicial power of the Commonwealth cannot be vested. The body established as a result of the Kerr Committee's recommendations was the Administrative Appeals Tribunal, which exercises a mix of original and appellate merits-review jurisdiction.

[21] J. R. Kerr, *Commonwealth Administrative Review Committee Report August 1971*, Parliamentary Paper No. 144 of 1972 (Canberra, Government Press, 1971).
[22] See Sir A. Mason, 'Administrative Law Reform: The Vision and the Reality' (2001) 8 *Australian Journal of Administrative Law* 135.
[23] See P. Cane, 'Merits Review and Judicial Review: The AAT as Trojan Horse' (2000) 28 *Federal Law Review* 213 at 213–19.

Comparison of the Australian with the English and US models
Against this constitutional background, the distinction between merits review and judicial review is very sharply drawn in Australian administrative law. In English law, by contrast, although it is often said that judicial review is concerned with procedure and not merits, the distinction is of more theoretical than practical importance because nothing much turns on it. A good illustration of the consequent difference of approach is found in the doctrine of jurisdictional error. The doctrine of jurisdiction is a device for preventing judicial review interfering too much with the decision-making autonomy of the executive: so long as the executive decision-maker stays within the area of its 'jurisdiction', what it does pertains to 'the merits', with which courts are wary of interfering. The doctrine of jurisdiction can, then, be seen as primarily concerned with the allocation (and, consequently, the separation) of power. In England, the doctrine is more or less dead. English courts now claim ultimate authority over all questions of *law* decided by bodies subject to judicial review. Whether a decision of *fact* is reviewable, and the intensity of review, depends not on whether the fact in question went to jurisdiction, but on the nature of the interests at stake in the decision. In Australia, by contrast, the doctrine of jurisdiction has considerable life left in it. It plays an important part in marking the line where judicial review ends and merits review begins.[24] Fidelity to constitutional separation of powers requires this boundary to be carefully observed. In England, by contrast, focus on the rule of law and the protection of individual interests (as opposed to issues of institutional design) has fatally undermined the doctrine of jurisdiction.

In the United States, the law has taken a different turn, despite the constitutional entrenchment of separation of powers. As we have noted, multifunctional regulatory agencies were originally attacked

---

[24] The approach of Mason CJ to error of fact in *Australian Broadcasting Commission v. Bond* (1990) 170 CLR 321 is based directly on the need to distinguish between judicial review and merits review. Concerning error of law, a distinction is drawn between 'tribunals' and 'inferior courts' (both of which are subject to judicial review): *Craig v. South Australia* (1995) 84 CLR 163. The theory of jurisdiction still applies to inferior courts, but it does not apply to tribunals. In relation to federal tribunals, this distinction neatly tracks the constitutional theory that tribunals, being part of the executive, have no power conclusively to decide questions of law. Errors of law made by inferior courts within jurisdiction can be corrected if they are 'on the face of the record'. But the force of this qualification to the theory of jurisdiction is lessened by the narrowness of the definitions of 'law' and 'record'.

for breaching separation-of-powers principles. However, the Supreme Court eventually found it possible to accommodate the conferral of federal judicial power on bodies that were not federal courts within the terms of the Constitution, by holding that constitutional separation of powers was satisfied if a federal court had the power to review decisions of such bodies made in exercise of federal judicial power. The explanation for this difference of approach may lie deep in a cultural difference between Australian and US law. Under the pervasive influence of legal realism, US lawyers, both practising and academic, take a more instrumental approach to law than their Australian counterparts, who have inherited a more analytical English tradition. Around the time of the New Deal, it became clear to US lawyers that a strict theory of constitutional separation of powers could not meet the needs of an activist and interventionist administrative and regulatory state attempting to deal with complex social problems. This realisation generated a new concern with the control of multifunctional agencies through institutional design.

In Australia, by contrast, the Constitution has been understood in a more literal way as demanding, in theory at least, that a rigid barrier be erected between executive and judicial power. Just as importantly, the Australian understanding of judicial power is derived largely from nineteenth-century English cases that were decided in contexts, and for purposes, far removed from developing a workable concept of separation of powers under a written constitution. As a result, the High Court has, for almost a century, been engaged in a fruitless search for a definition of what judicial power *is*, rather than for a useful account of what it, and the constitutional imperative to keep it separate, are *for*. Judicial power is understood historically in terms of the sorts of things English courts have traditionally done. The most absurd and inconvenient results have been avoided by distinguishing between functions that are exclusively judicial (of which trying criminal charges is one) and functions that may be either judicial or executive according to context (i.e. convenience).

It was against this background that the Kerr Committee took the view (which remains more-or-less unchallenged to this day) that judicial review and merits review of executive decisions are fundamentally different functions, the former being an exercise of the judicial power, and the latter an exercise of the executive power. Unlike a court conducting a judicial review, a tribunal conducting a merits review (it is said) 'stands in the shoes of the original decision-maker'. In theory, at least, whereas judicial review is concerned with whether the challenged decision was *lawful*, merits review is concerned with whether the decision was '*the correct and preferable one*'.

An Indian public-interest-based, social-justice model

In India, social and political conditions have given judicial review yet a different complexion and set of functions.[25] By developing what is called 'social action' or 'public interest' litigation, the Indian Supreme Court has established itself as a respected and trusted *political*[26] institution. Various juridical innovations have been used to this end. First, the Court has adopted extremely generous standing rules. For instance, in one case a prison inmate was given standing to draw the attention of the court to torture inflicted by prison authorities on another inmate. In another, workers in a public sector industry were allowed to challenge the propriety of selling an old plant at a low price. In another, lawyers had standing to petition the court against the politicisation of appointments and transfers of judges of the High Courts and the Supreme Court. The Court has even, on occasion, issued notices to the general public giving information about the hearing of a matter and inviting interventions.[27]

Secondly, the Court has adopted informal and inquisitorial procedures for dealing with public interest litigation. '[W]hat the courts expected from the respondent, which was the State in most of the cases, was that instead of taking an adversary position, and merely denying the allegation, it should help the Court to find the truth.'[28] The Court has also held, in effect, that public interest litigation cannot be settled – even if the petitioner withdraws, the claim continues.[29]

Thirdly, the Court has taken a very broad view of justiciability, being prepared to entertain highly political disputes. Most dramatically,

---

[25] In this section, I am heavily dependent on S. P. Sathe, *Judicial Activism in India: Transgressing Borders and Enforcing Limits* (Oxford, Oxford University Press, 2002). See also A. H. Desai and S. Muralidhar, 'Public Interest Litigation: Potential and Problems' in B. N. Kirpal (ed.), *Supreme But Not Infallible: Essays in Honour of the Supreme Court of India* (Oxford, Oxford University Press, 2000).

[26] Sathe distinguishes between being non-political and being apolitical: Sathe, *Judicial Activism*, pp. 293–4. Judges cannot be apolitical, but they can be non-political in the sense of being guided by considerations of principle rather than power. Here, 'political' is used in contrast to 'non-political'. John Griffith, by contrast, thinks that 'laws are merely statements of a power relationship and nothing more': J. Griffith, 'The Political Constitution' (1979) 42 *Modern Law Review* 1 at 19.

[27] Sathe, *Judicial Activism*, pp. 17–18.   [28] *Ibid.*, p. 207   [29] *Ibid.*, p. 232.

perhaps, it has reviewed decisions made by the President of India under section 356 of the Constitution dismissing state governments (a not infrequent occurrence).[30] The Court has also been prepared to resolve polycentric disputes in a legislative manner. It has, for instance, laid down norms for the appointment of judges and ordered the government to establish an all-India judicial service in order to create uniform conditions of service for judges throughout the country. In one case, the Court was asked to set free all remand prisoners who had been in custody for long periods. It gave directions as to which prisoners should be released and as to how the backlog of cases could be reduced. In another case, it issued directions about how the Central Bureau of Intelligence should be structured.[31] In a case involving the corrupt allocation of government housing to public servants, the Court laid down a detailed scheme for undoing the illegal allocations. In another case, instead of merely striking down a law that prohibited the issuing of rickshaw licences to non-operating owners, it put in place a scheme that enabled rickshaw operators to borrow the funds needed to acquire rickshaws from their owners. It has laid down guidelines for inter-country adoptions, and to outlaw sexual harassment of women at work – in both cases filling a legislative vacuum.[32] In such cases, the judicial role is much closer to (and perhaps drew inspiration from) that played by US courts in (for instance) the prison reform litigation described by Malcolm Feeley in his essay – with the very important difference that, unlike its US counterparts, the Indian Court lacks the facilities and resources needed for active involvement in the implementation process.

Fourthly, the Court has assumed the role of champion of the poor and the politically powerless. By allowing challenges to government action to be made by socially concerned petitioners on behalf of (for instance) pavement dwellers, bonded labourers, prison inmates, accused criminals and communities displaced by development projects, the Court has sought to give a voice to groups too small or weak to make an impact

[30] Up till 1991, 'President's rule' had been imposed ninety-five times.
[31] The case concerned delays in the investigation of alleged offences by high politicians. Sathe says: '[B]ecause . . . intervention in matters of corruption was unknown in India . . . the people, having lost faith in other organs of government, chose to take recourse to judicial process even though it meant governance by judiciary.' Sathe, *Judicial Activism*, p. 145.
[32] *Ibid.*, pp. 240 and 250–1. See also *ibid.*, pp. 309–10. 'The Court seems to have taken upon itself the function of correcting . . . systemic malfunctioning . . . to go into what is generally known as the area of political questions.' *Ibid.*, p. 128.

in the political process. It has even been prepared to allow litigation to be initiated merely on the basis of letters addressed to the Court by members of the public.[33]

Despite its extreme activism, the Court is held in high regard, and orders of the Court are accepted as deserving of respect and obedience by the government as much as by the citizenry. This is partly because of the low esteem in which politicians have been held in India since the passing of the generation that was involved in the struggle for independence, and especially since the state of emergency declared by Indira Ghandi in 1975.[34] The breadth of support for the Court is indicated by the fact that, on occasions, governments have, in effect, used the judicial process to resolve issues that the political system was incapable of handling peacefully. 'For example, the controversial decision to reserve 27 per cent of public service jobs for the backward classes, which triggered a fierce agitation by young men and women of the forward classes and seems to have brought India to the verge of civil war, was accepted without protest after the Supreme Court endorsed it by majority.'[35]

> There has been talk of streamlining judicial activism but the political establishment has not had either moral courage or political strength to strip the courts of their newly acquired power. This is because the court has carved out for itself a niche in the hearts of the people . . . Although the system of justice continues to be inegalitarian and inaccessible to a large number of people and hence [public interest litigation] seems to be nothing more than tokenism, the people have reposed greater faith in judges than in politicians . . . [N]either the political establishment nor the lay people have raised any objections against judicial activism.[36]
> The political players as well as the people in general feel that in matters involving conflict between various competing interests, the courts are

---

[33] *Ibid.*, pp. 203–7. See also J. Cassels, 'Judicial Activism and Public Interest Litigation in India: Attempting the Impossible?' (1989) 37 *American Journal of Comparative Law* 495 at 508: between 1 January 1987 and 31 March 1988, the Supreme Court received almost 24,000 letters. 'Public interest litigation in the late 1970s and early 1980s was dominated by petitions on behalf of oppressed people . . . The liberal rules of access from which public interest litigation emanated enabled the courts to reach victims of injustice who so far had remained invisible.' Sathe, *Judicial Activism*, p. 209. Sathe's view is that judicial activism of the extreme sort practised by the Indian Supreme Court is only justifiable when it is done to help those who lack the power to participate effectively in the political process: *ibid.*, pp. 281–3.

[34] *Ibid.*, pp. 254–64.   [35] *Ibid.*, p. 21. See also *ibid.*, pp. 270–7.

[36] *Ibid.*, p. 247. See also *ibid.*, pp. 283–5 and 307.

better arbiters than the politicians.[37] Judicial process is expensive, dilatory, and technical and if it is preferred despite such inherent defects, it is only because the other avenues of redressal have become ineffective and unreliable.[38]

Discussion

The basic reason for setting up these four models of judicial review is to establish a relationship between the research agenda for impact studies of judicial review and the functions of judicial review. My argument is that each of the models suggests, and indeed demands, a different set of research questions about the impact of judicial review. Impact studies of judicial review are likely to be most illuminating and useful when they are based on and informed by a fine-grained and contextualised understanding and enunciation of the purposes and functions of judicial review. For instance, within a rule-of-law framework, the most obvious questions are how effective judicial review is at protecting individual rights and at reducing government lawlessness.[39] From an institutional-design perspective, obvious questions concern the impact of judicial review on the participation of interests in the rule-making process,[40] on agency rule-making procedure, and on the substance of agency policy-making. The sharp distinction between judicial review and merits review in the Australian hybrid system suggests that judicial review should not be the only, or even perhaps the main, focus of attention for studies of the protection of individual interests and the control of bureaucratic decision-making. The emphasis in the public interest model on improving the lot of the poor and underprivileged suggests a quite different set of research questions concerned as much with distributive justice as with the rights of individuals or the behaviour of government agencies.

The other point to make here is that because the nature and characteristic functions of judicial review differ significantly from one

---

[37] *Ibid.*, p. 251.   [38] *Ibid.*, p. 285.

[39] It is in this context that the attitudes of administrators to judicial review are most relevant. See e.g. M. Sunkin and K. Pick, 'The Changing Impact of Judicial Review: The Independent Review Service of the Social Fund' [2001] *Public Law* 753–9; R. Creyke and J. McMillan, 'Executive Perceptions of Administrative Law – An Empirical Study' (2002) 9 *Australian Journal of Administrative Law* 163.

[40] For a research agenda related to the decision of the US Supreme Court in *Vermont Yankee* (see note 12 above), see R. B. Stewart, 'Vermont Yankee and the Evolution of Administrative Procedure' (1978) 91 *Harvard Law Review* 1805 at 821–2.

jurisdiction to another, we need to be very careful in drawing conclusions about the likely impact of judicial review in one jurisdiction from impact studies undertaken in another jurisdiction. A good illustration of this point is John McMillan and Robin Creyke's finding that, in about 60 per cent of cases in which the Australian Federal Court set aside an agency's decision, the applicant ultimately obtained a favourable outcome.[41] Compare this with Peter Schuck and Donald Elliott's finding that remand of decisions back to US agencies resulted in 'major changes' in the petitioner's favour in 40 per cent of cases.[42] At the same time, the proportion of cases remanded by courts to agencies was roughly the same in both studies. I have no idea what the explanation might be for this significant difference in outcomes, but I am fairly confident that, whatever it is, it is not simple or obvious, if only because the institution of judicial review in the US differs significantly from its Australian counterpart. It is, therefore, impossible to say whether – or, at least, to what extent – these studies reinforce one another, even though the authors of both consider that their results run counter to a widely held view about bureaucratic response to adverse court decisions, namely that administrators usually can and do find some way to reach the same conclusion again despite the defects found by the court in the original decision.

STUDYING THE IMPACT OF JUDICIAL REVIEW ON BUREAUCRATIC BEHAVIOUR

It should be clear from the discussion so far that the concept of the 'impact' of judicial review is a complex one. For instance, in relation to a review body that has the power to substitute its decision for that of the original decision-maker, 'impact' might refer simply to the proportion of reviews that are decided, respectively, in favour of and against the person challenging the decision. By contrast, because judicial review does not typically entail the power of substitution, studying impact in that context might lead us to ask how often a review decision in favour of the challenger actually leads to a decision in that person's favour when the case is reconsidered by the original decision-maker. Again, if our interest were in judicial review as a mechanism for handling individual

---

[41] See Chapter 6 below.
[42] P. H. Schuck and E. D. Elliott, 'To the Chevron Station: An Empirical Study of Federal Administrative Law' [1990] *Duke Law Journal* 984 at 1059–60.

grievances (whether in terms of protecting individual rights or in terms of policing the legal boundaries of public powers), 'impact' would most obviously refer to the ultimate outcomes for applicants of individual judicial review proceedings. On the other hand, if our interest were in judicial review as a mechanism for addressing systemic bureaucratic failings, the fate of individual complaints would not be nearly so important. Impact in the first of these senses is the prime subject of the large empirical project undertaken by Robin Creyke, John McMillan and Denis Pearce.[43] On the other hand, Simon Halliday describes the aim of his research into the administration of homelessness legislation as being 'to provide empirical data which can contribute towards an assessment of the effectiveness of judicial review as a way of regulating the administrative process';[44] and Genevra Richardson and David Machin describe their research into the Mental Health Review Tribunal as being 'primarily designed to examine the ability of judicial review to influence the future behaviour of respondent authorities'.[45]

The general point is that study of the concept of the 'impact' of judicial review is not, and cannot be, isolated from the purposes that are ascribed to it. One view is that it is only when we understand the impact(s) of judicial review that we can meaningfully engage in (normative) debate about its functions.[46] On the other hand, we might

[43] See Chapter 6 below. See also R. Creyke, J. McMillan and D. Pearce, 'Success at Court – Does the Client Win?' in J. McMillan (ed.), *Administrative Law under the Coalition Government* (Canberra, Australian Institute of Administrative Law, 1997).

[44] S. Halliday, 'The Influence of Judicial Review on Bureaucratic Decision-Making' [2000] *Public Law* 110. T. Mullen, K. Pick and T. Prosser, *Judicial Review in Scotland* (Chichester, Wiley, 1996), p. 113, say: 'Ultimately, the most important test of review . . . is the extent to which it shapes and influences the administrative process, in particular whether it makes it more likely that administrative decisions are routinely in accordance with law.' For an earlier study of the administration of homelessness legislation, see I. D. Loveland, *Housing Homeless Persons: Administrative Law and the Administrative Process* (Oxford, Clarendon Press, 1995).

[45] G. Richardson and D. Machin, 'Judicial Review and Tribunal Decision Making: A Study of the Mental Health Review Tribunal' [2000] *Public Law* 494. The studies reported by Lorne Sossin and Yoav Dotan in this volume (Chapters 5 and 7 respectively) pursue a similar agenda. Sossin's paper also alerts us to the useful distinction between impact on high-level policy-making and impact on 'street-level' implementation. Sossin focuses on soft law. For a study that includes 'hard' law, see M. Loughlin and P. M. Quinn, 'Prisons, Rules and Courts: A Study in Administrative Law' (1993) 56 *Modern Law Review* 497.

[46] This seems to be the position of G. Richardson and M. Sunkin, 'Judicial Review: Questions of Impact' [1996] *Public Law* 79 at 80–1.

think that, by choosing to study particular impacts of judicial review and not others,[47] researchers (whether explicitly or implicitly) ascribe particular functions to judicial review and seek to discover how good it is at performing those functions. Such functions are often found in normative constitutional theory, presumably on the basis that judicial review is an institution of governance. But the concept of function may also refer to the uses to which people actually put judicial review, understanding judicial review as a strategic resource. For instance, judicial review may be seen as a good source of publicity, or as a way of getting an issue onto the political agenda, or as a component of a larger political strategy.[48] In other words, the intended functions of judicial review can be viewed from a practical as well as from a normative perspective. Because various functions can be ascribed to judicial review, and because it can be used for various purposes, it is obvious that there is no single sense in which we can speak of the 'impact' of judicial review. Moreover, any particular instance of judicial review may serve different functions for different interested parties, and more than one function for any one party. Just as there is no single perspective on the function of judicial review, so there can be no single perspective on its impact.

In addition to the complexity related to the various purposes of judicial review intended (i.e. aimed at) by its providers and consumers, difficulty in studying its impact arises from two other sources. First, it is one thing to identify 'impacts' or 'consequences' consisting of changes in bureaucratic behaviour, but quite another to establish that they are causally related to judicial review. In a case where an agency reconsiders and changes an individual decision following a successful judicial review application by the person directly affected by the decision, the causal link may be easily enough established. But, where the impact is a

---

[47] For instance, research so far has tended to focus on cases in which the applicant for judicial review has been successful, and on the impact of judicial review on those to whom the norms of administrative law are addressed as opposed to their intended beneficiaries. Indeed, the choice to study the impact of enforcement of the norms of administrative law through judicial review as opposed to the impact of the norms themselves is a significant one.

[48] A classic study is T. Prosser, *Test Cases for the Poor: Legal Techniques in the Politics of Social Welfare* (London, Child Poverty Action Group, 1983). This functional complexity is well captured by Sathe in relation to Indian public interest litigation: Sathe, *Judicial Activism*, p. 246. See generally C. Harlow and R. Rawlings, *Pressure Through Law* (London, Routledge, 1992).

change in more general modes of working, the contribution of judicial review may be much harder to trace. It is a commonplace of research in this area that administrative decision-making is a product of various and diverse pressures and influences of which the law in general, and judicial review in particular, is only one.

Secondly, even if it is established that a particular change in bureaucratic behaviour is attributable to judicial review, there may be disagreement about whether the change provides an example of judicial review performing one of its intended functions or whether it is, on the contrary, an unintended and undesirable side-effect. A good example is found in ongoing and ultimately unresolvable debates about the imposition of procedural requirements on executive decision-makers. It is widely accepted that regulating bureaucratic procedure in order to improve the quality of administrative decision-making is an appropriate function for judicial review, but also – as Martin Shapiro's account (in Chapter 9 of this volume) of judicial review of agency rule-making lucidly shows[49] – that procedural requirements can be counter-productive if they reduce the efficiency of the administrative process too much. What there is less agreement about is the optimum balance between procedure and efficiency. More importantly, it is unlikely that this disagreement could be resolved by empirical evidence about the impact of judicially imposed procedural requirements on agency behaviour because the concepts of quality and efficiency, and views about the optimum balance between them, are evaluative, not empirical.

Or consider Rosemary O'Leary's study of the impact of judicial review on the US Environmental Protection Agency,[50] which neatly illustrates the adage that one person's meat is another's poison.[51] She

[49] Shapiro's paper in this volume (Chapter 9) focuses on the impact of judicial review on the behaviour of the regulated population rather than on the behaviour of the regulators. For a public-choice-inspired analysis of the same phenomenon, see J. L. Mashaw, *Greed, Chaos and Governance: Using Public Choice to Improve Public Law* (New Haven, Yale University Press, 1997), Chapter 7.

[50] R. O'Leary, 'The Impact of Federal Court Decisions on the Policies and Administration of the US Environmental Protection Agency' (1989) 41 *Administrative Law Review* 549.

[51] Another illustration emerged in the discussion of Malcolm Feeley's paper at the conference for which the essays in this volume were originally prepared. For Feeley, the possibility that judicially engineered improvements in prison conditions might have made courts more willing to impose custodial sentences was an undesirable side-effect, whereas for Shapiro it was a good outcome.

distinguishes between 'positive' and 'negative' effects of judicial review. Amongst those effects she identifies as negative are 'increased power of legal staff' and 'decreased power and authority of scientists'. More pointedly, several of the effects she identifies appear in very similar form on both sides of the ledger. For instance, she cites reduction in the power of the Office of Management and Budget as a negative effect, and the 'lifting of . . . prolonged OMB review' as a positive effect.[52] Redistribution of resources within the agency appears as a negative effect from the point of view of the losers, and as a positive effect from the point of view of the winners.

None of this would matter so much if our only interest in studying impact were descriptive. But, because law is a purposive social institution, underlying many empirical studies of law and legal institutions is an evaluative or teleological agenda aimed at justifying and improving legal systems and practices. The possibility that judicial review might be intended to serve various purposes at the same time, and that it might have negative effects, raises the possibility (for instance) that it might serve one of its intended purposes better than it serves the other(s), or that the costs of its negative effects may outweigh the benefits of its positive effects. Both possibilities complicate very considerably the normative arguments for and against judicial review. Obviously, too, difficulty in tracing casual connections between particular effects and judicial review is highly relevant to the project of drawing normative conclusions from empirical observations.

It might help, in thinking about studying the impact of judicial review, to examine an area of the law in which there is a longer history of theoretically self-conscious, impact research, and a considerably larger body of empirical data – namely tort law. Even though there has been considerable debate about the impact of tort liability and litigation on bureaucratic behaviour, the value of studying what we know about the impact of tort law lies not in any direct comparison between tort law and the rules and principles of judicial review,[53] but rather in the fact that the empirical data about tort law has been subjected to detailed and systematic goal-oriented analysis which is relevant beyond its particular subject matter. The empirical data available as of 1995

---

[52] O'Leary, 'Impact of Federal Court Decisions', p. 567.

[53] As far as I am aware, the impact of tort liability on bureaucratic behaviour has not been rigorously investigated. The classic study in an instrumentalist vein is P. H. Schuck, *Suing Government: Citizen Remedies for Official Wrongs* (New Haven, Yale University Press, 1983).

has been carefully analysed by Dewees, Duff and Trebilcock[54] in terms of the three most widely ascribed objectives of what they call 'accident law' – deterrence, compensation and corrective justice. In terms of judicial review, compensation translates into the function of resolving individual grievances (i.e. obtaining a positive outcome for a complainant), and deterrence translates into altering patterns of bureaucratic behaviour to reduce the incidence of legitimate grievances.

So far as compensation is concerned, research into accident law has dealt with questions such as:

- In the relevant universe of adverse events (say, personal injury), what proportion of events theoretically fall within the scope of 'accident law', thus qualifying for compensation?
- In the universe of theoretically compensatable adverse events, what proportion of events actually attract compensation through accident law?
- In the universe of adverse events that actually attract compensation through accident law, what proportion go to trial and what proportion are settled? In what proportion of cases is legal process issued, and what proportion are set down for trial?
- How long does it take to get compensation? What is the time gap between the occurrence of the compensation-attracting events and the receipt of compensation? How does accident law compare in this respect with other 'compensation systems' such as social security?
- How does accident law compare with other compensation systems in terms of the administrative costs of delivering compensation and in terms of the amounts of compensation received?
- What happens to people after they receive compensation? Is the compensation adequate for the purposes for which it is given? How do claimants feel about the 'compensation experience'? Do attitudes vary at different times?
- In terms of these various issues, do cases that are settled differ significantly and relevantly from cases that go to trial?

So far as deterrence is concerned, questions such as the following have been asked by impact researchers:

- What impact does accident law have on the incidence of adverse events that theoretically fall within its scope?

[54] D. Dewees, D. Duff and M. Trebilcock, *Exploring the Domain of Accident Law Taking the Facts Seriously* (New York, Oxford University Press, 1996).

- What is the cost of achieving this impact?
- How does accident law compare with other relevant regulatory mechanisms on a cost–benefit basis?
- Does the regulatory impact of accident law vary according to the causes of adverse events? For instance, is tort law better at deterring dangerous driving than environmental pollution?
- What is the regulatory impact of the risk of being sued – as opposed to actually being sued, whether successfully or not?
- Does accident law have undesirable collateral regulatory effects? For instance, does it encourage 'defensive' behaviour, and does it reduce participation in certain activities to sub-optimal levels?
- What is the relationship between the deterrence function and the compensation function of accident law? What is the impact of insurance on the deterrence function?

With appropriate modifications, each of these questions about the compensatory and deterrent functions of accident law could be asked in relation to judicial review. Merely listing the questions is enough to show that, relative to the investigation of the impact of accident law, the study of the impact of judicial review is in its infancy. The Dewees, Duff and Trebilcock review and discussion of the empirical evidence about the consequences of accident law runs to more than 400 pages. It is unlikely that a similar review of research into the impact of judicial review would justify such lengthy analysis. This is not meant in any way as a criticism of public lawyers or of the state of empirical research into public law. There are, no doubt, various excellent reasons and explanations for this state of affairs. Nor am I suggesting that we can draw any conclusions about the impact of judicial review from studies about the impact of tort law. My only point is that empirical researchers in the public law area might find the tort-law research suggestive and helpful when it comes to designing fruitful agendas of research into the impact of judicial review.

The third function ascribed to accident law by Dewees, Duff and Trebilcock is corrective justice. Amongst theorists who understand and analyse accident law in terms of corrective justice, the concept itself is a contested one. However, all corrective justice theories share at least two characteristics. First, they are non-instrumentalist in orientation. Corrective justice is based on ideas such as justice, morality and responsibility. From this perspective, tort law must be judged according to how closely it conforms to a particular normative conception of interpersonal and social rights and obligations rather than in terms of how well it achieves social goals such as compensation and deterrence. In other words, corrective justice is a theory about the legal doctrine and the values embodied in it, and about the architecture of legal institutions, not about the impact of law and legal institutions.[55]

Secondly, all corrective justice theories stress the bilaterality or correlativity of accident law. In accident law, the rights of the injured person are defined in terms of the obligations of the injurer, and *vice versa*. In this respect, accident law is fundamentally different from, on the one hand, compensation systems such as social security and, on the other, regulatory systems such as the criminal law. In this respect, too, the corrective-justice approach is very different from the instrumentalist approach of scholars such as Dewees, Duff and Trebilcock. For them, the key to understanding and assessing accident law lies in disaggregating the various functions ascribed to accident law and examining in turn how well it serves each. For the corrective-justice theorist, the result of this strategy of disaggregation is that what is being studied and evaluated is not accident law, because looking at compensation in isolation, or at deterrence in isolation, involves ignoring one of the two inextricably linked poles of accident law doctrine.

The importance of this debate can be seen in the way Dewees, Duff and Trebilcock deal with corrective-justice theory. They refuse to engage with it as a non-instrumental theory, and, to the extent that they consider it, they do so in terms of the goals of compensation and deterrence. On this basis, accident law is bound to score badly: because corrective justice looks to both sides of the equation at the same time, assessing accident law instrumentally as a vehicle of corrective justice involves saddling it with the sum of its compensatory and deterrent deficiencies. What Dewees, Duff and Trebilcock do not contemplate is that there might be a non-instrumentalist justification for accident law. Such a justification would not, of course, entail that accident law was

---

[55] Note, however, that the non-instrumentalist approach does not entail that tort law performs no social function. For example, embodying (and enforcing) sound principles of personal responsibility can itself be seen as a social function of tort law. The crucial difference between the instrumentalist and the non-instrumentalist lies in where they look to discover whether law is performing its functions. The instrumentalist looks to its impact on behaviour whereas the non-instrumentalist looks at its content and institutional structure. For both, the question of whether tort law is performing its functions is an 'empirical' one, but the evidence relevant to answering that question differs as between the two points of view.

normatively justified regardless of its consequences. But it would entail that in judging the value of accident law, *all things considered*, it would be legitimate and indeed necessary to take account of non-instrumental as well as instrumental factors. Putting the point crudely, for the non-instrumentalist tort law might be valuable even if it scored badly as a compensation and deterrence mechanism, by virtue of the fact that it embodied certain values and expressed them in (enforceable) principles of personal responsibility.

This discussion, I would argue, is just as relevant to judicial review law as to accident law. One aspect of the now-iconic distinction, originally drawn by Carol Harlow and Rick Rawlings, between red-light and green-light theories of administrative law[56] is that red-lighters tend to understand and assess administrative law non-instrumentally in terms of its congruity with constitutional values such as parliamentary sovereignty, individual rights, the rule of law and separation of powers. By contrast, green-lighters tend to view administrative law instrumentally in terms of the contribution it can make to 'good governance' and the furtherance of the projects of governance. Scholars who study the impact of judicial review are, of course, instrumentalist in approach, whether their interest is in judicial review as a grievance-handling mechanism or as a means of modifying bureaucratic behaviour.[57] But the two perspectives – the instrumental and the non-instrumental – are not mutually exclusive. Saying that the consequences of judicial review are important to its assessment and justification does not entail that only its consequences are important. Nor, in the public-law context, can the non-instrumental approach be subsumed, without remainder, under the instrumental, any more than it can be in the accident-law context. For non-instrumentalists, the justification of administrative

---

[56] C. Harlow and R. Rawlings, *Law and Administration*, (2nd edn, London, Butterworths, 1997), Chapters 2 and 3.

[57] Instrumentalists tend to be more interested in legal institutions than in legal doctrine, perhaps because it seems easier to study the impact of norm-enforcement than of the norms themselves. But both Genevra Richardson and Maurice Sunkin in their essays in this volume (Chapters 4 and 2 respectively) discuss the hypothesis that norms of procedural legality are more likely than norms of substantive legality to affect bureaucratic behaviour. Because law is largely dependent for its effectiveness on compliance-without-enforcement (enforcement is pathological in a well-functioning legal system: K. Hawkins, *Law as a Last Resort: Prosecution Decision-Making in a Regulatory Agency* (Oxford, Oxford University Press, 2002)) focusing on enforcement institutions – courts and tribunals – provides a limited perspective on law's impact.

law does not depend solely on its ability (such as it is) to resolve individual grievances against public functionaries favourably to complainants, or to improve bureaucratic procedures and compliance with the law, but also, to some extent at least, on the very constitutional values that the rules of administrative law embody and that the institutions of judicial review are available to vindicate.

THE LIMITS OF IMPACT STUDIES

This conclusion is not purely of theoretical importance. One of the most significant lessons to be learned from (and about) empirical research in law concerns ignorance and uncertainty. Research into the behavioural impact of law and legal institutions is very expensive, time consuming and methodologically difficult. Even in areas such as accident law, where there is quite a large body of empirical data, we know relatively little about the impact(s) of the law. In relation to judicial review, many impact studies begin by saying how little we know, and explain that the work being presented makes only a small contribution to filling the gap in our knowledge. Moreover, the conclusions of impact studies of judicial review are typically modest in scope and hedged about with numerous qualifications and caveats. Researchers warn that it is much harder to trace the impact of judicial review on patterns of bureaucratic behaviour than on the outcome of individual cases, partly because bureaucratic behaviour is influenced by so many factors.[58] Reaching generally valid and useful conclusions about the impact(s) of judicial review is difficult partly because a wide variety of functions and institutions are subject to judicial review, and the number of cases available to be studied in relation to any one of them is relatively small.[59] We must face the fact that, for the foreseeable future, our knowledge of the impact(s) of judicial review will be partial and patchy, to say the least.[60] The same is surely true of institutions that might be seen as alternative or supplementary to judicial review.

[58] E.g. Mullen, Pick and Prosser, *Judicial Review in Scotland*, p. 115.

[59] On the issue of macro versus micro research, see P. H. Schuck and E. D. Elliott, 'Studying Administrative Law: A Methodology for, and Report on, New Empirical Research' (1990) 40 *Administrative Law Review* 519 at 529.

[60] I do not mean to cast doubt on the importance of empirical research, but only to counsel caution in drawing conclusions from it broader than the evidence supports. Certainly, the fact that empirical research often raises more questions than it answers does not lessen its value in stimulating and informing debate.

It seems to me, therefore, that, even if one took a purely instrumental approach to assessing judicial review, according to which its justification depended entirely on a cost–benefit analysis of its effects, the extent of our ignorance and uncertainty about those effects would require guesses to be made, on the basis of what is often called 'intuition', about whether the game was worth the candle. (Incidentally, impact studies rarely go beyond ascertaining the consequences of judicial review to engage in such a cost–benefit analysis. In this respect, the literature on accident law is somewhat in advance of the public law literature.) My hypothesis[61] is that 'intuition' is typically a euphemism for non-instrumental judgments about the value of judicial review. When the evidence runs out, value judgment takes its place. People who think that there are good non-instrumental arguments for judicial review (who, in other words, think that the norms and institutions of judicial review embody and are based on sound constitutional values) will tend to fill gaps in the evidence in such a way as to support the conclusion that the impact of judicial review is positive, and those who do not will tend to fill them in such a way as to support the conclusion that the impact of judicial review is negative or non-existent.

Of course, not everyone thinks that judicial review is to be justified and assessed in purely instrumental terms. For such people, although the facts about the impact of judicial review are certainly relevant, they cannot be conclusive because judicial review embodies values that deserve to be observed and promoted for their own sake. Law can be important not only on account of what it practically achieves but also on account of what it symbolically stands for. In politics, as in life, symbols can be important regardless of their actual impact on the world. Under the public interest model, judicial review may be seen to express the aspiration of a distributionally just(er) society. Under the rule-of-law model, it may be seen to promote a vision of a fair relationship between governor and governed. Under the separation-of-powers model, it may be seen to embody politically sound principles of institutional design. Judicial review can perform such non-instrumental symbolic functions simply by existing and being available. Judicial review is symbolically important for the values it embodies and protects. From this perspective, judicial enforcement of administrative-law norms has value independently of its behavioural impact.

---

[61] Which is, of course, itself capable, in theory at least, of being empirically tested.

41

CONCLUSION

The basic point that I have sought to make in this paper is that study of the impact of judicial review (as of other bodies of law and legal institutional arrangements) takes place against the background of assumptions and assertions (both express and implied) about the purposes and functions of judicial review. Views about such purposes and functions affect the choice and definition of the impacts to be studied, and the conclusions drawn from the data collected. These various links between views about functions and purposes on the one hand, and studies of impact on the other, underline the importance of taking care in defining the term 'judicial review' in the phrase 'the impact of judicial review'. There are many technical and practical obstacles in the way of the impact researcher; and it is, of course, extremely important to address these. But it is just as important for the impact researcher to address and articulate the normative foundations on which the research, and the conclusions drawn from it, are based.

However, I have also suggested that because, for the foreseeable future, our knowledge of the impact of judicial review is likely to be quite limited, it is important to acknowledge the role of non-instrumental understandings of judicial review in assessments of its function and value. Just as each of the models of judicial review generates a different impact-research agenda, so each of the models suggests a distinctive non-instrumental understanding of judicial review. In the face of ignorance and uncertainty about what judicial review can achieve, such understandings of what judicial review is and is for are just as important as impact studies to the task of deciding whether it is a good thing or not.

CHAPTER TWO

CONCEPTUAL ISSUES IN RESEARCHING THE IMPACT OF JUDICIAL REVIEW ON GOVERNMENT BUREAUCRACIES

MAURICE SUNKIN

INTRODUCTION AND BACKGROUND

Attempts to understand the impact of judicial review are undertaken for a variety of reasons, most generally because such an understanding tells us something about the ways in which courts matter. This, of course, is of interest for a multitude of reasons to those working in a broad range of contexts across a spectrum of disciplines from constitutional law, political science, and socio-legal studies to organisational and political theory. The rich variety of approaches that may be adopted when studying impact offers researchers considerable scope, but it carries dangers particularly for those attempting to make use of research that may have been undertaken within particular disciplinary frameworks[1] or in the context of other jurisdictions. In the previous chapter, Peter Cane argued, for example, that the impact of judicial review can be effectively researched only in the light of the assumed or asserted purposes and functions of judicial review and that these are likely to vary depending on jurisdictional factors and the approach being taken.

Given the opportunities for researchers and the risks that are associated with cross-disciplinary and cross-jurisdictional research, it is important for those working in this field to be clear about the nature and purpose of their research as well as the ground to be covered.

---

[1] See e.g. the debates surrounding G. N. Rosenberg's *The Hollow Hope: Can Courts Bring About Social Change* (Chicago, University of Chicago, 1991) in D. A. Schultz (ed.), *Leveraging the Law: Using the Courts to Achieve Social Change* (New York, Peter Lang, 1998).

Perspectives, approaches and goals may vary widely, but clarification, particularly in relation to the basic conceptual building blocks of the work to be undertaken, should always be sought when designing research.[2] The attempt to satisfy this elementary requirement will provide a useful rigour at the planning stage. It will also help to ensure that the data generated are reliable and valid and of use to those seeking to draw from the research findings. As McCann has observed, while there is ample room for different frameworks and approaches, 'it is the careful specification of basic concepts and theoretical frames that is most important. After all no study can examine all the effects of legal action, or even all the important effects.'[3]

In this paper I shall survey some of the main conceptual issues raised when seeking to identify what research into judicial review and bureaucratic impact might be about. While I hope that the issues raised will be of value across jurisdictions, as a UK public lawyer I shall draw for illustration upon the UK legal system in general and my own empirical work in particular. The chapter will consider two main sets of issues. The first concerns what might be described as issues of territory: what ground is to be covered in research on the impact of judicial review on bureaucracy? This involves identifying the terrain to be covered and defining its features. In this context, two basic questions may be asked: (a) the impact of what? and (b) the impact on what?[4] The second set of issues are evaluative and analytical in nature. They are concerned, in particular, with the problems associated with investigating and understanding 'impacts' as well as issues of causation.

In drawing a distinction between matters of definition and evaluation, I am conscious that these issues are not always easily distinguished, especially when definitions are themselves dependent on the evaluative approach taken. To take one example: some might argue that one cannot define what is meant by terms such as 'impact' or 'judicial review' in the abstract without regard to one's analytical approach or broader research methodology. Halliday, for instance, has argued that

---

[2] Concepts may be defined as being 'categories for the organisation of ideas and observations': M. Bulmer, 'Facts, Concepts, Theories and Problems' in M. Bulmer (ed.), *Social Research Methods* (London, Macmillan, 1984). See generally A. Bryman, *Social Research Methods* (Oxford, Oxford University Press, 2001), Chapter 2.

[3] M. W. McCann, 'Law and Political Struggles for Social Change: Puzzles, Paradoxes, and Promises in Future Research', in Schultz, *Leveraging the Law*, p. 336.

[4] G. Richardson and M. Sunkin, 'Judicial Review: Questions of Impact' [1996] *Public Law* 79.

one cannot properly understand the nature of the impact of judicial review on administrative procedures without first understanding the nature of administrative procedures. He says that, since administrative procedures involve a process of interpretation and reinterpretation of influences such as judicial review, the 'impact' of judicial review continuously mutates.[5] Indeed, adopting this interpretivist approach, it might be said that the meaning of judicial review itself is likely to change as the process of reinterpretation occurs so that, when viewed from the perspective of the administrator, the concept of judicial review is bound to be indeterminate rather than fixed. I shall return to these observations later in this chapter, and this is certainly not the place to dispute them. Nonetheless, as I have already indicated, it is convenient, at least for the moment, to assume that we can distinguish between definitional issues on the one hand and analytical or evaluative issues on the other.

Before moving on, an example might help to focus on some of the practical issues that might arise at the initial stages of research planning. Let us imagine that researchers are designing a project on the impact of judicial review. They are working in a single jurisdiction and share a similar conception of the broad constitutional and political purpose of judicial review. Nonetheless, at an early stage in the planning, questions arise as to what precisely is to be studied. The broad plan is to focus on the impact of several key judicial decisions concerned with immigration. But, within this plan, what is it about these decisions that is to be investigated? Are the researchers interested in the impact of the decisions themselves, or with other matters such as the effectiveness of the remedies issued by the court, the significance or otherwise of the principles or norms contained within, or established by, the judgments? During these early discussions, it emerges that the researchers might also be interested in why the claimants went to court and what they hoped to achieve. It was also suggested that it would be worthwhile investigating the dynamics of the litigation process, including, for instance, how the defendant public bodies responded to the challenges and whether, for example, there were attempts to secure settlements and, if so, why (and why did they fail in these instances?). Even before the researchers started considering the types of impact they were expecting to study it was apparent that key decisions must be made

[5] S. Halliday, 'Researching the "Impact" of Judicial Review on Routine Administrative Decision-Making' in D. Cowan (ed.), *Housing: Participation and Exclusion* (Dartmouth, Aldershot, 1998), p. 196.

about the focus and priorities of the project. One very basic reason for this is that research into the impact of court decisions is likely to be a very different exercise to undertaking research into access to, and use of, the court system, not to mention undertaking an investigation of the dynamics of litigation, including reasons why parties handle cases in the way they do and why some matters are settled and others fail to be resolved by the courts. While a single well-designed project might enable each of these aspects to be explored successfully, that research would almost inevitably be extremely complex and involve compromises. Where the real interest is in impact, this needs to be clear from the outset even if this means that other tantalising issues have to be left for another day (or another academic lifetime).

In presenting the situation in this way I do not mean to imply all the relevant issues will be apparent at the outset of research. The situation is often the opposite of this. Many of the most important and interesting conceptual questions may only arise during the research as issues emerge or once the research has been undertaken and sense is being made of the data. After all it is in the nature of research that we cannot always anticipate what will be found. Nonetheless, there is, as they say, no substitute for careful planning.

MAPPING THE TERRITORY

The impact of what?

Cane has already provided an overview of a range of constitutional functions performed by judicial review. He has shown that the nature of this institution, and the expectations associated with it, vary widely. Researchers must therefore be sensitive to the constitutional and jurisdictional context. This, of course, is not to say that the nature of judicial review remains constant even within specific jurisdictions. Changes occur over time. Some of these will flow from constitutional reforms, such as the enactment in the United Kingdom of the Human Rights Act 1998 or devolution. Others will be associated with less tangible factors including the way legal issues and rights questions are viewed within society, the extent to which the courts are used to achieve policy reform by pressure groups, the activism or otherwise of the judiciary, and the general political responses to judgments.

The British constitutional setting is, of course, famous for being subject to incremental change, and over the past few decades developments in judicial review and its role in relation to government have been especially dynamic. In the context of this paper, a key feature of this period of judicial review in the United Kingdom is neatly captured by the contrasting observations to be found in de Smith's *Judicial Review of Administrative Action*. In each of the five editions of this work, it is said that: 'Judicial review provides just one of a number of legal controls of administrative action and its role is inevitably sporadic and peripheral.' However, in the fifth edition the editors thought it necessary to add that: 'the effect of judicial review on the practical exercise of power has now become constant and central.'[6]

There is much in these statements to interest the empirical researcher of impact. If the influence of judicial review on the exercise of power has shifted from being peripheral to being central and constant, what explanations are there for this? Is it in fact the case? If so, in what sense, or senses, is the importance of judicial review now central and constant? More generally, how does this growth in the importance of judicial review affect such matters as the content of policy, the structure of administrative systems, the behaviour of officials, and so on? I shall return to some of these questions, but before doing so I propose to look at three ways of viewing the institution of judicial review that may be relevant to researchers across jurisdictions, namely: as a process; as specific judicial decisions; and as a system of values and legal norms.

Judicial review as process
Despite the traditional preoccupation of legal academics with judicial decisions, it is well established that the whole process of litigation may be of interest to those concerned with bureaucratic reactions to judicial review. Gambitta,[7] for example, has shown that litigation provides access to the government arena, helps to elicit answers and information from public agencies and achieves publicity, and can legitimate claims even if they are ultimately unsuccessfully pursued in the courts. Both macro and micro issues are raised by accounts such as this.

At a macro level such accounts raise the broad question of the ways in which judicial review may be mobilised by individuals or groups to challenge government and secure constitutional, political and social change. Related to this is a host of questions about the effectiveness

---

[6] S. A. De Smith, H. Woolf and J. A. Jowell, *Judicial Review of Administrative Action* (5th edn, London, Sweet & Maxwell, 1995), p. vii.

[7] R. Gambitta, 'Litigation, Judicial Deference and Policy Change' in R. Gambitta, M. May and J. Foster (eds.), *Governing Through Courts* (New York, Sage, 1981).

of using the courts to lever reform and to generate publicity or raise awareness about issues of debate. These in turn raise important questions about the ways in which government and their political strategists view the courts and prepare for and respond to litigation. When a politician criticises the judges in the press following an embarrassing failure in the courts (as the Home Secretary, David Blunkett MP, did immediately following Collins J's decision in R. (on the Application of Q and others v. Secretary of State for the Home Department,[8] declaring the government's asylum procedures to be unlawful[9]), is this to be understood as an unplanned outburst by a frustrated politician? Or is it part of a deliberate strategy designed to undermine the judges generally or this judge in particular and thereby reduce the political impact of the decision and inhibit the making of similar decisions in the future?

Threats of litigation At the micro level Gambitta reminds us that specific challenges to governmental decisions may exert influences even before final judicial determinations are made and even if the case is withdrawn before that stage is reached. As we shall see in a moment, the mere threat of challenge may exert an inhibiting effect on policy and influence decision-making, and the degree to which it does so is likely to vary depending on the precision of the threatened challenge, the nature of the litigant and the sensitivity of the issues involved. Legal challenges that call into question sensitive areas of executive policy and/or which are instituted by those represented by lawyers with a reputation for mounting well-directed challenges or which are brought by experienced and respected interest groups are likely to be approached by public bodies with particular care.[10] Certainly the need to respond to legal challenge will absorb resources and emotional energy. As James puts it, 'the very business of going to court is fraught with danger and inconvenience for officials'.[11]

---

[8] 19 February 2003, upheld by the Court of Appeal, [2003] EWCA Civ. 364; [2003] 3 WLR 365.

[9] The Daily Mail, not a natural supporter of the Labour Government, joined with the Home Secretary in criticising this decision. Under a headline that covered the front page, the paper asked: 'So What Have Our Judges Got Against Britain?' (Daily Mail, 20 February 2003, p. 1).

[10] M. Sunkin and K. Pick, 'The Changing Impact of Judicial Review: The Independent Review Service of the Social Fund' [2001] Public Law 736 at 757 (hereafter referred to as the IRS study).

[11] S. James, 'The Political and Administrative Consequences of Judicial Review' (1996) 74 Public Administration 613–37 at 619.

In some situations challenge will activate internal procedures aimed at reviewing the original decision or policies and procedures in order to plan either for settlement out of court or an unfavourable judicial decision.[12] Machinery for reconsidering decisions that are being appealed against or challenged in judicial review proceedings is probably now commonplace. How effective this machinery is in correcting error is open to question, however. For instance, it has been noted in the context of social security appeals in the United Kingdom that in 1997 social security appeal tribunals overturned 35 per cent of appeals against adverse decisions that had already been reviewed by Benefits Agency officials.[13] Nonetheless, there can be little doubt that significant resources are, for a variety of reasons, invested in such internal procedures and that their presence may have implications for decision-makers within the system as well as for the way the system 'internalises' judicial review norms and values. Sunkin and Pick's research on the Independent Review Service of the Social Fund (the IRS study), for example, illuminated the care that is taken within the IRS to reconsider decisions that have been challenged and the range of factors taken into account when deciding whether or not the decisions should be changed. In addition to the substantive or procedural quality of the decision, these included factors such as the importance of the issue, the resource implications, and the perceived value of obtaining clarification of the law. There is in addition an important personal dimension. It is clear from this research that, while the original decision-makers will feel supported when the organisation decides to defend a challenge, the decision to concede may provoke strong feelings, ranging from puzzlement to abandonment, amongst even experienced and case-hardened decision-makers. These feelings are likely to be particularly strong if the decision-maker feels that an adequate explanation has not been given to him or her for the body's decision.[14]

---

[12] An example is provided by the government's response to R. (on the Application of Q and others) v. Secretary of State for the Home Department [2003] EWCA Civ. 364; [2003] 3 WLR 365. By the time this case had reached the Court of Appeal, the relevant procedures were being 'radically overhauled', a factor that was clearly relevant to that court: see [2003] EWCA Civ. 364, [2003] 3 WLR 365 at para. 120.

[13] R. Sainsbury, 'Social Security Decision-Making and Appeals: Chequered History, Uncertain Future?' in N. Harris (ed.), Social Security Law in Context (Oxford, Oxford University Press, 2000), p. 208.

[14] Sunkin and Pick, 'The Changing Impact', p. 757.

This personal dimension may be especially important to those concerned with the effects of judicial review on the attitudes and behaviour of officials. In this context one of the striking features of the IRS research was the contrast between the way Social Fund Inspectors with personal experience of judicial review were likely to approach challengeable decisions and the approach of those with no direct personal experience of judicial review or its threat. Broadly speaking, the former group indicated that they were much more likely to be cautious and to adopt a defensive approach and much readier to seek advice. In other words, the data indicated that the behaviour of the Social Fund Inspectors did appear to change as the incidence of scrutiny (both internal and external) increased, and it appeared to do so independently of general organisational considerations. This implies that there may in fact be a link between the actual incidence of challenge and the behaviour and attitude of decision-makers. This finding is significant given that judicial review will be an extremely rare event for most officials, the vast majority of whom will never have direct contact with the process.

Settlement Settlement is also a significant element of judicial review litigation, and warrants brief comment.[15] Certainly it is now recognised to play a key role within the British system. Thus, by the mid-1990s only approximately one-sixth of all judicial review claims in England and Wales reached a substantive hearing. Approximately one-third was refused permission to proceed, and approximately 50 per cent were withdrawn following a settlement.[16] As well as being important from the point of view of case flow, the process of settlement raises a number of issues of principle. The first concerns the quality of settlements reached, given the typically 'informal' nature of negotiation between an individual or group on the one hand and a public body, that may be far better resourced and experienced in these matters, on the other. Settlement also raises issues of more general significance. The ability to settle is, for example, an ability to keep controversial public interest issues or sensitive issues of policy out of court. This

---

[15] See generally M. Sunkin, 'Withdrawing: A Problem in Judicial Review?' in P. Leyland and T. Woods (eds.), *Administrative Law Facing the Future: Old Constraints and New Horizons* (London, Blackstone Press, 1997).

[16] See L. Bridges, G. Meszaros and M. Sunkin, 'Regulating Judicial Review' [2000] *Public Law* 651 at 666–9. See also *The Impact of the Human Rights Act on Judicial Review* (London, Public Law Project, 2003).

may be extremely valuable for public authorities and especially for those that are regularly challenged by judicial review proceedings.[17] For the researcher of impact this raises a host of issues associated with the way public bodies organise themselves to prepare for settlements: how they decide what cases to concede and what to fight; how lawyers and policy-makers work together in making such decisions; and how, if at all, such decisions are monitored and controlled. Perhaps the most important issues are concerned with the relative influence of settled outcomes as contrasted with judicial decisions. Apart from saving resources, one of the most common reasons for settling a public law case is assumed to be the ability to resolve a specific problem without risking the integrity of the system or the policy that gave rise to that problem. But, does this mean that settlements have no effects within the system beyond the instant case? Is settlement a process that generates purely unique events? If these questions were to be explored empirically it is likely that the findings would indicate that settlements, and the processes that lead to settlements, do have influences within the organisations and that they are complex and subtle; how they differ from the influence of court decisions themselves would also be interesting to explore.

Judicial review as judgments

Not surprisingly, much of the work on impact has focused on reaction to particular decisions or a series of decisions in particular contexts. However, researchers have rarely explained why they have chosen to concentrate on decisions rather than on other aspects of the litigation process. Halliday is an exception. He tells us that he focused his work on what he called 'extreme case' scenarios in order to test 'the hypothesis that judicial review has a "hortatory role"'.[18] He also argued that administrators' experience of the effects of final judgments, '*symbolizes* the fullest immersion of the administrative decision-making process into the legal world'.[19]

---

[17] Cf. T. Daintith and A. Page, *The Executive in the Constitution* (Oxford, Oxford University Press, 1999), who consider governmental attitudes to settlement in the context of their discussion of whether the executive adopts a strategic approach to litigation, especially at pp. 341–3.

[18] S. Halliday, 'The Influence of Judicial Review on Bureaucratic Decision-Making' [2000] *Public Law* 110 at 111.

[19] Halliday, 'Researching the "Impact" of Judicial Review', p. 192.

When working from judgments two preliminary issues suggest themselves. The first concerns the range and type of judgments to be included in the study. Researchers might, for example, be concerned with a sample of decisions, say, over certain periods; with decisions in particular areas such as immigration or housing; with decisions that have particular constitutional or policy dimensions; with decisions of particular courts, or even decisions of particular judges. Whatever the sample, when selecting cases it is important to remember that doctrinal importance is not necessarily an indication of bureaucratic importance. For administrators the significance of decisions will be determined by how easy a decision is to live with rather than by whether it breaks new legal ground. 'Liveability' will depend on factors such as whether the decision dictates the introduction of a new policy framework, the establishment of new procedures, or the adoption of new approaches to decision-making.[20] The House of Lords decision in *Khawaja*[21] is a good illustration of a landmark legal decision that held that the Home Office had acted unlawfully, but which appeared to have relatively little impact on the administration. It was held that the power to deport an 'illegal entrant' meant that the authorities had to establish that a person was actually an 'illegal entrant' before they deported him and that they could not rely on their belief, no matter how reasonably held, that he fell within this category. This decision therefore called for new fact-finding rigour, but it did not call for a new policy framework and its effect on the administration was therefore minimal.[22]

A related point is that the impact of decisions is not necessarily directly linked to the legal success or otherwise of the challenge.[23] It certainly cannot be assumed that decisions that support a public body will necessarily have less impact than decisions that go against it. For one thing, the actual decision on the particular facts may be less significant to the parties than, say, the guidance offered by judges on the approach to be taken to cases in the future,[24] or the approach taken

---

[20] M. Sunkin, 'Judicial Review's Liveability' [1989] *Legal Action* 10.

[21] *R. v. Home Secretary, ex parte Khawaja* [1984] AC 74.

[22] Richardson and Sunkin, 'Questions of Impact', p. 91.

[23] Gambitta, 'Litigation'; R. O'Leary, 'The Impact of Federal Court Decisions on the Policies and Administration of the US Environmental Protection Agency' (1989) 41 *Administrative Law Review* 549.

[24] E.g. in the context of the Social Fund, the decision of Brooke J in *R. v. Social Fund Inspector, ex parte Ali* (1994) 6 Admin LR 205 was perceived to be 'particularly useful'

by judges to interpretational issues. Moreover, it cannot be assumed that a failure in the courts will necessarily be altogether unwelcome. The decision, while unwelcome on the facts, may bring clarification of the law. Judicial decisions, whether favourable or not, may also confer legitimacy on a body that can show that its actions are founded on a legal rather than a non-legal base. These two factors, the provision of clarity and legitimacy, were certainly claimed by the Independent Review Service of the Social Fund to be as important as success or failure in the courts during its early days.[25] Failure in the courts may even vindicate the real views or aims of the body or section most directly concerned.

These observations indicate that context may be extremely important to any assessment of the impact of judgments. The publicity associated with controversial decisions, for instance, may appear to be as important as (or even more important than) the decision itself, especially when the judgment concerns high-level executive policy or issues that are socially or ethically controversial. Where judgments, for example, become the focus for public campaigns, attract media attention or lead to questions in Parliament, it is inevitably important to distinguish between the direct impact of the case on those immediately affected by it and its broader more amorphous indirect impacts. This in turn raises issues associated with the nature of impact and causation, to which I shall return.

One of the implications of the above discussion is that researchers may be unable to rely exclusively on the law reports or on doctrinal discussions in order to select the decisions to be investigated. In many situations, some preliminary field work will be useful in order to identify decisions that the relevant authorities believe have had the most significant impact. In sampling it might then be useful to explore any differences there may be between decisions that have attracted the attention of commentators or the press and those which appear to be significant to the relevant organisations.[26]

---

in so far as it reminded inspectors of the need to look at the needs of the family in the round without being deflected by any particular factor: Social Fund Commissioner's Annual Report 1992–3, para. 5.4. cited in Sunkin and Pick, 'The Changing Impact', p. 746 n. 40.

[25] Sunkin and Pick, 'The Changing Impact'.

[26] A contrast between decisions that are doctrinally important and decisions that are perceived to be of importance to public bodies might itself make an interesting study.

Legal norms, values and principles

A further set of issues concerns the complexity of judgments and the messages they convey.[27] After all, there is much more potential interest in judgments than the decision itself. Indeed, for some researchers the real interest lies in the impact and influence of general principles, or the legal values and norms enunciated or implied in judicial decisions. In this context their concern might be with the ways in which notions such as legal rationality or judicial conceptions of fairness or natural justice are accommodated by, or infused within, bureaucratic systems and administrative cultures.[28] To what extent, for instance, can one meaningfully speak of the rule of law as institutional morality[29] or of managerial systems satisfying the requirements of 'bureaucratic justice'?[30]

The interests of others might be focused upon the impact of particular legal doctrines or requirements, such as the developing principles regarding substantive legitimate expectations, the giving of reasons, or, in the United Kingdom, the impact of the emerging principle of proportionality, and the requirement to comply with human rights.[31] Others might be interested in the impact of particular forms of relief such as the differences if any between the effects of declaratory orders, injunctions or orders to pay compensation.[32] This particular aspect might be of particular interest in the context of the study of whether the form of remedial relief affects compliance; an issue that is of considerable interest in a system such as that of the United Kingdom where it is often claimed that the relationship between courts and government is ultimately based on trust rather than coercion.[33]

There has certainly been much speculation that the impact of judicial decisions depends on the legal principles involved. Feldman, for

---

[27] Cf. Galanter's assertion that judicial decisions contain messages that 'are resources that parties use in envisioning, devising, pursuing, negotiating, and vindicating claims': M. Galanter, 'The Radiating Effects of Courts' in K. O. Boyum and L. Mather (eds.), *Empirical Theories about Courts* (New York, Longman, 1983), pp. 117–42.

[28] McCann, 'Law and Political Struggles'.

[29] J. Jowell, 'The Rule of Law Today' in J. Jowell and D. Oliver (eds.), *The Changing Constitution* (4th edn, Oxford, Oxford University Press, 2000).

[30] J. Mashaw, *Bureaucratic Justice* (New Haven, Yale University Press, 1983).

[31] L. Clements and R. Morris, 'The Millenium Blip: The Human Rights Act 1998 and Local Government' in S. Halliday and P. Schmidt (eds.), *Human Rights Brought Home: Socio-Legal Perspectives on Human Rights in the National Context* (Oxford, Hart Publishing, 2004).

[32] See Chapter 8 below.

[33] Lord Woolf in M. v. *Home Office* [1993] 3 All ER 537 at 567b.

example, has argued that the courts have evolved three techniques for 'controlling' administrative behaviour: directing, limiting and structuring.[34] His argument is that different sets of legal principles work differently to control administration. For example, the traditional *ultra vires* doctrine directs bodies by imposing specific controls on the scope of permissible action. By contrast, rules concerned with common law fairness provide more *ex ante* guidance and are likely to have a wider impact on administrative procedures than the narrower *ultra vires* principles. While issue may be taken with the particular typology used, it is certainly plausible that the impact of decisions depends on the legal principles being enunciated. It has, for example been widely speculated that process-based values may have a greater long-term impact on administrative systems than substantive principles. Richardson and Sunkin, for example, have raised the possibility that:

> Although the ability of juridical norms to infiltrate administrative cultures is likely to be limited, it may be that certain values, those associated with process for example, are more readily internalised than others.[35]

Issues of this sort will be of central concern for some researchers and may require careful consideration of the precise legal content of judgments. Richardson and Machin, for example, found it essential to understand the nature and scope of judicial decisions in order to understand the impact of judicial review on the Mental Health Review Tribunals.[36] To this end, they identified three categories of judicial review decision: that concerned with the statutory criteria used by the tribunals; that concerned with the powers of the tribunal; and that concerned with procedural requirements. These categories, they argued, reflect the different roles attributed to judicial review in the literature. Thus, they argued that the first and second categories concern the court's role as the final arbiter of the meaning of statutory provisions and the scope of the tribunal's legal powers respectively. The third category is concerned with the court's role in promoting 'better decision-making

---

[34] D. Feldman, 'Judicial Review: A Way of Controlling Government?' (1988) 66 *Public Administration* 21.

[35] Richardson and Sunkin, 'Questions of Impact', p. 103. It has been said that '[t]he development of the IRS certainly resonates with that proposition': T. Buck, 'Judicial Review and the Discretionary Social Fund' in T. Buck (ed.), *Judicial Review and Social Welfare* (London, Pinter, 1998), p. 129.

[36] G. Richardson and D. Machin, 'Judicial Review and Tribunal Decision Making: A Study of the Mental Health Review Tribunal' [2000] *Public Law* 494 at 496.

by insisting on fair, inclusive and open procedures'.[37] This threefold classification then provided the framework for evaluating the impact of judicial review on the Mental Health Review Tribunals. In passing, it may be noted that Richardson and Machin found that procedural values did not effectively penetrate a system dominated by medical values and culture. This finding challenged the assumption that procedural values are likely to penetrate (and therefore influence) non-legal environments more effectively than more substantive legal requirements.

The impact on what?

It is by no means original to liken the impact of courts to the radiating ripples caused when a stone is thrown into water.[38] Of course the analogy should not be pushed too far. In some cases, the impact of decisions is limited to the parties themselves, and even then the effects may be specific and short-lived. In other situations, the ripples may be apparent way beyond the stone's point of entry. In such situations, researchers may discern impacts extending beyond the specific parties, influencing, for instance, government policies and possibly more general social change and cultural attitudes. As we shall see in the next section at various points, difficult questions of causation arise when we seek to identify linkages between what the courts do and what happens elsewhere.[39] For present purposes, my focus is more specific. It is upon the bureaucratic impact of judicial review, and for this reason I shall consider certain features of bureaucratic organisations and processes that may warrant consideration by researchers of impact.

Bureaucracy

This is not the place to enter upon a lengthy discussion of the nature of bureaucracy. Suffice to say that, as with the meanings of judicial review, there are clearly different ways of understanding and defining 'bureaucracy' depending on our disciplinary context and perspective. For present purposes, a safe starting point might be to assume that our primary research interests are with the impact of judicial review on the

---

[37] *Ibid.*, p. 497.   [38] Galanter, 'The Radiating Effects'.

[39] Such issues are often approached by drawing a distinction between direct impacts and indirect impacts. Broadly speaking, the term 'direct' impacts refers to specific effects that appear to be directly caused by judicial decisions. The term 'indirect', by contrast, refers to influences or reactions that are more diffuse and indeterminate in nature and which may have no immediate linear connection with specific judgments. Cf. McCann, 'Law and Political Struggles', p. 334.

process of *public* administration and the organisations within which this process occurs.[40] This definition is broad enough to cover matters of process as well as the study of public sector organisations themselves. In the United Kingdom, these organisations would include central government departments, local authorities and other bodies established by statute to perform public functions, including tribunals. This list, of course, potentially includes a vast array of particular bodies that are unified by little more than the fact that they operate in the public sector and must act in the public interest. Nonetheless, despite its breadth, this focus on public administration and public organisations will not necessarily suit all researchers. Some, for example, might argue that it fails to acknowledge the fragmented nature of government where lines between public and private are often blurred and many public functions are performed by private organisations.[41] This being so, some will regard a focus on 'public' bureaucracy as being arbitrary and unduly narrow. There is certainly a plausible argument that the impacts of judicial review, or at least the norms and values that it encapsulates, on powerful private organisations are worthy of study. After all, it might be argued that lines between public and private should not act as a barrier to the investigation of the way law regulates power where that power is not being formally exercised by the state and its agents. Having said this, those who are concerned with the bureaucratic impact of judicial review are likely to be principally concerned with those bodies that are the principal and immediate targets of judicial review litigation.

Organisational contexts

When considering the bodies to be investigated, researchers should have regard to variables such as the nature of organisations, the contacts they have with judicial review, and the general procedural environment, including their age and the resource and cultural context in which they operate.[42]

---

[40] See D. Beetham, *Bureaucracy* (2nd edn, Buckingham, Open University Press, 1996), especially at pp. 3–4.

[41] See generally M. Taggart (ed.), *The Province of Administrative Law* (Oxford, Hart, 1997).

[42] Another significant variable is an organisation's ability to respond to judicial decisions. For instance, while central government departments may have relatively ready access to legislation (both delegated and primary) should a judicial decision call for a legislative response, other bodies such as tribunals and local authorities will be unable

As I have just indicated, even where the focus is on the public sector a vast array of organisations, processes and relationships may be investigated. Within British central government, to take one sector, departments vary considerably in size, responsibility, internal organisation, and culture.[43] They vary also in their experience of judicial review litigation. While departments such as the Home Office have regular daily direct contact with judicial review litigation involving issues such as immigration and to a lesser extent prisons or the criminal justice system, other central government departments may have contact with judicial review only a few times a year.[44] The experience of local government is equally sporadic. In areas such as housing judicial review is commonplace, but significant regional variations exist with metropolitan inner city authorities attracting the bulk of litigation.

The experience that particular departments have of judicial review may also change over time, sometimes quite rapidly. The prison service in the United Kingdom provides a striking example. It was not until the end of the 1970s that the courts were prepared to judicially review decisions of the prison authorities.[45] Prior to this the service regarded itself as being effectively insulated from external legal scrutiny. As one official put it, it had 'a tendency to consume its own smoke'.[46] When the courts first held that they could review certain disciplinary decisions, parts of the service experienced a sense of crisis and some senior officials apparently thought 'that the roof had fallen in on them'. Over the next few years the number of judicial reviews of prison decisions grew, as did the degree to which they intruded. Not surprisingly, the impact of this new legal environment on prisons has been the subject of several studies.[47] The changing influence of judicial review was also a theme of

to use legislation in order to secure changes to the legal framework within which they operate: James, 'The Political and Administrative Consequences', p. 620.

[43] For an overview, see P. Hennesey, *Whitehall* (2nd edn, London, Fontana, 1990), especially Chapter 10 ('The Geography of Administration').

[44] See L. Bridges, G. Meszaros and M. Sunkin, *Judicial Review in Perspective* (2nd edn, London, Cavendish, 1995), especially Chapter 3.

[45] *R. v. Hull Prison Board of Visitors, ex parte St Germain (No. 1)* [1979] QB 425.

[46] Quoted in M. Sunkin and A. Le Sueur, 'Can Government Control Judicial Review' (1991) 44 *Current Legal Problems* 161–83 at 168.

[47] E.g. M. Loughlin, 'The Underside of the Law: Judicial Review and the Prison Disciplinary System' (1993) 46 *Current Legal Problems* 43; M. Loughlin and P. Quinn, 'Prison Rules and Courts: A Study of Administrative Law' (1993) 56 *Modern Law Review* 497; S. Livingstone, 'The Changing Face of Prison Discipline' in E. Player and M. Jenkins (eds.), *Prisons After Woolf: Reform Through Riot* (London, Routledge,

the work Pick and I did on the IRS. Here, however, we were interested in exploring how judicial review impacted upon a newly established agency as it developed during the first ten years of its existence.[48]

Another variation concerns the nature of the procedures adopted. At one extreme are bodies that employ adjudicative processes, which are similar to the courts and which are staffed by decision-makers with a high degree of technical expertise, possibly including legal expertise. While it has been suggested that reviewing courts might have a greater impact on the behaviour of such bodies than on other types of agency,[49] as we have already noted, Richardson and Machin's work indicates that the extent to which this impact is felt appears to depend on the expertise of the body and the cultural context within which it operates.

By contrast much public administration is undertaken using no judicial processes by decision-makers who (at most) are likely to have only the most general awareness of judicial review and only very limited direct contact with lawyers. Often they will be working at the street level in high-pressure environments seeking to make complex decisions about how to allocate scarce resources such as housing or welfare benefits. In such contexts, the decisions might be regarded as classic examples of administrative decisions,[50] and one might expect law and legal values to be distant and the likelihood of judicial review exerting an impact correspondingly remote. For these very reasons, some will regard such environments as being particularly suitable for investigating the ways in which judicial review and legal norms impinge upon the world of administration.[51]

Types of impact

Even within particular organisational contexts, researchers are likely to have a variety of concerns when exploring impacts. While some will

---

1994); and S. Livingstone, 'The Impact of Judicial Review on Prisons' in B. Hadfield (ed.), *Judicial Review: A Thematic Approach* (Dublin, Gill and Macmillan, 1995).

[48] Sunkin and Pick, 'The Changing Impact'.

[49] S. M. Sterett, *Creating Constitutionalism? The Politics of Legal Expertise and Administrative Law in England and Wales* (Ann Arbor, University of Michigan Press, 1997).

[50] *Kingsley v. UK* (2002) 35 EHRR 177 at 302; also Lord Hoffmann in *Begum v. Tower Hamlets London Borough Council* [2003] UKHL 5, [2003] 2 AC 430 at paras. 55 and 56.

[51] E.g. I. Loveland, *Housing Homeless Persons* (Oxford, Oxford University Press, 1995); and Halliday, 'Researching the "Impact" of Judicial Review'. Cf. also the work on prisons noted above at note 47.

simply be interested in knowing what goes on within organisations in relation to judicial review, asking questions such as how organisations spot potential challenges, how they handle litigation, how judicial decisions are interpreted and explained to officials, others may have more specific interests, focusing, for instance, on aspects such as policy[52] or legal frameworks, on management systems, attitudes and behaviour, on the way legal and non-legal norms interact and on what meanings are given to values such as fairness or equality. For the purposes of illustration, I shall briefly consider two broad matters: first, impacts on frameworks, structures and system design; and, secondly, impacts on management and decision-making.

Impact on frameworks, structures and system design   The traditional view is that, in the UK system, the courts are not permitted to review the legality or constitutionality of primary legislation. This inevitably inhibits judicial review's *direct impact* on the structures, systems and procedures that are established by primary legislation. For instance, in the context of prison discipline, Richardson and Sunkin distinguish between the statutorily ordained structure of prison discipline on the one hand and the procedures adopted during prison disciplinary adjudications and the actual decisions in these adjudications on the other. Although the impact of judicial review on procedural matters has been significant, its impact on the statutory provisions is inevitably limited.[53] This is not to say that judicial review can never have a direct impact on systems established by statute. Courts possess considerable interpretational latitude, and 'the truth is that courts are inescapably possessed of some degree of legislative power'.[54] The decision in *Anisminic v. Foreign Compensation Commission*[55] is the classic example of a decision that effectively redrafted legislation and required parliamentary action in response.[56] More recently and more controversially, the series of decisions questioning aspects of government policy

---

[52] E.g. M. Hertogh, 'Coercion, Cooperation, and Control: Understanding the Policy Impact of Administrative Courts and the Ombudsman in the Netherlands' (2001) 23 *Law and Policy* 47–67; also D. Barak-Erez, 'Judicial Review of Politics: The Israeli Case' (2002) 29 *Journal of Law and Society* 611–31.

[53] Richardson and Sunkin, 'Questions of Impact', p. 93.

[54] F. Bennion, *Statutory Interpretation* (2nd edn, London, Butterworths, 1992), p. 94.

[55] [1969] 2 AC 147.   [56] Foreign Compensation Act 1950.

on asylum also provoked government to nullify the effect of judgments by primary legislation.[57]

In the United Kingdom, the Human Rights Act 1998 requires that, 'so far as it is possible to do so', legislation should be read and given effect in a way which is compatible with human rights.[58] If the courts cannot find an interpretation that is human-rights-compatible, the higher courts may grant a declaration of incompatibility.[59] These developments will increase the potential impact of court decisions on statutory systems and procedures, and in future there is likely to be much scope for work on this aspect.

Even prior to the Human Rights Act 1998, judicial review exerted a potentially significant *indirect* influence on the design of statutory systems. In some instances, this influence affected the nature of the agencies established, and their powers, procedures and manner of operations. The Independent Review Service of the Social Fund is one example. The IRS was created with judicial review in mind as a compromise solution when the social fund scheme was established in the mid-1980s.[60] This scheme essentially established a budget out of which financial support was to be provided to those already dependent on the state for their basic needs who found themselves facing unexpected expenses that could not be met from their normal resources. The decisions as to whether expense claims were to be made were taken by officers in local branches of the Benefits Agency. When the scheme was first proposed, it contained no method for appealing against these local decisions. The government argued that an appeal system would be incompatible with a budgetary-based scheme because if an appellate body allowed an appeal this would affect the budget that had to be maintained by the local offices of the Benefits Agency. The absence of an appeal mechanism attracted widespread criticism and the government

---

[57] R. v. Secretary of State for Social Security, ex parte Joint Council for the Welfare of Immigrants [1997] 1 WLR 275 held that regulations restricting access of asylum seekers to income support were invalid. The decision was nullified by s. 11 of the Asylum and Immigration Act 1996. In R. v. Westminster City Council, ex parte M. (1997) 1 CCLR 85, the Court of Appeal held that asylum seekers deprived of benefits were still entitled to residential assistance from local authorities under the National Assistance Act 1948. This decision was in turn nullified by s. 116 of the Immigration and Asylum Act 1999.

[58] Human Rights Act 1998, s. 3.   [59] Human Rights Act 1998, s. 4.

[60] See generally T. Buck, *The Social Fund* (2nd edn, London, Sweet and Maxwell, 2000).

eventually conceded by introducing a review process that could look at the legality of the process by which decisions were taken but which was not a full-scale appeal on the merits. This review was to be undertaken by Social Fund Inspectors who are officials based in the IRS, rather than by independent tribunals, and no further appeal was to be permitted from their decisions. Judicial review was therefore important in two practical ways. First, it provided the model for the inspectors' powers. In effect, the task of the inspectors was to judicially review decisions of the Benefits Agency, although the inspectors were not lawyers, let alone judges. Secondly, since there were no appeals permitted, the only way of challenging decisions of inspectors was by way of judicial review.

Management and decision-making within organisations It is when we turn to consider judicial review's impact on internal procedures and decision-making that some of the most difficult but most interesting research issues arise. Here we are getting very close to the heart of the relationship between law and bureaucracy. But, as we do so, the problems of researching and identifying impacts of judicial review grow, principally because few of us will have an insider's knowledge or experience of the system and access may give rise to problems.

One – albeit rough – distinction that is useful in this context is that between formal and informal reactions to judicial review. Broadly speaking, a *formal* reaction is one that has been formalised in a rule or in a formal decision, and an *informal* reaction is one that is represented in other ways, such as in attitudes and feelings of officials.[61] More will be said about researching such matters in a moment; suffice to say that, by contrast to *informal* reactions, formal changes are likely to be relatively easy to detect and verify, although, as always, care will need to be taken before they are causally linked to judicial review.[62]

One potentially serious difficulty for researchers is that the influences of judicial review are unlikely to be fully reflected in such things as formal pronouncements or in changes to rules or procedures. It has been observed that:

[61] In practice, however, not all reactions can be easily distinguished into formal or informal. For instance, if management introduces a change of approach that is contained in guidance or in an internal policy statement, officials may treat these as being as binding as any formal rule change.
[62] Richardson and Sunkin, 'Questions of Impact', pp. 93–4.

[t]he most profound and enduring influences of judicial review are not to be found by examining the statute book, or by seeking formalised and public shifts of policy in response to litigation. Rather they are to be found in the effects of litigation on the less accessible aspects of government: the internal and informal working practices of departments, their management systems and decision-making culture.[63]

Those concentrating on formal responses to judicial review, for example, might have missed some of the most interesting developments within British central government over the past two decades or so in relation to judicial review. Prior to the mid-1980s, central government's reaction to judicial review litigation was typically case-based, reactive and pragmatic. The impression from the little work that is available is that up to this period government responded to challenges as they came. It had few, if any, facilities for anticipating litigation, and contingency planning for failure in the courts was on occasion very rudimentary.[64] This was perhaps a typically British, pragmatic approach that was rooted in, and sustained by, the generalist nature of a civil service in which few administrators were trained in law. At this time, government lawyers tended to play a relatively peripheral role and were rarely involved at the stage when policy or strategy was being formulated. The overall picture was one that in retrospect appears to have been exceedingly complacent.

From the mid-1980s, the overall approach within central government started to change so that planning for judicial intervention was to become more proactive and systemic. The responses have since been well documented and include the establishment of programmes of education and training, the publication of pamphlets such as the *Judge Over Your Shoulders*,[65] the more careful monitoring of judicial review in general and the earlier use of lawyers within departments. In this context, Daintith and Page note that the coming together of lawyers and administrators has been seen, positively, as a means by which legal ideas and values have been spread to administrators.[66]

---

[63] Sunkin and Le Sueur, 'Government Control', p. 162.   [64] *Ibid.*

[65] 'Judge Over Your Shoulder: Judicial Review: Balancing the Scales' (London, Cabinet Office, 1994).

[66] Daintith and Page, *The Executive*, p. 345. On the other hand, Daintith and Page say that it is at least arguable that 'the opposite could happen' and that 'lawyers could find their independence of mind being eroded by their more intimate involvement in, and commitment to, the political purpose of the department'. See further at *ibid.*, p. 346.

The IRS study also revealed influences that would not have been apparent had the research concentrated on *formal* reactions to judicial review. Certainly, some of the most interesting aspects to emerge from the IRS study concerned the way managerial attitudes and policy towards judicial review altered over the period studied. During the early life of the IRS, the influence of judicial review on management priorities and goals appears to have been substantial. The IRS was established in a political storm. As well as the general controversy surrounding the creation of the Social Fund, there was specific criticism levelled at the original absence of any system of appeal from decisions taken by the Benefits Agency. As already indicated, the IRS was created to mollify this criticism. Nonetheless, many critics regarded this new agency with suspicion and its establishment as a window-dressing exercise. Given this political context, it is perhaps unsurprising that one of the early priorities of the IRS was to enhance its perceived legitimacy. In this context judicial review was both a foe and a friend. It was a foe in so far as critical decisions of the court could further undermine the credibility of the IRS. It was a friend in so far as the courts could provide guidance to the new body and reinforce its claim to be independent from government. Interestingly, the desire to establish legal legitimacy was also reflected in management's concern to ensure that the IRS functioned as an institution modelled on legal procedures and legal values. This emphasis on judicial review declined as the IRS became more established and as managerial priorities altered from an initial concern to establish the legitimacy of the IRS to a later concern to improve the efficiency of service delivery.

RESEARCHING AND ASSESSING IMPACTS

Up to now I have been exploring how researchers might conceptualise judicial review and bureaucratic impacts. The focus has been essentially definitional. It has been concerned with showing various ways in which the main building blocks of research in the area may be approached. The assumptions have been that judicial review and bureaucratic impact can be understood in isolation from each other and that doing so is an important element in research design. However, the study of judicial review's impact is the study of a relationship, and its principal aim is to investigate whether, to what extent and in what ways judicial review influences bureaucratic organisation, practice or attitudes. This being so, the most interesting and difficult issues for researchers are not definitional; rather they have to do with the way that these influences are investigated, identified and assessed. In this part of the chapter I shall look briefly at some of the research issues involved.[67]

I shall start with two elementary observations. First, as with any relationship, that between judicial review and bureaucracy can be viewed from more than one perspective and its nature will differ, or at least appear to differ, accordingly. Secondly, whatever the perspective adopted, there is more than one way of researching impact and more than one way of understanding basic matters including the nature of impact itself and what constitutes evidence of relevant causal connections between judicial review and bureaucratic change.

Different perspectives: positivism and interpretivism

We shall first consider perspective. A basic distinction is often made in the literature between 'court-centred' or 'top down' approaches to the study of legal impact on the one hand, and community- or society-based or 'bottom up' or 'impact-based' approaches on the other.[68] The former tends to visualise the relationship between courts and change in society (or, more specifically, in our present context, between the courts and changes in bureaucracy) as an essentially one-way affair in which the courts initiate change and others react to this. Those adopting this approach are often taken to assume that the influence exerted by the courts can be identified amongst a range of other influences and that this influence is both special and distinctive. It is taken to be special in the sense that the influence exerted by the courts possesses an authority that is rooted in law and the constitutional standing of the courts. It is assumed to be distinctive both in the sense that law and legal values are considered to be distinctive[69] and in the sense that the influence of the courts remains 'visible' and therefore traceable to points where impacts may be discerned. This in turn implies an interface, or a point

---

[67] See further Chapter 10 below.

[68] R. Cotterrell, 'Judicial Review and Legal Theory' in G. Richardson and H. G. Genn (eds.), *Administrative Law and Government Action* (Oxford, Oxford University Press, 1994); cf. McCann's critique of the approach taken by Rosenberg in *The Hollow Hope*: McCann, 'Law and Political Struggles'.

[69] Wade and Forsyth provide a classical example of this when they tell us that the mental exercise of the judge and the administrator are fundamentally different: H. W. R. Wade and C. F. Forsyth, *Administrative Law* (8th edn, Oxford, Oxford University Press, 2000), p. 41.

of meeting or even collision (of impact), between the legal and the non-legal.[70]

This language of impact, with its connotation of the interaction between physical things, does not necessarily imply that all who take a court-centred approach are necessarily rooted to an epistemological position that is positivistic in character and which draws inspiration from research in the natural sciences. Nonetheless, one of the contrasts between this perspective and the society-based approach to be described more fully in a moment is that techniques informed by positivism are much more likely to be adopted, consciously or unconsciously, by court-centred researchers than by those adopting alternative perspectives.

In its ideal form, a positivist approach to the study of impact calls for a research design that enables potential impacts to be investigated in an experimental setting in which variables can be carefully controlled and causal links accurately determined by measurable objective evidence. An example of a near perfect situation would be one in which researchers could compare two bureaucratic systems that were identical save that one was affected by a court decision. By measuring the differences between the two systems after the decision, researchers would be able to accurately determine what impact, if any, it had. In practice, of course, producing conditions of this type is impossible. Nonetheless, this type of experimental model forms the positivist ideal to which research in the real world should so far as it is possible conform. Thus researchers have been encouraged to develop methods that effectively control for 'plausible rival hypotheses'[71] as to what might explain the

[70] Of course, the view that the law is distinctive and influences the non-legal is not monopolised by those who adopt a court-centred approach to the study of legal impact.

[71] R. Lempert, 'Strategies of Research Design in the Legal Impact Study: The Control of Plausible Rival Hypotheses' (1966) 1 *Law and Society Review* 111–32. 'A legal impact study represents an attempt to ascertain how a particular law affects the conduct and attitudes of those individuals . . . or other relevant units located in jurisdictions where that law is in force. By its very nature such a study involves one essential comparison: the comparison between actual patterns in jurisdictions having the law in question and the behaviour patterns which would have existed in the same jurisdictions had the law in question never been enacted. Since this comparison is one which by definition cannot actually be made, the problem for the legal impact theorist is how to estimate best what the behaviour patterns would have been in a certain jurisdiction had the law in question never existed there.' *Ibid.*, p. 111.

changes in behaviour or practice following a judicial decision and to ensure that their conclusions are based on measurable and objective evidence rather than desire or ideological belief.[72] From this perspective, one cannot say that a decision has had this or that impact unless at least persuasive evidence exists to support the claim that there is a causal connection between the decision and the impact. As the debates surrounding Rosenberg's *Hollow Hope* illustrate, what constitutes such evidence might be a matter of intense disagreement. The essential reason for this disagreement lies in the fundamental difference between positivistic approaches and non-positivist approaches to the study of impact.

Those adopting what I for convenience call the 'society-based' approach argue that it is impossible to fully understand the role and influence of judicial decisions from the perspective of the courts alone. Attempts to do so are unlikely to provide insights into the complex and subtle ways in which the influence of the courts is experienced within society by individuals, groups and organisations and in turn how the courts themselves are influenced by society. From this perspective, the search is for a more nuanced appreciation of the way judicial decisions are received and understood. Such an approach sits unhappily with a notion of impact that implies clashes between the legal and the non-legal; rather the concern is to explore more subtle interactions, influences and interpretations.[73] From this perspective, judicial decisions need, for example, to be understood not as isolated events but in the context in which they are delivered. Judicial decisions have a history. A legal challenge to a decision refusing a person asylum, for instance, will often be part of a broader political debate about the merits of asylum policy in general or the appropriateness of the decision-making procedures more specifically. Given the existence of this debate, it is likely that any decision will be widely reported in the press and the media and that these reports will feed into the political environment. Each of these events will themselves generate reactions and influences that might ultimately lead to changes in policy or governmental practice or procedure. Within this milieu, the particular influence exerted by the

---

[72] See G. N. Rosenberg's defence of his *Hollow Hope* in his chapter, 'Knowledge and Desire: Thinking about Courts and Social Change' in Schultz, *Leveraging the Law*, pp. 251–91.

[73] For some, the very line between legal and non-legal influences on behaviour is indistinct.

judicial decision itself is exceedingly difficult to isolate and indeed it might be fruitless to attempt to do so.[74]

Positivistic approaches do not permit issues such as these to be explored. After all, as many sociologists have pointed out, people and organisations are not objects of natural science and their behaviour cannot be understood in the ways that natural scientists seek to explain how natural objects are affected by external forces. For this purpose, approaches based broadly on what we might refer to as interpretivism are now widely used by investigators of impact. This approach owes much to Max Weber's description of sociology as a 'science which attempts the interpretive understanding of social action in order to arrive at a causal explanation of its course and effects'.[75] Crucially, unlike research in the natural sciences which is essentially concerned to examine how external forces operate on objects, here the task is to obtain an interpretive understanding of the way those actually involved in social action make sense of and give meaning to the world around them. Such an understanding might be missed by those who reject links simply because they appear not to be established by statistically reliable evidence.[76] In the specific context with which we are concerned, this implies that we can only meaningfully study the way judicial review impacts upon bureaucracy from the point of view of those involved in bureaucratic decision-making. This is something that is particularly important if our aim is to understand what I earlier described as the informal impact of judicial review, that is to say its impact on the attitudes and actual behaviour of administrators in their day-to-day work.

The above comments may be illustrated by Halliday's approach to the impact of judicial review on administrative procedures. For

---

[74] See e.g. D. Schultz and S. E. Gottlieb's criticism of Rosenberg's *Hollow Hope* in 'Legal Functionalism and Social Change: A Reassessment of Rosenberg's *The Hollow Hope*' in Schultz, *Leveraging the Law*, pp. 192–6, in relation to the nature of historical explanation.

[75] M. Weber, *The Theory of Social and Economic Organization* (New York, Free Press, 1947), quoted by A. Bryman, *Social Research*, p. 14.

[76] Cf. for example, Schultz and Gottlieb commenting on statistical reliability of evidence of causality: 'To say an event will come about in 5% of the cases is to say that it usually will not come about. Statistical tests for the confidence of predictions screen out many such findings as too unreliable to justify the statistical conclusion that the act or event under scrutiny is a "cause" for the result being examined. But that statistical lack of confidence is not equivalent to a finding that the preceding event was not a cause of the following event.' Schultz and Gottlieb, 'Legal Functionalism', p. 183.

Halliday, the very nature of impact in this context is problematical. In particular, he argues that one cannot properly understand a simple linear relationship between judicial review and administration in which the former has discrete impacts on the latter. The relationships between the two are much more fluid and subtle. Halliday argues that decision-making 'should be conceptualized as a continually developing process of social construction'. It is 'a subtle and shifting affair which is a matter of seemingly endless human interpretative work'.[77] Likewise, he points out that the 'impact' of judicial review should be 'recognised as being dynamic, organic and changing'. As administrators continually engage in the process of interpretation and reinterpretation, so the 'impact of judicial review mutates'. He goes on to say that:

> The risk in talking about 'impact' is to conceive of a process of decision-making as comprising a series of discrete and overly straightforward cause–effect relationships between 'informing factors' and decision outcomes. Under this model of decision-making, judicial review (cause) may be deemed to have a fixed and determinant effect on decision-outcomes. Under this notion the relationship between judicial review and decision-outcomes is one of linear cause and effect. However, if we conceptualize the 'context' of decision-making as being internal rather than external to the decision-making process [Emerson-Paley, 1992], as being fluid and having multiple possible constitutions, it becomes potentially misleading to talk about the *impact* of various factors upon decision-making. A picture of 'factors' external to the 'decision' sustaining a discrete cause–effect relationship to the 'decision' becomes problematical. Rather . . . [t]he question of what impact judicial review has may, then, be better conceived as one of how the influence of experience of judicial review interacts with other informing influences.[78]

The importance of the administrator's perspective

These important insights have significant implications for research design, methodology and analysis for those working on administrative procedures (the implications may differ for those undertaking work on adjudicative procedures, for example). First, they indicate the importance of seeing judicial review from the perspective of the administrator. But, how can this be achieved given that most researchers are

---

[77] Quoting R. Baldwin and K. Hawkins, 'Discretionary Justice: Davis Reconsidered' [1984] *Public Law* 570–99 at 581.

[78] Halliday, 'Researching the Impact', p. 196. Citations omitted.

not within the system? One way of managing this problem is by the adoption of an ethnographic approach.[79] Researchers will need to have direct contact with those involved. They will need to hear what officials have to say and, ideally, observe what they do. Interviews can go some way to this end and qualitative data gained following semi-structured interviews with decision-makers can certainly provide valuable insights. But interviews have well-known limitations, and are unlikely to provide a complete view of 'how [administrative law and judicial review] is operationalised in the routine work of bureaucrats'[80] or how judicial review actually influences particular decisions in contexts such as tribunal hearings. For this, some form of observation is necessary if this is permissible or practical given issues such as confidentiality or the sensitive nature of decision-making in certain areas of governmental work.[81] Several recent projects have used a variety of forms of observation. These include Richardson and Machin's work on Mental Health Review Tribunals and Loveland and Halliday's separate studies of homelessness decision-making in local housing authorities. In the Mental Health Review Tribunals study, the researchers observed tribunals in action (including the preliminary meeting, the hearing and the deliberations) and interviewed patients' representatives, tribunal members and members of tribunal staff. In the latter studies, the researchers spent significant periods of time in the relevant offices and augmented this by semi-structured interviews and access to case files.[82]

Also noteworthy is Buck's work on the IRS, which was in part based on his experience of the system as legal advisor within the IRS. This

[79] See e.g. M. Hammersley and P. Atkinson, *Ethnography: Principles in Practice* (2nd edn, London, Routledge, 1995); P. Brewaer, *Ethnography* (Buckingham, Open University Press, 2000).

[80] Halliday, 'The Influence of Judicial Review', p. 111.

[81] Participant observation may be defined as: 'the method in which the observer participates in the daily life of the people under study, either openly in the role of researcher or covertly in some disguised role, observing things that happen, listening to what is said, and questioning people, over some length of time.' H. Becker and B. Geer, 'Participant Observation and Interviewing: A Comparison' (1957) 16 *Human Organisation* 28, quoted in M. Denscombe, *The Good Research Guide* (Buckingham, Open University Press, 1998), p.148.

[82] Loveland says that he spent 'intensive periods of several months at each site, with subsequent follow up visits. Data was collected from analysis of case files and of policy documents, from semi-structured and informal interviews with administrators at all levels . . . and from observation of decision-making procedures.' Loveland, *Housing Homeless Persons*, p. 4.

provided unique insights into a range of debates that were occurring within the management of the IRS relating, for example, to the types of letter that should be written to explain decisions. While early managerial policy had emphasised the need for complete reasoning so that letters could be defended if necessary in judicial review proceedings, the emphasis later shifted to providing clear and succinct accounts. These were not so legally watertight, but they were thought to be easier for applicants to understand and cheaper and quicker to write. The management saw these as being benefits worth obtaining despite the legal risks involved. Buck evidently disagreed with this approach, arguing that it constituted a shift from an approach based on principles of legality and was a concession to a new managerial culture.[83]

The contingent meaning of law in the bureaucracy

Secondly, Halliday shows that from an interpretivist perspective neither fixed and immutable judicial review values or principles nor the existence of a single hard edge separating judicial review and administration can be assumed.[84] The meaning attached, for example, to ideas such as fairness or natural justice are likely to alter as the messages emanating from the courts are received, interpreted and reinterpreted within the administrative system.[85] Thus one might plausibly suggest that the principles and values that lawyers associate with judicial review change as they are mixed with the innumerable other factors (resources, policies, personal pressures and so on) to form part of an administrative soup of influences on decision-making.[86] The result

---

[83] T. Buck, 'Discretionary Social Fund', p. 115.

[84] Having said this, at certain points the edges may be harder than at others and it would be interesting to study where these hard edges exist. One might speculate, for instance, that the role of the government lawyer in interpreting the implications of decisions is critical to the process by which administrative meanings are given to judgments.

[85] See Chapter 3 below.

[86] At the risk of over-egging the culinary metaphor, if we were to seek to identify elements of judicial review within this soup we might find that they have been dissolved, as when street-level decision-makers fail to recognise judicial review principles. Alternatively, we might find that they have become reconstituted. That is to say, they appear to resemble judicial principles but they are not recognised as such by the administrators or they are based on outdated legal requirements. Another possibility, evident in the IRS study, is that procedures may contain aspects of legal rationality or fairness but are principally designed to satisfy the demands of administrative efficiency or other managerial objectives.

is that understandings of judicial review and its requirements are likely to differ between communities of decision-makers across organisations as well as between levels within single organisational structures.

This in turn implies that researchers should be cautious in the way they attribute meaning. The language used within bureaucracies may be the language of judicial review but the meanings intended or assumed may be very different to the meanings that a judge or a lawyer would expect. But the contrary is also possible. Procedures and approaches may well conform to the requirements of legality even when the procedures have not been explicitly designed with judicial review in mind or when decision-makers are not consciously employing judicial review standards or techniques. In the IRS study, for example, many officials denied having been trained in judicial review. This was puzzling given that we knew that all the officials had in fact received training in how to approach decisions using judicial review principles. The reality was that our interviewees simply did not associate the training they had received in, for instance, how to handle a case fairly and how to provide a reasoned decision as training in judicial review. For them, judicial review was something external and distant rather than a set of norms to be applied in their everyday work.

Dynamic interactions between the courts and bureaucracy
Halliday's observations also draw attention to the dynamic nature of the interactions involved in the relationship between judicial review and administration. Neither judicial review nor the administrative process are static. Each is dynamic, as is the relationship between them.[87] Judicial review principles develop over time and new principles emerge while established principles are given new meanings by the judges. The fluidity of this process, which has been particularly evident in the United Kingdom over the past few decades, means that understandings of the requirements of judicial review ideally should be constantly revisited in order to ensure that current practice complies with current judicial expectations. At the same time, the administrative environment is also dynamic as policy and resource priorities alter. All this creates a situation in which there is considerable potential for administrative processes and judicial requirements to diverge,

---

[87] One of the findings of the IRS study was that the influence of judicial review changes over time as the IRS evolved in response to changes in the environment in which it functioned, its own organisational maturity and changing policy priorities.

resulting in tension and potential conflict between legal and non-legal norms.

This in turn highlights the inherent difficulty of attempting to isolate the influence of judicial review where decision-makers are continuously reacting to multiple constraints. This problem exists even where the influence of judicial review is acknowledged[88] and where causal links are plausible, but it is particularly acute in routine decision-making where judicial review has no direct or explicit role.[89] In such a situation, positivists might not be the only ones forced to conclude that they can discern no meaningful impact of judicial review on day-to-day administration.

CONCLUDING COMMENTS

The relationship between judicial review (or indeed the law and legal procedures more generally) and government is an important and rich area for empirical investigation. It offers considerable opportunities for researchers across a range of disciplines adopting a variety of research techniques. This paper has sought to map out some of the most basic conceptual matters that researchers may find useful to address when designing and planning research. It has briefly touched on some key methodological issues including the difficulty of identifying causal links between what emanates from judges and what happens within government. In closing, it may be noted that the study of impact is now important not only for academic scholars but also for hard-nosed legal practitioners involved in the hard graft of working the law. Two recent specific examples from the UK legal context illustrate this well.

One flows from the Court of Appeal's recent call[90] for a new approach to the conduct of public law litigation and its castigation of the prevailing litigation culture. In essence, the Court of Appeal criticised lawyers for seeking to 'over-judicialise' administrative procedures when mounting challenges to public bodies in the courts. Particular criticism

---

[88] Cf., for example, the comments that '[c]ertainly proximity in time between judicial intervention and the reform of rules or structures cannot, without more, establish a causal link between judicial review and change even at a formal level'. Richardson and Sunkin, 'Questions of Impact', p. 93.

[89] Such as in the context in which Halliday was working: routine decision-making by housing officers.

[90] R. (on the application of Cowl and others) v. Plymouth City Council (Practice Note) [2002] 1 WLR 803.

was made of their 'unfortunate' tendency to insist on 'arguing about what had occurred in the past' rather than 'focusing on the future' and 'on what matters', that is to say on whether disputes can be resolved without the need to resort to judicial review. This call is typical of the changing litigation culture in the United Kingdom, in which litigation is regarded as being a last resort to be employed only where alternative means of dispute resolution have failed. In the context of judicial review, this implies an obligation upon lawyers and public bodies to work more closely together to resolve disputes by informal means if necessary. Where matters are brought to the courts, the judges will do their utmost to encourage settlement. All this reinforces the importance to lawyers and judges of understanding how public agencies will respond to legal challenge.

The second example is provided by a recent paper delivered by the Attorney General in which he calls upon lawyers in the Government Legal Service to marshal arguments that will persuade the courts to develop the notion of deference to the executive in judicial review and human rights matters. To this end, he calls on government lawyers and those representing the government to adopt a much more co-ordinated, or strategic, approach to arguing the merits of deference. This approach includes carefully selecting cases that show the need for deference and the careful preparation of arguments that are designed to pick up and reinforce several key themes. Two of these are particularly pertinent here. One is his call to ensure that arguments for deference are based on evidence rather than on assertion. Another is the belief that judges must be educated about the need to show deference in cases where they might otherwise interfere with policies that have polycentric effects without understanding the ramifications of doing so:

> We [government lawyers] must think about how best to present [cases] ... It is here that the question of evidence – especially of policy background and considerations – becomes absolutely crucial. That evidence is essential to bring home to the court the complexity of the policy background, *and the ramifications of unsettling policy decisions in what may, superficially at least, appear to be a discrete area capable of being ring-fenced.*[91]

[91] Lord Goldsmith, 'New Constitutional Boundaries' (paper delivered by the Attorney General to a Government Legal Service Conference on Current Developments in Administrative Law, 22 March 2002), p. 15. Lord Goldsmith also spoke of the need to 'be on a constant look out for cases which offer the opportunity to develop the lines and guiding principles' to which he referred: *ibid.*, p. 14.

Here, then, is a call for government lawyers to ground claims for deference in evidence and to develop litigation strategies designed to influence judges to adopt less invasive approaches to review by better enabling them to appreciate the impact of their decisions across policy areas. There can be no better illustration of the constitutional importance of understanding the impact of judicial review than this. This is a task that in the United Kingdom clearly now confronts not only academics and government lawyers, but also those representing claimants and the judges.

CHAPTER THREE

STUDYING BUREAUCRATIC IMPLEMENTATION OF JUDICIAL POLICIES IN THE UNITED STATES: CONCEPTUAL AND METHODOLOGICAL APPROACHES

BRADLEY C. CANON*

DEVELOPMENT OF AMERICAN IMPACT AND IMPLEMENTATION RESEARCH

American scholars have been studying the impact of court decisions for almost half a century.[1] One impetus to doing this was the dramatic defiance mounted in southern states to the US Supreme Court's landmark *Brown v. Board of Education* (1954)[2] decision declaring segregated schools unconstitutional. Southern resistance was followed by opposition and evasion of other major new policies adopted by the Court under Chief Justice Earl Warren (1953–69), for example, striking down prayers in public schools, prohibiting the introduction of illegally seized evidence in criminal trials, and requiring the police to inform suspects of their rights before questioning them.[3]

The 'behavioural revolution' in American political science also produced considerable attention to judicial impact. Around 1960, many scholars began investigating actual behaviour as they sought

---

* My thanks go to my colleague Richard W. Waterman for suggestions he offered on an earlier draft of this chapter and to Peter Cane and the other participants at the Tilburg conference where the papers in this volume were mutually discussed.

[1] The earliest such study seems to be G. Patric, 'The Impact of a Court Decision: Aftermath of the *McCullom Case*' (1957) 6 *Journal of Public Law* 455–64. See also F. Sorauf, '*Zorach v. Clauson*: The Impact of a Supreme Court Decision' (1959) 53 *American Political Science Review* 777–91; and W. Murphy, 'Lower Court Checks on Supreme Court Power' (1959) 53 *American Political Science Review* 1017–31.

[2] 347 US 383 (1954).

[3] *Abington Township v. Schempp*, 374 US 203 (1963); *Mapp v. Ohio*, 367 US 643 (1961); *Miranda v. Arizona*, 384 US 436 (1966), respectively.

explanations for the making of public policies (including judicial decisions), how they were implemented, who was affected, and how. Researchers began testing hypotheses and developing more general theories. By 1970, Stephen Wasby had gleaned 135 hypotheses from the impact literature.[4] The study of what happened following court decisions flourished in the 1970s and afterwards. Numerous political science dissertations focused on impact, and most political science conventions devoted a panel or two to it. In 1984, Charles A. Johnson and I published *Judicial Policies: Implementation and Impact*.[5] It organised the studies by 'populations' impacted,[6] and offered an array of general theories that seemed to explain at least some forms of impact. Most studies looked at the impact of US Supreme Court decisions, but some examined those of state supreme courts or lower federal courts. These studies focused mainly on what happened following a judicial decision: to what extent did a ruling lead people to change their behaviour or, alternately, did the ruling shape behaviour to accord with the court's policy preferences or requirements. While political scientists took the lead, especially in theory development, sociologists and other social scientists, as well as law professors, also engaged in important impact research.[7]

Findings about the impact of judicial policies[8] in the United States are mixed. A broad analysis of the research and results is beyond the

---

[4] S. L. Wasby, *The Impact of the United States Supreme Court: Some Perspectives* (Homewood, IL, Dorsey Press, 1970), Chapter 8.

[5] C. A. Johnson and B. C. Canon, *Judicial Policies: Implementation and Impact* (Washington, CQ Press, 1984).

[6] We noted four populations: the interpreting population (mostly lower court judges), the implementing population (usually government agencies), the consumer population (those directly or potentially affected by the decision) and a residual or secondary population (persons not directly affected by the decision such as newspaper editors or legislators). Of course, the composition of the populations changed with the nature of the judicial decision.

[7] Another focus, sometimes called the 'law and society' approach, takes a 'bottom up' strategy (as opposed to 'top down' studies of the impact of a particular decision) asking how do ordinary people interact with the law. Many articles in the *Law and Society Review* over the last twenty years exemplify this approach which is as much the province of sociologists, anthropologists and law professors as it is of political scientists. For a succinct description of the bottom-up approach, see M. W. McCann, 'Reform Litigation on Trial' (1993) 18 *Law and Social Inquiry* 715 at 729–35.

[8] American impact scholars often use the term 'judicial policies' instead of 'judicial review'. In the US the term 'judicial review' is usually applied to court decisions determining whether a legislative enactment or an agency rule or action violates a provision of the US Constitution. There is no counterpart to this in the United

scope of this chapter and I refer the reader to Canon and Johnson's second edition.[9] Some decisions have altered little, perhaps generating more in the way of impassioned argument than real change. Indeed, some US Supreme Court cases such as desegregation or removing prayers from the public schools have met considerable resistance or evasion. But these same decisions, along with *Roe v. Wade* legalising abortion,[10] have changed the behaviour of millions of people.

THE FOCUS OF THIS CHAPTER

This chapter focuses on one aspect of the broader study of the implementation and impact of American judicial policies: their implementation by government agencies. It is, moreover, not so much a review of the literature (although much is cited) as it is a discussion of how we should conceptualise implementation research. That is, what concepts or models should we use to guide our investigations, and what theories should structure our research designs?[11] This discussion constitutes the bulk of the chapter. The last section then discusses the major research methods used by American scholars who study bureaucratic implementation of judicial decisions.

I begin by noting that not all judicial policies are implemented by government agencies. For example, many important decisions finding tort liability where none had existed before affect private corporations. Presumably, non-governmental organisations will alter their

Kingdom (except to the extent that certain courts were recently authorised to review Parliamentary Acts for compliance with the European Convention on Human Rights – see s. 4 of the Human Rights Act 1998) or some other Western countries that lack written constitutions or have ones that do not provide for a final judicial interpretation of its provisions. Many major American judicial policies are a result of judicial review. But some result from statutory interpretation. Constitutional judicial review cannot be altered by a legislative body while statutory interpretation can be overridden with new legislation.

[9] B. C. Canon and C. A. Johnson, *Judicial Policies: Implementation and Impact* (2nd edn, Washington, CQ Press, 1999).

[10] 410 US 113 (1973).

[11] Elements of the model are drawn from Canon and Johnson, *Judicial Policies*. For a useful earlier discussion, see L. A. Baum 'Implementation of Judicial Decisions: An Organizational Analysis' (1976) 4 *American Politics Quarterly* 86–114. See also M. Hertogh, 'Coercion, Cooperation and Control: Understanding the Policy Impact of Administrative Courts and the Ombudsman in the Netherlands' (2001) 23 *Law and Policy* 47–67.

behaviour to avoid liability.[12] (Of course, in some circumstances, government agencies are liable for tort damages.) Or public law decisions may directly give persons the legal right to do something they heretofore could not do. For example, *Roe* v. *Wade* held that pregnant women had a right to obtain an abortion, an act that was then a felony in almost all American states. No government agency 'administered' the new right. Likewise, decisions narrowing the definition of obscenity allowed book and video stores to sell material that had previously been banned.

Even so, many major judicial policy changes are mediated through government bureaucracies – they affect the behaviour of a consumer population only after an agency has implemented them. Here the court orders or directly implies that the agency (or type of agency) must change its behaviour in order to secure convictions, avoid fines or contempt citations or diminish liability, or in order to avoid some other undesirable consequence.[13]

A government agency can react[14] in three basic ways to a court decision[15] that orders or strongly implies that the agency should change its policies or processes. First, it can give the decision a *positive* reception. Agency leaders may welcome a decision that allows them to

[12] Whether organisations actually change their behaviour to avoid liability is, of course, an empirical question that has not been well explored.

[13] In this paper, I treat the agency as a unit and do not discuss the internal consequences within an agency that might follow from a judicial decision such as a shift of power from one subunit to another, e.g., from field workers or scientists to legal or financial staffs. For a good discussion of this aspect, see R. O'Leary, 'The Impact of Federal Court Decisions on the Policies and Administration of the US Environmental Protection Agency' (1989) 41 *Administrative Law Review* 549–69.

[14] Agencies can also act in anticipation of a likely judicial decision if an issue is litigated, as Maurice Sunkin discusses in the English context in Chapter 2 above. There is some empirical work on this in the US. In a study of US Army Corps of Engineers' grants of wetlands use permits, B. Canes-Wrone shows that the Corps will adjust its behaviour on the basis of a likely judicial decision given various courts' ideological composition and/or their prior decisions in the environmental area. See B. Canes-Wrone, 'Bureaucratic Decisions and the Composition of Lower Courts' (2003) 47 *American Journal of Political Science* 205–14. See also S. Hunter and R. W. Waterman, *Enforcing the Law: The Case of the Clean Water Acts* (Armonk, NY, M. E. Sharpe, 1996), pp. 114–20, who note greater Environmental Protection Agency enforcement activities in regions where the courts levy higher fines on violators.

[15] In this paper I use judicial decision in the singular. However, my comments apply equally to a set of two or more consistent decisions advancing the same policy. Bureaucracies sometimes face such a situation.

implement a policy they want to undertake, but which has heretofore been legally off-limits.

Secondly, the agency can be *indifferent* to the judicial decision. Its leaders[16] see the court's action as having little important effect on the agency's goals or functioning. Some behavioural adjustments seem to be required, but they arouse neither enthusiasm nor much resistance.

Thirdly, an agency can react *negatively* to a judicial decision. Its leaders perceive that the court's demands will make it more difficult to fulfil agency goals or perhaps prohibit the agency from pursuing the goal altogether. Or the leaders may think the judicial requirements will be dysfunctional to its routines and processes, thus draining resources and impairing efficiency. Or they may believe that abiding by the judicial decision will cause the agency to lose popularity with political funding sources or with the public. Or agency leaders may simply believe that the court's decision amounts to bad public policy that ought to be resisted for its own sake. When a court makes a relevant decision, agency leaders respond with what I call an 'acceptance decision'.[17] This is a psychological reaction. It can be conceptualised as a location on a continuum ranging from total acceptance to total rejection.[18] The acceptance decision also has an intensity component, i.e., people who dislike a decision may or may not feel strongly about it. Acceptance decisions are affected by a person's prior attitudes, if any, towards the judicial policy's subject matter, the degree of legitimacy or respect he or she accords the court making the decision, the perceptions of the consequences of the decision, and how the new policy will affect the agency's role in society or his or her own role in the agency.

A 'behavioural adjustment' follows from the acceptance decision. Unlike an acceptance decision, the behavioural adjustment is an observable change (or non-change) in agency behaviour. Change that

---

[16] I generally talk of agency leaders in this paper. Agency leaders, however, do not always reflect the views of lower ranking personnel or staff. When there is a divergence, leaders' decisions may be poorly implemented.

[17] The acceptance decision and the behavioural adjustment noted in the next paragraph are discussed more fully in Canon and Johnson, *Judicial Policies*, pp. 24–6.

[18] Some decisions can have different holdings or components some of which may be accepted and others rejected. But for this conceptual discussion, I treat decisions as single holdings.

occurs may be minuscule or it may be sweeping. While an agency's behavioural adjustment is usually closely linked with the nature of the acceptance decision, it does not necessarily mirror it. Agency leaders may mask or temper their rejection (or enthusiasm) for political or organisational reasons. Even so, if there is strong intensity behind their acceptance decision, we would expect leaders to maximise their efforts to implement a judicial policy or minimise their efforts to comply.

This chapter concentrates on the indifferent and hostile agencies. While resource problems may impede implementation of a decision that an agency welcomes, there is no failure of agency will. But when an agency finds a judicial decision unwelcome or sees implementation as dysfunctional, it is tempted to minimise compliance or forego it altogether. In such instances, judicial decisions may have a muted impact on the agency – and on society – or perhaps none at all.

Courts do not have many powers to effect implementation of their policy decisions. Initially, a court hopes to persuade the losing agency and others similarly situated of the rightness or wisdom of its decision through its accompanying opinion. There is no research about the impact of American courts' opinions on agency acceptance decisions (or on anyone else's for that matter). However, there is little intuitive reason to think they are very persuasive against entrenched agency policies or behaviour patterns, at least in the short run.

Courts have some more direct powers, but they are quite limited. They can, of course, find agencies or their leaders in contempt, but as a practical matter this occurs only in the most blatant instances of non-compliance. In some instances courts may 'take over' agencies as when federal district judges appointed masters to supervise prisons, school systems resistant to desegregation, or child welfare agencies. Studies by Malcolm Feeley and Edward Rubin and by Susan Mezey indicate that these trial-level courts occasionally reform bureaucratic policies or practices.[19] But this, too, is relatively infrequent. It violates the American separation-of-powers concept and happens only in cases of

---

[19] M. M. Feeley and E. L. Rubin, *Judicial Policy Making and the Modern State: How the Courts Reformed America's Prisons* (New York, Cambridge University Press, 1998); and S. Gluck Mezey, *Pitiful Plaintiffs: Child Welfare Litigation and the Federal Courts* (Pittsburgh, University of Pittsburgh Press, 2000). Feeley's chapter in this volume, Chapter 8, argues that American federal judges have a greater ability to alter bureaucratic behaviour significantly than is commonly believed.

adamant agency opposition or woefully inadequate agency resources. As noted earlier, damages awards in tort suits may encourage behavioural adjustment, but much depends upon the agency's perceptions of its future liability.

The problem of obtaining compliant implementation is exacerbated when a judicial decision affects thousands of separate agencies, as occurs in a federal system like the US. There may be only one Internal Revenue Service, but there are thousands of independent school systems and police departments around the country.

So in good part courts have to depend upon non-judicial factors to gain agency compliance. A major factor is a general respect for the courts. Overt resistance to court decisions is usually seen as a version of 'outlawry', something that respectable citizens and government agencies should not do lest they undermine the rule of law. Closely related, we normally accord legitimacy to court decisions, that is, our understanding of the system of government tells us that the court had a right to make the decision it did. Like umpires or referees in ball games, the courts may occasionally make a bad call, but we must live with the system. As a part of the government, agencies presumably are particularly likely to see court decisions as legitimate. More generally, the public and its elected representatives are also likely to look askance at agency outlawry. Public agencies must worry about their reputation. It is not in their interest to be seen as rogue or self-serving units. Agencies engaged in 'outlaw' activities may sometimes trigger a 'fire alarm' that generates unwelcome attention from the relevant legislative oversight committees.[20]

Consequently, there is an expectation that indifferent or hostile agencies will normally implement unwelcome court decisions to a greater or lesser extent. However, experience tells us that a few decisions will arouse a sufficiently high degree of non-acceptance to overcome a sense of respect or legitimacy and lead an agency, especially when its opposition is shared by legislators and the public, to defy or evade court decisions or implement them in the most narrow and begrudging fashion. And even agencies that are more indifferent than opposed to a court decision may need prodding before engaging in implementation.

[20] See M. D. McCubbins and T. Schwartz, 'Congressional Oversight Overlooked: Police Patrols Versus Fire Alarms' (1984) 28 *American Journal of Political Science* 165–79.

A HEURISTIC MODEL OF AGENCY REACTIONS[21]

At the outset, I will reiterate Maurice Sunkin's reminder that 'doctrinal importance is not necessarily an indication of bureaucratic importance'.[22] While the substance of a judicial policy can be important to an agency, its reaction may be affected even more by a decision's 'liveability'. That is, how inconvenient is it for the agency to implement the decision?

Numerous demands besiege administrative agencies. Clients, sometimes powerful ones, expect services and often expect the agency to act as their advocate in the councils of government. Legislators expect the agency to function efficiently yet inexpensively. They also expect it to abide by both the specific policies they set out for the agency and by the laws that apply to administrative agencies generally. Presidents or cabinet secretaries often want agencies to follow specific policies that advance (or at least do not hinder) the administration's political goals. Legislators, executive superiors and the public do not want an agency to engage in policies that are unpopular or threatening. Often an agency is required or expected to coordinate with other government agencies to accomplish some desirable goal.

Moreover, agencies have their own internal dynamics to consider when meeting external demands. They need to maintain or improve employee morale by instilling a sense of mission and accomplishment,

---

[21] In recent years, American political scientists have used principal–agent theory to model the reaction of subordinates to supervisors, i.e., to investigate to what extent subordinates in the field feel obligated to apply superiors' (including legislators') policies and to what extent they can or will alter these policies. The seminal work is T. Moe, 'The New Economics of Organization' (1984) 28 *American Journal of Economics* 739–77. Principal–agent theory is sometimes used to study the responses of lower courts to US Supreme Court decisions. See D. R. Songer, J. A. Segal and C. M. Cameron, 'The Hierarchy of Justice: Testing a Principal–Agent Model of Supreme Court–Circuit Court Interactions' (1994) 38 *American Journal of Political Science* 673–96. So far as I am aware, this theory has not been directly used to study bureaucratic responses to judicial decisions, although a few scholars have measured the influence of multiple 'principals' on their agency activities through questionnaires (e.g., R. W. Waterman and A. Rouse, 'The Determinants of the Perceptions of Political Control of the Bureaucracy and Venues of Influence' (1999) 9 *Journal of Public Administration Research and Theory* 527–70). I do not use principal–agent theory in this chapter. In my judgment – indeed an underlying theme in this chapter – most agencies are too hierarchically distant from the courts to be fairly considered their agents.

[22] See Chapter 2 above.

to develop logical and efficient routines, and to acquire and preserve resources. Demands that appear subversive to these dynamics pose problems.

Court decisions requiring new agency policies or behaviour come into this mix of more permanent demands and dynamics only occasionally. Such decisions are analogous to strangers, they are the 'new kid on the block'. As such, they have the potential for upsetting an agency's mix of policies and routines, of jeopardising its relationships with clients, legislators, employees, etc. Naturally, the greater the potential, the more wary or even hostile an agency becomes. Put otherwise, court decisions are at best just one of many demands upon a bureaucracy, often of low-level importance in the agency's overall scheme of things and occasionally upsetting or even dysfunctional. Such demands are likely to get as minimal attention or be candidates for as minimal behavioural adjustment as seems possible.

Given the many demands upon agencies and the potential problems a judicial decision can produce, agencies that are indifferent or hostile to it usually go through three steps when considering how to implement a judicially mandated change. Step 1 occurs when the agency leaders interpret what the court requires of it. For various reasons discussed below, court decisions are usually open to differing interpretations or at least differing understandings of their application. Step 2 comes when the agency searches for ways of changing its policies or processes in a manner that will minimally satisfy what the court is perceived as requiring while minimally altering its goals, functions, *ésprit de corps*, and relationships with the rest of the government and with the public. Step 3 is the agency's choice of an actual implementation strategy (which can be different in practice from that on paper). These three steps, which form the heart of my model, are quite similar to those Marc Hertogh develops in his study of the impact of courts and the National Ombudsman on two government agencies in the Netherlands.[23]

[23] Hertogh, 'Coercion, Cooperation and Control'. I had not read Hertogh's article when I developed these steps. Hertogh calls his steps information, transformation and processing. The steps are set in a continuum of cooperative versus coercive relationships between the courts or ombudsman and the agency. The ombudsman, who has few real coercive powers, usually takes a cooperative approach to settle complaints while the courts, which have virtually no informal interactions with the agency, usually take a coercive approach. Hertogh suggests that cooperation produces more impact than coercion. I do not use a cooperation versus coercion continuum in my model. There is no American counterpart to the European

I discuss these steps separately below. I should note that, while the steps are conceptually separate and to some extent linear, they can be closely interwoven in thought processes. Indeed, at times the requirement of an immediate response to a judicial stimulus telescopes them into one process.

Step 1: interpretation

An agency's normal first step is to interpret how a court decision applies to its own actions. Quite often this is not clear from the court's opinion. The opinion may set forth a general change in policy, but give little guidance as to behavioural details. Or it may set forth details about its application to one agency, but leave its application to other agencies unclear. Or an opinion, especially one drafted by a collegial court, may by the nature of its creation lack clarity or precision or even seem partly self-contradictory. Some opinions contain caveats, exceptions or warnings against too broad an interpretation. Or a decision may seem at odds with another decision by the same or a higher court, leaving an agency unsure about which is applicable.

Agency leaders and attorneys must make educated guesses about what the court decision asks of them. Sometimes this is relatively easy and often done in good faith. But their interpretations can be coloured by their acceptance decision. This is all the more so as the intensity of rejection increases. In high-intensity situations, an agency may deliberately interpret the court's decision to find it inapplicable to itself by using convoluted reasoning, citing other authority or invoking unusual circumstances. Or an agency may ignore the decision – perhaps through a process of non-decision or a 'let sleeping dogs lie' attitude – and hope that no one challenges its failure to act. It can take years for this to happen, and in some cases may never occur.[24]

More often a process of cognitive dissonance[25] will set in and an agency will interpret the decision as inapplicable, or to apply only in

Ombudsman, and, like Dutch courts, those in the US do not normally negotiate with agencies.

[24] Some school administrators followed this strategy regarding *Abington Township* v. *Schempp*, 374 US 203 (1963), which barred led prayers in public schools. See K. M. Dolbeare and P. E. Hammond, *The School Prayer Decisions: From Court Policy to Local Practice* (Chicago, University of Chicago Press, 1971). Even four decades later, federal courts are occasionally called upon to enjoin organised prayers in rural public schools in the American South.

[25] Cognitive dissonance theory holds that individuals reduce mental tensions by subconsciously seeking consistency between their beliefs and the demands of others. In

minor or limited instances.[26] The degree to which deliberate rejection or minimisation through cognitive dissonance occurs may depend upon how absorbed agency leaders are in the agency's own culture or in a local culture rather than a national one.

At times, agencies, especially smaller ones (e.g., rural school systems, small-town police departments) are not aware of the details of a court decision.[27] They learn about it from television, newspapers or by word of mouth. Media coverage – especially thirty-second sound-bites on television news programmes – may over-emphasise the scope of a court decision, ignore certain aspects of the decision, or even misreport the decision or its major implications. Thus agency leaders may believe a decision says something different than it actually does. A study of American network coverage of the Supreme Court found that the Court's refusal to hear a case was sometimes reported as a definitive decision on the merits, or that important Court decisions sometimes went unreported if there were a lot of other major news stories that day.[28]

Even when agency leaders understand a decision, their knowledge may not be communicated very well to staff or field workers. This can be deliberate, or the leaders may not believe the decision is important enough to merit particular attention. Or the decision's behavioural requirements may be disseminated, but not its rationale or examples of its application, thus leaving workers unsure of its whys and wherefors. Cognitive dissonance can set in so that the staff misinterpret what the agency leaders tell them. Sometimes ordinary agency mechanisms for

the case of a judicial decision, this can be done by misperceiving its nature, scope or requirements. For an application of this theory to agency reactions to the US Supreme Court's decision in *Abington Township* v. *Schempp*, 374 US 203 (1963), see W. K. Muir, Jr, *Prayer in Public Schools: Law and Attitude Change* (Chicago, University of Chicago Press, 1967). As Muir shows, an alternate resolution to cognitive dissonance is for agency personnel to accept the decision's rightness and make behavioural adjustments accordingly. This often occurs, but it may take unusual leadership and/or considerable time.

[26] Such interpretations are not always 'wrong' in the controlling sense, but are more likely than not to be rejected by the court that made the decision if presented to it.

[27] In *Small Town Police and the Supreme Court: Hearing the Word* (Lexington, MA, DC Heath, 1976), S. L. Wasby, using questionnaires and interviews, reported inadequate communication of criminal justice decisions to small police departments in the 1960s and 1970s.

[28] E. Slotnick and J. A. Segal, *Television News and the Supreme Court: All the News That's Fit to Air?* (Cambridge, Cambridge University Press, 1998).

communicating its own policy changes may be poorly structured for disseminating judicial policy changes.[29]

As a consequence, agencies may have a different interpretation of a
judicial decision than the judges intended or than a lower court is likely
to make in a lawsuit. When the court decision is not highly visible,
agency misinterpretations may go unquestioned for years. In sum, what
the court proclaims is not always what the agency understands.

Step 2: the agency search

When agency leaders believe that the court decision calls for a
behavioural response, the next step is determining what that response
will be. As noted above, intense non-acceptance or inertia may lead the
agency to maintain its policies and accompanying behaviour patterns
and wait for a court, the legislature or an executive branch superior to
force changes upon it. But most agencies would rather avoid imposition
of change by outsiders. So if this seems to be a possibility, an agency
searches for ways of changing its behaviour that will minimally satisfy
what the court requires while minimally altering behaviour that serves
its goals or functions. So the first part of the search process is evaluating the extent to which the decision will affect the agency. When a
decision's requirements do not seem comprehensive or threatening, the
agency may comply reasonably well. But a search for a minimal adjustment will occur when the decision endangers core goals and functions
or is likely to drain resources devoted to those goals.

In its search, an agency must consider how change will affect its
relationships with outside groups. Its clientele is one such group. For
many agencies, service to clients is their *raison d'être*, for example, the
Department of Commerce and businesses. If a court decision makes
such service more difficult, the agency will seek a minimal implementation strategy. Conversely, for agencies that have no need to please
their clients, for example, prisons and inmates, a decision that enhances
clientele power will trigger a search for minimal implementation.

Agencies must also consider the positions of political bodies or offices
that fund or govern it: how will Congress, the president, etc., react to
full implementation or to virtually no implementation? Agencies seldom want to invite the wrath of their benefactors. Note that this can

---

[29] Creyke and McMillan, in Chapter 6 below, discuss the dissemination of administrative law decisions to Australian agencies at some length based upon agency staff and
officer responses to questionnaires.

work both ways: some legislators or executives may favour full compliance with the court decision even though it hurts the agency's clientele or otherwise disrupts its functions, while other legislators or executives may demand that an agency minimise implementation of politically unpopular decisions. Likewise, agencies must consider public reactions (and those of the media whose coverage can influence the public) because these ultimately influence legislative and executive positions.

Agencies will also calculate the decision's potential impact on its own resources. One found liable in a tort suit (or seeing itself as vulnerable when another agency loses a case) is more willing to make resource-preserving behavioural adjustments than is a losing agency not faced with monetary liability. This is particularly the case in a litigious society like the US where thousands of lawyers are ready to swoop down like hawks on vulnerable deep pockets. By contrast, when full compliance with a judicial decision requires a significant expenditure of its own funds, the agency will look for ways to avoid implementation or do it 'on the cheap' (conversely, the high cost of defending litigation can lead some agencies to view compliance as the best way to preserve resources[30]).

In the main, agency searches will follow 'utility theory', a rough cost–benefit analysis. A kind of individual utility calculation was first advanced by the eighteenth-century British philosopher Jeremy Bentham and is a theoretical mainstay (often termed rational choice theory) guiding the research of present day economists. The theory was first applied to responses to judicial decisions by Robert Stover and Don Brown.[31] Put simply, agency leaders will calculate the benefits the agency gains by little or no implementation plus the costs to the agency of such non-compliance and weigh them against the benefits to the agency of full or nearly full implementation plus the costs of compliance. This can be expressed in the inequality:

$$B(N) + C(N) <?> B(I) + C(I)$$

---

[30] See E. J. Ringquist and C. E. Emmert, 'Judicial Policy-Making in Published and Unpublished Decisions: The Case of Environmental Civil Litigation' (1999) 52 *Political Research Quarterly* 7–37; and R. Kagan, 'Adversarial Legalism and American Government' in M. Landy and M. A. Levin (eds.), *The New Politics of Public Policy* (Baltimore, Johns Hopkins University Press, 1995).

[31] R. Stover and D. Brown, 'Understanding Compliance and Noncompliance with the Law: The Contributions of Utility Theory' (1975) 56 *Social Science Quarterly* 363–75.

where B = benefits, C = costs, (N) = non-implementation and (I) = implementation. Non-implementation can be expected if the net value on the left side of the equation exceeds that on the right and implementation is expected if the reverse is true.[32] Note that utility theory is centred on costs and benefits to the agency itself and not to government or society more generally.

Utility theory does not incorporate immeasurable psychic costs very well.[33] In this sense, agency leaders or cultures can have a greater or lesser sense of 'law abidingness', a belief that it is wrong to disobey the law even though it might be advantageous to do so.[34] If 'law abidingness' is high, leaders and employees might not be willing to undergo the psychic tensions of disobedience. This is especially so if the defiance is visible or made so by the media. Differences in agency cultures and their leaders' sense of 'law abidingness' can produce different responses even when the agencies' clientele or political or resource utilities are similar.

Stover and Brown present utility theory largely in terms of compliance or non-compliance. Sometimes agencies have no other choices, but most often agency responses do not have to be dichotomous. Some degree of partial implementation is possible and even likely. This is illustrated in Figure 3.1. Point A is the agency's policy preference on a one-dimensional policy continuum and Point C is what the court decision commands. B1, B2 and B3 are alternative policies the agency can adopt, some closer to its own preferences and some closer to the court's.[35]

[32] Stover and Brown use the terms 'compliance' and 'noncompliance'. I think 'implementation' is a word more descriptive of the range of agencies' choices. I have altered their equation and discussion in this manner.

[33] Stover and Brown include psychic costs in utility theory. This can be done in a conceptual sense, but in my judgment psychic costs are too immeasurable to test in the real world. Moreover, their inclusion would tempt researchers to attribute outcomes deviating from those predicted by measurable utility theory variables to psychic considerations. Utility theory would then become meaningless because in explaining everything, it would not be subject to falsification.

[34] The concept is discussed in the agency setting by H. R. Rodgers Jr and C. S. Bullock, *Law and Social Change: Civil Rights Laws and Their Consequences* (New York, McGraw-Hill, 1972). See also R. Johnson, *The Dynamics of Compliance* (Evanston IL, Northwestern University Press, 1967), which focuses on American school system responses to the *Schempp* case (no prayer in public schools).

[35] The figure is adapted from C. A. Johnson, 'Judicial Decisions and Organizational Change' (1979) 11 *Administration and Society* 27–51.

A_____B1_____B2_____B3_____C

Figure 3.1 *Policy gap between agency and court*

The most likely outcome in the longer run is that a hostile or indifferent agency will select a 'compromise' in the B range.[36] Its choice depends upon its perceptions of a number of factors, most notably how committed the agency is to its own policy, the resources necessary to comply, the agency leaders' attitudes towards the court decision, the risks of judicial enforcement and the severity of sanctions, and pressures from clientele groups, legislators, bureaucratic superiors and the public. Of course, an agency's compromise is not necessarily static; it can change over time as threats to its goals and functions materialise or fade, cost estimates rise or fall and political interest in the court's policy preferences increases or decreases. For example, following *Miranda* v. *Arizona*, American police departments were at first quite resistant to notifying suspects of their right to be silent, to have an attorney present, etc., but within a few years found that most suspects waived their rights after routinised warnings.[37]

As is true of all policy decisions, judicial rulings can have consequences that are not anticipated by either the court or the agency, especially when implementation becomes more problematic or technology changes, or as changes in the political or economic climate alter pressures on the agency. As these consequences become apparent, compliant agencies may become resistant, or *vice versa*. As a result, courts will sometimes alter their policies or allow agencies greater deference in their implementation. For example, the Environmental Protection Agency, an agency created in 1971 to enforce a newly adopted broad federal policy commitment, was whipsawed by changes in administration and subjected to changing and debatable technical considerations

---

[36] The 'compromise' is unilaterally chosen, at least at first. The agency does not negotiate with the court. But in an indirect sense a compromise may be negotiated over a few rounds of litigation.

[37] *Miranda* v. *Arizona*, 384 US 436 (1966) held that evidence obtained through interrogation of an in-custody suspect was not admissible in court unless the suspect had been told of his rights and waived them. Many detectives became quite skilled at obtaining waivers. See R. A. Leo, '*Miranda*'s Revenge: Police Interrogation as a Confidence Game' (1996) 30 *Law and Society Review* 259–88. See also the discussion in Canon and Johnson, *Judicial Policies*, pp. 82–4 and 103–5.

in the 1970s and 1980s. It also had to deal with vagueness and 'loop-holes' in its enabling statute.[38]

In closing the discussion of Step 2, I need to make the point that the search process is usually much less rational than the above description implies. A rational calculation of utilities requires considerable information. In reality, information is often acquired haphazardly or can be virtually absent during agency searches. The costs of obtaining information can be high and detract from other agency functions, and so unless the court decision is of primary importance, the agency will settle for imperfect information. It may even search on the basis of leaders' mere speculations. Moreover, an agency may have to make an initial response to a court decision before it has time to collect and rationally review information on alternate choices. An initial response can some-times become a fixed policy to which an agency may cling for reasons of inertia or pride.

Step 3: implementation of behavioural response

A search by an indifferent or hostile agency will settle on one of five basic behavioural responses. One, already noted, is to *do nothing* due to ignorance, misperception, the seeming unimportance of responding, intense opposition to the decision as a matter of policy preference, or because of its negative impact on the agency's functioning.

However, if an agency finds non-response difficult or impossible, a second strategy is to comply only in a particular case when directly threatened with a sanction such as a contempt citation. Legal schol-ars call this *non-acquiescence*. Using this tactic, the agency will com-ply with direct court orders but not much else. Although some federal agencies had engaged in this practice in earlier administrations, sev-eral major agencies used non-acquiescence during the Ronald Reagan presidency. The Social Security Administration was perhaps most noto-rious. Under pressure to save money, it generally refused to apply federal court policies allowing liberal eligibility for disability awards, but would do so if the applicant actually filed a suit. Indeed, the agency openly announced its non-acquiescence policy and instructed staff and admin-istrative law judges to ignore certain judicial precedents. The Internal Revenue Service was similarly open about its non-acquiescence while the National Labor Relations Board (NLRB) and the Occupational

---

[38] R. Shep Melnick, *Regulation and the Courts: A Study of the Clean Air Act* (Washington, Brookings Institution, 1984).

Safety and Health Administration (OSHA) were less visible in their defiance. Fewer than 5 per cent of the Social Security and OSHA applicants appealed the adverse agency decisions to the courts. While external fiscal pressures primarily motivated Social Security, the NLRB's resistance was motivated by an intensely negative acceptance of decisions regarding judicial policies. Beyond fiscal or policy considerations, an agency will sometimes adopt non-acquiescence as it waits to see whether the court decision will 'stick' or be overturned by Congress, or because it seems too much effort to retrain staff, rewrite manuals and reprogram computers around the country.[39]

Similarly, a study by Martin Shapiro revealed that the US Patent Office had much lower standards for obtaining a patent than did the Supreme Court.[40] The Patent Office would obey particular Court decisions, but would not change its standards to accommodate the more stringent requirements called for in Court opinions. While the Court might reverse the most egregious patent grants, it obviously could not supervise the office's everyday operations. A strong commitment to its own standards motivated the Patent Office (a non-political agency).

Non-acquiescence is much riskier when the agency needs the cooperation of the courts on a continuing basis. The police usually want convictions and thus must conduct searches and interrogations in accordance with such famous US Supreme Court due process decisions as *Mapp* and *Miranda* and their progeny. On occasion, however, when the police carry out a search or an arrest for the purposes of harassment rather than for prosecution purposes, they can pay little attention to judicial constrictions on their behaviour.[41] As discussed earlier, such resistance is also more problematic when an agency risks civil liability by refusing to implement a judicial decision. A number of American

[39] D. Maranville, 'Nonacquiescence: Outlaw Agencies, Imperial Courts and the Perils of Pluralism' (1986) 39 *Vanderbilt Law Review* 471–538; and S. Estreicher and R. L. Revesz, 'Nonacquiescence by Federal Administrative Agencies' (1989) 98 *Yale Law Journal* 679–772. Hertogh, 'Coercion, Cooperation and Control', reports similar behaviour by the Dutch Tax Authority, while Creyke and McMillan, in Chapter 6 below, note that the Australian Immigration Authority tries to settle cases it might lose in order to avoid the establishment of an adverse precedent.
[40] M. Shapiro, *The Supreme Court and Administrative Agencies* (New York, Macmillan, 1968), pp. 143–226.
[41] Based on his field participation with the police, Jerome Skolnick reports that officers often simply harass gamblers, prostitutes and sometime drug dealers to keep them in check or to make their activities more inconvenient. See J. Skolnick, *Justice Without Trial* (New York, Wiley, 1966).

police departments, for example, who followed a policy of strip-searching arrestees for minor offences (including traffic stops) even after federal and state courts had ruled such searches illegal in cases involving other departments and their cities (e.g., Chicago and Louisville, Kentucky) eventually wound up paying hefty compensation to settle class action suits.[42]

In a third strategy one step up, an agency may accept the need for general change, but implement it only in a *pro forma* sense. A 'window-dressing' policy change is adopted to give the appearance of doing something without really doing very much. Here agency leaders more or less intend to maintain the *status quo* or they may be indifferent about how subordinates respond. *Pro forma* change occurs when an agency is hostile to the decision, but, unlike the Patent Office, is more subject to judicial review or even to external political pressures and thus must appear to make a general behavioural adjustment. As noted, after *Miranda* most police departments gave the required warnings during interrogations, but they developed ways of doing it that discouraged suspects from invoking their rights. As a practical matter, relatively few suspects completely refused to answer police questions.

A *pro forma* approach can also happen when the agency, although not necessarily hostile to the decision's values, concludes that real implementation will be somewhat dysfunctional or consume too many resources. For example, American school systems often held 'quickie' hearings after the Supreme Court ruled that students could not be suspended without a hearing.[43] A hundred or more suspensions may occur every week in a large urban school system, so real hearings would be quite time-consuming. Moreover, formal hearings might encourage a 'litigious' mindset in pupils or parents. So school administrators began conducting them more or less on the spot with minimal due process.

A fourth strategy that an agency hostile to a judicial decision can follow is to take *minimal steps* to implement it. Agency leaders recognise the need to make some general change, but believe that it ought to be as little as they can get away with. In a classic example, many Southern school systems adopted 'freedom of choice' plans after *Brown v. Board*

[42] Note that it was not the police departments but the cities that ended up paying, so there was no great incentive to the police to alter their policy. On the other hand, police departments are supervised by municipal officers (and attorneys) who certainly should have foreseen the consequences.

[43] The case was *Goss v. Lopez*, 419 US 565 (1975). Suspensions usually range from one day to two weeks.

of Education allowed students to enrol in any school in the system. The expectation was that all whites would sign up at the former all-white schools and that social pressures would keep all but a handful of blacks enrolled in the formerly legally black schools.[44]

In some circumstances, minimal implementation can also involve using what Lorne Sossin calls 'soft law'.[45] Most agencies must exercise some discretion in administering policies, and this is particularly true of those that handle a large number of clients in a wide variety of circumstances such as the police, the Immigration and Naturalization Service or the Internal Revenue Service. Administrators' discretion is shaped by tradition, by the policies of unit heads or by internal agency guidelines or working definitions. Soft law usually results in settlements, lowered charges, or other compromises that are not formally visible to appellate courts. When courts do consider soft law cases, they often show deference to such practices if they seem to have superficial compatibility with their policy decisions. In short, some agencies are in a position to utilise soft law to 'soften' 'hard' judicial law considerably.

Fifthly, an agency – even when it dislikes the decision – may engage in *full or nearly full implementation*. This can occur when agency leaders have a sense of law-abidingness. Or it can happen when sanctions for not doing so seem likely. This is particularly true when an agency faces tort liability, as some do in the US. For example, after Supreme Court decisions that made government agencies liable for sexual harassment,[46] some agencies tried to foreclose future lawsuits by creating offices to handle complaints and instituting training sessions on harassment for all employees. Sometimes, the monetary or reputational costs of litigation itself can induce a high degree of compliance.[47] A *pro forma* response would be simply to adopt a formal policy and post a few notices about it. Likewise, police departments are sometimes subject to liability for excessive use of force. Some will make a real effort to prevent or punish such behaviour and others will not.[48] In the case of the police,

---

[44] The Supreme Court struck this strategy down in *Green* v. *School Board of New Kent County*, 391 US 430 (1968).

[45] See Chapter 5 below.

[46] *Faragher* v. *City of Boca Raton*, 524 US 775 (1998); and *Davis* v. *Monroe County School Board*, 526 US 629 (1999).

[47] See Ringquist and Emmert, 'Judicial Policy-Making'; and Kagan, 'Adversarial Legalism'.

[48] See S. Walker and L. Fridel, 'The Forces of Change in Police Policy: The Impact of *Tennessee* v. *Garner* on Deadly Force Policy' (1993) 11 *American Journal of Police*

professional isolation and often police unions may enhance resistance to real implementation.[49]

FACTORS AFFECTING CHOICE OF ADJUSTMENT BEHAVIOUR

How an agency adjusts to a judicial decision depends upon a number of factors. I have alluded to them already, but offer a brief but summary overview here.

There are two main internal factors. One is the *policy tension* that exists between the judicial mandate and the agency's goals and functions. Judicial decisions that require an agency to forego pursuing some of its core goals, that drain significant resources away from these goals or that require behaviour that impedes achieving these goals naturally create tensions among agency leaders and personnel. Normally bureaucratic agencies are committed to preserving their goals and functions. The greater the demand for change, the greater the tension and the more likely an agency is to resist. Good examples of this come from American federal courts' decisions in the 1970s and 1980s ordering major changes in the way prisoners were treated. Both guards and prison administrators viewed these decisions as seriously dysfunctional and bitterly resisted them. The Texas prison system, which had a particularly isolated culture, limited legal information and help to the prisoners, retaliated against prisoners who expressed interest in obtaining legal help and even countersued some attorneys trying to implement judicial reforms. It often took repeated court decisions to accomplish minimal change.[50]

97–112. In *Garner*, 471 US 1 (1985), the Supreme Court found the police liable under federal civil rights laws for denying due process when an unarmed burglar was shot while running away after ignoring an officer's command to stop. More generally, see L. B. Edelman, 'Legal Ambiguity and Symbolic Structures: Organizational Mediation of Civil Rights Law' (1992) 95 *American Journal of Sociology* 1401–40.

[49] Skolnick, *Justice Without Trial*, discusses the isolated culture of police officers.

[50] See, e.g., B. W. Crouch and J. Marquart, '*Ruiz*: Intervention and Emergent Order in Texas Prisons' in J. J. DiIulio (ed.), *Courts, Corrections and the Constitution: The Impact of Judicial Intervention in Prisons and Jails* (New York, Oxford University Press, 1990). The case was *Ruiz v. Estelle*, 503 F Supp 1265 (SD Tex., 1980). See also S. Ekland-Olson and S. J. Martin, 'Organizational Compliance with Court-Ordered Reform' (1988) 22 *Law and Society Review* 359–87. Feeley's chapter in this volume, Chapter 8, argues that judicially mandated changes in prisons were more easily accomplished.

The other internal factor is *inertia* – the tendency of organisations, especially large ones, to continue their policies and functions with little change. Inertia in agency routines and culture is a fact of organisational life; a staple part of organisational theory. An agency can be particularly inertial when its employees are professionals and do much of their work without direct supervision, for example the police or social workers. Such workers develop a culture and norms of behaviour that cannot be easily controlled by supervisors. Beyond that, however, agency workers try to retain old habits for convenience's sake. Few are willing to learn new ways to behave unless a carrot or stick is visible. Inertia can be overcome, of course, sometimes due to a fear of sanctions or the lure of rewards and sometimes by dynamic leaders. This is particularly true when agency personnel are relatively indifferent to the substance of the judicial decision. But inertia is an 'anti-force' to be reckoned with.

Agency adjustment is also affected by external factors. We have already noted the *political factors* that can influence an agency's response – the policy preferences of presidents and legislators, and the impact of public opinion. When these run in the opposite direction to the judicial decision's requirements, an agency can suffer from a policy tension similar to that noted above, even if the agency itself does not feel strongly negative about the decision.

But agencies can also be affected by *community pressures* – expectations from those with whom agency personnel regularly interact. Client communities work closely with regulatory agencies, for example agribusinesses and the Department of Agriculture or telecommunications companies with the Federal Communications Commission.

Many agencies, or at least their crucial personnel, will also take cues from professional communities whose standards and norms can be quite independent of both court decisions and political or clientele pressures and perhaps of geographical influence as well. Physicians, academics and to a lesser extent military officers, for example, are quite often highly influenced by their training, ethics and the expectations of their peers as communicated through professional journals and conferences. This will influence reactions to judicial decisions by public hospitals, universities and the armed services.

Finally, agency staff can be influenced by the predominant values of geographical communities in which they work. While professionals are more likely to respond in accordance with their professional norms, lower level staff are usually affected by the local culture. Agency personnel in Washington or San Francisco, rather liberal cities, may react differently to some court decisions than staff in more conservative locales like Phoenix, Arizona, or Omaha, Nebraska.

RESEARCH METHODS[51]

Systematic data on the impact of judicial decisions on bureaucracies are obtained in much the same way as are other data concerning agency responses to external policies – that is, largely from agency records, administering surveys, conducting interviews, and occasionally by observation.

Bureaucracies by their very nature keep lots of records, and a good proportion of those records are public or can be accessed by scholars. With many agencies, the data are available in the aggregate, but privacy concerns bar access at the individual level, for example student or welfare client records. The reliability of records (i.e., whether they reflect what actually happened) is normally quite good, although occasionally a few are problematic.[52] More frequently, questions of validity arise when records are used as a surrogate for the agency behaviour that actually interests the researcher. For example, in my study of the impact of the Supreme Court's 1961 *Mapp* v. *Ohio* decision that illegally seized evidence could not be introduced in criminal trials, I collected arrest data for crimes in which the evidence was usually obtained by police searches and seizures (e.g., drug possession, concealed or illegal weapons).[53] These data, however, do not actually indicate whether the searches were illegal. I made the assumption (based upon my interviews and the research of others) that a reasonably high proportion of these searches were illegal prior to *Mapp* and thus any significant decline in arrests reflected a decline in illegal searches by the police. While I believed the assumption was a good one, it nonetheless remained an

---

[51] This section relies on my earlier work, B. C. Canon, 'Courts and Policy: Compliance, Implementation and Impact' in J. B. Gates and C. A. Johnson (eds.), *The American Courts: A Critical Assessment* (Washington, CQ Press, 1991).

[52] For example, some police departments raise or lower charges on borderline felony–misdemeanour crimes such as shoplifting. Lowering charges makes their record of crime control look better while raising them can support an argument that crime is on the rise so the department needs more officers or other support.

[53] *Mapp* v. *Ohio*, 367 US 643 (1961). B. C. Canon, 'Is the Exclusionary Rule in Failing Health? Some New Data and a Plea Against a Precipitous Conclusion' (1974) 62 *Kentucky Law Journal* 651–730.

assumption. Where surrogate records are used, researchers must decide how well such agency records reflect the agency behaviour that they are investigating. Of course, researchers have a natural tendency to accept surrogate variables as valid because recorded evidence of the behaviour they are really interested in is non-existent. Finally, as Peter Cane points out, even when valid, data that correlate do not in themselves conclusively demonstrate causality, especially when bureaucrats are under multiple pressures.[54]

Sometimes records cannot be obtained or do not exist. And in non-response or non-acquiescence situations, there may be little or no causality to determine, so the investigator's task is to find out why the agency did not respond. When records are absent, scholars must generate impact data by asking agency personnel about their acceptance decisions and behavioural adjustments. Indeed, acceptance decisions are basically mental and not usually found in records. Even when agency records are plentiful, scholars should enhance their validity by gathering information directly from agency personnel whenever possible.

Most often researchers pursue this by sending questionnaires to agency leaders and/or to a sample of rank-and-file personnel seeking such information in the wake of a judicial decision affecting the agency. These surveys are sometimes sent to hundreds of respondents and enable scholars to acquire a broad set of reactions from persons in a number of agencies and in far-flung locations. Sizeable datasets give confidence in the results.[55] Of course, the researchers must take care to craft the questions so as to obtain useful answers – a task that may require considerable sophistication when the responses could put the agency in a bad light.

Although they cannot reach the number of respondents that surveys can, interviews with agency personnel enable investigators to obtain significantly more detailed and colourful knowledge about how agencies are reacting to a court decision. They can probe the psychic cost considerations, the acceptance decision process and the development of a behavioural adjustment policy better than can questionnaires. Three studies that relied largely on interviews (and some observation)

[54] Chapter 1 above.
[55] The pioneering work is F. H. Way, Jr, 'Survey Research on Judicial Decisions: The Prayer and Bible Reading Cases' (1968) 21 *Western Political Quarterly* 189–205. Few American bureaucratic response datasets are available and almost none comparable to that which Creyke and McMillan (see Chapter 6 below) have collected.

produced an in-depth understanding of how rural school systems reacted to *Schempp*, the school prayer decision.[56] Another noted how several state agencies' leaders implemented what they viewed as problematic state supreme court decisions.[57] Interviews with leaders of local agencies in different towns, such as police departments, are often useful in developing an understanding of the range of responses to court decisions.[58] Of course, interviews are a greater drain on researchers' time and resources than are survey instruments, so they are undertaken less often.[59]

Direct observation of relevant behaviour provides the most reliable impact data. However, this is quite often impossible or at least impractical on any continuing basis. And, at best, observation can produce only a minute and non-random sample of the universe of agencies' responsive behaviour. Even so, the findings can be highly illuminating and suggestive of theory to guide more widespread research. Two observational studies of police interrogation of suspects shortly after the *Miranda case* produced classic insights into police responses that have coloured researchers' and writers' images of police behaviour to this day.[60] A combination of observation and interviews can be even more revealing,[61] as can participant observation.[62]

[56] Muir, *Prayer*; Dolbeare and Hammond, *School Prayer Decisions*; and Johnson, *The Dynamics*.

[57] Johnson, 'Organizational Change'.

[58] On police reaction, see Wasby, *Small Town Police*; and N. Milner, *The Court and Local Law Enforcement* (Beverly Hills, CA, Sage Books, 1971).

[59] Except when they are supported by at least a modest-sized grant, interviews of agency personnel are usually done by graduate students writing their dissertations.

[60] M. S. Wald, R. Ayers, R. Hess, M. Schanz and C. Whitebread, 'Interrogations in New Haven: The Impact of *Miranda*' (1967) 76 *Yale Law Journal* 1519–648; and R. Medalie, L. Zeitz and P. Alexander, 'Custodial Interrogation in Our Nation's Capital: The Attempt to Implement *Miranda*' (1968) 66 *Michigan Law Review* 1347–422.

[61] A good example is F. Wirt, *The Politics of Southern Equality: Law and Social Change in a Mississippi County* (Chicago, Adline, 1970). Wirt 'hung around' the county, studying not only the implementation of desegregation in the schools but its impact on the political and social life of the county.

[62] A classic if seldom replicable example of participant observation occurred when a scholar served as a prison guard in Texas following *Ruiz* v. *Estelle*, 503 F Supp 1265 (SD Tex., 1980), a decision requiring the prison system to drastically alter many of its policies. See Marquart and Crouch, 'Intervention and Emergent Order'. Another is Skolnick, *Justice Without Trial*. Skolnick was not a sworn officer, but he accompanied the police on their routines for over a year – to the point that his identity as a scholar was forgotten.

CONCLUSION

Systematic empirical research about how administrative agencies implement judicial policies does not occur all that frequently in the US.[63] It is an area of scholarly adolescence lying in a 'no man's land' between the studies of public administration and judicial politics; it is of interest to both of these disciplines (and others), yet peripheral to each of them. We need to encourage more research here, especially studies that can be connected theoretically with each other and with those of the past. Only in this way can we develop and build theories of bureaucratic response that will guide further studies and give us confidence in the theories' validity. This paper is a step towards this end.

I have developed a conceptual model here that offers a structure for organising research into the implementation of judicial decisions by public bureaucracies. The model is based largely upon intuition as gained by an experiential understanding of human reactions and a scholarly familiarity with judicial and bureaucratic interactions. It is also informed by a number of empirical studies, many of which are noted.

My model is not particularly innovative. It has guided some of my previous research and writing as well as that of others, particularly Charles Johnson. But earlier work has largely been focused on reporting particular research or on giving a broad synthesis of others' findings. The model has not been developed conceptually or heuristically to the extent I do here. But it is hardly the last word. I invite comment, refinement and improvement.

---

[63] The chapters in this volume by Sossin and by Creyke and McMillan report a dearth of empirical research in Canada and Australia respectively.

PART TWO

INTERNATIONAL CASE STUDIES

CHAPTER FOUR

IMPACT STUDIES IN THE UNITED KINGDOM

GENEVRA RICHARDSON

INTRODUCTION

This chapter is designed to provide a brief overview of the empirical research conducted on the impact of judicial review on bureaucratic decision-making in the UK.[1] While both impact and judicial review are terms which require further definition, an extensive analysis has been provided in Part 1 of this volume and there is therefore no need to dwell too long on matters of definition here. Nonetheless, before describing the existing research, it is necessary to place both judicial review and impact within a UK context, and the first part of this chapter provides some introductory background. The second part then presents a brief survey of the relevant research in the UK, and the third part further analyses some of the data to emerge from a study conducted by the author and a colleague in 1997–9. Finally, the fourth part considers how far these findings can be applied in other decision-making contexts. A concluding part indicates some possible ways forward for impact research in the UK.

---

[1] For the purposes of this chapter, the term 'United Kingdom' (or 'UK') is being used very loosely. The brief description of judicial review given deals almost exclusively with the position in England. Any full consideration of the implications of devolution has been left to others. However, 'United Kingdom' has been retained in the title because not all the empirical work has been done in England.

SETTING THE CONTEXT

Judicial review

The purpose of judicial review

As is abundantly evident from other contributions to this volume, judicial review not only performs different formal tasks within different jurisdictions and constitutional arrangements, but it is also the subject of different aspirations and expectations. There is no universally agreed purpose of judicial review. Certainly in the UK the fundamental justification for judicial review is hotly contested.[2] This theoretical uncertainty, however, need not inhibit empirical investigation. Indeed, it could be argued that data emerging from empirical studies of impact at a variety of different levels of decision-making can only serve to improve the quality of that theoretical debate.[3] However, as Cane points out,[4] the impact of judicial review cannot be isolated from the purposes that are ascribed to it. So to some extent the choice of impact to be studied by empirical researchers will be governed by the purpose ascribed to judicial review.

The relevance of jurisdictional context

Certainly the constitutional and formal legal role of judicial review differs from jurisdiction to jurisdiction and will be influenced by a variety of familiar constitutional factors. To some extent, therefore, inter-jurisdictional comparisons must be treated with considerable caution.[5] However, it is arguable that, while this caution is most appropriate in relation to impact studies involving legislative or 'high' policy reactions to judicial review, it is of less relevance to studies of front-line bureaucratic decision-making where constitutional and jurisdictional factors are unlikely to be so significant.

Judicial review in the UK

In the UK, judicial review is the primary judicial mechanism available to challenge the decisions of public bodies, and is the only mechanism which has been specifically developed to test the legality of public

---

[2] C. Forsyth (ed.), *Judicial Review and the Constitution* (Oxford, Oxford University Press, 2000).

[3] G. Richardson and M. Sunkin, 'Judicial Review: Questions of Impact' [1996] *Public Law* 79.

[4] See Chapter 1 above.   [5] *Ibid.*

bodies in public law. It is therefore unsurprising that it has attracted special attention from those interested in the relationship between courts and government in the broadest sense. The power of the High Court in the UK to consider the legality of the decisions of inferior bodies by way of judicial review derives from the common law. It is part of the court's inherent power and as such is not dependent on any legislative authority. Traditionally judicial review is said to be concerned with the lawfulness of a decision in public law. The precise criteria by which this lawfulness is judged have been developed over time by the judiciary themselves and, in the interests of constitutional propriety, the judiciary have been anxious to emphasise the limits of their reviewing power, particularly in relation to the exercise of discretion by public bodies. Obviously in recent years membership of the European Union and the passing of the Human Rights Act 1998 have radically altered the constitutional and political landscape within the UK. Nonetheless, the essential role of the reviewing courts within the constitution has not changed. Parliament remains legislatively supreme and the courts' primary role is still to interpret and enforce the will of Parliament. Under the Human Rights Act, if a court decides that a particular statutory provision fails to comply with the UK's obligations arising under the European Convention on Human Rights (ECHR), the court cannot quash that provision, it can merely issue a declaration of incompatibility.

These formal characteristics of judicial review in the UK are relevant to the conduct of impact studies in two main respects. In the first place, according to the orthodox constitutional theory described above judicial review is limited to enforcing the will of Parliament. Thus there is a formal limit to what the courts can achieve. While the developments of recent years have served to shift those formal limits in areas where ECHR rights are engaged or where EU law applies, the courts in the UK still have no general power to impugn the legality of an Act of Parliament. Any attempt to assess the impact of judicial review on legislative policy must be understood within that constitutional context. Secondly, the traditional grounds for judicial review remain quite limited, particularly in relation to the control of the exercise of discretion, and this may lead to a divergence between the law as understood by lawyers and the law as understood by those potentially subjected to it. Again, any attempt to assess the practical impact of judicial review must be fully aware of that relationship.

Judicial review as an institution
Finally, there may be a distinction to be teased out between the principles underpinning judicial review and the institution of judicial review which enforces those principles. With reference to Cane's distinction between instrumental and non-instrumental approaches to judicial review, a non-instrumental approach might be more relevant to the underlying principles. These principles could relate both to the existence of judicial review and to the nature of its requirements, the juridical norms it applies. Thus, for example, the very existence of judicial review might be said to reflect broad principles of the rule of law and good government, while the juridical norms relating to procedural fairness might have a non-instrumental base in dignatory theory or full participation.[6] In contrast, resort to judicial review as a mechanism for the enforcement of such juridical norms might be seen in largely instrumental terms, either as an 'hortatory' device[7] to encourage improved decision-making or as a means of redress of individual grievances.

Impact
This volume and consequently this chapter is primarily concerned with the bureaucratic impact of judicial review: the impact of judicial review on the behaviour of those subject to it. Again some preliminary explanation is required.

Potential respondents[8] in the UK
Judicial review is considered by some to have the ability to influence the behaviour both of the parties directly affected by particular court decisions and of those potentially subject to review by the High Court: the direct and indirect impact of judicial review. In the UK, the list of potential respondents has expanded in recent years in order to reflect the changing patterns of governance and the flexibility of the boundary between public and private. Whatever the precise test, however, the list of potential respondents in the UK includes all the obvious public sector bodies such as local authorities, government ministers and

---

[6] G. Richardson, *Law, Process and Custody: Prisoners and Patients* (London, Weidenfeld and Nicolson, 1993); D. Galligan, *Due Process and Fair Procedures* (Oxford, Oxford University Press, 1996); J. Mashaw, *Due Process in the Administrative State* (New Haven, Yale University Press, 1985).

[7] S. Halliday, 'The Influence of Judicial Review on Bureaucratic Decision-Making' [2000] *Public Law* 110.

[8] The term 'respondent' is being used in a general, non-technical sense.

departments and most tribunals. It does not include superior courts or Parliament.

Impact within a bureaucracy

Just as the meanings attributed to judicial review evolve and change over time and differ between public agencies and between individuals within those agencies, so too will the nature of its impact differ as individuals and agencies change over time. In the first instance, the impact of judicial review will be felt by *individuals* working within a public agency. All such individuals will be subject to a wide range of personal influences and pressures whatever their specific role within the organisation, and the relative significance of judicial review within that bundle of influences will vary both between individuals and across time.

The nature of any impact will also vary depending on the particular *task* affected. Senior officials responsible for the articulation of agency policy might be directly influenced by a single court judgment on a particular statutory provision in such a way as to alter the formal statement of that policy in the future. The same judgment might also indirectly influence legislators who might wish to avoid similar difficulties in the future, the UK version possibly of what Tushnet calls 'judicial overhang'.[9] In contrast, the impact of a particular judgment on those concerned with the daily implementation of agency policy rather than its formulation might be more diffuse and informal. In this context, the perceived constraints imposed by judicial review may be accorded no special significance by routine decision-makers and may even be in opposition to other value systems and demands.

Thus impact may be direct or indirect, and it may vary across time, between individuals and, perhaps most significantly, between tasks. It may lead to formal changes in policy or simply to a realignment of the factors considered in the course of routine decision-making.

IMPACT STUDIES IN THE UK

It has become quite common now in UK academic circles to bemoan the absence of systematic empirical research on the bureaucratic impact of judicial review.[10] Given the complexity of the notion of impact and

[9] M. Tushnet, *Taking the Constitution Away from the Courts* (Princeton, Princeton University Press, 1999).

[10] R. Cranston, 'Reviewing Judicial Review' in G. Richardson and H. Genn (eds.), *Administrative Law and Government Action* (Oxford, Clarendon Press, 1994);

the diversity of the potential respondents to judicial review, this scarcity of empirical data is perhaps unsurprising. Nonetheless, there is now a modest body of research from which it is possible to draw out some common themes. Writing in 1998, Simon Halliday suggested that the then existing body of work fell into three categories:

- studies which propose links between judicial decisions and administrative reaction;
- works reflecting on the impact of judicial review by way of personal professional experience; and
- empirical studies designed to investigate the impact of judicial review on administrative decision-making.[11]

Four years further on, that classification can still usefully be applied.

The first category contains work which has proposed direct links between judicial decisions and formal administrative or executive reaction. Typically, the links are made simply through the examination of documents after the event, and so, to some extent, causal relationships have to be implied through chronology alone. As Sunkin notes,[12] the attribution of causal effects to judicial review can pose considerable difficulties for the interpretation of empirical data, and these documentary studies suggest that such difficulties are not limited to the interpretation of data in relation to routine decision-making. Examples of work in this first category include a study of the official reaction to test cases in the field of welfare benefits,[13] and several accounts of the evolution of prison policy[14] and of mental health policy.[15] These accounts

---

R. Rawlings, 'Litigation as Political Action' in I. Loveland (ed.), *A Special Relationship? American Influences on Public Law in the UK* (Oxford, Clarendon Press, 1996); S. Livingstone, 'The Impact of Judicial Review on Prisons' in B. Hadfield (ed.), *Judicial Review: A Thematic Approach* (Dublin, Gill and McMillan, 1995); G. Richardson and M. Sunkin, 'Judicial Review: Questions of Impact' [1996] *Public Law* 79; S. Halliday, 'Researching the Impact of Judicial Review on Routine Administrative Decision-Making' in D. Cowan (ed.), *Housing, Participation and Exclusion* (Aldershot, Dartmouth, 1998); T. Daintith and A. Page, *The Executive in the Constitution* (Oxford, Oxford University Press, 1999).

[11] Halliday, 'Researching the Impact'.   [12] See Chapter 2 above.

[13] T. Prosser, *Test Cases for the Poor: Legal Techniques in the Politics of Social Welfare* (London, Child Poverty Action Group, 1983).

[14] M. Loughlin and P. Quinn, 'Prisons, Rules and Courts: A Study of Administrative Law' (1993) 56 *Modern Law Review* 497; Richardson, *Law, Process and Custody*; Livingstone, 'The Impact of Judicial Review'.

[15] Richardson, *Law, Process and Custody*.

concentrate on the formal and tangible effects of judicial review. Of these effects, some can be regarded as positive in so far as they further the spirit of the court's decision. Some adjustments to prison policy in relation to transfers, letters etc., would fall into this category.[16] In contrast, some reactions recorded are obviously negative, as in the case of legislative reversal.[17] Still others are at best neutral, as when the impugned decision is taken again and the same outcome reached.[18] However, because these studies concentrate on tracing direct links between judicial decisions and the formal reactions of the respondent bureaucracy, they provide little systematic data either on the extent of indirect impact outside the specific target agency, or on the more diffuse and informal impact on decision-makers further from the formulation of agency policy.

More recently, in the flurry of debate which has accompanied the introduction of the Human Rights Act, there has been a degree of speculation about the likely impact of human rights litigation on legislators and policy-makers more generally.[19] Fredman, for example, has suggested that the arguments put by litigators can occasionally filter back into the legislative process.[20] This suggests that our notion of judicial review should be expanded to include the arguments put by applicants, even if those arguments are formally rejected by the court. Of course, in jurisdictions where constitutional rights litigation in one form or another is well established, the debate about its impact on both legislators and the executive is rather further developed.[21]

The second category is the smallest and most specific, covering accounts of the impact of judicial review provided by those with direct

---

[16] S. Livingstone and T. Owen, *Prison Law* (2nd edn, Oxford, Oxford University Press, 1999).

[17] Prosser, *Test Cases*.

[18] C. Harlow, 'Administrative Reaction to Judicial Review' [1976] *Public Law* 116.

[19] T. Campbell, K. D. Ewing and A. Tomkins (eds.), *Sceptical Essays on Human Rights* (Oxford, Oxford University Press, 2001).

[20] S. Fredman, 'Scepticism Under Scrutiny: Labour Law and Human Rights' in Campbell, Ewing and Tomkins, *Scepticism*.

[21] Tushnet, *Taking the Constitution*; M. Tushnet, 'Scepticism about Judicial Review: A Perspective from the United States' in Campbell, Ewing and Tomkins, *Scepticism*; W. Sadurski, 'Rights-Based Constitutional Review in Central and Eastern Europe' in Campbell, Ewing and Tompkins, *Scepticism*; W. Sadurski, 'Judicial Review and the Protection of Constitutional Rights' (2002) 22 *Oxford Journal of Legal Studies* 275.

professional experience.[22] While there is some suggestion in these accounts that the impact of judicial review has been predominantly positive and has helped to improve the quality of departmental decision-making, significant reservations are also expressed. Hammond is certainly the most positive, describing the beneficial effects of judicial review in terms of improved decision-making procedures, enhanced statutory provisions and better training and guidance. He concludes that 'the rule of law has been strengthened considerably and greater protection against the abuse of power has been afforded to all citizens'.[23]

Such undiluted optimism is not reflected by Kerry or James. Although Kerry agrees with Hammond that departmental officials are now more aware of judicial review, he accepts that an awareness of rules is not sufficient on its own to alter behaviour. He also provides evidence of the evolving nature of judicial decisions, even within the judicial system itself, by citing the generous interpretations of *Conway* v. *Rimmer* by subsequent courts. James comments that the principles enunciated by judicial review are too vague usefully to guide future behaviour and reaffirms the point made earlier by Harlow that formal compliance with certain judgments can be easily achieved without altering the substance of the impugned decision. In this context, however, it is interesting to note the positive reactions on the part of respondent agencies in Australia recorded by Creyke and McMillan in their more systematic and rigorous study described in Chapter 6 below.[24]

The third category is perhaps the most relevant to the question of bureaucratic impact. Broadly defined, this category includes studies of the reaction to single cases and thus includes Prosser's study of the *Atkinson* case[25] and Bridges *et al.*'s account of the Fare's Fair litigation.[26] It can also encompass studies such as Loveland,[27] Obadina,[28] and

---

[22] S. James, 'The Political and Administrative Consequences of Judicial Review' (1996) 74 *Public Administration* 613; M. Kerry, 'Administrative Law and Judicial Review' (1986) 64 *Public Administration* 163; A. Hammond, 'Judicial Review: The Continuing Interplay Between Law and Policy' [1998] *Public Law* 34.

[23] Hammond, 'Judicial Review', p. 43.   [24] See Chapter 6 below.

[25] T. Prosser, 'Politics and Judicial Review: The Atkinson Case and Its Aftermath' [1979] *Public Law* 59.

[26] L. Bridges, C. Game, J. McBridge, O. Lomas and S. Ranson, *Legality and Local Politics* (Aldershot, Gower, 1987).

[27] I. Loveland, *Housing Homeless Persons* (Oxford, Oxford University Press, 1995).

[28] D. Obadina, 'Judicial Review and Gypsy Site Provision' in T. Buck (ed.), *Judicial Review and Social Welfare* (London, Pinter, 1998).

Daintith and Page,[29] where the bureaucratic impact of judicial review provides a significant, but not the primary, theme. Finally, the empirical studies which focus primarily on the impact of judicial review on front-line decision-makers include Mullen, Pick and Prosser,[30] Buck,[31] Halliday,[32] Richardson and Machin,[33] and Sunkin and Pick.[34] While these studies remain relatively few in number and narrow in the range of respondents studied, certain common themes are beginning to emerge, particularly from the final group of studies.

In the first place, all the studies in this final group, with the exception of Richardson and Machin, were concerned with administrative and largely routine decision-making in relation to either homelessness or aspects of the social security system. In one way or another, all were designed to examine the impact of judicial review on bureaucratic behaviour:

- Halliday: 'how law and the experience of litigation are understood and translated into bureaucratic behaviour';[35]
- Buck: 'the effects of judicial review on the behaviour, development and culture of the [Independent Review Service]';[36]
- Sunkin and Pick: 'to look more closely . . . at the attitudes of the [Social Fund Inspectors] and others within the [Independent Review Service] towards both judicial review litigation and juridical norms more generally';[37]

---

[29] T. Daintith and A. Page, *The Executive in the Constitution* (Oxford, Oxford University Press, 1999).

[30] T. Mullen, K. Pick and T. Prosser, *Judicial Review in Scotland* (Chichester, Wiley, 1996).

[31] T. Buck, 'Judicial Review and the Discretionary Social Fund: The Impact on a Respondent Organisation' in T. Buck (ed.), *Judicial Review and Social Welfare* (London, Pinter, 1998).

[32] Halliday, 'The Influence of Judicial Review'; and Halliday, 'Researching the Impact'.

[33] G. Richardson and D. Machin, 'Judicial Review and Tribunal Decision-Making: A Study of the Mental Health Review Tribunal' [2000] *Public Law* 494; G. Richardson and D. Machin, 'Doctors on Tribunals: A Confusion of Roles' (2000b) 176 *British Journal of Psychiatry* 110.

[34] M. Sunkin and K. Pick, 'The Changing Impact of Judicial Review' [2001] *Public Law* 736.

[35] Halliday, 'The Influence of Judicial Review', p. 111.

[36] Buck, 'Discretionary Social Fund', p. 115.

[37] Sunkin and Pick, 'The Changing Impact', p. 742.

- Mullen *et al.*: 'the impact of judicial review inside public authorities'.[38]

The majority of these studies focused primarily on the general, indirect effect of judicial review on decision-making within a bureaucracy, while Mullen *et al.* looked more specifically at the impact of a direct experience of litigation.[39]

In terms of research methods, Mullen *et al.* and Sunkin and Pick relied primarily on the review of documents, including case files, and interviews. Sunkin and Pick were also able to observe relevant meetings. Buck, who served as a consultant legal advisor within his subject agency, managed to combine documentary research with participant observation in a very literal sense. Halliday adopted a more consciously sociological approach. His aim was to identify the influence of judicial review by building up an understanding of the social construction of administrative reality within his subject bureaucracies. He therefore conducted three months of participant observation within each of his three local authorities, supplemented by subsequent interviews with key personnel.[40]

There is not the space here to do justice to all the findings which have emerged from these studies, but it is possible to identify certain common themes. In the first place, the research reaffirms the view that judicial review should be seen as a sequence of steps, not as a single event.[41] Indeed, the data-gathering by Mullen *et al.* was specifically designed to identify the effects of the various stages of judicial review litigation.

Secondly, and perhaps most strikingly, all these studies emphasise the limited ability of judicial review to influence administrative decision-making. Even Buck, who is the most positive with regard to the internalisation of judicial norms by individual administrators (in his case, within the Independent Review Service), draws attention to the inability of judicial review to achieve the consistency of decision-making required to inspire public confidence.[42] Both Loveland and Halliday in presenting their studies of homelessness decision-making within local authorities describe the other pressures bearing on individual decision-makers:

[38] Mullen, Pick and Prosser, *Judicial Review*, p. 114.   [39] *Ibid.*, pp. 114–15.
[40] Halliday, 'Researching the Impact', pp. 190–5.   [41] See Chapter 2 above.
[42] Buck, 'Discretionary Social Fund', pp. 129–30.

In different ways, professional intuition, systemic suspicion, bureaucratic expediency, judgments about the moral desert of applicants, inter-office relations, financial constraints and other values all played a part in how judicial review impacted upon decision-making in the three local authorities.[43]

Halliday further points out that the tendency of judicial review to focus on a single decision out of the multiple exercises of discretion which characterise the typical administrative process also serves to reduce its ability to influence that process.

In their study of the Independent Review Service (IRS) of the Social Fund, Sunkin and Pick also confirm the difficulties involved in identifying the precise influence of judicial review among all the other factors which bear on routine decision-making within a complex organisation.[44] But perhaps the most arresting conclusion which they draw relates to the changing impact of judicial review. In the early years of the IRS when the organisation was anxious to establish its own legitimacy, judicial review was 'of central importance'.[45] Then, as the organisation's goals shifted to a concern to ensure efficient service delivery, so the influence of judicial review declined. Judicial review it seems can be used instrumentally to encourage compliance with juridical norms when such compliance coincides with broader agency goals, but as agency goals shift so the incentive to comply will diminish.

Another theme to emerge from these studies, with the possible exception of Buck and Mullen *et al.*, relates to the potentially negative impact of judicial review. The term negative is being used here to refer to apparent reactions to judicial review within bureaucracies which run counter to the instrumental ideal of judicial review as a mechanism through which bureaucratic decision-making can be improved. Such possibly negative consequences can be seen in Halliday's suggestion that increased exposure to judicial review might reduce the extent to which organisations scrutinise themselves.[46] Further research regarding the internal review of Scottish homelessness decision-making, however, has led him to believe that organisations will always scrutinise themselves but that the emphasis of that scrutiny may not always reflect the values of judicial review.[47] These findings reinforce the description

---

[43] Halliday, 'The Influence of Judicial Review', pp. 116–17.

[44] Sunkin and Pick, 'The Changing Impact'.   [45] *Ibid.*, p. 759.

[46] Halliday, 'The Influence of Judicial Review'.

[47] S. Halliday, 'Internal Review and Administrative Justice' (2001) 23 *Journal of Social Welfare and Family Law* 473.

of the modern state as containing complex layers of accountability[48] and serve to illustrate further the relatively low priority which can be given to juridical norms in the context of routine bureaucratic decision-making.

Other evidence of negative impact can be seen in Loveland's conclusion that in two of the three authorities studied the moves towards increased compliance with the legal requirements were defensive. They were designed to safeguard decisions from legal challenge, not to improve routine decision-making in any real sense.[49] In a similarly negative vein, Sunkin and Pick record a concentration on detail and formality at the possible expense of substance on the part of some inspectors. While they do not claim a direct association between judicial review and this increase in formalism, they do conclude 'that a concern to ensure that their decisions would survive judicial scrutiny did lead the inspectors to place stress on matters of detail and form to the possible cost of substance'.[50] In their rather different study of the executive, Daintith and Page also draw out a possibly negative consequence:

> Familiarity with judicial review, it is said, has indeed bred contempt . . . : as judicial review becomes a regular element of administrative process . . . ministers are increasingly willing to take the legal risks pointed out to them by their advisors.[51]

This brief discussion of existing impact research in the UK makes no attempt to do justice to the rich and complex data that these studies have produced. It is by any standards a highly selective account of some of the conclusions that have been derived. Nonetheless, however selective the above account, I would argue that the data emerging from these studies do suggest that the instrumental potential of judicial review should not be overestimated, particularly in the context of routine bureaucratic decision-making. There are too many other influences at play. In addition, those studies which have concentrated on front-line decisions suggest that there is nothing particularly significant about judicial review; it is likely to be simply one of a number of factors

---

[48] C. Scott, 'Accountability in the Regulatory State' (2000) 27 *Journal of Law and Society* 38.
[49] Loveland, *Housing Homeless Persons*, Chapter 11.
[50] Sunkin and Pick, 'The Changing Impact', p. 748.
[51] Daintith and Page, *The Executive*, p. 337.

within what Sunkin describes as 'an administrative soup of influences on decision-making'.[52]

As Halliday concludes in his 2000 account:

> these research findings demonstrate that, despite extensive and prolonged exposure to judicial scrutiny, unlawful decision-making was rife in each authority. In different (and sometimes subtle) ways the local authorities' administrative processes displayed considerable evidence of values and priorities which were in conflict with the norms of administrative law.[53]

On this basis, if we really want to understand the influence of judicial review on bureaucratic decision-making, we may have much to learn from the more general literature on bureaucratic decision-making and the exercise of discretion.

THE IMPACT OF JUDICIAL REVIEW ON A TRIBUNAL SYSTEM

In 1997–9, with the help of a grant from the ESRC, David Machin and I conducted an empirical study of the impact of judicial review on the decision-making of the Mental Health Review Tribunal (MHRT). The findings have been described elsewhere,[54] and the present discussion will concentrate merely on those aspects of the research which may be particularly relevant to the general concerns of this volume.

In the UK, tribunals are part of the judicial not the administrative branch of government, but as 'inferior bodies' they are subject to the supervision of the High Court by way of judicial review. Thus, while they may differ significantly in formal constitutional terms from the bodies which were the subjects of the research described above, tribunals are still potential respondents of judicial review.

The primary task of the MHRT is adjudicative. It is required to review the legality of a patient's detention in hospital for assessment or treatment for mental disorder, and to direct the discharge of those to whom the statutory discharge criteria apply. As the subject of research into the impact of judicial review, the MHRT has a number of advantages. In the first place, there has been some suggestion in the literature that

---

[52] See Chapter 2 above.   [53] Halliday, 'The Influence of Judicial Review', p. 122.
[54] Richardson and Machin, 'Judicial Review'; and Richardson and Machin, 'Doctors on Tribunals'.

the decisions of reviewing courts might have a greater influence on the behaviour of adjudicatory, rather than administrative or executive, bodies.[55] Secondly, it might be assumed that MHRTs would be particularly aware of the requirements of judicial review because each panel is chaired by a lawyer, legal representation is common and the tribunal has had direct experience of judicial review on several occasions. MHRTs are also particularly attractive as research subjects because they provide the opportunity to examine the law's ability to influence behaviour within an environment where powerful systems compete. The research described above has already provided evidence of the law's limited ability to influence behaviour by way of judicial review in a number of different contexts, and of the importance of 'values and priorities which were in conflict with the norms of administrative law'.[56] The MHRT, which has to operate in an environment possessing its own powerful medical and therapeutic values, provides an excellent opportunity to study how, if at all, juridical norms influence behaviour. The tribunal's primary role of reviewing the legality of a patient's detention in hospital and directing a discharge if the statutory criteria are met is, formally at least, a strictly legal task.[57] However, the statutory discharge criteria which the tribunal is required to apply refer expressly to questions of psychiatric diagnosis, patient welfare and public safety. Thus the strictly legal task cannot be performed in isolation from therapeutic and other values.[58] As suggested above, judicial review can be seen as a mechanism for imposing legal norms and values, juridical norms, and it was hoped that by studying its impact on the decision-making of the MHRT something more could be discovered about the law's relevance in a highly contested environment.[59]

Finally, from a research point of view, a tribunal has certain pragmatic advantages. Three people come together on a single occasion to

---

[55] S. Sterett, *Creating Constitutionalism? The Politics of Legal Expertise and Administrative Law* (Ann Arbor, University of Michigan Press, 1997).

[56] Halliday, 'The Influence of Judicial Review', p. 122.

[57] G. Richardson and D. Machin, 'A Clash of Values? Mental Health Review Tribunals and Judicial Review' (1999) 1 *Journal of Mental Health Law* 3.

[58] N. Eastman and J. Peay, *Law Without Enforcement: Integrating Mental Health and Justice* (Oxford, Hart, 1999); P. Bartlett and R. Sandland, *Mental Health Law: Policy and Practice* (London, Blackstone, 2000); J. Peay, *Decisions and Dilemmas: Working with Mental Health Law* (Oxford, Hart, 2003).

[59] G. Teubner, A. Bankowska, R. Adler and Z. Bankowski, *Law as an Autopoietic System* (Oxford, Blackwell, 1993); and M. King, 'The "Truth" about Autopoiesis' (1993) 20 *Journal of Law and Society* 218.

review information relating to a specific task, to discuss that information and to reach a decision. Of course, the factors which influence the individual tribunal members and thus the final decision will extend beyond those visible on the day, but the researcher with adequate access will be in an unusually good position to observe the whole interactive process leading to the decision. The research method adopted, therefore, concentrated primarily on the observation of tribunal hearings, the private discussion prior to the hearing and the deliberations following the hearing itself. As a preliminary exercise, all the judicial review decisions involving the MHRT since the introduction of the current legislation were analysed in order to identify the nature and scope of the resulting judgments. A sample of 300 files from the tribunal offices were also examined, and interviews were conducted with patient representatives, tribunal members and members of the tribunal staff. But the most significant data were gathered during the observation of fifty hearings and their attendant deliberations. These data were organised using data-collection instruments designed to enable the recording of legal and procedural matters. While the primary aim was to study the extent to which the law appeared to influence the tribunal's decision-making, it was also considered essential to understand the whole context within which the tribunals were acting.[60] At the hearing itself, the nature of all the issues raised and the identity of the questioner and the respondent were recorded, while during the private meetings before and after the hearing particular attention was paid to any reference to legal requirements, either procedural or substantive.

Three particular aspects of the research findings will be discussed here: different juridical norms, different impacts; competing values; and reason giving.

Different juridical norms, different impacts

The legal literature has suggested that the potential of judicial review to influence future behaviour will vary depending on the nature of the juridical norm imposed.[61] More particularly, there has been an assumption in some of the literature that process values have a better chance of penetrating non-legal systems than do other types of legal

[60] Richardson and Machin, 'Doctors on Tribunals'.

[61] D. Feldman, 'Judicial Review: A Way of Controlling Government?' (1988) 66 *Public Administration* 21; R. Rawlings, 'Litigation as Political Action' in I. Loveland (ed.), *A Special Relationship? American Influences on Public Law in the UK* (Oxford, Clarendon Press, 1995).

norm.[62] With this in mind, the relevant case law was analysed, and the results indicated that the subject matter of the decisions fell into three categories: the statutory criteria; the powers of the tribunal; and procedural requirements, both common law and statutory.

Statutory criteria
Traditionally, judicial review has been regarded as the proper and final arbiter of statutory meaning. Thus, in view of the uncertain wording of the statutory criteria central to the work of the MHRT, it is perhaps surprising that only a few of the relevant decisions directly addressed those criteria. We therefore had little opportunity to assess the impact of any judicial statements of meaning. Indeed, we encountered very little discussion of the statutory wording in the course of our fieldwork, and certainly no expectation that judicial review would be able to provide clarification if any were needed. In interview, both the legal presidents and the patient representatives were insistent that judicial review could never provide adequate clarity given the nature of the statutory criteria. At the hearings themselves, the little discussion there was of the criteria related either to the statutory requirement that psychopathic disorder be treatable or to the degree of illness required to justify continued detention. In both these contexts, tribunal members were inclined to adopt the meaning which they felt coincided with the 'correct' outcome. The tribunal's treatment of the phrase 'nature or degree' can be used as an example. That phrase was directly relevant in eight of the observed hearings. In striving for the 'correct' outcome five tribunals adopted a conjunctive approach and three a disjunctive. The formal legal position was not clarified until after the completion of the fieldwork when the High Court finally ruled that the words should be read disjunctively. Obviously, we can only speculate on whether this ruling will attract compliance, but our data certainly suggested that tribunals prefer a conjunctive approach.

While the problems raised when legal meanings are imposed by courts have been recognised in other contexts,[63] they may be

---

[62] G. Teubner, 'Substantive and Reflexive Elements in Modern Law' (1983) 17 *Law and Society Review* 239; M. Loughlin, *Public Law and Political Theory* (Oxford, Clarendon, 1992); J. Black, 'Constitutionalising Self Regulation' (1996) 59 *Modern Law Review* 24.

[63] J. Black, 'Reviewing Regulatory Rules' in J. Black, P. Muchlinski and P. Walker, *Commercial Regulation and Judicial Review* (Oxford, Hart, 1998); P. Craig, *Administrative Law* (4th edn, London, Sweet and Maxwell, 1998).

particularly acute in the case of the MHRT because of the adoption by statute of words which possess an established meaning outside law. The issue is discussed further below.

Powers of the tribunal

Decisions in this category related to the interpretation of the tribunal's precise powers to delay or defer a discharge or to the nature of the conditions it could impose. Here the data, from both the interviews and the hearings, do suggest that tribunals were aware of and compliant with such judgments, even when those judgments were restrictive of their powers. In some sense, therefore, judicial review may be seen to have influenced subsequent behaviour here, and it is interesting to consider why this might be, particularly since such high levels of compliance were not observed across all categories of decision. It is possible that the obligation to obey the law had been internalised to the extent that the tribunal chairs, as legal actors, regarded themselves as bound to comply with the rulings of the High Court even though there was no threat of challenge. In which case, judicial review would be regulating behaviour in advance without the need for enforcement.

Such an interpretation of the data, however, does not explain why this particular category of judgment should attract such respect. Certainly, the court rulings on the tribunal's powers are very specific and, in some cases, very clear, and this might serve to intensify the chairs' perceived obligation to comply. But these same characteristics of specificity and clarity would also add to the ease with which non-compliance would be revealed on the face of the written record. In which case, the high levels of compliance might flow simply from an appreciation that non-compliance will be obvious and highly vulnerable to subsequent challenge via judicial review. Classic deterrence literature suggests that it is the certainty of the imposition of the sanction which exercises the strongest influence on behaviour.[64]

Procedural requirements

Three procedural issues had attracted the attention of the reviewing courts: the patient's ability to challenge factual allegations appearing

---

[64] A. Von Hirsch, A. Ashworth and M. Wasik, *Fundamentals of Sentencing Theory: Essays in Honour of Andrew Von Hirsch* (Oxford, Clarendon Press, 1998), pp. 44–87.

in his or her medical records; the role of the medical member of the tribunal; and the adequacy of the reasons given. The last is dealt with separately below. The reviewing courts had established that patients should be permitted to challenge factual allegations where relevant to matters relating to the statutory criteria. The accuracy of such allegations was an issue in ten of the fifty observed hearings, and in all cases the patient was permitted to challenge the disputed allegation. No reference was made to the relevant judicial ruling during any of the observed hearings or private deliberations, but in interview the tribunal chairs gave the impression that the need to allow patients to question allegations was accepted as part of the normal legal process. Perhaps here the specific substance of the juridical norm, rather than simply the obligation to obey the law, had been fully internalised by the legal actors, and the threat of subsequent enforcement by judicial review was indeed irrelevant.

By contrast, the legal requirements of fairness with regard to the role of the medical member of the tribunal were almost invariably breached. Each MHRT has a psychiatrist member, and the rules require this doctor to examine the patient prior to the hearing in order to assess his or her mental condition. This presents problems in relation to the common law duty to act fairly. It is a fundamental principle of the common law that all evidence which is likely to influence the outcome of a decision be made available to all parties. Thus the courts have held that, if the tribunal doctor takes a different view of the patient's condition to that taken by any other medical witness and that view is likely to influence the outcome, then the tribunal doctor should reveal his or her opinion in the course of the hearing. Interview data suggested that the legal chairs were generally alive to the problems of fairness, and to some extent their concern was shared by the medical members themselves. However, the observation data indicate that tribunal doctors rarely, if ever, expressed an opinion openly during the hearing: in not one of the observed hearings did the tribunal doctor directly express a clinical opinion. On the other hand, the data indicate that tribunal doctors regularly expressed clinical opinions during the private deliberations, and in some cases these opinions could be determinative of the outcome. Case No. 4 provides a clear example:

> All the evidence given during the hearing supported the patient's discharge on the basis that he was willing to remain as a voluntary patient. Only the medical member felt firmly that the patient was still a high risk,

but this was not revealed during the hearing and came as a surprise to the other tribunal members when it was disclosed during the deliberations. In the event the patient was not discharged.

In other words, even though the juridical norms were familiar to and understood by the tribunal members, non-compliance with those norms was commonplace.

The doctor is on the tribunal as an expert, and as a doctor will have examined the patient. As a member of the tribunal he or she is acting as a legal actor and is expected to respect legal values, specifically the duty to act fairly. However, our data suggest that these requirements of fairness, contrary to the expectations in the literature referred to above, do not manage to penetrate the medical member's way of viewing the task. Perhaps as a doctor these procedural obligations appear irrelevant, particularly since much of the discussion at the hearing more closely resembles a clinical case conference than a formal legal adjudication. The research on administrative decision-making described above has clearly established that the law is but one of a number of ingredients within the 'administrative soup of influences' relevant to each decision. These present data suggest that this might be equally true in an adjudicative context and even in relation to process norms. The significance of a competing system of values, however, must now be considered.

Competing values

As explained above, the MHRT has to negotiate a path between the often competing demands of law, medicine and public safety. While the tribunal's primary role of reviewing the legality of a patient's detention is essentially a legal task, that task cannot be performed in isolation from therapeutic and other value systems. In terms of judicial review and its potential to influence behaviour, the presence of these alternative systems becomes significant at two main points.

Statutory meaning

There were data suggesting that tribunals will not adopt court-imposed meanings if they do not reflect what the tribunal regards as the correct outcome. The highly contested area of psychopathy and treatability can be used as an example. At the time of the fieldwork the prevailing case law indicated that a tribunal was not obliged to release a patient simply because his or her condition was not treatable. In two of the observed hearings this issue was raised and, although it was not determinative of the outcome in either hearing, both legal chairs seemed to assume that if a patient with psychopathy was not treatable he or she should be discharged. To an extent this is unsurprising. Essentially, the tribunal has to ensure that the right people and only the right people are detained in hospital for treatment. If right is to be defined legally, it will turn on whether the detention is lawful or unlawful, while, if a medical definition is to prevail, it will turn on whether the patient is well or unwell, treatable or untreatable. If there were a perfect match between the legal and the medical, court intervention to establish clarity would be welcomed and the resulting definition respected. In the absence of such a match, compliance with a court-imposed definition is less likely.

Within the legal literature the term 'juridification' is used to describe the 'process by which relations hitherto governed by other values and expectations come to be subjected to legal values and rules'.[65] Arguably, the introduction of a statutory framework to govern the provision of mental health care and a tribunal to police that system provides a clear example of such a process of juridification at work. The presence of judicial review to oversee the decisions of the tribunal merely reinforces the process. Juridification, it is said, carries the risk that the law will be stretched too far and will cease to provide a useful basis for structuring relations. In these circumstances, there is a danger that the law will either be ignored altogether or will start to destroy the activity it seeks to regulate.[66] These risks are reduced when there is a reasonably good fit between the legal values and those of the system which the law seeks to regulate, but are increased when the law seeks to introduce unfamiliar values and concepts. Thus the MHRT, which is multidisciplinary and is familiar with the reality of mental health care, may attribute a meaning to the statutory wording which reflects that reality, while the High Court by contrast may favour a meaning which does not 'fit' so well. Both the literature and our data suggest this latter meaning will attract less support.[67]

The doctor on the tribunal
The presence of a doctor on the MHRT is explained by the desire to give the tribunal access to sufficient professional expertise to enable it

[65] Scott, 'Accountability', p. 19; M. Loughlin, *Legality and Locality: The Role of Law in Central-Local Government Relations* (Oxford, Oxford University Press, 1996).
[66] Scott, 'Accountability'; G. Teubner, *Enterprise Corporatism: New Industrial Policy and the 'Essence' of the Legal System* (Florence, European University Institute, 1987).
[67] Scott, 'Accountability'; Black, 'Reviewing'.

adequately to assess the medical arguments before it. The doctor is therefore expected to behave as both doctor and legal actor. As legal actor he or she should be anxious to comply with the juridical norms imposed by the High Court but, at least in so far as the requirement to reveal his or her clinical opinion is concerned, the data indicate that these juridical norms do not prevail. Perhaps this is unsurprising given the context of the tribunal's decision, the fact that the doctor is obliged to conduct a clinical examination of the appellant/patient, and the possible medical consequences of the tribunal's decision. Perhaps in such circumstances only lawyers would expect juridical values to prevail. Whatever view is taken, however, the data are clear: even the process values imposed by judicial review in a relatively formal adjudicatory forum were unable to penetrate a well-entrenched system of non-legal values.

The giving of reasons

MHRTs are under a statutory duty to give reasons. For the purposes of assessing the impact of judicial review, the way in which this duty is fulfilled is directly relevant in two respects. In the first place, the reviewing courts have amplified the statutory obligation and an examination of the reasons provided against these court-expressed requirements could furnish one measure of tribunal compliance with the requirements of judicial review. Secondly, the written reasons constitute the only formal record of the tribunal's decision and thus provide a vital source of evidence in any subsequent attempt to challenge that decision by way of judicial review.

In an attempt to assess tribunal compliance we examined the relevant case law and recorded five requirements relating to reasons. However, these requirements lacked rigour and clarity to such a degree that it was extremely difficult to establish whether a given set of reasons was compliant or non-compliant. Indeed, when we examined the reasons given in the fifty observed tribunals, in only two cases was it possible to determine with confidence that the reasons given were non-compliant. The vast majority of tribunal decisions turn on matters of opinion or clinical judgment and frequently involve predictions as to the patient's future conduct: does his or her condition amount to a psychopathic condition under the Act? Will he or she continue to take medication if the section is lifted? In such circumstances, it is hard to understand from the reported case law precisely what level of detail the law requires the reasons to provide. Judging from these conclusions alone, therefore, the rulings emanating from judicial review are woefully ill-equipped to provide guidance for future tribunals. However, in fairness to the courts, several interviewees accepted that the High Court's ability to produce positive guidance on reason-giving is limited by its primary role of *ex post* adjudication. The judicial review court is simply asked to determine the legality of a single set of reasons and if it upholds them as lawful that ruling on its own will provide little specific guidance to future tribunals. We also examined the quality of the reasons as a record of the tribunal's proceedings, and concluded that as a record of those proceedings most reasons given were partial and provided an inadequate basis on which to judge the legality of a tribunal's decision-making. In particular, the reasons routinely failed adequately to record the emphasis placed on risk during the course of the hearing.

Finally, much of the legal literature emphasises the likely instrumental benefits to be derived from the giving of reasons in terms of better administrative decision-making.[68] Sociologists, on the other hand, tend to emphasise how rules are used to construct *post hoc* accounts of decisions rather than actually to constrain them.[69] Thus, if the instrumental benefits claimed for them are to be made out, the obligation to provide reasons would have somehow to elevate the importance of rules within the decision-making process. In an attempt to investigate the instrumental claim further, we recorded the sequence of the discussion during the private deliberations between the three tribunal members as they came to a decision following the close of the hearing. If the duty to give reasons did in fact elevate the importance attached to the legal rules as a constraint on the decision we would have expected the deliberations of the panel to start with the statutory criteria and to allow the outcome to follow. In the event, 28 per cent started with the statute, 10 per cent with the desired outcome, and 62 per cent moved between the two. In terms of the instrumental effects of an obligation to give reason, these data can be interpreted in a number of ways. In the first place, it might be assumed that, if the decision-maker starts with the statutory criteria and moves to the outcome (28 per cent), that outcome will be dictated by the legal criteria and to that extent could be described as legally rigorous. On the other hand, if the tribunal moves from outcome

---

[68] *Administrative Justice: Some Necessary Reforms: Report of the Committee of the Justice/All Souls Review of Administrative Law in the United Kingdom* (Oxford, Clarendon Press, 1998).

[69] D. McBarnet and C. Whelan, 'The Elusive Spirit of the Law: Formalism and the Struggle for Legal Control' (1991) 54 *Modern Law Review* 848–73.

to statute (10 per cent), there might be less legal rigour. Here, just as the sociological literature would suggest, the law is secondary and is used to justify rather than to dictate the outcome: an agreed medical or therapeutic outcome is identified first, then justified in terms of the statutory criteria. However, while the statute-to-outcome model might be more rigorous in the legal sense, in the context of the MHRT it might not lead to a better outcome in any broader sense when account is taken of the possible mismatch between law and medicine mentioned above. Indeed, the outcome-to-statute model might lead to a more relevant interpretation of the statute.[70] Thus, while the obligation to give reasons may, in some cases, elevate the importance of the statutory criteria during the decision-making process, such legal rigour may not necessarily lead to better decision-making.

LEARNING FROM THE SPECIFIC

The MHRT cannot be regarded as a typical public bureaucracy. It is an adjudicatory rather than an administrative body, it is operating in an area fraught with conflicting values, and it is making decisions which directly impact on the most fundamental rights of individuals. In these circumstances, it would be most unwise to draw any generalisations from the above data and attempt to apply them even to other adjudicatory tribunals, far less to non-adjudicatory agencies. Nonetheless, these data emerging from a small study of the MHRT do tend to support and even to amplify some of the themes which have emerged from the research on other agencies described above. This is particularly true with regard to the evidence from the other studies which suggests that judicial review can have only a limited impact on bureaucratic decision-making.

In the case of the MHRT where a relatively formal adjudication is involved, lawyers are present, and fundamental rights are at stake, it might be assumed that juridical norms would be accorded particular respect. However, as the above data indicate, the influence of judicial review on the decision-making of the MHRT 'is patchy at best, even with regard to procedural fairness'.[71] Admittedly, compliance with certain judicial requirements was high, but wherever there was a conflict between medical and juridical norms the former tended to prevail, even where the juridical norm related to process. It is obviously

---

[70] Black, 'Reviewing'.   [71] Richardson and Machin, 'Judicial Review', p. 514.

arguable that the MHRT is exceptional in the degree of reliance it has to place on disciplines other than the law. But it is not unique in having to relate to other systems, and reviewing courts must regularly issue rulings which could be expected to apply across competing systems. On the basis of the data from the MHRT, the influence of such rulings on subsequent bureaucratic decision-making is likely to be minimal unless some attempt is made to accommodate alternative value systems. In the first place, the courts must recognise the 'range of interpretations' that statutory words may possess and must be prepared to accept that there may be no uniquely correct interpretation.[72] There is also a need to encourage the reviewing courts where possible to allow their rulings to reflect and build on structures which are already in place. Thus, for example, the fairness requirements imposed on and largely ignored by tribunal doctors might have more chance of success if they were presented as an extension of the therapeutic relationship.[73] Doctors need to be open with their patients if they are to win their trust. Finally, it is possible that, in other areas where judicial rulings need to be interpreted before they are conveyed to routine decision-makers, soft law can be used to facilitate the communication between law and other systems. Judicial rulings can be reinterpreted through soft law to make them match more closely the needs of non-legal structures.[74]

Since the completion of the fieldwork described here, the Human Rights Act 1998 has come into force, and a number of cases relating to the MHRT and the obligations contained in Articles 5 and 6 of the ECHR have already been decided.[75] It would certainly be interesting to examine the impact of such cases on current MHRT decision-making. At the moment, the relevant decisions have related primarily to process issues, and it might be revealing to compare the impact of such cases to the impact of pre-Act process rulings. Eventually, more cases may be brought which raise questions of the compliance of the substantive statutory criteria with the ECHR, and here the issue of congruence between law and medicine will again be relevant.

---

[72] Black, 'Reviewing'.
[73] Richardson, *Law, Process and Custody*, pp. 251–2; D. B. Wexler and B. W. Winick (eds.), *Law as a Therapeutic Key: Developments in Therapeutic Jurisprudence* (Durham, NC, Carolina Academic Press, 1996).
[74] See Chapter 5 below.
[75] The Public Law Project, *The Impact of the Human Rights Act on Judicial Review: An Empirical Research Study* (Oxford, Nuffield Foundation, 2003).

FURTHER STUDY

One thing is clear from all the studies considered here and elsewhere in this volume: the notion of impact is so complex and contingent that great care must be taken both in the description of what is being studied and in the scope of any empirical claims made.

Judicial review has many characteristics which make it particularly interesting in political and constitutional terms. It has also been subject to significant claims from the judiciary as to its likely instrumental impact. It is, undeniably, an attractive subject for empirical research. But it is only another branch of the law and, in so far as any putative instrumental effect is concerned, it can be seen simply as a form of judge-made regulation. In studying its bureaucratic impact, therefore, we should draw upon all that is already known about law and discretion in general and regulation in particular. Research on the impact of judicial review must be properly informed by the lessons gleaned elsewhere in relation to discretionary decision-making within bureaucracies and the impact of different forms of regulation. There is now an extensive literature on regulation as a legal and as a social phenomenon, its origins,[76] the forms it can take[77] and its limitations.[78] In addition, there is a rich seam of research designed to study the practice of enforcement through which regulation is implemented,[79] the relationship between the regulators and the regulated and the various styles of enforcement practice adopted by the regulatory agencies. This body of work suggests first that the extent to which regulation is capable of influencing bureaucratic behaviour will be constrained by the general difficulties experienced by law when it attempts to penetrate other systems; but

---

[76] J. G. Francis, *The Politics of Regulation: A Comparative Perspective* (Oxford, Blackwell, 1993); R. Baldwin and M. Cave, *Understanding Regulation: Theory, Strategy, and Practice* (Oxford, Oxford University Press, 1999).

[77] A. I. Ogus, *Regulation: Legal Form and Economic Theory* (Oxford, Clarendon Press, 1994); J. Black, *Rules and Regulators* (Oxford, Clarendon, 1997); I. Ayres and J. Braithwaite, *Responsive Regulation: Transcending the Deregulation Debate* (Oxford, Oxford University Press, 1992).

[78] Teubner, Bankowska, Adler and Bankowski, *Law as an Autopoietic System*; J. Black, 'Regulatory Conversations' (2002) 29 *Journal of Law and Society* 163.

[79] K. Hawkins, *Environment and Enforcement* (Oxford, Oxford University Press, 1984); K. Hawkins and J. Thomas, *Enforcing Regulation* (Boston, Kluwer-Nijhoff, 1984); Ayres and Braithwaite, *Responsive Regulation*; B. Hutter, *Compliance: Regulation and Environment* (Oxford, Clarendon, 1997); M. Hertogh, 'Coercion, Cooperation and Control: Understanding the Policy Impact of Administrative Courts and the Ombudsman in the Netherlands' (2001) 23 *Law and Policy* 47–67.

that certain forms of regulation might be more successful than others and that certain non-legal systems might be more receptive than others. It also emphasises the significance of enforcement and the enforcement style adopted. We must therefore allow the lessons from this literature both to influence our expectations of the likely impact of judicial review and to inform any future research in the field.

It is also important to ensure that the methodology adopted is suitable to the particular impact under scrutiny. While certain types of impact can best be studied through quantitative, survey-based research,[80] others demand the use of more qualitative, observational techniques. This chapter has concentrated mainly on the latter, and there is certainly a case to be made for more, small-scale, observational studies. Such studies might cover a range of different bureaucratic contexts in an attempt to identify both common and distinguishing features. These could, for example, include areas where there is much soft law and areas where there is little, or areas where the decision-making is essentially administrative and those where it is more adjudicatory in nature. Then, following on from the MHRT research in particular, it might be valuable to compare the impact of legal norms in areas where established non-legal values are strong with those areas where no obvious alternative value system prevails. Finally, such studies might also consider the relative influence of different types of legal norm: do certain norms transfer more readily than others? The bureaucratic impact of judicial review can only be understood in all its variety through the conduct of more, carefully targeted and predominately qualitative, empirical studies.

[80] See Chapter 6 below.

CHAPTER FIVE

THE POLITICS OF SOFT LAW: HOW JUDICIAL DECISIONS INFLUENCE BUREAUCRATIC DISCRETION IN CANADA

LORNE SOSSIN*

INTRODUCTION

There is remarkably little literature in Canada on the influence of judicial decisions on bureaucratic discretion. Since the enactment of Canada's Charter of Rights and Freedoms in 1982,[1] scholarly interest has focused primarily on the influence of the Charter on the policy-making process (notably the rise in importance of the federal and provincial justice ministries),[2] and the legislative process,[3] rather than

* I wish to acknowledge the generous financial support of this research by the Social Science and Humanities Research Council of Canada, the Connaught Foundation and the University of Toronto, Faculty of Law. Many of the ideas in this paper were developed through collaboration with the participants of the workshop on judicial impact held in Tilburg, the Netherlands in November 2002. I am grateful to all of the participants, and particularly so to Simon Halliday and Marc Hertogh who provided comments on an earlier draft of my paper, and to Robin Creyke and John McMillan who commented on the paper at the workshop. I am also indebted to the many colleagues who shared their comments and insights on this work, including Sharryn Aiken, Joseph Arvay, Annie Bunting, Ian Greene, James Kelly, Janet Mosher and Bruce Ryder. Aaron Delaney and Laura Pottie have provided superb research assistance throughout this research.

[1] See http://laws.justice.gc.ca/en/charter/.

[2] See J. Kelly, 'Bureaucratic Activism and the Charter of Rights: The Department of Justice and Its Entry into the Centre of Government' (1999) 42 *Canadian Public Administration* 478.

[3] See P. Hogg and A. Bushell, 'The Charter Dialogue Between Courts and Legislatures (Or Perhaps the Charter of Rights Isn't Such a Bad Thing After All)' (1997) 35 *Osgoode Hall Law Journal* 75. See also K. Roach, 'Constitutional and Common

on the impact of judicial decisions on the exercise of administrative discretion. For these observers, it is as if the court's decision is the end of the story of a legal challenge to government action, rather than the beginning of a complex, new chapter. The aim of this paper is to shift the focus of the analysis to the process by which judicial decisions influence the exercise of discretionary authority by front-line decision-makers.

There is good cause to be suspicious of the assumption that, once a court has issued a ruling, public officials simply comply with it, and, if they do not, further litigation (or the threat of it) serves as an adequate alternative remedy. Front-line discretionary decision-makers typically will not have the time, the expertise or the inclination to read and digest case law, even when judicial orders or reasons directly relate to their decision-making. The remoteness of the judicial action is accentuated when the decision at issue is general in nature, dealing with broad principles of statutory interpretation rather than a particular factual circumstance. In such circumstances, it may be possible to construe a court's findings in broad or narrow terms, with significant or trivial consequences for administrative decision-makers. The task of interpreting judicial standards often resides with government lawyers, but the task of disseminating those standards usually falls to the policy-making apparatus of government. Neither of these groups, however, can guarantee how these standards will be received and applied by front-line decision-makers.

Principally, judicial standards are disseminated to front-line decision-makers through a variety of informal guidelines, circulars, operational memoranda, directives, codes and oral instructions which, collectively, may be characterised as 'soft law'.[4] Soft law is distinct and broader

Law Dialogues Between the Supreme Court and Canadian Legislatures' (2001) 80 *Canadian Bar Review* 481. For an earlier approach, see J. Hiebert, 'Determining the Limits of Charter Rights: How Much Discretion Do Governments Retain' (Toronto University, PhD dissertation, 1991).

[4] The term 'soft law' is one of several terms adopted to convey a range of non-legislative guidelines, rules and administrative policies. It was adopted in the context of codes of ethics in A. Campbell and K. C. Glass, 'The Legal Status of Clinical and Ethics Policies, Codes, and Guidelines in Medical Practice and Research' (2001) 46 *McGill Law Journal* 473–89; and L. Sossin and C. Smith, 'Hard Choices and Soft Law: Ethical Codes, Policy Guidelines and the Role of the Courts in Regulating Government' (2003) 40 *Alberta Law Review* 867. Soft law should not be confused with binding guidelines or with binding rules. Occasionally, a statute will delegate to

than the power afforded some administrative bodies to issue delegated legislation or quasi-legislation.[5] As employed here, the term encompasses the full range of influences over discretionary authority, including both formal instruments and ingrained administrative practices.[6] While soft law reflects a diverse set of legal and policy constraints operating on decision-makers, these constraints must be seen in a contextual light. Determining the impact of judicial decisions through soft law requires due attention to the dynamics of administrative culture and institutional relations as well as the predilections and convictions of individual decision-makers.[7]

The aim of this study is to examine the impact of judicial review on bureaucratic action through an analysis of soft law. Three case studies will be presented in order to illustrate the impact of judicial decisions on the exercise of discretionary authority. The first case study involves the 'spouse-in-the-house' provision in Ontario's social welfare legislation, which was struck down by the Ontario Divisional Court in *Falkiner* v. *Ontario (Ministry of Community and Social Services)*,[8] a decision upheld on slightly different grounds in the Ontario Court of Appeal.[9] The second case study considers the statutory authority for immigration and refugee decision-makers to grant a statutory exemption to individuals

an administrative body the authority to issue guidelines or rules which may bind decision-makers (see, for example, section 27(2) of the Canadian Human Rights Act, which confers this authority on the Canadian Human Rights Commission). See generally D. Mullan, *Administrative Law* (Toronto, Irwin, 2001), pp. 375–9; and F. Houle, 'La zone fictive de l'infra-droit: l'integration des regles administratives dans la categorie des textes reglementaires' (2001) 47 *McGill Law Journal* 161.

[5] See G. Ganz, *Quasi-Legislation: Recent Developments in Secondary Legislation* (London, Sweet & Maxwell, 1987), pp. 16–22.

[6] For a discussion of the proper classification of various non-legislative instruments, see R. Baldwin and J. Houghton, 'Circular Arguments: The Status and Legitimacy of Administrative Rules' [1985] *Public Law* 239–84. See also Houle, 'La zone fictive', pp. 180–5.

[7] Simon Halliday refers to these as 'non-legal' influences which 'co-exist' with concerns of legality in the decision-making process, and include 'professional intuition, systemic suspicion, bureaucratic expediency, judgments about the moral deserts of applicants, inter-office relations, financial constraint and other values and pressures [which] all played a part in how judicial review impacted upon decision-making': S. Halliday, 'The Influence of Judicial Review on Bureaucratic Decision-Making' [2000] *Public Law* 110 at 117.

[8] [2000] OJ No. 2433 (Div. Ct).

[9] [2002] OJ No. 1771 (CA). Leave to appeal to the Supreme Court was granted in March 2003.

based on 'humanitarian and compassionate considerations'. The nature and scope of this authority was considered by the Supreme Court of Canada in *Baker* v. *Canada (Minister of Citizenship and Immigration)*.[10] Finally, the third case study analyses the discretionary determinations of customs officials in seizing material at the border based on its infringement of the standard of 'obscenity' under the Customs Act. In *Little Sisters Book and Art Emporium* v. *Canada (Minister of Justice)*,[11] the Supreme Court of Canada considered the constitutional implications of how this discretion was exercised. Each case examined below involved a statutory setting characterised by broad discretion, an important appellate court decision resulting from a challenge to state action, and a subsequent attempt to use soft law to inform front-line decision-makers of new criteria or standards arising out of the appellate decision. Further, each of these three appellate decisions also considered, to varying degrees, the role of soft law more generally in the legal regulation of discretionary authority.

METHODOLOGY AND CONTEXT

This research consists primarily of an analysis of the various soft law instruments chosen to disseminate the judgments in the three cases introduced above. These range from a questionnaire to solicit information from welfare applicants in the 'spouse-in-the-house' setting, to policy guidelines in the immigration context, and a technical operations manual used by customs officials to determine whether material is obscene. In each case, however, the form and content of the instruments chosen, and the manner of their development and application, tell only a partial, although important story. It is also important to understand how these instruments interact with administrative culture, training and in-house education, institutional relations and personal values.

   The case studies I have selected all deal with written guidelines of one kind or another, which were designed to assist with discretionary decision-making. While the scope of soft law, in my view, extends to less formal instruments and to administrative practices, discerning the impact of judicial review in these types of soft law is especially problematic, and would require greater resources than were available for this

---

[10] [1999] 2 SCR 817.   [11] [2000] 2 SCR 1120.

research.[12] However, in an attempt to capture the less formal dynamics of judicial impact, I have interviewed selected informants from inside and outside government who were involved either in the three cases I am analysing and/or in the subsequent process of disseminating new standards or criteria for the exercise of discretion in the light of the judicial decisions. While this study does not purport to do justice to the complexity of the relationship between judicial review and soft law, my aim is to highlight the centrality and importance of this relationship.

The study forms part of a larger research project on the legal regulation of public administration funded by the Social Sciences and Humanities Research Council of Canada. The first part of this research considered the dynamics of discretion from the standpoint of the relationship between bureaucrats and citizens.[13] The second part of the research explores the legal regulation of public administration.[14] This paper is one of two which will consider the interplay between soft law and the impact of judicial review.[15]

ORGANISATION OF ANALYSIS

This analysis is divided into three sections. The first section outlines the role of soft law both in informing judicial standards regarding

---

[12] What would be required, in my view, is a survey initiative along the lines of what Robin Creyke and John McMillan undertook in Australia, discussed in 'Executive Perceptions of Administrative Law – An Empirical Study' (2002) 9 *Australian Journal of Administrative Law* 163–90.

[13] This research received additional funding from the Law Commission of Canada, and was published as L. Sossin, 'Law and Intimacy in the Bureaucrat–Citizen Relationship' in N. des Rosiers (ed.), *No Person Is an Island: Personal Relationships of Dependence and Independence* (Vancouver, University of British Columbia Press, 2002), pp. 120–54 (also published in translation as 'Le juridique et l'intime dans le rapport entre fonctionnaires et citoyens' in N. des Rosiers (ed.), *Les rapports de dependance et d'interdependance* (Quebec City, Les Presses de l'Universite Laval, 2002), pp. 109–50), and L. Sossin, 'An Intimate Approach to Fairness, Impartiality and Reasonableness in Administrative Law' (2002) 28 *Queen's Law Journal* 809–58.

[14] Two papers written thus far examine the legal status of soft law: L. Sossin, 'Discretion Unbound: Reconciling the Charter and Soft Law' (2002) 45 *Canadian Public Administration* 465; and Sossin and Smith 'Hard Choices'.

[15] The second of these papers is L. Sossin, 'The Rule of Policy: *Baker* and the Impact of Judicial Review on Administrative Discretion' in D. Dyzenhaus *et al.* (eds.), *The Unity of Public Law* (London, Hart, 2004) (forthcoming). This chapter was based on a presentation at a conference on 'The Authority of Reasons: A New Understanding of the Rule of Law?', held at the University of Toronto, 3–5 January 2003.

discretionary decision-making and in disseminating new or modified standards to front-line decision-makers. In this sense, I argue that it may be seen as forming a conduit between the executive and judicial branches of government, through which both legal and administrative influences on discretionary authority may be articulated. The second section examines the role soft law has played in three case studies involving major cases of public law litigation in Canada. Finally, in the third section, I discuss how the impact of judicial review on bureaucratic decision-making is difficult to ascertain and more difficult still to evaluate. I conclude that the *form* of judicial review's impact on bureaucratic action may well be as important as the content. Where judicial standards are communicated transparently through instruments of soft law, and the interpretation of those standards by policy-makers and front-line decision-makers is made equally transparent, the result will be greater coherence and accountability in discretionary action.[16]

SOFT LAW AS AN EXECUTIVE–JUDICIAL DIALOGUE ON DISCRETION

Soft law is a particularly significant window into the relationship between judicial and bureaucratic decision-making. As alluded to above, I believe that soft law may serve as a conduit for a dialogue between the executive and judicial branches of government. At first glance, this dialogue may appear more like a monologue, in that significant judicial decisions are most often disseminated to front-line decision-makers through the use of soft law. These non-legislative instruments also embody the policy choices of decision-making bodies, including the interpretation and application of new judicial standards. Under Canadian administrative law, such discretionary standards and guidelines, in turn, are considered as part of the decision-maker's 'expertise', which attracts deference from the court when discretionary decisions are challenged.[17] In other words, where a particular

---

[16] While it is beyond the scope of this essay, it is worth highlighting another key indicator of coherence and accountability in exercising discretion, which is clear and precise statutory language creating the discretion. In a sense, each of the court cases I discuss herein may be traced to ambiguous and vague grants of discretion.

[17] Much of Canadian administrative law since *CUPE, Local 963* v. *New Brunswick Liquor Corporation* [1979] 2 SCR 227 has focused on the proper scope and degree of curial deference to administrative decision-makers. In *CUPE*, the Supreme Court held that, where legislation includes a privative clause purporting to restrict judicial

interpretation or application of statutory authority is discussed in a guideline or reflected in an administrative practice, this will inform the judicial understanding of what constitutes a reasonable exercise of discretion.[18] In settings of discretionary decision-making in Canada, it is simply not open to the court to supplant its view for that of the decision-maker.[19] Thus, the decision-maker, and by implication the policy-maker, have as significant a voice in the dialogue on discretionary standards as does the court.

While courts have been willing to look to soft law as part of the administrative context of decision-making, they have been reluctant to see these instruments as part of the legal framework of decision-making.[20] The court's dichotomous understanding of statutory law on the one hand, and soft law on the other, has waxed and waned over the

intervention, this is an indication that the legislature wished the expertise of the decision-maker to be respected by the Court, and judicial intervention will be warranted only where the construction given to a statutory power is 'patently unreasonable.' The Supreme Court has developed a nuanced 'pragmatic and functional' approach to determining the standard of judicial review for administrative determinations. The existence of statutory discretion typically will suggest that at least some deference is required. For a recent discussion of the high level of deference appropriate in discretionary settings, see *Suresh* v. *Canada (Minister of Immigration and Citizenship)* 2002 SCC 1, paras. 26–41; and *Pezim* v. *British Columbia (Superintendent of Brokers)* [1994] 2 SCR 577 at 607, where Iacobucci J explained that a reviewing court should not disturb a decision based on a 'broad discretion' unless the tribunal has 'made some error in principle in exercising its discretion or has exercised its discretion in a capricious or vexatious manner' (para. 34). Only when those choices are shown to be unreasonable or beyond the jurisdiction of the decision-maker will the Court be justified in intervening. The Court has accepted that this analysis should be informed by an understanding of the decision-making context, in which soft law instruments are considered alongside the applicable statutory provisions. An example of the Court according such treatment to policy guidelines is discussed with respect to *Baker* v. *Canada* [1999] 2 SCR 817.

[18] This may be distinguished from Julia Black's notion of 'conversational regulation' or circumstances in which executive decision-makers or policy-makers may mediate dialogues between government and those affected by discretionary decision-making. See J. Black, 'Constitutionalising Self-Regulation' (1996) 59 *Modern Law Review* 24. See also L. Sossin, 'Redistributing Democracy: Authority, Discretion and the Possibility of Engagement in the Welfare State' (1994) 26 *Ottawa Law Review* 1.

[19] See *Suresh* v. *Canada (Minister of Immigration and Citizenship)* 2002 SCC 1, paras. 26–41.

[20] The first Supreme Court case to consider the status of soft law was *Martineau* v. *Matsqui Institution* [1978] 1 SCR 118, in which a narrow majority of the Court held that directives issued to guide a parole board were merely 'administrative' and thus could not bind the board. Four dissenting justices held that the directives were 'law'

years.[21] It has enjoyed a recent resurgence as a result of the Supreme Court's judgment in *Little Sisters Book and Art Emporium* v. *Canada (Minister of Justice)*.[22] In *Little Sisters*, the Court was asked to respond to the argument that a customs operational manual, developed to guide customs officers in exercising their statutory discretion to identify and seize obscene material being imported into Canada, was the source of discriminatory acts undertaken against a gay and lesbian bookstore. The Court had already concluded that the impugned provision of the Customs Act, which simply afforded officials a discretion to seize material deemed to be 'obscene', was not unconstitutional. Binnie J, for the majority, addressed the soft law issue in the following terms:

> It is the statutory decision, however, not the manual, that constituted the denial. It is simply not feasible for the courts to review for Charter compliance the vast array of manuals and guides prepared by the public service for the internal guidance of officials. The courts are concerned with the legality of the decisions, not the quality of the guidebooks, although of course the fate of the two are not unrelated.[23]

The Court's distinction between statutes and guidebooks, of course, is not really one of feasibility (there is a similarly vast array of regulations prepared by the public service but these are all subject to judicial scrutiny if impugned under the Charter) so much as one of legitimacy.

since they were authorised by the Act and affected the rights of an individual. Pidgeon J, writing for the majority, concluded that: 'In my opinion it is important to distinguish between duties imposed on public employees by statutes or regulations having the force of law and obligations prescribed by virtue of their condition of public employees. The members of a disciplinary board are not high public officers but ordinary civil servants. The Commissioner's directives are no more than directions as to the manner of carrying out their duties in the administration of the institution where they are employed.'

[21] See *Ainsley Financial Corporation* v. *Ontario Securities Commission* (1995) 21 OR (3d) 104 (CA) at 108–9; *Hopedale Developments Ltd.* v. *Oakville (Town)* (1965) 1 OR 259 at 263 (Ont. CA); *Maple Lodge Farms Ltd.* v. *Canada* [1982] 2 SCR 2 at 6–7; *Capital Cities Communications Inc.* v. *Canadian Radio-Television Commission* (1978) 81 DLR (3d) 609 (SCC) at 170; *Friends of Oldman River Society* v. *Canada (Minister of Transport)* [1992] 1 SCR 3 at 35; *Pezim* v. *British Columbia (Superintendent of Brokers)* [1994] 2 SCR 557 at 596; and Law Reform Commission of Canada Report 26, *Report on Independent Administrative Agencies: Framework for Decision Making* (1985), pp. 29–31.

[22] [2000] 2 SCR 1120. This case is discussed in more detail in the case study on 'obscenity' determinations by customs officials.

[23] *Ibid.*, para. 85.

Legislation and regulations are subject to parliamentary accountability and procedural formality (they must be enacted or issued in a particular fashion, subject to the Statutory Instruments Act,[24] published in a particular form and vetted for compliance with constitutional strictures, and are subject to parliamentary debate). Soft law is subject to no such criteria.

The distinction between legislation and regulations on the one hand, and soft law on the other, is formal rather than functional in origin. It is rooted in the separation of powers. Courts cannot treat guidelines as 'law' because to do so would recognise that public administration is subject to laws of its own design rather than subordinate to the will of Parliament.[25] Thus, if guidelines or practices are formally treated as 'binding', this would constitute an unlawful fettering of administrative discretion.[26] However, by the same token, if guidelines are ignored by a decision-maker, this may be considered evidence that the decision was unreasonable[27] or unfair[28] or both. This leaves soft law in a legal and administrative limbo which cannot easily be resolved. If

---

[24] See RSC 1985, c. S-22. For a discussion of this Act and its significance, see Houle, 'La zone fictive'.

[25] Canada's separation-of-powers doctrine appears to be gaining in importance. For discussion, see L. Sossin, *Boundaries of Judicial Review* (Toronto, Carswell, 1999), pp. 9–19. In the context of discretionary authority, the Supreme Court recently used this doctrine to justify curial deference to ministerial decision-making. In *Suresh v. Canada (Minister of Citizenship and Immigration)* 2002 SCC 1, which concerned the discretion to deport a suspected terrorist, the Court observed that (*ibid.*, para. 38): 'Parliament's task is to establish the criteria and procedures governing deportation, within the limits of the Constitution. The Minister's task is to make a decision that conforms to Parliament's criteria and procedures as well as the Constitution. The court's task, if called upon to review the Minister's decision, is to determine whether the Minister has exercised her decision-making power within the constraints imposed by Parliament's legislation and the Constitution. If the Minister has considered the appropriate factors in conformity with these constraints, the court must uphold her decision. It cannot set it aside even if it would have weighed the factors differently and arrived at a different conclusion.'

[26] See *Ainsley Financial Corporation v. Ontario Securities Commission* (1995) 21 OR (3d) 104 (Ont. CA) at 109, in which the Ontario Court of Appeal referred to the 'Rubicon between a non-mandatory guideline and a mandatory pronouncement having the same effect as a statutory instrument'.

[27] See *Baker* [1999] 2 SCR 817.

[28] See *Bezaire v. Windsor Roman Catholic Separate School Board* (1992) 9 OR (3d) 737 (Div. Ct) (in which a school board's decision to close nine schools was quashed because neither ministerial nor school board policy guidelines, which called for consultations with affected parties, were followed). See also *Hammond v. Association*

guidelines are subject to coherent procedural and substantive standards, as I have advocated elsewhere,[29] there is a risk of undermining the flexibility needed to guide discretionary judgments and adding yet another layer of formalism to the judicial–executive dialogue over discretionary authority.[30] Yet, to permit public authority to be exercised according to internal and sometimes secret principles and policies, not subject to meaningful forms of public review, undermines the integrity of public administration and the rule of law.[31]

Notwithstanding its uncertain legal status, or perhaps because of it, soft law represents a flexible and effective mechanism for disseminating judicial standards to decision-makers. Soft law instruments can adapt diffuse or abstract judicial commentaries into usable, relevant decision-making criteria. Depending on the context, a judicial standard may be presented to decision-makers as a checklist of relevant factors, a commentary on what principles, rules or exceptions should guide a decision, or as a fact-based illustration of how to apply a standard from which decision-makers may reason from analogy. A further, potential benefit of soft law as a means of disseminating judicial standards is that most guidelines and directives are now available to the public, or can easily be made public, either through ministry websites or by responses to freedom-of-information requests. Since decision-makers in high-volume discretionary settings rarely have the resources to issue detailed written reasons for their determinations, publicly available guidelines, which incorporate relevant judicial standards, may provide an important (and, often, the only) window to affected parties about how a particular discretionary decision was reached, and what basis may be available to challenge it.[32]

---

of *British Columbia Professional Foresters* (1991) 47 *Administrative Law Reports* 20 (BCSC).

[29] See Sossin, 'Discretion Unbound'.

[30] See D. Dyzenhaus, 'Constituting the Rule of Law: Fundamental Values in Administrative Law' (2002) 27 *Queen's Law Journal* 445 at 471–80.

[31] For a discussion of this principle, see U. H. Richardson, 'Administrative Policy-Making: Rule of Law or Bureaucracy?' in D. Dyzenhaus (ed.), *Recrafting the Rule of Law* (London, Oxford University Press, 1999).

[32] Of equal importance is the fact that guidelines may sometimes reflect input and negotiations between affected parties and decision-makers. For example, in *Capital Cities, Communications Inc.* v. *Canadian Radio-Television Commission* (1978) 81 DLR (3d) 609 (SCC) the Supreme Court held that, while existing regulations would prevail against policy statements, absent any regulation, the CRTC was obliged to consider its policy statement in making the determination at issue. In reference to the policy

Whereas statutes and regulations are meant to define the boundaries and mandates of public authority, soft law is intended to ensure coherence and consistency in the implementation of those mandates. In his landmark study of administrative discretion, K. C. Davis advocated for rule-making as an important tool both for confining discretionary power and for structuring it.[33] His main concern was countering the potential for arbitrary or oppressive uses of administrative discretion. For Davis, plans, rules, findings, reasons, precedents and a fair informal procedure were all variations on the same theme of greater transparency and accountability. This democratic justification for clear standard-setting has served as a touchstone for much administrative law scholarship on discretionary authority,[34] and has met with some judicial favour in Canada.[35]

The dilemma in using soft law instruments such as guidelines and manuals to convey judicial standards is that judicially determined standards are binding on decision-makers. Thus, we have a situation in which inherently binding standards are mostly conveyed through inherently non-binding instruments of soft law. This dilemma is yet another reason to prefer forms of soft law which convey judicial standards in a clear and transparent fashion. It also reflects an inherent flaw in the formalist position. Rather than parse over whether the form of a guideline is binding, the more germane issue appears to be whether the content of the guideline should be accorded the force of law by decision-makers.[36] Of course, this distinction is not always so clear either. Because judicial standards themselves are subject to interpretation and may not apply in

guidelines under discussion, Laskin CJ, writing for the majority, referred approvingly to democratic input as a justification for giving weight to the guidelines, noting that 'the guidelines on this matter were arrived at after extensive hearings at which interested parties were present and made submissions'.

[33] K. C. Davis, *Discretionary Justice: A Preliminary Inquiry* (Baton Rouge, Louisiana State University, 1969).

[34] See the discussion of Davis' influence in D. Galligan, *Discretionary Powers: A Legal Study of Official Discretion* (Oxford, Clarendon Press, 1986), pp. 170–7; and K. Hawkins, 'The Uses of Legal Discretion: Perspectives from Law and Social Science' in K. Hawkins (ed.), *The Uses of Discretion* (Oxford, Clarendon, 1992), pp. 16–17.

[35] See, for example, *Re Hopedale Developments Ltd v. Town of Oakville* (1964) 47 DLR (2d) 482.

[36] See Houle, 'La zone fictive'; see also H. Janisch, 'The Choice of Decision-Making Method: Adjudication, Policies and Rule-Making' in *Administrative Law: Principles, Practices and Pluralism* (Scarborough, Ont., Carswell, 1992).

the same way to different legal and factual contexts, this suggests that it may be open to a decision-maker legitimately to disagree with the communication of a judicial standard in a guideline and to approach that standard unfettered by the guideline. In this sense, while the underlying judicial standard may be binding, the manner in which policy-makers conclude that the standard should affect decision-makers may not be. Precisely how those standards will bind decision-makers would seem to fall to the discretion of policy-makers (advised, presumably, by government lawyers). Whether judicial standards are presented as an interpretive commentary or a checklist, for instance, reflects important assumptions about the policy implications of case law, and about the judicial role in the discretionary process. At the end of the day, the form and content of soft law cannot be so easily disentangled.

While soft law has the potential to serve as a conduit between the executive and judiciary for exchanging knowledge about legal and administrative aspects of discretionary authority, I suggest that the ambiguity surrounding the legal status of soft law has impaired the fulfilment of this potential. It has also meant that the development and application of soft law has been subject to little or no accountability, with little or no guarantee of consistency. Interviews with legal, policy and operational staff in several different ministry settings reveal that, while the importance of soft law to the discretionary process is universally recognised, standards for its use simply do not exist. Guidelines, manuals and directives may be designed in an *ad hoc* or well-planned manner, they may be disclosed to the public or kept secret, they may or may not be vetted by lawyers, and they may be based on the input of affected parties or drafted behind closed doors. To the extent soft law serves as a vehicle for communicating judicial decisions to front-line decision-makers, no supervisory process exists to ensure that this is done in an effective and expeditious fashion or to ensure that it captures the spirit as well as the letter of the judicial determination (except, of course, by way of further litigation).

In the following section, I explore the potential and limitations of soft law through three case studies on the impact of judicial review on bureaucratic discretion. These cases suggest that the distinction between 'law' and 'policy' often is invoked strategically, both by courts and administrative decision-makers, in order to support desired outcomes in particular cases. The result is that courtroom victories, elusive as they often may be, can turn bittersweet as litigants witness administrative decision-makers respond to judicial orders with defiance, confusion or indifference. It remains to be seen, however, whether this instrumental approach to soft law can be supplanted by a transparent and constructive exchange of perspectives between courts, policy-makers and decision-makers.

LITIGATION, SOFT LAW AND BUREAUCRATIC DISCRETION: THREE CASE STUDIES

The three case studies selected for this study have a good deal in common. All involve controversial, discretionary settings which resulted in high-profile litigation. In each case, the administrative scheme, including the instruments of soft law, were considered by the court as well as the statutory provision whose constitutionality or proper interpretation was being challenged. Ultimately, though, it is the differences with respect to the impact of judicial decisions on bureaucratic action in each setting which I believe is most revealing.

Social welfare eligibility determinations: the 'spouse-in-the-house' rule

The first case study considers a legal setting which has long been subject to the vicissitudes of administrative discretion – the determination of eligibility for social welfare for single mothers. In Canada, as in the US, beginning with the first mother's pensions in the 1920s, the administration of social welfare to has also served as a mechanism for social control.[37] Determining eligibility for different kinds of social programmes is a means of distinguishing the deserving from the undeserving poor. A particularly pernicious chapter in welfare administration involves the 'spouse-in-the-house' rule. Originally, the concern of welfare administrators for the sexual and intimate relationships of female recipients of benefits arose out of the statutory requirement that recipients be 'proper' or 'suitable'. Later, this definition was refined to exclude women who lived 'as husband and wife'. Finally, as much for reasons of fiscal austerity as social engineering, women who lived with a person with whom she shared financial responsibility were deemed to be 'spouses' and eligible only for benefits as a couple, not as an individual, and one of them

---

[37] See M. Little, *No Car, No Radio, No Liquor Permit: The Moral Regulation of Single Mothers in Ontario, 1920–1997* (Toronto, Oxford University Press, 1998); and L. Gordon, *Pitied But Not Entitled: Single Mothers and the History of Welfare* (Toronto, The Free Press, 1994).

would be deemed the 'head of the household' (most often the male), who would be the recipient of the monthly cheque.[38]

The definition of 'spouse' was contained in a regulation to the Ontario Works Act, and left much to the discretionary determinations of case workers. Regulation 366 provided that a 'spouse' was:

> (d) a person of the opposite sex[39] to an applicant or recipient who is residing in the same dwelling place as the applicant or recipient if
>
>   (i) the person is providing financial support to the applicant or recipient,
>   (ii) the applicant or recipient is providing financial support to the person, or
>   (iii) the person and the applicant or recipient have a mutual agreement or arrangement regarding their financial affairs
> and the social and familial aspects of the relationship between the person and the applicant or recipient amount to cohabitation.

What constituted 'a mutual agreement or arrangement' for the purposes of a spousal determination? What evidence of 'social and familial' relationships would be sought, and from what source? Where an applicant shared a dwelling with another person, the applicant has to fill out a detailed questionnaire seeking personal and financial information. Welfare officials were provided with a comprehensive set of administrative directives for interpreting the results of the questionnaire. As the testimony of officials in the *Falkiner* decision revealed, these questionnaires were integral to the eligibility determination.[40] However, officials were careful to emphasise, as did the ministry directives, that no particular answer to a particular question would lead to a particular finding. Rather, cases were considered as a whole, based on a mix of subjective and objective factors.[41] While the government argued that caseworkers

---

[38] For a discussion and critique of the policy rationale underlying this initiative, see M. Little and I. Morrison, 'The Pecker Detectors Are Back' (1999) 34 *Journal of Canadian Studies* 110–36.

[39] In 2000, following a ruling of the Supreme Court that common law spousal definitions violated the Charter of Rights, all provincial statutes, including the regulations to this Act, were amended to provide parallel 'same sex partner' definitions, to which the same rights, obligations and privileges would apply.

[40] Cross-examination of Dianne Metzell, Record of Proceedings, *Falkiner* v. *Ontario* (Court of Appeal) pp. 218–21.

[41] *Ibid.*

went through an 'extensive training programme', it appeared that only two hours of training were provided, which was focused mostly on the process for terminating benefits, not how to weigh answers to the questionnaire.[42] The phrasing of Regulation 366 created this discretion, but it was the questionnaire, the directives, the institutional culture of welfare caseworkers and their instincts which determined the exercise of this discretion.[43] A further influence on both policy-makers and front-line decision-makers was the partisan politics of the time. In 1995, when this regulation was issued, a neo-liberal Conservative government had just been elected in Ontario, for whom a fundamental restructuring of the welfare system was a major campaign plank. The 'spouse-in-the-house' rule was one of the first policy initiatives of the new government, following an across-the-board 21 per cent cut to welfare benefit rates.[44]

The new 'spouse-in-the-house rule' almost immediately resulted in substantial numbers of people having their benefits curtailed or cancelled, mostly women with children. The definition was challenged under the equality provision of the Canadian Charter of Rights and Freedoms on the basis that it was overbroad and discriminated against sole support mothers on social assistance.[45] The applicants were successful before the Social Assistance Review Board (now called the Social Benefits Tribunal), but rulings by this administrative tribunal have no binding effect beyond the particular decision being challenged. An appeal was taken by the government to the Ontario Divisional Court. The Divisional Court struck down the 'spouse-in-the-house', regulation as unconstitutional.[46]

---

[42] See Affidavit of Kevin Constante and evidence of Lynett Cumming, Record of Proceedings, in *ibid.*

[43] The complex influences on discretionary decision-making are the subject of a vast literature. For the seminal works, see M. Lipsky, *Street Level Bureaucracy: Dilemmas of the Individual in Public Services* (New York, Russell Sage, 1980); and J. Handler, *The Conditions of Discretion: Autonomy, Community Bureaucracy* (New York, Russell Sage, 1986).

[44] This cut was unsuccessfully challenged as a constitutional infringements of the rights of welfare recipients in *Ontario (Ministry of Community and Social Service) v. Masse* [1996] OJ No. 363 (Div. Ct) (leave to appeal to the Ontario Court of Appeal refused). In this case, as in others challenging government welfare policy, the Court reiterated that, in Canada, welfare is a privilege, not a right.

[45] A related aspect of the litigation challenged the interpretation of the spousal definition to individuals who were disabled.

[46] *Falkiner v. Ontario* [2000] OJ No. 2433 (Div. Ct).

Following the Divisional Court decision, the ministry now faced several vexing legal and administrative problems. First, it had to take steps to bring the administration of welfare benefits into compliance with the Court's ruling.[47] Secondly, the government had to consider whether to address other substantially similar spousal definitions in other parts of the social welfare statutory scheme, as well as whether to appeal the Divisional Court's ruling. Thirdly, the government had to consider whether to provide redress for former recipients whose benefits had been terminated as a result of the 'spouse-in-the-house' rule. Interviews with lawyers representing the applicants in *Falkiner* suggest that the Court's ruling was met, initially at least, with a response of delay and deflection. The ministry issued a memorandum to all regional directors and programme managers.[48] The main thrust of the ministry's response was to suspend new 'spouse-in-the-house' determinations and to appeal the Divisional Court's ruling.

In May 2002, the Court of Appeal upheld the Divisional Court's ruling that the definition of 'spouse' in Regulation 366 was discriminatory and therefore unconstitutional, although on slightly different grounds.[49] With respect to the administration of the scheme, the Court of Appeal recognised the importance of the questionnaire and directives, but treated these simply as evidence of the problems with the spousal definition, rather than the source of the discriminatory government action. Laskin JA, writing for the Court of Appeal, emphasised the Court's concerns with the administration of the scheme in the following terms:

> Finally, the administration of the definition is highly intrusive of the privacy of single persons on social assistance. They are subjected to heightened scrutiny of their personal relationships. They are required

---

[47] The government applied for a stay of the order of the Divisional Court while the decision was under appeal. This was denied (decision issued 22 September 2000).

[48] The memorandum dealing with *Falkiner* simply indicated that the regulation had been struck down, and that 'new' cases were not to be decided.

[49] The Court of Appeal held that the 'spouse-in-the-house' rule discriminated against the applicants on grounds of sex and marital status and on the basis of being recipients of social welfare. This latter holding represents the first time in which an appellate court in Canada recognised social welfare recipients as a discrete minority entitled to equality protection under the Constitution. The Court was particularly concerned that the over-wide breadth of the definition could capture women who were just 'trying on' new, intimate relationships or individuals who were sharing expenses on an equal basis as roommates.

to complete a detailed questionnaire on their personal living arrangements. The questionnaire includes the following questions:

Do you and your co-resident spend spare time at home together?
Do you go to church, temple, synagogue, etc. with your co-resident?
How do you and your co-resident address each other's parents?
Who takes care of you and your co-resident when either of you are ill?
Do you ask your co-resident for advice regarding the children?
Does your co-resident buy them birthday or other presents?

These and many other questions on the questionnaire touch on highly personal matters. Far from negating any discrimination as the government contends, administering the challenged definition by requiring social assistance recipients to complete this questionnaire further suggests that the definition undermines human dignity.[50]

Following the Court of Appeal decision, the government responded with a new regulation incorporating a revised definition of 'spouse',[51] which was accompanied by a new set of guidelines and questionnaire.[52] The revised directives and questionnaire do not mention the *Falkiner* decision by name. The stated intent of the new policy is to 'clarify' the definitions of spouse and same-sex partner. These clarifications include addressing specific scenarios raised by the Court of Appeal, for example where cohabiting individuals split expenses on a 'fair share' basis. The scope of the discretionary authority, however, remains unchanged and, in the eyes of the *Falkiner* litigants, little had changed. The policy decision of the ministry, in the eyes of those familiar with the case, was to respond to the Court's decision minimally and grudgingly. While the impact of the Court's decision can be clearly discerned in some parts of the soft law scheme (i.e. the 'fair share' clarification in the directives), it pervades other parts in a more subtle fashion. The questionnaire, for

---

[50] *Falkiner* [2002] OJ No. 177 (CA), para. 104.

[51] The new language leaves caseworkers with a similar discretion based on similar factors, but provides for a three-month 'grace' period before the inquiry is begun into whether a person and recipient are spouses. The new regulation also removes the low economic threshold which characterised the old definition, and which was singled out as unconstitutionally overbroad by the Court of Appeal. The regulation provides that two people living together should be treated as spouses where 'the extent of the social and familial aspects of the relationship' and the 'extent of the financial support provided by one person to the other or the degree of financial interdependence between the two persons' is consistent with cohabitation.

[52] Ontario Disability Support Program Policy Bulletin 011-2002, dated 12 July 2002, p. 4, on file with the author.

example, no longer contains probing questions regarding the details of daily life (e.g. 'When you go out with your co-resident, how do you introduce him/her?'), but rather asks, in more bureaucratic fashion, for applicants to tick a series of 'yes' and 'no' boxes to indicate whether the applicant and the person with whom they are cohabitating are 'known' as spouses by any public agencies, school, bank, place of worship, etc., or whether they have 'presented each other' as parents of any children residing in the household. The result of these revisions is a less 'intrusive' administrative scheme – although whether this evidences a legislative scheme better able to preserve the human dignity of applicants, as the term is used in the *Falkiner* decision, remains unclear.[53]

Falkiner also stands as a stark reminder of the limitations of judicial review in effecting meaningful change in discretionary authority. The litigation has been going on for seven years (with an application for leave to appeal to the Supreme Court of Canada pending), and has absorbed substantial resources from all parties. Will the change in the directives and in the form of the questionnaire lead to different outcomes in the exercise of the 'spouse-in-the-house' discretion? Certainly, in a small number of cases, it will. However, even to the extent that the Court's concern with the administration of the 'spouse-in-the-house' rule is addressed, the form in which it does so fails, in my view, to take advantage of soft law's potential. Neither the directives nor the questionnaire speaks to the *Falkiner* decision in clear or transparent terms. Neither contains a justification for the important legal and policy choices made in responding to the Court of Appeal's reasons. The impact of judicial review on bureaucratic discretion must be read between the lines, and in the margins of the directives and the questionnaire. By contrast, in the following case study, the impact of judicial review occupies a central place in the soft law instruments intended to guide discretionary decision-making.

Immigration determinations: 'humanitarian and compassionate' grounds

While the 'spouse-in-the-house' setting reflects a policy of what might be described as minimal compliance, this approach does not

[53] Interestingly, one caseworker with whom I spoke indicated that, under the old questionnaire, it was possible to informally coach sympathetic applicants to provide answers which would keep them outside the spousal definition. The new questionnaire is seen as removing much of this discretion and has resulted in a process which is more 'bureaucratic'.

characterise all discretionary settings in Canada. An example of a policy setting which has embraced a more open engagement with judicial decisions is the 'humanitarian and compassionate' exemption under the Canadian Immigration Act.[54]

This statutory provision contained no criteria for the determination of humanitarian and compassionate grounds. The regulation issued pursuant to this provision is similarly broad and undefined.[55] Guidelines were issued as part of the Inland Processing Manual No. 5 ('IP5'), which were developed in order to guide the exercise of this broad discretion.[56] Nonetheless, as in the case of the 'spouse-in-the-house' rule, the essence of the determination of 'humanitarian and compassionate' grounds rested with the subjective conclusions of individual immigration officers. In *Baker* v. *Canada (Minister of Immigration and Citizenship)*,[57] one such determination led to years of litigation, and arguably to a sea change in the treatment of soft law in Canada.

---

[54] Section 114(2) of the Immigration Act read: 'The Governor in Council may, by regulation, authorize the Minister to exempt any person from any regulation made under subsection (1) or otherwise facilitate the admission of any person where the Minister is satisfied that the person should be exempted from that regulation or that the person's admission should be facilitated owing to the existence of compassionate or humanitarian considerations.' This section was amended by the Immigration and Refugee Protection Act 2002, in part as a consequence of the *Baker* decision, discussed herein, and now reads: '(1) The Minister shall, upon request of a foreign national who is inadmissible or who does not meet the requirements of this Act, and may, on the Minister's own initiative, examine the circumstances concerning the foreign national and may grant the foreign national permanent resident status or an exemption from any applicable criteria or obligation of this Act if the Minister is of the opinion that it is justified by humanitarian and compassionate considerations relating to them, taking into account the best interests of a child directly affected, or by public policy considerations.'

[55] Immigration Regulations 1978, SOR/78-172, as amended by SOR/93-44, 2.1: 'The Minister is hereby authorized to exempt any person from any regulation made under subsection 114(1) of the Act or otherwise facilitate the admission to Canada of any person where the Minister is satisfied that the person should be exempted from that regulation or that the person's admission should be facilitated owing to the existence of compassionate or humanitarian considerations.'

[56] Apart from integrating interpretive principles from case law, as discussed further below, this Manual also served to transmit the decisions and interpretations of the immigration and refugee board, which, unlike judicial decisions, are not binding apart from the particular case at issue before the board. For a discussion of this 'cohering' function of guidelines, see Houle, 'La zone fictive', pp. 183–5.

[57] [1999] 2 SCR 817.

Mavis Baker was an illegal immigrant who had had four Canadian-born children during the eleven years she had lived illegally in Canada. The question for the immigration officer was whether the prospect of separating Mrs Baker from her children constituted humanitarian and compassionate grounds for exempting her from being deported pursuant to the Immigration Act. The immigration officer denied her application, disclosing in his reasons a number of biases against Mrs Baker. The following passage from those reasons illustrates the complex mix of personal judgments, objective evidence and immigration policy which figured in the determination:

> PC is unemployed – on Welfare. No income shown – no assets. Has four Cdn-born children – four other children in Jamaica – HAS A TOTAL OF EIGHT CHILDREN Says only two children are in her 'direct custody'. (No info on who has ghe [sic] other two). There is nothing for her in Jamaica – hasn't been there in a long time – no longer close to her children there – no jobs there – she has no skills other than as a domestic – children would suffer – can't take them with her and can't leave them with anyone here . . . Lawyer says PS [sic] is sole caregiver and single parent of two Cdn born children. PC's mental condition would suffer a setback if she is deported etc. This case is a catastrophy [sic]. It is also an indictment of our 'system' that the client came as a visitor in Aug. '81, was not ordered deported until Dec. '92 and in APRIL '94 IS STILL HERE! The PC is a paranoid schizophrenic and on welfare. She has no qualifications other than as a domestic. She has FOUR CHILDREN IN JAMAICA AND ANOTHER FOUR BORN HERE. She will, of course, be a tremendous strain on our social welfare systems for (probably) the rest of her life. There are no H&C factors other than her FOUR CANADIAN-BORN CHILDREN. Do we let her stay because of that? I am of the opinion that Canada can no longer afford this kind of generosity. However, because of the circumstances involved, there is a potential for adverse publicity. I recommend refusal but you may wish to clear this with someone at Region. There is also a potential for violence – see charge of 'assault with a weapon'.[58]

The decision of the officer was quashed by the Supreme Court on the basis of bias and on the grounds that it was an unreasonable exercise of discretion. In this part of the decision, the Court considered the ministry guidelines which officers were supposed to rely upon. Guideline 9.05,[59] for example, directed officers to carefully consider all aspects of

---

[58] *Ibid.*, para. 5.   [59] Issued as part of the Inland Processing Manual.

the case, using their best judgment and asking themselves what a reasonable person would do in such a situation. It also states that, although officers are not expected to delve into areas which are not presented during examination or interviews, they should attempt to clarify possible humanitarian grounds and public policy considerations even if these are not well articulated. According to the Court, the guidelines also set out two bases upon which the discretion conferred by the Act and the regulations should be exercised: public policy considerations and humanitarian and compassionate grounds. Public policy reasons included marriage to a Canadian resident, the fact that the person has lived in Canada, has become established, and has become an 'illegal de facto resident', and the fact that the person may be a long-term holder of employment authorisation or has worked as a foreign domestic. Humanitarian and compassionate grounds included whether unusual, undeserved or disproportionate hardship would be caused to the person seeking consideration if he or she had to leave Canada.

L'Heureux-Dube J, writing for the Court in *Baker*, characterised the Minister's guidelines as 'great assistance to the Court in determining whether the reasons . . . are supportable . . . They are a useful indicator of what constitutes a reasonable interpretation of the power conferred by the section.'[60] At another point in the judgment, she acknowledged that these guidelines 'constitute instructions to immigration officers about how to exercise the discretion delegated to them',[61] and set out the criteria on which discretion should be exercised. In general, the Court's approach in *Baker* suggests that soft law may serve to delineate the scope of what will be accepted by a court as a reasonable exercise of discretion.[62] That the decision taken in *Baker* was at odds with the guidelines was one of several grounds cited by the Supreme Court for quashing it as an unreasonable exercise of discretion.[63]

Following the decision in *Baker*, humanitarian and compassionate determinations (specifically those involving children) were left in a state of limbo. This is telling because, in normal circumstances, policy staff would begin working on contingency arrangements for adverse judicial rulings early on in the litigation process.[64] Finally, a year after the Supreme Court's decision, the ministry published an

---

[60] [1999] 2 SCR 817, para. 72.   [61] *Ibid.*, para. 16.
[62] *Ibid.*, paras. 67 and 72.   [63] *Ibid.*, paras. 74–5.
[64] Interview with CIC policy official, 16 July 2002. The cause of delay was characterised first as 'a breakdown in communications', and later as 'bureaucratic drift'.

'operational memorandum' on *Baker* and its implications for future decision-making.[65] This memorandum was divided into separate sections on 'case details', 'court's reasons for deciding to return for redetermination', 'summary of issues and impact on CIC [the ministry]' and 'conclusion [which included a web link to the full text of the decision]'. The memorandum points out those policies and practices which the Court affirmed as legally sufficient (for example, the Court's finding that note-taking met the legal requirement for 'reasons') as well as those which the Court held to be legally deficient (for example, the failure to take proper consideration of the best interests of the children). The memorandum concludes with a passage on 'why the Baker decision was not upheld'. In this section, the memorandum details the basis for the Court's ruling that the decision-maker's exercise of discretion was both unreasonable and biased.[66] The memorandum employs a mixture of summary, paraphrasing, quoting and analysing of the Supreme Court reasons, in order to remain faithful to the text but also to be clear about the broader relevance of the judgment for discretionary decision-making. This approach to disseminating a new judicial standard highlights the potential of soft law to facilitate judicial–executive dialogue. Of course, simply providing a useful summary of a case is not in and of itself likely to have a significant impact on bureaucratic action. After all, the 'biased and unreasonable' reasons offered in *Baker* (which were not, strictly speaking, reasons at all, but rather an internal recommendation from a junior to a senior immigration officer) were not exceptional – they were drafted in a fashion which suggested shared assumptions about the immigration system, an impression confirmed by the fact that the reasons were not only accepted by the senior immigration officer, but also deemed appropriate to provide to the applicant.

[65] See *Baker* [1999] 2 SCR 817; and 'Issues Addressed and Impact on Citizenship and Immigration Canada', www.cic.gc.ca/manuals-guides/english/om-web/2000/ip/ip00-08e.html (issued 10 July 2000, OM #00-08) (accessed 13 May 2002). Approximately three to four cases each year are the subject of operational memoranda. These are subsequently incorporated into revised manuals. Most memoranda are issued following significant Supreme Court decisions, but they may follow lower court rulings as well. Some are issued as a 'one-time instruction only', while others are eventually incorporated into the text of the manual. Based on interviews with ministry staff, the decision when to issue a memorandum, and what content the memorandum should contain, is subject to no general standards, and appears to be a policy judgment made collectively by the legal services and policy branches of the ministry, often on the advice of the litigation team who argued the case.

[66] *Ibid.*, p. 4.

Rather than serve as a clarion call to immigration decision-makers, the judgment in *Baker* may just as easily serve as a 'roadmap' showing how decision-makers can phrase 'reasons' in order to avoid successful judicial review in the future.

Perhaps with such concerns in mind, the ministry undertook an unusual pilot project in February 2001 in the Toronto region. With the assistance of York University's Centre for Practical Ethics, the ministry organised a day of workshops and lectures on the Supreme Court's judgment, entitled 'Baker and Beyond'. Approximately 100 front line decision-makers from the Toronto region attended the event, and heard from academics, lawyers and ministry staff on the significance of the decision. More importantly, those attending had an opportunity in workshops and 'breakout session' to discuss the case and hypothetical scenarios raising similar issues.[67] The discussion at these small group meetings was revealing. Decision-makers disclosed that they often viewed their own government lawyers as adversaries, and offered anecdotes about how judicial reviews of their decisions succeeded only because they were not allowed by their lawyers to put the 'real story' before the court. Decision-makers emphasised that the guidelines, even when summarising case law, were simply a reference tool, and that their decisions were a product of individual judgment based on the evidence and could not be fettered by blind adherence to guidelines. A lawyer involved in the case later mentioned as an aside that the independence of decision-makers typically is raised at the moment the discussion turns to their accountability for decision-making.[68]

The impact of judicial review on bureaucratic discretion in the 'humanitarian and compassionate' setting as a result of *Baker* has been, on the one hand, dramatic. Procedurally, applicants are now routinely entitled to written reasons for decisions (although, interestingly, only if written reasons are formally requested). Substantively, many applicants with children have had more favourable 'humanitarian and compassionate' determinations as a result of the Court's direction. However, it is more difficult to conclude that the values underlying the biased and unreasonable reasons in *Baker* have been changed by the Court, and indeed the inadvertent effect of the decision may be that reasons for discretionary decisions in the future may be far less candid. At a minimum,

---

[67] I should disclose that I participated in the 'Baker and Beyond' retreat, giving a lecture on the 'reasons' requirement arising out of the Supreme Court decision.
[68] Interview with lawyer involved in *Baker*, 9 July 2002.

however, by choosing to engage with the *Baker* case directly in the Operations Memorandum, and through subsequent training workshops, both policy-makers and decision-makers have been able to participate in a frank dialogue with the Court regarding the scope and content of their discretionary authority. This kind of venue for exchanging knowledge and perspective is particularly important in settings where officials are charged with applying 'community' standards, as in the following case study relating to the determination of when material crossing the border is 'obscene'.

Customs seizure determinations: the definition of 'obscenity'

The Customs Act authorises customs officers to seize material that is obscene. While obscenity is not defined, the Act incorporates by reference the 'obscenity' provision in the Criminal Code – the proper interpretation of which was discussed at length by another Supreme Court decision, *R. v. Butler*.[69] The incorporation of the *Butler* standard in the customs manual – Memorandum D9-1-1 – constitutes a middle ground between the incorporation of case law in the 'spouse-in-the-house' in which there is no mention of the case, and the express memorandum on *Baker* in the setting of 'humanitarian and compassionate' grounds for decision-making.

Memorandum D9-1-1 included a section on 'Jurisprudence and Revenue Canada's interpretive policy for the administration of Tariff Item No. 9899.00.00 on goods deemed to be obscene under subsection 163(8) of the Criminal Code'. This section mentions no judicial decision by name. Rather, references to the findings of 'courts' are used to clarify the standard customs officials were to apply in exercising the 'obscenity' discretion. For example, the 'jurisprudence' section emphasises that, 'The Courts have found that certain material that Revenue Canada deals with is "more difficult to evaluate" . . . The officer must make a subjective assessment of whether, in the context of the whole work, the exploitation of sex is "undue" and further, whether the exploitation of sex is overcome by an artistic, literary, or other similar purpose.' This section also included a discussion of the different roles

---

[69] [1992] 1 SCR 452. In *Butler*, the Court adopted a 'harm' principle, by which material is deemed to be obscene if the dominant characteristic of the work is the undue exploitation of sex or the portrayal of sex in contexts of crime, horror, cruelty and violence.

that the courts and customs officials play in prohibiting obscenity, and highlights that officials must 'judge' each case on its merit and in its entirety. Elsewhere in the Memorandum, a more detailed list of particular acts and depictions which would meet the threshold of obscenity is presented, including graphic visual depictions.

The obscenity decision-making process was the setting for the Supreme Court's most significant ruling on the scope and significance of soft law, *Little Sisters Book and Art Emporium* v. *Canada (Minister of Justice)*.[70] Little Sisters is a bookshop in Vancouver specialising in lesbian and gay material, whose owners claimed that their Charter rights were violated by customs officers who targeted the bookstore for seizures of imported materials over a period of years. After a complex trial, the judge concluded not only that customs officials had wrongly delayed, confiscated, destroyed, damaged, prohibited or misclassified materials imported by the appellant on numerous occasions, but that these errors were caused 'by the systemic targeting of Little Sisters' importations in the [Vancouver] Customs Mail Centre'. The trial judge found that the Customs Act, to the extent it violated Charter rights, was a reasonable infringement and therefore saved under section 1 of the Charter, but that the exercise of this discretionary authority against the Little Sisters bookstore did violate both the equality (section 15) and freedom of expression (section 2(b)) guarantees. In other words, because the discretion created by the Customs Act was capable of being interpreted in a manner which complied with the Constitution, it was not the legislation but rather the administrative decision-making that was held to be responsible for the breach of the rights of the bookstore owners.

Binnie J, writing for the majority, characterised the administration of the Customs Act as 'oppressive',[71] and concluded that its effect – whether intended or not – was to isolate and disparage the appellants on the basis of their sexual orientation. Binnie J took note of the general bureaucratic culture as well. Officials were chosen to screen imported material for obscenity as a means of 'paying their dues' or as a form of informal punishment. The officials were overburdened and under-resourced which meant having too little time to judge the artistic merit

---

[70] [2000] 2 SCR 1120. For a broader discussion of the significance of *Little Sisters*, see L. Sossin, 'Discretion Unbound'. See also B. Ryder, 'Case Comment on Little Sisters' (2001) 39 *Osgoode Hall Law Journal* 207.

[71] *Little Sisters* [2000] 2 SCR 1120, para. 40.

of a work, and most often resulted in skipping to the allegedly obscene sections and comparing them to the examples of obscenity set out in the manual. The court recognised that a source of the targeting of Little Sisters lay in Memorandum D9-1-1. To take but one example, the Manual suggested that all acts of anal penetration violated the obscenity standard in direct contradiction to the standard set out in the previous *Butler* decision, and affirmed by directives from the Department of Justice.[72] Notwithstanding the evidence that customs officers followed the Manual in most if not all instances, Binnie J was unwilling to subject this non-legislative instrument to Charter scrutiny, in part because, as mentioned earlier, he took the position that Memorandum D9-1-1 was merely a 'guidebook'. On the relevance of the Manual, he concluded:

> The trial judge concluded that Customs' failure to make Memorandum D9-1-1 conform to the Justice Department opinion on the definition of obscenity violated the appellants' Charter rights. However, I agree with the British Columbia Court of Appeal that the trial judge put too much weight on the Memorandum, which was nothing more than an internal administrative aid to Customs inspectors. It was not law. It could never have been relied upon by Customs in court to defend a challenged prohibition. The failure of Customs to keep the document updated is deplorable public administration, because use of the defective guide led to erroneous decisions that imposed an unnecessary administrative burden and cost on importers and Customs officers alike. Where an importer could not have afforded to carry the fight to the courts a defective Memorandum D9-1-1 may have directly contributed to a denial of constitutional rights. *It is the statutory decision, however, not the manual, that constituted the denial.*[73]

The attempt to construct a watertight boundary between what constitutes deplorable public administration and what constitutes a denial of constitutional rights, is a complex and perhaps artificial exercise. Binnie J himself appeared to acknowledge this, observing elsewhere in his reasons that:

[72] Binnie J found that: 'The evidence established that for all practical purposes Memorandum D9-1-1, and especially the companion illustrated manual, governed Customs' view of obscenity. The Customs' view was occasionally intransigent. Reference has already been made to the opinion from the Department of Justice that depiction of anal intercourse was not as such obscene. That opinion was ignored for at least two years while imported materials depicting anal intercourse continued to be prohibited on the basis of the outdated D9-1-1 Memorandum.' *Ibid.*, para. 85.

[73] *Ibid.* (emphasis added).

The public service responds to ministerial direction with no less alacrity than it responds to statute or regulation. In short, an importer's rights may be protected in fact by statute, regulation, ministerial direction or even departmental practice. What is crucial, at the end of the day, is that Charter rights are in fact respected. The modalities for achieving that objective will vary with the context.[74]

Following the judgment in *Little Sisters*, Memorandum D9-1-1 was revised, and complaints regarding the discriminatory exercise of discretion under the 'obscenity' provision of the Customs Act have been substantially reduced.[75] These changes have come in two forms: first, some of the depictions of obscenity which were inconsistent with the judicial definition were removed or modified; and, secondly, the section of the Manual dealing with 'jurisprudence' was revised. While the Court was unwilling to subject the Memorandum itself to constitutional scrutiny, Binnie J observed that further litigation was always available as a means of ensuring that the administrative process improved. Such further litigation has now been launched by Little Sisters, after a series of comic books were stopped at the border on obscenity grounds.[76] It is thus too early to say whether the apparent improvement represents a temporary curtailment of enforcement in the wake of the Supreme Court's judgment, cosmetic revisions to the relevant guidelines to immunize them from further judicial criticism, or a more substantial change in the decision-making values of the customs agency. What the 'obscenity' setting reveals, however, is the fact that the judicial–executive dialogue on discretionary authority is rarely static. Cycles of litigation, policy development and administrative renewal overlap and become intertwined. Only a framework of analysis which sheds light on this dynamic set of institutional and individual relationships has the capacity to illuminate the impact of judicial decisions on bureaucratic action. It is to a preliminary sketch of such a framework that I now turn.

TOWARD A SOCIO-LEGAL APPROACH TO SOFT LAW

Socio-legal approaches to both judicial review and bureaucratic decision-making begin from the premise that neither judicial statements nor bureaucratic statements should be taken as self-evident or

---

[74] *Ibid.*, para. 138.   [75] See Ryder, 'Case Comment', n. 39.
[76] This information was provided by Joe Arvay, counsel for Little Sisters.

straightforward. The exercise of administrative discretion constitutes both a complex social process and a 'collective enterprise'[77] which neither a particular judicial decision nor a policy guideline can control. However, both judicial review and administrative policy provide a valuable measure of accountability for discretionary decision-making – in some cases, the only such measure – and for this reason merit deeper scrutiny. Judicial review presents an opportunity not only to prevent abuse but also to shed light on the proper scope and purpose of discretionary authority.[78] As the three case studies discussed above illustrate, soft law serves as a site of interpretation and contestation over the meaning of judicial review, and, by extension, as a forum for administrative bodies both to inform courts and to respond to them regarding the proper criteria for discretionary decision-making.

Prevailing wisdom holds that judicial review is not an effective means of changing bureaucratic action, and that its utility, if any, lies in focusing public attention on particularly oppressive or discriminatory decision-making settings.[79] However, it is worth observing that the reverse may sometimes be true as well – in certain discretionary settings, judicial review is welcomed as an easy crutch to avoid the difficult and sometimes unpopular work of policy-making. For example, the determination of eligibility for charitable status in Canada under the Income Tax Act is a highly discretionary process which invites policy-makers and decision-makers to craft a principled approach to defining the scope of what constitutes a 'charity'.[80] Rather than take up this challenge, officials have simply deferred to the courts, and, in so doing, have transformed judicially developed principles intended to guide administrative decision-making into rigid, legal

---

[77] This characterisation of administrative discretion is borrowed from Hawkins, 'The Uses of Legal Discretion', p. 27.

[78] For a broader discussion of the relationship between law and discretion in the Canadian context, see N. des Rosier and B. Feldthussen, 'Discretion in Social Assistance Legislation' (1992) 8 *Journal of Law and Social Policy* 204; L. Sossin, 'The Politics of Discretion: Toward a Critical Theory of Public Administration' (1992) 36 *Canadian Public Administration* 364.

[79] See P. Robson, 'Judicial Review and Social Security' in T. Buck (ed.), *Judicial Review and Social Welfare* (London, Pinter, 1998), p. 105; see also generally L. Bridges, G. Meszaros and M. Sunkin, *Judicial Review in Perspective* (London, Cavendish, 1995).

[80] For an analysis of administrative decision-making in this area, see L. Sossin, 'Regulating Virtue: A Purposive Approach to the Administration of Charities in Canada' in J. Phillips, B. Chapman and D. Stevens (eds.), *Charities: Between State and Market* (Kingston, Ont., McGill-Queen's Press, 2001), pp. 373–406.

requirements.[81] Neither indifference nor blind obedience to courts is likely to improve the quality and coherence of discretionary decision-making. But what role should courts play in the bureaucratic process?

On the one hand, it is important to highlight, as Peter Cane does in his contribution to this volume, that different legal and bureaucratic cultures approach the impact of judicial review in different ways.[82] Further, I share his caution that 'we need to take seriously the possibility that we may never know enough about the impact of judicial review to enable us to make properly informed, instrumentally based policy choices about the desirability of, or how best to design, judicial review institutions'.[83]

Not only is it difficult to agree on what we mean by the 'impact' of judicial review on bureaucratic decision-making, and more difficult still to assess it, but assuming we overcome these conceptual challenges, a further hurdle is encountered in ascertaining whether greater or lesser impact is *desirable*. I would suggest that, at least in the Canadian setting, notwithstanding chronic problems of delay, cost and access associated with litigation, judicial review continues to hold promise as a means of constructive influence on bureaucratic decision-making. By clarifying the criteria for the reasonable exercise of discretion, courts may serve as a catalyst, as in *Baker*, for reflection by policy-makers and decision-makers about the principles which ought to underlie the exercise of discretion. Further, by subjecting soft law and the decision-making process itself to scrutiny, as in the cases of *Falkiner* and *Little Sisters*, the court shines a spotlight on a corner of the bureaucratic process which too often is left in the shadows.

In terms of a conceptual framework to guide our understanding of the impact of judicial review, other contributors to this volume have addressed this question in greater depth. Maurice Sunkin, for example, organises a framework around three, discrete aspects of judicial review:

- the impact of the *process of judicial review litigation* (including the threat of litigation);
- the impact *of judgments* in particular cases or in a series of decisions; and
- the impact of the *principles or values* enshrined in judicial review.[84]

---

[81] Those standards are conveyed to decision-makers using yet another form of 'soft law' – a set of guidelines, contained as part of an 'Employees Handbook', which summarise the judicial case law in the field of charitable eligibility; discussed in *ibid.*

[82] See Chapter 1 above.   [83] *Ibid.*   [84] See Chapter 2 above.

Rather than focus on different aspects of review, I have approached the issue from a framework which seeks to distinguish between different *types* of judicial influence, different *methods* of judicial influence and, finally, different *degrees* of judicial influence.

Judicial review appears to influence bureaucratic decision-making in at least three ways. First, judicial review may serve in an individual dispute resolution role – a judicial order may uphold, modify or quash a particular administrative decision, and may apply directly to others in the same position. In this way, judicial review maps the boundaries of administrative discretion in individual cases or classes of cases. Secondly, judicial reasons may offer a new, changed or definitive interpretation of a legal standard which has broader implications for bureaucratic decision-making. Here, the reach of the judicial decision may extend far beyond the particular dispute. In this fashion, judicial review influences the direction of administrative policy. Finally, judicial review may also influence bureaucratic practices. Bureaucrats may attempt to avoid judicial review by complying with previously established judicial standards, even if this compliance is cosmetic and expressly intended to insulate discretionary decision-making from judicial accountability.

Classifying various kinds of influence, however, does not shed light on the method of the influence. Developing a framework for understanding *how* judicial review influences bureaucratic decision-making requires an examination of at least three sequential methods of judicial influence in the administrative process.[85] First, a policy decision is made as to whether any soft law instruments require revision in light of a particular case, and, if so, what the content and degree of the revision should be. While judicial review may be pursued with adversarial zeal by government lawyers, those same lawyers generally work to ensure bureaucratic compliance with judicial decisions.[86] Secondly, a further policy decision is made as to the form of the revision – whether the case itself is to be discussed as in the case of *Baker*, whether the jurisprudence is to be summarised more generally as in the obscenity context following *Little Sisters*, or whether the relevant guideline is to be revised

---

[85] This sequential – or serial – view of discretion builds on the approach to discretion which views each exercise of discretionary authority as part of a sequence of decisions occurring in a network of legal relationships. For discussion of this 'holistic' view, see Hawkins, 'The Uses of Legal Discretion', pp. 28–32.

[86] See A. Hammond, 'Judicial Review: the continuing interplay between law and policy' [1998] *Public Law* 34 at 40–1.

without mention of the case, as in the 'spouse-in-the-house' setting. Based on my interviews, this determination appears to be made most often on institutional and situational grounds – the consensus is that, due to bureaucratic inertia, revisions to guidelines tend to follow the same form as their predecessors. Finally, the third aspect of the administrative process which must be considered is the reception of policy change by front-line decision-makers. For example, in *Little Sisters*, the revisions to Memorandum D9-1-1 appear to have resulted in positive change in the context of front-line decision-making but it is not easy to figure out why. Changing social perceptions of gays and lesbians has played a role, as has improved training for customs officials, key revisions to Memorandum D9-1-1, and the strategic desire to avoid embarrassment and internal criticism by virtue of further litigation.

While it is difficult to reach any conclusion regarding the degree of judicial impact,[87] which may turn on the perspectives of individual decision-makers across diverse settings, the case studies I have analysed suggest that front-line discretion is influenced in a significant fashion by judicial decision-making, but often not as quickly, as comprehensively or as coherently as litigants and the courts would wish (and sometimes with unintended consequences which may turn out to be more pernicious than the original mischief which the court intervened to remedy).[88]

Discretion spans the divide between law and policy. Based on these brief case studies, I argue that soft law has significant potential to serve as a conduit for judicial–executive dialogue concerning the nature and scope of discretionary authority. To fulfil this potential, however, the form and content of the soft law must reflect an authentic attempt

---

[87] Bradley Canon suggests four degrees of response: (1) defiant non-compliance; (2) evasion or avoidance; (3) cosmetic acceptance; and (4) full compliance. See Chapter 3 above.

[88] To take but one example, the attempt to reign in discretionary authority in the context of social welfare in the 1960s (in order to counter the arbitrary and discriminatory standards used to determine eligibility), brought about in large measure as a response to vigorous 'welfare rights' litigation and new judicially crafted procedural standards, contributed to a 'clericalisation' of the welfare bureaucracy and a sharp increase in complexity and delays in processing applications. On this phenomenon, see W. Simon, 'Legality, Bureaucracy and Class in the Welfare System' (1983) 92 *Yale Law Journal* 1198; and J. Handler, 'Dependent People, the State and the Modern/Postmodern Search for the Dialogic Community' (1988) 35 *UCLA Law Review* 999.

to engage with the judicial reasons and rulings.[89] This requires that policy-makers and decision-makers be explicit and transparent regarding their interpretation of judicial standards, and that courts be explicit and transparent regarding the basis for and extent of their deference to the expertise of policy-makers and decision-makers. While it may be impossible fully to measure bureaucratic compliance with judicial standards, it is in my view desirable that the process of complying with those standards be as open as possible, and capable of justification on normative as well as pragmatic grounds.[90]

Soft law should be understood as a site for this exchange of executive and judicial perspectives to take place. It is also, of course, a site of tension and conflict – where the delicate and shifting balance between rules and discretion is played out, and the tenuous institutional relationship between front-line decision-makers, policy-makers and courts most visibly takes shape. The key to better understanding the impact of judicial decisions on bureaucratic discretion, I have suggested, lies in better understanding the politics of soft law.

---

[89] An authentic attempt to engage implies more than simply citing or paying lip-service to a decision. For a discussion of 'authenticity' in the context of bureaucratic discourse, see J. Vining, *The Authoritative and the Authoritarian* (Chicago, University of Chicago, 1986). For Vining, 'a statement or document is "authentic"' when it can be taken seriously. If a statement is to be taken seriously the author of it must mean what he says. He must be speaking in what we call good faith and not thinking only of the reaction to what he says. He must not deliberately mean two incompatible things, be deliberately ambiguous with the intention of choosing later, after the reaction, the meaning best for his interests and treating that as if he had meant it all along' (*ibid.*, p. 42). This is a theme also pursued in slightly different terms in J. Mashaw, *Due Process in the Administrative State* (New Haven, CT, Yale University Press, 1985), pp. 87–93.

[90] This procedural emphasis is consistent with a broader movement in Canadian administrative law, and beyond, towards transparency in discretionary decision-making. A significant watershed in this regard was the Supreme Court's decision in *Baker*, discussed above, which recognised a common law duty for discretionary decision-makers to provide written reasons. For a discussion of this 'culture of justification', see D. Dyzenhaus, M. Hunt and M. Taggart, 'The Principle of Legality in Administrative Law: Internationalization as Constitutionalization' (2001) 1 *Oxford University Commonwealth Law Journal* 5.

CHAPTER SIX

THE OPERATION OF JUDICIAL REVIEW IN AUSTRALIA

ROBIN CREYKE AND JOHN McMILLAN*

JUDICIAL REVIEW IN AUSTRALIA

The fabric to create an administrative law system was part of the invisible baggage brought by the first settlers to the Australian colonies after 1788. The first legal step taken to establish a colony – Governor Phillip's Proclamation at Sydney Cove – can, with contemporary eyes, be classified as an executive instrument, a species of subordinate legislation. Judicial review of government action, another mainstay of administrative law, was also an activity engaged in early by the fledgling court system. In an early public law case in 1825, the Chief Justice of the colony of New South Wales, Sir Francis Forbes, in a case brought by emancipated convicts against court officers who had failed to empanel them in jury lists, ruled that:

> every court has of necessity a power to compel [the executive] to execute its process. This is a power necessarily incidental to the creation of courts.[1]

When the British colonies were reconstituted at the turn of the twentieth century to form the new nation of Australia, the Constitution

---

* The statistical material and empirical data included in this chapter first appeared in a related article, R. Creyke and J. McMillan, 'Judicial Review Outcomes – An Empirical Study' (2004) 11 *Australian Journal of Administrative Law* 82 at 83–6 and 97–9.

[1] *R. v. Wentworth, Campbell and Dunn* (1825), http://www.law.mq.edu.au/scnsw (27 October 2000).

they adopted included a unique constitutional guarantee, section 75(v), which conferred upon the High Court of Australia a jurisdiction to grant three administrative law remedies to restrain federal agencies and officials from exceeding the limits of their power. While the practical significance of that guarantee has since been overshadowed by the comprehensive administrative law framework established by the legislature, the constitutional and common law foundation for administrative law retains its importance. The effectiveness of the judicial role is underscored by the additional function discharged by Australian courts, of scrutinising the constitutional validity of legislation – a role not shared in all countries by common law courts exercising judicial review.[2]

Administrative law in Australia nowadays rests principally on a statutory basis. Progressively since 1975, the Australian Parliament has created one of the most comprehensive systems of administrative law in the world.[3] The major elements of the system are the Federal Court, which undertakes judicial review of executive action under the Administrative Decisions (Judicial Review) Act 1977 (Cth); administrative tribunals undertaking merit review, such as the Commonwealth Administrative Appeals Tribunal, the Migration Review Tribunal, the Social Security Appeals Tribunal and the National Native Title Tribunal;[4] the Commonwealth Ombudsman; the Human Rights and Equal Opportunity Commission, and individual Sex, Race and Disability Discrimination Commissioners; and a system of open government, grounded in the Freedom of Information Act 1982 (Cth) and the Privacy Act 1988 (Cth). A right to a written statement of the reasons for a decision was granted to those eligible to bring a judicial review action[5] or an application for merits review.[6] These changes have been followed in many of the Australian states and, even broader, have attracted international attention and emulation.

---

[2] Cf. the position in the United Kingdom (see Chapter 4 above).

[3] The Australian system was established primarily upon the recommendation of four reports to government, that are analysed in R. Creyke and J. McMillan (eds.), *The Kerr Vision of Australian Administrative Law – At the Twenty-Five Year Mark* (Canberra, ANU Centre for International and Public Law, 1998) (see law.anu.edu.au/aial/publications). The major report of the four was the *Report of the Commonwealth Administrative Review Committee* (1977) (Kerr Committee Report).

[4] For constitutional reasons, Australian courts exercising federal judicial power are precluded from undertaking merit review of administrative decisions (see Chapter 1 above).

[5] Administrative Decisions (Judicial Review) Act 1977 (Cth), section 13.

[6] E.g., Administrative Appeals Tribunal Act 1975 (Cth), section 28.

THE JUDICIAL REVIEW PROJECT

A central aim of administrative law – to ensure that government acts lawfully – depends ultimately for its realisation on the effectiveness of the system for judicial review of administrative action. The process commences with an aggrieved person challenging a decision in an independent forum. If the action is successful, the matter will usually be remitted to an agency to implement the court ruling, often by reconsidering the earlier decision. Whether the court's ruling is respected, and whether more broadly there is any normative change in government administration, are matters that lie beyond the courtroom and, to all intents and purposes, out of the public eye.

The effectiveness of judicial review rests in part on a blend of faith and assumption – matters that had not been put to the test in any concerted way in Australia[7] or, indeed, elsewhere.[8] It is ironic that this aspect of administrative justice should be so little studied. Most legal systems have an elaborate and sophisticated structure defining how a person goes about challenging a decision and obtaining an order, but no follow-up mechanism to assess how effectively the review system operates. There is usually no published record (certainly no published series) to which one can turn to find the ultimate outcome in the dispute between citizen and government. There is no statutory procedure

---

[7] An Australian government research body, the Administrative Review Council, had commenced but abandoned two studies, a cost–benefit analysis of administrative law, and a study of the impact on agencies of judicial review: see, respectively, Administrative Review Council, *Ninth Annual Report 1984–85*, para. 38; and *Sixteenth Annual Report 1990–91*, para. 29.

[8] There is some overlap between our study and other foreign studies, but they nevertheless cover different ground: e.g., L. Bridges, G. Meszaros and M. Sunkin, *Judicial Review in Perspective* (2nd edn, London, Cavendish Publishing, 1995); S. Halliday, 'The Influence of Judicial Review on Bureaucratic Decision-Making' [2000] *Public Law* 110; G. Richardson and D. Machin, 'Judicial Review and Tribunal Decision Making: A Study of the Mental Health Review Tribunal' [2000] *Public Law* 494; B. Hadfield and E. Weaver, 'Trends in Judicial Review in Northern Ireland' [1993] *Public Law* 12; and T. Mullen, K. Pick and T. Prosser, *Judicial Review in Scotland* (Chichester, John Wiley and Sons, 1996), p. 110 at p. 132. For United States studies, see P. H. Schuck and E. D. Elliott, 'To the Chevron Station: An Empirical Study of Federal Administrative Law' [1990] *Duke Law Journal* 984; M. Shapiro, *Who Guards the Guardians? Judicial Control of Administration* (Athens, GA, University of Georgia Press, 1988); R. O'Leary, 'The Impact of Federal Court Decisions on the Policies and Administration of the US Environmental Protection Agency' (1989) 41 *Administrative Law Review* 569.

for agency reporting of what occurs following the court decision. Nor does any official have the function of monitoring the outcome of a court decision to ensure it is implemented as between the particular parties, or that its principles are applied in other, similar cases considered by the agency.

This dearth of knowledge about the impact of judicial review is an obvious ground for criticism. There are public expectations that the review system will deliver justice, just as there are government expectations that the system will be efficient and cost-effective. Justification for the system needs to rise above the level of anecdotal history. For these reasons the authors, together with Emeritus Professor Dennis Pearce, obtained a grant from the Australian Research Council to study the eventual outcome for those who were successful in a judicial review action.[9]

This paper reports the findings of that study, in the process shedding some light[10] on the extent to which judicial review achieves its core objectives, of yielding a positive outcome for the individual, and 'addressing systemic bureaucratic failings'.[11] The findings are a mixture of statistics that record the survey responses from applicants and agencies, and commentary provided by the survey participants. A brief description is given also of the research methodology, and the profile of cases covered by the study. The article concludes with the authors' personal reflection on the empirical data.

METHODOLOGY

The objective of the project was to track the administrative history of all decisions of the Federal Court of Australia, over a ten-year period, in which the Court had made a decision favourable to the plaintiff, that is, a decision setting aside a government agency decision. No comparable

---

[9] With additional funding support from the Council, we also conducted a follow-up study into the attitudes held by government officials concerning the impact of court and tribunal rulings on government administration: see R. Creyke and J. McMillan, 'Executive Perceptions of Administrative Law – An Empirical Study' (2002) 9 *Australian Journal of Administrative Law* 163.

[10] The findings go some way towards refuting the suggestion by Peter Cane (see Chapter 1 above) that it may not be possible to obtain sufficient information about the impact of judicial review 'to enable us to make properly informed, instrumentally based policy choices about the desirability of, or how best to design, judicial review institutions'.

[11] See Chapter 1 above.

study had been undertaken in Australia. Two hypotheses were being tested: first, whether court rulings that set aside administrative decisions and (in the normal case) require those decisions to be reconsidered are respected by agencies; and, secondly, whether the eventual outcome in individual cases is favourable to applicants, or is instead no different, either because an agency has remade the same decision or because of some other intervening act, such as legislative change. In short, the core purpose was to test whether judicial review is beneficial for those who utilise it, or whether instead it is ultimately a fruitless and unsuccessful enterprise. If the latter is the case, deeper questions arise concerning both the attitude of government agencies and the underlying premise of judicial review itself.

Consistently with the purpose of the research project, the only decisions being examined were those in which a ruling favourable to the applicant had been made. An added feature of this group of cases is that they were more likely to be those with precedential value for public administration. The study did not include decisions that were favourable to an applicant as a result of a settlement or consent order; the difficulty of identifying and tracing those cases was the main reason. Many, for example, are subject to a confidentiality order.

Boundaries of the study

The cases in the study were those decided by the Federal Court in the ten-year period 1984–94. That lengthy period was chosen so as to obtain a reasonable sample of cases. A feature of this period was that the simplified system of judicial review introduced by the Administrative Decisions (Judicial Review) Act 1977 (Cth) (the 'ADJR Act') had commenced shortly before (in October 1980). Prior to that Act commencing operation, there had been a paucity of judicial review cases in Australian courts.[12]

The initial sample of cases involved 4,159 entries in the Federal Court database, many of which were interim procedural rulings by the Court, sometimes in cases that were later settled or abandoned. Filtering of the entries identified 714 cases that went to a final hearing. In 292

---

[12] Lindsay Curtis noted that the index of the *Commonwealth Law Reports* for the period 1960–75 reveals only 'seventeen reported cases (other than industrial relations matters) which can be classified as administrative review cases', and that a similar outcome applied in most states: L.Curtis, 'The Vision Splendid: A Time for Re-appraisal' in Creyke and McMillan, *The Kerr Vision*, pp. 39–40.

(40.9 per cent) of those cases, the Court made a ruling setting aside the decision under review, sometimes by consent of the parties. The most usual order (in 74 per cent of cases) was a remittal of the case to the decision-maker for reconsideration; the decisions made in other cases included declarations on a point of law, orders quashing a decision, the grant of an extension of time, or a direction that a statement of reasons be provided. Some of the cases in the study were the subject of an unsuccessful appeal[13] by the government agency – forty-three cases appealed to the Full Federal Court, and four to the High Court.

Information about the cases in the survey was elicited in two ways. First, the subsequent administrative history of each of the 292 cases was traced, principally by a questionnaire and interviews administered to the solicitors and government officials involved. Next, each court judgment was analysed against a template designed to pick up key elements of the judgment, and to record the information in a form that was entered into a specially designed database constructed to allow manipulation of the data by reference to some of the main variables in judicial review cases. Not all of the 292 cases could be included in this part of the survey, as not all judgments were accessible; some judgments from this period were not published on the web, and no single court registry or library had an archive of all unreported judgments.

Contacting agencies and solicitors

The most ambitious element of the project was to contact, for each of nearly 300 cases, the legal representatives for the individual applicant and the agency – close to 600 overall. Once the solicitor and official involved in each case were identified, a questionnaire was sent to the named individual asking:

1. Was the application reconsidered in accordance with the order of the Court?
2. If so, what was the final outcome?
3. Was there any change in the law or in the agency's practice of which you are aware that flowed from this decision?
4. Are there any other aspects of the case that are relevant to our project?

---

[13] Decisions that were reversed on appeal were not included in the 292 cases in the study.

Many of the solicitors and agencies were also contacted by telephone either to elicit or to clarify a response. The information obtained was entered into the database. Contacting the solicitor and the agency enabled us to check the accuracy of the data, particularly as to the final outcome (questions 1 and 2), and to seek answers to questions 3 and 4 which focused on whether the decision had broader implications for the agency, administrative law, or agency practice.

Practical barriers to research

We expected difficulty in obtaining information from applicants, but perhaps not as great as occurred. Some cases had been concluded more than ten years previously, and details of subsequent action were sketchy; busy solicitors did not always regard it as a high priority to allocate time to assist a university research project; secretaries would screen out calls; solicitors claimed legal professional privilege; and some solicitors had changed firms, moved interstate, retired, taken leave and, at the extreme, died. A reply was nevertheless received from applicants in over 80 per cent of cases and a substantive response was given in nearly two-thirds of cases (Table 6.1).

Government agencies gave valuable assistance to the project, but were either unable or reluctant for workload reasons to trace the history of all cases in the survey. A common problem noted by agencies was that file management problems made it difficult to trace the subsequent history of a case: the reasons included that the file could not be located; officers with corporate knowledge of the system had moved on; or the title of the case or name of the plaintiff was not a reliable pointer to the file recording the subsequent agency action. An added difficulty in some agencies, particularly those with a large national operation, was that implementation of a court order may not have been handled by a central legal section, but at the decision-making (often regional and sometimes overseas) level. One agency frankly noted that its files in the matter were 'in complete disarray'. Midway through the project we thought it pragmatic not to press agencies for a response in those cases where an applicant response had been received. Overall, we received a substantive response to the survey questions from agencies in roughly one-third of cases (but an acknowledgment reply in a greater number): see Table 6.1.

In the final tally, we received a reply from either the applicant, the agency, or both, in all but fourteen (5 per cent) of the 292 cases in the survey; in a further twenty-one (7 per cent) the reply was not

Table 6.1 *Responses to survey questions from applicants and agencies*

	Yes %	No %	Other %	No. of responses received
1. Did agency reconsider the application?				
• Applicants	74.8	5.0	20.2	242 cases
• Agencies	80.1	2.5	17.4	121 cases
2. Was the outcome in favour of the applicant?				
• Applicants	58.3	16.7	25.0	240 cases
• Agencies	60.0	15.0	25.0	120 cases
3. Any change in the law or agency practice?				
• Applicants	26.2	48.9	24.0	233 cases
• Agencies	46.1	40.4	13.5	89 cases
4. Any other aspects relevant to this project?				
• Applicants				146 cases
• Agencies				44 cases

substantively helpful, usually because details were unknown or a claim of legal professional privilege was made. In summary, the survey yielded a sizeable volume of data covering a substantive period. Immigration cases represented the largest number of cases sampled in the study (just over 50 per cent : see Table 6.2).

The applicant and agency response were mostly for different cases, and this difference in the sample has to be borne in mind in evaluating the responses. There were roughly thirty cases in which a response was received from both parties. The responses in those cases were generally consistent, save that the precedential importance of a decision was sometimes viewed differently.

STATISTICAL ANALYSIS

The statistical information containing the core findings of the project is contained in Table 6.1. The table covers only those cases for which a response was received. As the figures indicate, in a few cases a response was received for one question but not another.

The category 'other' refers to cases for which a response was received, but the response was not illuminating in a substantive way. This was usually for one of three reasons: the solicitor claimed legal professional privilege in roughly 20 per cent of these cases; the solicitor did not have the information to answer the question in another 40 per cent; and in many of the remaining cases the issue in dispute or the order of the court was such that 'reconsideration' by the agency was not the appropriate way to implement what the court ordered. In a few cases, the issue in dispute was still under consideration by a government agency.

For Questions 1 and 2 – the key questions – the applicant and agency responses were very similar. In answer to Question 1, 80.1 per cent of agencies (compared to 74.8 per cent of applicants) claimed that the decision was reconsidered in accordance with the court order. In answer to Question 2, 60 per cent of agencies (compared to 58.3 per cent of applicants) claimed that agency reconsideration of the decision delivered an outcome favourable to the plaintiff. The other side of that coin – an outcome that did not favour the applicant – also yielded a similar response: 15 per cent for agencies, and 16.7 per cent for applicants. This degree of consistency reinforces the research findings.

Putting the 'other' category to one side, the response to Question 1 indicates that the administrative decision under review was reconsidered by an agency in accordance with the court order in nearly every instance. The small percentage of cases (5 per cent) where this did not occur were mostly ones in which the applicant's circumstances overtook the court decision, making reconsideration either inappropriate or pointless (for example, the applicant moved employment). In only two cases (a health and an immigration case) did the applicant allege that the agency undermined the court decision by using other statutory powers to achieve the disputed objective – causing the solicitor for one applicant to claim that the agency 'ignored the effects of the Federal Court decision [and] thumbed its nose at the Court'.

Overall, therefore, the picture that emerges is a positive one: agencies generally do comply with a court order and reconsider a matter, notwithstanding that there is no formal mechanism (other than a fresh court application by the applicant) to ensure that the order is carried into effect. This may not seem surprising to those who would expect no less of a government agency: nonetheless, to have it confirmed that the rule of law is being respected is an important finding in its own right.

Question 2 was the more significant in terms of the objectives of this study. Significantly, over half of applicants (58.3 per cent) confirmed that the outcome, after agency reconsideration, was favourable.[14] The figure, in fact, was almost certainly higher, since it seems sensible to assume that there would have been a similar pattern of resolution in the 'other' category of cases (mostly being cases in which a reconsideration had not been finalised or the solicitor declined to answer on grounds of legal professional privilege). Assuming a similar pattern in those cases, possibly as high as 78 per cent of cases would, in the applicants' view, have been resolved favourably.

There was a noticeable but explainable difference in the responses to Question 3. While agencies noted a change to the law or agency practice in a far higher proportion of cases (46.1 per cent, compared to 26.2 per cent for applicants), the base figure was different (89 cases for agencies, and 233 cases for applicants). The question also referred to changes 'of which you are aware' – suggesting that the figure would be lower for applicants, a point confirmed by the higher agency response. Yet in some instances there was also a clash of opinion: an agency indicated that a change in practice had eventuated, whereas the applicant's comments suggested that the agency was intransigent and unmoved by the legal proceedings. Comments that elaborate that disparity are given below. For the moment, however, the noteworthy point is that, in close to one-third of judicial review cases in this study, one or other of the parties were of the view that, in one way or another, the decision caused a subsequent change to the law or agency practice. It was more common, by a factor of nearly 2:1, for the impact of the decision to relate to agency practice rather than the law.

In answer to Question 4, over half of the applicants (58.3 per cent), and nearly as many agencies (48.9 per cent), responded by providing comments on other aspects of the case that were considered relevant to our project. (The responses to questions 3 and 4 are combined in this paper.)

---

[14] The percentage of applicants who were ultimately successful exceeds those in Bridges, Meszaros and Sunkin, *Judicial Review*, p. 127, which found that on average only 47 per cent of judicial review applications were successful. In the US, the Schuck and Elliott study, 'To the Chevron Station', found an ultimate success rate of around 40 per cent. The Mullen, Pick and Prosser project (*Judicial Review*, pp. 124 and 130) on judicial review applications of decisions by Scottish local authorities in relation to emergency housing were comparable to our figures, with applicants achieving some measure of success in 75 per cent of cases (fifteen of twenty petitions), but the size of the sample was limited.

COMMENTARY[15]

General observations

As indicated by the statistics, written comments were received from applicants and agencies in roughly two-thirds of the 292 survey cases. That in itself illustrates the helpful endeavour of many respondents to put the outcome of a case in context. In some instances, the dominant feature of that context was the respondents' sharp reaction (both positive and negative) to the lessons learnt from judicial review about the way government and the legal process work. At other times, the context was the broader complexity of a dispute, and the difficulty of drawing a simple cause–effect relationship between a case and an outcome.

In the one-third or so of cases in which a written comment was not provided, the respondent often explained that there was a difficulty in doing so. Legal professional privilege was one such difficulty. Settlement of a dispute on confidential terms was another. Staff changes also affected the capacity of many agencies to offer incisive comment. And generally, as noted earlier, agencies experienced some difficulty in locating the file that would record the subsequent history of the case.

As those points indicate, nothing turns on the proportion of respondents who commented on individual questions. However, to augment the statistical flavour of this report, we can say that, on Question 1, written comments were provided by applicants in roughly 58 cases and agencies on 35; on Question 2, by applicants on roughly 185 cases and agencies on 98; on Question 3, on 119 and 56 cases respectively; and, on Question 4, on 148 and 45 cases respectively. Overall, therefore, in the bulk of cases some commentary was received and the following selection is necessarily selective.

The final introductory point to note is that we have usually not cited the author of a comment, though sometimes it is clear to which agency a comment relates. Partly the reason is that the respondents to the survey were promised confidentiality as regards the identification of individual cases. Furthermore, our central objective was to provide a whole-of-government picture on the operation of judicial review, not to sensationalise the performance of any particular agency.

---

[15] In some instances (indicated by a square bracket), we have inserted the name of an agency to provide the context for a remark. Generally, we have not indicated the amendment of a comment if the change was merely to capitalisation, spelling out an abbreviation, or such like.

Question 1: whether the application was reconsidered in accordance with the court order

Some applicants took the opportunity to express their appreciation of an agency's approach to reconsideration. Typical comments were: 'the agency was being reasonable and considering fresh evidence'; 'reconsidered quickly; was surprised at the cooperation received'; and the agency agreed of its 'own volition' that the decision had been wrong.

Not all comments, however, were so appreciative, and a number of applicants were critical of an agency's behaviour. A common complaint was that the agency took too long to reconsider the decision, and did so in some instances only after the applicant threatened further legal action. Of one department it was said:

> The respondent . . . endeavoured to ignore the effects of the Federal Court decision and to ensure that the practice of the department in such cases continually avoided the Federal Court's determination in order to pursue their policy which the Court had found to be inconsistent with the legislation.

And, of another:

> Yes eventually. Took a long time, threatened to go back to the Federal Court and eventually after several threats . . . and going to the Attorney-General to seek contempt orders got a proper reconsideration.

The commentary by agencies on this question was routine, to the effect that the agency complied with the court order. In a few cases the agency acknowledged that in reconsidering the case it had to apply a different legal test than hitherto, or that the facts had to be assembled and evaluated afresh in light of the court's ruling. The only additional colour came from one comment, that the agency disagreed with the legal ruling of the court, but decided that in light of the facts the agency would be unlikely to succeed on appeal.

Question 2: the final outcome in the case

We noted earlier that the eventual outcome for applicants was favourable in a majority of instances, possibly as high as 78 per cent. That meant, to give some examples, that deportation action was abandoned, a tax or customs payment recalculated, a regulatory code rewritten, a disciplinary inquiry terminated, an appeal panel reconstituted, or a search warrant not executed.

In some cases, the cause–effect relationship was direct and attributable to the judicial review action. In other cases, the factual context was more complex and the favourable decision rested as much or more on other legal or factual considerations that post-dated the court's decision (a common example being the grant of residency status following upon a subsequent change in either the law or the situation of the applicant). Even in those cases, however, it can at least be said that the judicial review action erased an adverse decision and cleared the way for a favourable outcome.

Applicant responses

Applicants who were positive about the process were usually those whose cases had been resolved through a negotiated settlement either during the hearing or after the court's decision. Comments included: 'the applicant got a payout and left the agency; negotiations amicably resolved the situation'; 'they realised they had made an error in their original decision-making'; and 'the applicant appealed which was then settled favourably for him; there were significant sums of money involved and the applicant was satisfied with the settlement'. In at least one instance the applicant accepted that the initial decision had been the result of a one-off error, stating that 'the original decision was manifestly flawed and an aberration and unlikely to happen again'.

The majority of applicants were critical of the relevant agency and in some cases of the administrative reconsideration process generally. Some stated that the favourable decision only occurred because the court left the agency with no choice. As one applicant commented: 'the court made a declaration which was binding; the fact that the agency complied is no indication that they were being "good"'.

A frequent complaint was the length of time taken to get a result, both initially from the review body and then from the agency following the review. The comments included: 'has been a very slow process'; 'went into a black hole and six years later still deciding'; and 'getting money out of the department was a struggle; from the date of judgment it took two years to get the money and even then it came in instalments'. The impact of delay on the applicant is indicated by instances in which the outcome was negated, for example, by the fact that the applicant had left the country by the time the reconsideration occurred; or because a licence had expired before judgment was delivered. In one licensing case, the applicant claimed the agency deliberately delayed the hearing so that 'by the time the case went ahead the time in which to transfer the licence had expired and the original transferor could not apply'. The expiration of time was also a factor in personnel employment cases, in several of which the applicants had, by the time of the court decision, left the employment in which the dispute originated. But perhaps the most poignant example of a pyrrhic victory was one in which the animals the subject of a quarantine order had already been destroyed by the time the court set aside the quarantine order.

Many applicants complained about the difficulty of obtaining reconsideration by the agency. One observed: 'It seemed the application had been put in a vacuum once the Federal Court remitted it. The applicant was required to send lots of letters and make many phone calls. During this time there was a high turnover of staff and this case fell into the "too hard basket".' In two immigration cases, the applicants stated that the agency was still considering the decisions four and six years respectively after the court order. But in at least one other case this delay worked in an applicant's favour, as 'by the time the application went back a new special [visa] category had been introduced and then the applicant applied via that and was approved'.

In a few instances additional court or tribunal hearings were required to enforce the initial court order. Comments included: 'they went to court a second time for compensation which was later negotiated; it took a long time'; 'the applicant eventually won after going back to court three times'; 'ended up going back to court to determine whether the agency had to pay interest on the amount owing'.

Other applicants complained that the agency was deliberately obstructionist after the court decision. Comments included: 'the agency made life very difficult for the applicant'; 'the agency refused the relevant certificates and refused to make the decisions; they changed their arguments in an attempt to override the court's determination'; and 'the Minister declined the visa relying on different grounds'. In one instance the applicant claimed that the agency 'was very difficult and did not apply the law properly in the majority of cases; they mostly applied their own usual practice to any decision'. A few applicants referred to the difficulties that arose if an agency resorted to other statutory procedures to circumvent a court decision, with one complaining that 'the department did precisely what it had done before'.

Faced with these problems, in two cases applicants resorted to the media as a more effective means than the court process of obtaining the outcome they sought. In one such instance, press reports led to the relevant Minister agreeing to review the decision, while in the other the applicant claimed that only the threat of going to the media resulted in the agency finally complying with the determination of the Federal Court.

Agency responses

For the most part, the agency comments were along the lines that a case was reconsidered on its merits as required by the court, sometimes resulting in the same decision as before, at other times resulting in a different and favourable outcome for the applicant. The added complexity of the dispute by the time of reconsideration was noted in a few instances. This was sometimes given as a reason why the outcome was favourable for the applicant: for example, a proposal to revoke a doctor's certificate was abandoned 'due to perceived administrative difficulties and the cost involved in establishing a committee with special expertise to properly reconsider the matter'.

Agencies were sometimes sceptical about a link being drawn between an applicant's success in the judicial review application, and a subsequent positive outcome for the applicant. One agency stated that the applicant got what he wanted 'but not necessarily as a result of the judicial review action'; and another that the 'judicial review action was entirely peripheral to the substantive issue'. There were also cases where the agency considered that the applicant had had a technical win, but without any meaningful benefit, for example enforcing a right to an adequate statement of reasons. In another case, the law had been changed in the interim by a differently constituted court, and the new ruling was applied on reconsideration to the detriment of the applicant.

Perhaps the most complex of the cases was one in which a decision that invalidated a schedule of benefit entitlements was construed by the agency as having a similarly invalidating effect on some earlier schedules, thus reviving a much older schedule. Benefit payments totalling millions of dollars had been paid under items introduced by the invalid schedules, though the agency decided that 'recovery of this technical overpayment would not be practicable'.

In a few instances, subsequent litigation between the parties went against the applicant. Sometimes the later case involved a challenge to the decision made by the agency after reconsideration of the decision. On the other hand, in one instance the agency said that it conceded during further litigation because it would have been embarrassing had the case been listed for hearing.

In a significant proportion of cases, the agency stated that it either did not have or could not find records that adequately substantiated the final outcome. A common reason, particularly in immigration cases, was that the file had been remitted to the decision-making area following the court's decision. The similarity of the names of many litigants added to the difficulty. Equally, in a customs case it was not possible to trace which claimants benefited from the making of a new tariff concession order.

Questions 3 and 4: subsequent change in law or agency practice; and other relevant aspects of the case

It was earlier noted, in the statistical overview, that agencies and applicants reported a subsequent change to the law or agency practice in roughly one-quarter of the 292 cases covered by this study. The general pattern that emerges is that administrative law litigation often has an impact on law and government that extends far beyond the circumstances of the individual case. Sometimes the change is general and administrative in nature – for example, the instigation of specialist training for decision-makers, or of revised instructions on how the law is to be applied and decisions are to be made. In other instances, the change may be more specific, yet hold implications for numerous other decisions to be made thereafter (for example, legislative amendment of a specific statutory provision, or administrative amendment of a policy manual). Our study also turned up many examples of change that was momentous in scale, such as the complete restructuring of a legislative scheme, or the revamping of tender procedures. There are also comments from both applicants and agencies on the impact of judicial review generally.

That positive summation of the findings was contradicted by other comments that are reported below. Some of the applicant comments were severely critical of agencies, claiming that the agency was intransigent to change or failed to draw an obvious lesson from the court proceedings. Likewise, some agencies described a different context for change, observing that the agency's conviction that it had acted properly had not been shaken, even if the court outcome suggested otherwise.

Agency responses
We start by providing a selection of the agency comments that illustrate a major reconsideration of agency policy or practice:

Following the decision an inquiry was held into the procedures followed. This resulted in revamping of tender procedures [for broadcasting licences], new procedures for seeking legal advice on proposed decisions from the department's lawyers and a restructuring of the department's legal section.

Several of the cases led to a revised construction of the agency's guidelines with significant consequences for the operation of pharmacies.

The decision in this case – that the government has a duty to provide [quarantine] inspectors – has affected the agency's operations. The agency is now also promoting a system of inspection where such staff are actually employed by [those being regulated] as part of a quality assurance arrangement.

There was extensive discussions and training provided to [customs] decision-makers to facilitate compliance with the law as stated by the court.

[Led to the introduction of] seminars where staff present their views about what happened, why they lost/won and how to deal with the situation in the future.

Had potentially far-reaching effects on the administration of Australian's migrant selection procedures overseas.

Fish are now regulated under a different set of Orders as a result of changing legislative policies and new ways of conducting food inspection.

Internal guidelines were prepared and issued to Australian Taxation Office officers explaining the operation of the 'reasonable expectation' principle as enunciated in the case, and its impact on dealings between staff and taxpayers.

Similar examples were given of far-reaching legislative amendment, for example, to the tariff concession system, to the definition of 'subsidies' under the General Agreement on Tariffs and Trade (GATT), and to workplace health and safety standards. In many instances, agencies referred to changes made to policy manuals and ministerial guidelines. Among other specific changes were the expansion in membership of a health advisory committee, and the issue of a circular on the contents of statements of reasons. In a few instances, agencies noted that the proceeding was regarded as a test case and the court's ruling was thereafter applied in similar disputes: for example, after one such case a grant was provided to other applicants in the same position.

Another recurring mention was of modification in the style of decision-making in the agency. Specific mention was made in at least five cases of the impact that a natural justice ruling of a court had on agency practice, for example, leading to all referees being contacted thereafter, to referee reports being provided to applicants, and to visa applicants being granted a hearing prior to an adverse decision. Other observations about changed decision-making included: 'discretion must be exercised according to reason and justice and not arbitrarily'; 'relevant decision-makers are aware of the outcome of this case and take decisions accordingly'; and 'the authority took a far less restrictive approach to the construction and application of guidelines'.

One common theme was that agencies view judicial review positively, as providing a means for resolving legal ambiguity or differences of view within external review bodies, particularly tribunals. One agency, among many, commented that it 'tends to pursue actions before the court when it is seeking to use the court as arbiter in disputed areas and needs a strong precedent to guide it'.

Those comments are to be contrasted with other cases in which the agency did not perceive any need for change, despite its decision being overturned. The usual reason was that the decision was regarded as aberrant or unusual, turning on its 'particular facts and circumstances'. Another reason was that the issue under challenge had not arisen before and was unlikely to arise again, or there had simply been a mistake in the agency decision-making process. An interesting variation of that theme were instances in which the agency indicated, if somewhat obliquely, that the decision was flawed solely because of the officers in charge of the case, not because of any inherent problems with agency practice or the law. For example, 'the investigating officer had applied satisfactory guidelines too vigorously'; and 'cases of this kind would not be allowed to sit around or develop in the way that they had at the time; all the people in the section have now moved on'.

Finally, there were cases (illustrated by the following four observations) in which the agency was not enamoured with the court decision, but (begrudgingly, perhaps) acknowledged a need to make a change to agency practice:

> The court's decision made the department super cautious about adhering to process. They adopted a no risk policy which increased the complexity of the statement of reasons process and made the system more expensive. The expectation of intense scrutiny by the courts meant that a 'hell of a lot' more time was spent by the department on the process.

The action that flowed from the Federal Court's decision involved the agency rewriting their guidelines and issuing these to staff. Essentially the technical defects to procedural fairness were removed which had been raised in the judgment. The agency took the view that they had lost on a technicality which was not a substantial defect.

This decision had far-reaching resource implications, effectively by imposing on a decision-maker an obligation to verify the truth of all information supplied by the applicant.

There is a tendency now to avoid precedents and to treat each case on its merits.

The way in which officers learn about and understand the decisions of courts and tribunals is also an important issue. This will be influenced in part by the initiative shown by individual officers since court and tribunal decisions are now readily accessible on the web and in published reports. Agencies also have a strategic role to play and the written comments from officers bore out the reliance they place on their own agency to keep them informed of administrative law developments.

How well agencies responded to that need is indicated from the results of a survey of officers and agencies.[16] Roughly 60 per cent of officers overall indicated that agency methods were effective in informing them of decisions in which their agency was involved and an even higher percentage (three-quarters) of officers said they received information about key tribunal or court decisions. At the same time, and disturbingly, half the officers surveyed relied on informal discussion as the main method of obtaining information. At the same time, a majority of agencies considered there was room for improvement in the way they identify and evaluate the importance of recent court and tribunal decisions, the most frequent suggestion for change being that the agency should be more systematic in the way this function is handled.

Applicant responses
Applicants, like agencies, pointed to many subsequent changes in legislation (often to overcome a shortcoming exposed by the court decision) on matters as diverse as visa and passport eligibility, child support deductions, industry subsidy, customs duty, occupational standards, medical remuneration, radio transmission, and the transferability of

---

[16] This was an element of the External Review Project (referred to in note 9 above).

fishing licences. There were some suggestions, whether accurate or not, of broad-scale legislative change: 'this case changed the whole National Health Scheme'; another was said to have brought in '(i) the Protection Visa system; (ii) Bridging visas where applicants are not kept in detention any more; and also (iii) created the Refugee Review Tribunal'; and yet another was said to have prompted the legislative change requiring the mandatory detention of boat people.

Numerous examples were given of the important role played by individual decisions (in several cases as test cases funded by an agency), in clarifying the meaning of vague or unsettled legislative provisions, such as 'remaining relative', 'dependency' and 'normal value'. Other interesting examples of the impact that a decision can have beyond the immediate dispute included a new conflict-of-interest register being established, a different non-adjudicative model being adopted for calculating chemist fees, broader industry consultation being implemented, a different approach being adopted to taxation default assessments, and the implementation of a different procedure for environmental assessment. There was also some acknowledgment of a change in agency style: 'seem to be more aware of their legal obligations to consider proposals and refer [threshold issues] back to the relevant minister'; '[customs] has since been super careful [not to apply the wrong test]'; 'strengthened the resolve of DILGEA to "get it right" [and avoid challenge]'; and 'tendency now to avoid precedents and treat each case on its merits'.

However, so far as agency practice was concerned, the prevailing sentiment in the applicant comments was one of criticism, rising to the point of alleging 'blatant lies', 'personal bias', 'tyrannical', 'malicious' and even 'bad faith'. The following examples are more tempered but nevertheless illustrate the criticism:

> The department are still a law unto themselves! This case was put in the 'too hard' basket which is why the applicant was successful.

> Only when you have a winning decision from a court will you then have something to bargain with.

> There are some departmental people who try to interpret what the [veterans] law should be and undermine judicial determination of the Federal Court.

> An amendment was made to the regulations . . . Ended up with a case of 'overkill'.

The system that was arrived at by the agency merely put in place a form that had to be filled in yet still did nothing about addressing the [causative problem] and therefore missed the signals entirely.

The Minister tends to ignore decisions of the Federal Court where possible.

The officer who made this decision has not changed his behaviour and he continues to provide advice and make decisions which are inconsistent with Commonwealth legislation.

The decision-maker told me that he was determined to make a determination 'the way they usually did', even saying at one stage 'I don't care what the court says'.

The Medical Board are a law unto themselves.

Perhaps the most pointed criticism came in one case from an applicant's counsel who, being otherwise complimentary of the agency, claimed that the case in question was 'one of the worst cases of double dealing by the Commonwealth he had ever seen'. The agency had acknowledged an anomaly in the legislation, but rather than amend it, agreed to fund a test case, ostensibly to demonstrate that the tribunal that normally heard cases of this kind 'were a mob of cowboys'. The case was instead settled between the parties, the agency did not pay the applicant's fees as arranged, and the agency later engineered the change to the legislation it was seeking.

Applicants also criticised the use of consent settlements, particularly in immigration cases, to avoid an unfavourable judicial determination. That criticism is captured in the following observations:

The department usually concedes now after the first directions hearing. They seem to concede pretty quickly – worried about costs and bad precedents. If ANY issues arise they concede and send the application back. There is then less chance a judge will give them a hiding!

The general feeling is that there have been no changes in the practices of the [immigration] department. They often concede matters so they don't have to change their practices or procedures.

The department didn't want the point of law resolved and therefore settled.

It was an improper exercise of discretion – a point which would have won in court if the case was not conceded.

Table 6.2. *Subject area of case*

	Frequency	Percentage
Immigration	162	55.5 %
Customs	20	6.9 %
Taxation	15	5.15 %
Communications	14	4.8 %
Health	14	4.8 %
Primary industry	7	2.4 %
Veterans' affairs	7	2.4 %
Not specified	17	5.8 %
Miscellaneous	36	12.2 %

Another general criticism was that judicial review can be a waste of resources: 'the department remakes the same decision dressed up to get around the initial problem'. To similar effect was the view that decisions are largely subjective: 'decisions rest largely on the type of personality you are dealing with and who sits in the chair of the decision-maker'.

An interesting suggestion for reform was that matters resubmitted by a court to an agency for reconsideration should be given priority by the agency. Other suggestions included staff training, and creating a mechanism for enforcing Federal Court decisions within agencies.

Profile of the cases in the survey

As part of this study, a profile of the 292 cases under study[17] was prepared, listing matters such as the jurisdictional basis for the action, the subject matter of the dispute, the nature of the parties, and the ground of legal error. The main purpose to be served was to build a profile of judicial review in Australia. Some of the issues (such as source of jurisdiction) are of technical domestic interest only, and are not included in Table 6.2.

Table 6.2 shows that immigration cases dominated the study, comprising over half the cases. It is perhaps worth noting that immigration

[17] As explained earlier, the cases in the study were those in which the plaintiff was successful in challenging the validity of a Commonwealth administrative decision (40.6 per cent of administrative law cases heard by the Federal Court or the High Court in the period under study). It is possible, though we think unlikely, that on the issues covered in this profile, the successful group of cases exhibit differences to the unsuccessful group of cases.

cases are not necessarily representative of judicial review cases over-all; questions to do with the protection of individual rights tend to loom large in immigration cases, and it is claimed (though not with-out demur) that the litigation can be inspired by the tactical objec-tive of delay as much as by disagreement with the legal ruling under challenge.[18] The remaining cases, which are spread more evenly over Commonwealth responsibilities, provide a more representative picture of judicial review issues, such as licensing, the revocation of bene-fits, workplace grievances, taxation and environmental regulation. The 'miscellaneous' category included agencies with a limited exposure to judicial review such as the Department of Foreign Affairs and Trade, the Australian Federal Police, the Australian Electoral Commission and the Treasury.

Other figures that can be noted briefly, by way of indication of the data that can be collected in a survey of this kind, were as follows. The profile of the applicants for review was individual male (53.1 per cent), individual female (18.2 per cent), corporation (20.5 per cent), government agency (4.4 per cent) and non-government organisation (0.3 per cent). The respondent agency was a minister or department (74.0 per cent), a statutory authority (17.8 per cent) and other (for example, a magistrate) (1.7 per cent). Applicants were represented by a private solicitor or counsel (86.0 per cent), legally aided (5.5 per cent) and self-represented (1.7 per cent).

Clarity of the legal issues involved in a case

Conformably with the rule of law and the separation of powers, a judi-cial ruling on the legality of government conduct will often have prece-dential significance for subsequent administrative decision-making. It is therefore important that the legal principles involved in a case can be identified clearly from a court's reasons for its judgment. This study sought to test that proposition by analysing each judgment to gauge, firstly, whether it was easy to identify both the ground(s) of review advanced by the plaintiff, and, secondly, the ground(s) of legal error relied upon by the court in setting aside the decision.[19] The framework

18 E.g., see Senate Legal and Constitutional Legislation Committee, Parliament of Australia, *Migration Legislation Amendment (Judicial Review) Bill 1998* (1999); and Senate Legal and Constitutional References Committee, *A Sanctuary under Review: An Examination of Australia's Refugee and Humanitarian Determination Process* (2000).
19 In our companion article on executive perceptions of administrative law, govern-ment officers were asked to evaluate the reasons given by administrative law review

of analysis used for this purpose was the statement of grounds of review in section 5 of the ADJR Act (see Table 6.3). The analysis of each judgment was necessarily subjective,[20] but in any case replicates the process that necessarily occurs within government agencies in examining court judgments.

On the first issue, the finding was that in only 60.4 per cent of ADJR Act cases was the applicant's legal argument clearly stated by the court. This is a surprisingly low figure. These were, after all, a group of cases in which an administrative decision or action was found to be unlawful, with the case generally being remitted to the agency for reconsideration. In deciding what action was necessary to heed the finding of the court, an agency would frequently find it useful to know the surrounding context of legal argument in which the finding of the court was reached.

The statistics were further refined by analysing whether (on our evaluation) some judges were better than others in clearly stating the successful ground of review. Twenty-two members of the Federal Court decided five or more of the cases in the survey. The disparity was marked – ranging from one judge ranked as clearly stating the successful ground in seven out of eight cases (87.5 per cent), to another who did not state the ground clearly in any of six cases (0 per cent). If, for statistical reliability, we take a smaller sample of the six judges who decided thirteen or more cases, the clarity ranking was 10.7 per cent, 33.3 per cent, 46.2 per cent, 46.2 per cent, 50 per cent and 64 per cent. Only nine of the twenty-two judges had a clarity ranking of 50 per cent or more.

The results of the second issue are covered in Table 6.3. Table 6.3 tabulates the legal issues involved in each case in three ways: column 1 lists the percentage of cases in which a ground of review was noted by a court as a possible legal issue in the case; column 2 lists the percentage of such cases in which the court held that a breach of that ground had occurred, and accordingly set the decision aside; and column 3 lists the corresponding percentage of cases in which the argument was dismissed. The following points can be made about the results in Table 6.3:

bodies. The respondents to the survey expressed overall satisfaction with the quality of reasons (72.6 per cent approval), the length (55.1 per cent) and the comprehensibility (67.7 per cent): see Creyke and McMillan, 'Executive Perceptions', p.172.

[20] Senior law students employed on the project undertook the analysis. Although their legal education was incomplete, their legal competence was perhaps not much different to (and in many cases greater than) that of non-legally qualified public servants who would be expected to conform to any ruling in the judgment.

Table 6.3 *The legal error identified by a court in setting aside a decision*

	% of cases in survey in which ground raised	% of those cases in which ground upheld	% of those cases in which ground rejected
s. 5(1)(a): natural justice	38.5	34.2	65.8
s. 5(1)(b): breach of lawful procedure	12.2	17.1	82.9
s. 5(1)(c): no jurisdiction	4.2	41.7	58.3
s. 5(1)(d): decision not authorised by legislation	13.9	40.0	60.0
s. 5(1)(e): improper exercise of power	24.7	16.9	83.1
s. 5(1)(f): error of law	49.3	42.3	57.7
s. 5(1)(g): fraud; and 5.5(2)(d): bad faith	1.4	0	100.0
s. 5(1)(h): no evidence	18.4	26.4	73.6
s. 5(2)(a): irrelevant consideration	26.4	26.3	73.7
s. 5(2)(b): relevant consideration	48.3	35.3	64.7
s. 5(2)(c): improper purpose	1.0	33.3	66.7
s. 5(2)(e): dictation	2.8	25.0	75.0
s. 5(2)(f) inflexible policy	16.7	27.1	72.9
s. 5(2)(g): unreasonableness	31.3	21.1	78.9
s. 5(2)(h): uncertainty	1.4	25.0	75.0

- The total number of claims of breach of a ground of review represented in column 1 was 836. Hence, it was common for more than one ground of review to be argued (on average, three per case). Equally, in many cases more than one ground of legal error was found by the court in setting aside a decision. That illustrates the overlap between the grounds of review, and to that extent the difficulty of precision in categorising legal errors under one heading rather than another.
- The most frequently argued ground of review was error of law, in nearly half the cases in this part of the study. Part of the reason is that error of law can incorporate misinterpretation of legislation.

More significantly, perhaps, error of law is a malleable and umbrella concept in administrative law. The next two most frequently argued grounds were failure to take a relevant consideration into account (48.3 per cent of cases) and breach of natural justice (38.5 per cent of cases). A similar point can be made about those grounds, that they are indeterminate in scope and have much to offer an applicant.

- The grounds most relied upon by applicants were also among the grounds most likely to be upheld by a court (error of law in 42.3 per cent of cases, relevant consideration in 35.3 per cent and breach of natural justice in 34.2 per cent). This statistic can be viewed in either of two ways: an indeterminate ground is more likely to succeed; or an applicant is more likely to choose a ground that has a higher chance of being upheld. It is probable that both propositions are largely correct.

- Many of the grounds at the lower end of both scales are those that more easily connote bureaucratic turpitude or abuse of power (such as bad faith, improper purpose, improper exercise of power and unreasonableness). One possible interpretation of the low success rate on those grounds is that it is difficult to establish a grave breach of that kind. Another possible interpretation, however, is that judicial review is less a mechanism for correcting bureaucratic misbehaviour, and more a mechanism for correcting procedural deficiencies and for clarifying legislative vagary.

CONCLUSIONS

Anecdotal belief had long held that a successful judicial review action would most likely be followed by an agency remaking the same decision, though taking care to avoid the earlier legal error. That belief has now been disproved, at least in Australian judicial review in the period covered by this research project. If theories are built upon facts, then the value of judicial review in producing a favourable outcome to an applicant has been demonstrated. It was admittedly a minority of cases in which an applicant was successful at trial, yet the alternative interpretation of that fact is that applicants were mistaken in those cases in believing they were the victims of legal error. When their belief was more soundly based, judicial review was a promising mechanism for rectifying both the error and its impact.

Another feature of judicial review that is often overlooked in academic analysis but was highlighted by this study was the advantage accruing to an agency from judicial review. Agencies commented frequently that judicial review afforded them an opportunity to clarify the surrounding legal environment and to obtain definitive guidance on the meaning of legislation administered by the agency.[21] This is especially important if there have been conflicting lines of tribunal or judicial authority on an issue. Similarly, there were many instances in which agencies later changed their procedures or policies in light of a court decision, or sponsored legislative amendment (though some of those changes were designed to reinstate the view of the legislation held by the agency prior to the court ruling).

In many instances – albeit too few, according to applicants – agencies responded to and heeded the criticisms made by courts, despite any institutional mechanism in the administrative law system to require that response. Some of those changes were profound. The explanation for the change can differ from one case to the next, and sometimes be political in character, yet the commentary in this study suggested that in an appreciable number of cases the change was prompted by an agency's preparedness to accept the outcome and ruling in a judicial review case as a valuable and instructive incident.[22]

The negative comments made about agency behaviour were also an important product of the study. In some cases, an agency was alleged to have taken action to nullify the import of a court order.[23] Delay in implementing a court order – a frequent complaint – was a similar problem. Sometimes further court action was necessary to reassert the earlier success, or media exposure to highlight the battle.

---

[21] The consistency of comments to this effect appears to run contrary to the experience of Richardson and Machin in their examination of the Mental Health Review Tribunal in England (Richardson and Machin, 'Judicial Review'). An Australian feature that reflects the attention paid to judicial decisions is the plethora of well-regarded and up-to-date text annotations of legislation that is subject to high-volume review, such as social security, veterans' entitlements, and migration. There are also general report series, such as the *Administrative Law Decisions* and the *Administrative Law Bulletin* (Lexis-Nexis).

[22] These findings suggest that even the strong competing values within public administration did not neutralise the impact of administrative review (cf. Chapter 4 above).

[23] For an examination of the methods employed in the United States of nullifying the effect of a decision, see Chapter 3 above.

It was alleged that the strategy most commonly adopted by agencies to avoid an unwelcome precedent was to resolve a matter prior to a hearing. A court settlement prior to the hearing date could avoid a loss at court.[24] Although this provides a partial win at least for the applicant, the practice is apt to undermine other potential benefits from judicial review, notably a legal ruling and reasons that provide guidance and a precedent to others.

A significant finding was that agency records are sometimes inadequate when it comes to finding information relating to a specific case. Perhaps that is to be expected in agencies that have a large number of case files spread around Australia, but it does question whether judicial review cases, instead of being viewed as important threads in the fabric of law and government, are treated instead as discrete incidents having no broader contextual significance. A pleasing outcome of our study was that several agencies acknowledged (to the authors) that this was an important issue and that steps were being implemented by the agency to enable better tracking of cases. As that illustrates, an empirical study can have an impact on the data that are being collected. Indeed, the solicitor for at least one applicant suggested that our inquiries had provided the incentive for an agency to review a case that it had hitherto been neglecting, to the ultimate benefit of the applicant.

The part of the study that mapped the frequency with which different grounds of review figured in the cases was also significant. The statistics confirmed what many had intuitively assumed, that the more indeterminate legal standards were of growing importance in judicial review. This trend runs counter to the rule-of-law ideal that the legal standards that guide government decision-making should be clear and ascertainable. Of similar concern was the proportion of cases in which it was difficult to categorise by orthodox method the legal standard being raised or applied.

It is hoped, too, that the findings in this study have more universal relevance. Judicial review of executive action is found (albeit with jurisdictional differences[25]) in common law, civil law, and other legal systems, including that of China. There are many common features – the role of courts in evaluating the legality of executive action against

---

[24] See Chapter 4 above, where Richardson argues that preliminary action in a judicial review matter can influence the behaviour of agencies.

[25] *Ibid.*

pre-existing standards, the tendency of courts to remit a legally defective decision to an agency for reconsideration, the diversity of government action subject to judicial review, and the randomness of litigation across the spectrum of government decision-making. A similar question therefore arises in all systems as to whether judicial review is ultimately of benefit to the applicant in the individual case, and of broader impact in the scheme of law and government. If the Australian experience is anything to go by, the judicial review system is succeeding on both fronts.

CHAPTER SEVEN

LEGALISING THE UNLEGALISABLE: TERRORISM, SECRET SERVICES AND JUDICIAL REVIEW IN ISRAEL 1970–2001

YOAV DOTAN

INTRODUCTION

Courts in liberal democracies are often described as the guardians of human rights. Hardly anyone would argue against the proposition that one of the primary roles of courts in a democracy – if not their most important role – is to defend basic human rights. The question as to whether and to what extent courts manage to fulfil this constitutional role in reality remains, however, a much debated issue. The ability of courts to protect human rights is even more questionable when faced with situations of national emergency. There, the danger of a widening gap between high judicial rhetoric and the tough reality of abusing human rights 'on the ground' is constant.

In the current paper I deal with the behaviour of judicial institutions and the impact of their decisions in a situation of national emergency. The case study concerns the rulings of the Israeli Supreme Court in regard to the use by Israeli security services of torture during the interrogation of detainees suspected of hostile terrorist activity (HTA) between 1970 and 2001. The purpose of the paper is to present the different kinds of reaction of the Court to petitions regarding interrogation procedures during these years, and to examine the impact of each judicial doctrine on the procedures of the secret services and on the civil rights of detainees.

I will start by describing the institution of the Supreme Court and its general practices with regard to judicial review. Then, I will describe the developments of the procedures of interrogation of suspected terrorists over the years. Next, I shall examine the alternative judicial responses available to courts faced with the dilemma posed by the fight against terrorism and describe the choices made by the Israeli courts in that regard. The paper also includes an empirical analysis of the impact of the rulings of the Supreme Court on the human rights of suspected terrorists. I shall conclude by evaluating the relative impact of the different doctrines adopted by the Supreme Court during the research period.

BACKGROUND

The Supreme Court of Israel and judicial activism

The 'old Court': from establishment to 1980

The Supreme Court of Israel has always been considered an influential institution within the Israeli polity. A distinction should, however, be made between two principal stages regarding its overall involvement in political and bureaucratic decision-making. From the establishment of the State of Israel in 1948 to the late 1970s, the Supreme Court, while gradually and consistently developing a rich jurisprudence of judicial review, kept a fairly low public profile. Soon after Israel was established, the Court firmly established the principle of the rule of law and stated that requirements of legality applied to all governmental agencies. During the first three decades (1948–80), the Court also developed principles of human rights. In the absence of a formal written constitution,[1] the Court entrenched in its decisions basic liberties such as the right of free speech, freedom of procession and association, and freedom of trade.[2] It also exerted judicial supervision over

---

[1] Israel has no written constitution. Instead, the Knesset enacted a number of Basic Laws that enjoy a partial supremacy over regular legislation. Most of these Basic Laws, however, refer to structural issues and do not contain a Bill of Rights. Only in 1992 did the Knesset enact the 'Basic Law: Human Rights and Dignity' that specifically refers to the protection of fundamental human rights, such as the freedom of movement, privacy and human dignity. Still, many fundamental political rights (such as freedom of speech and political equality) are yet to be entrenched in Basic Laws. See Basic Law: Human Dignity and Liberty (translated in http://www.knesset.gov.il/main/eng/engframe.htm); C.A 6821/93, *Bank Ha'mizrachi* v. *Migdal* 39(4) PD 221 (translated in (1997) 31 *Israeli Law Review* 764); D. Barak-Erez, 'From an Unwritten Constitution to a Written Constitution: The Israeli Challenge in American Perspective' (1995) 26 *Columbia Human Rights Law Review* 309 at 309–22.

[2] HC 73 and 87/53, *Kol Ha'am* v. *Minister of the Interior*, 7, PD 871; HC 148/79, *Saar* v. *Minister of the Interior and the Police* 34(2) PD 169; HC 241/60 *Kardosh* v. *The Company Register* 15 PD 1151; HC 1/49, *Begerano* v. *Minister of Police* 2 PD 80;

the actions of most administrative agencies and governmental units. The development of judicial review was, however, done cautiously. The Court kept a low public profile, refrained from entering into sensitive political questions and avoided direct confrontation with the executive branch.

The cautious policy of judicial review was reflected primarily with regard to issues of national security and military activities. As early as 1948, the year of establishment, the Supreme Court ruled that the military and all security agencies are subject to the principle of the rule of law and the supervision of the courts. It ordered the release of an Arab resident of Jaffa who was detained according to a writ issued under emergency regulations, since it found that the appropriate procedure was not properly exercised prior to the arrest.[3] Judicial supervision in the area of national security was, however, extremely limited before 1980. The Court's review was extremely formal in nature. It was based on the question of the (strict) legality of the action at stake in accordance with the traditional (English) test of *ultra vires*. The Court overtly refrained from any attempt to second-guess (or even to examine) the discretion of the relevant decision-maker on substantive grounds. It also openly stated that, due to the sensitivity of national security claims, the scope of review in security matters would be narrower than that generally applied in other matters.[4] The limited nature of judicial review in areas of national security was further sustained by other doctrines regarding access to judicial review. Before 1980, the Court applied the doctrine of *justiciability* to ensure that sensitive questions in the area of foreign relations and national security could be kept off the Court's docket, under which doctrine the Court holds that such matters are 'unsuitable' for judicial determination.[5] This doctrine effectively enabled the Court to

HC 370/79, *Katalan v. The Prison Service* 34(3) PD 294; B. Bracha, 'The Protection of Human Rights in Israel' (1982) 12 *Israel Yearbook of Human Rights* 110; A. Zysblat, 'Protecting Fundamental Human Rights in Israel Without a Written Constitution' in I. Zamir and A. Zysblat (eds.), *Public Law in Israel* (Oxford, Oxford University Press. 1996), p. 47.

[3] HC 7/48, *El-Karbotli v. Minister of Defense* 2 PD 5 at 15.
[4] E.g., HC 46/50, *El Aiubi v. Minister of Defense* 4(1) PD 222; I. Zamir, 'Human Rights and National Security' (1989) 23 *Israeli Law Review* 375 at 401.
[5] The doctrine of justiciability was applied by Israeli courts in a way that was roughly equivalent to the use of the doctrines of 'political question', 'equitable discretion' and 'act of state' in the United States: see L. H. Tribe, *American Constitutional Law* (3rd edn, Foundation Press, New York, 2000), pp. 365 *et seq.* and n. 44.

avoid dealing with certain cases whenever the judges felt that intervention in a sensitive or controversial matter would endanger the Court's
reputation or autonomy.[6] Issues of national security were also hidden
behind a thick veil of secrecy. Therefore, in many instances, even if
the issue arrived at the courtroom, the public had no knowledge about
the very existence of the process.[7] Not surprisingly, before 1980, there
is hardly an Israeli court case that even refers to the existence of the
General Security Service.

The 'new Court': judicial activism since 1980
Since 1980, there has been a major shift in almost all of the aspects
of judicial review mentioned above. There was a dramatic change in
the principles concerning access to the courts. In its landmark decision
in *Ressler* v. *Minister of Defense*, the Supreme Court sharply reversed
its prior rulings on the issue of justiciability. Justice Aharon Barak
(currently Chief Justice) said:

> Any [human] action is susceptible to determination by a legal norm, and
> there is no action regarding which there is no legal norm determining it.
> There is no 'legal vacuum' in which actions are taken without the law
> having anything to say about them. The law encompasses any action . . .
> The fact that an issue is 'strictly political' does not change the fact that
> such an issue is also 'a legal issue'.[8]

[6] HC 561/75, *Ashkenazi* v. *Minister of Defense* 30(3) PD 309; HC 222/68, *Hugim
Leumiem* v. *Minister of Police* 24(2) PD 141.
[7] See e.g. the case of a former GSS officer who was convicted of murdering his colleague and served life imprisonment while even his name remained covert (Mr X): see
M. Reinfeld, Y. Melman and M. Nesher, 'Mordechai Kedar, "Mr X", Petitioned the
HCJ Demanding a Re-trial', *Ha'retz*, 5 January 1996.
[8] HC 910/86, *Ressler* v. *Minister of Defense* 42(2) PD 441 at 477. While this wide
concept of justiciability was not adopted in its entirety by all other justices of the
Supreme Court, it did mark a willingness on the part of the Court to substantially
widen the range of issues which were thereafter considered justiciable under the new
approach. Similar reform was conducted in regard to the standing requirement. Before
the 1980s, the petitioner was required to show a direct personal interest in the action
subject to judicial review. Since 1980, and particularly after the *Ressler* decision, the
Court acknowledged the standing of petitioners in matters of public importance even
if they had no personal interest in the decision at stake. This reform opened the
gate for many public action organisations and political groups to resort to litigation
as a vehicle to initiate social and political reforms: see Y. Dotan and M. Hofnung,
'Interest Groups in the High Court of Justice: Measuring Success in Litigation and in
Out-of-Court Settlements' (2001) 23 *Law and Policy* 1.

The reform of the rules concerning access to court was followed by a similar revision of the rules of judicial review. During the 1980s and the 1990s, the courts showed a growing tendency to expand the scope of judicial review. They developed new tools for judicial review and imposed new requirements on administrative authorities such as the duties of reasonableness, rationality of the decision-making process and proportionality.[9] More generally, the Court replaced the old methodology of strict formal analysis of the *legality* of the relevant governmental decision in favour of a 'soft', value-oriented analysis of *interest-balancing*.[10]

The activist trends of the Court during the last two decades have extended to petitions against military or other security agencies. As mentioned above, the Court had previously stated that the scope of judicial review would be narrower in cases involving security matters than in other cases of administrative discretion. More recently, however, the Court has stepped back from this position. For example, in a case in which the Court was asked to review a decision of the Military Censor not to allow the media to publish the name of the new Head of the Mossad (the Israeli intelligence agency), Justice Barak concluded:

> The security nature of the administrative discretion deterred judicial review in the past . . . Over the years it was made clear that there is nothing unique in security considerations . . . Judges can and should review the reasonableness of discretion in security matters as much as they can and should review administrative discretion in any other field. Hence, there are no special limits on the scope of judicial review in security matters.[11]

The Court also stated that a military authority may infringe on basic civil rights (such as the freedom of speech or the freedom of association)

---

[9] HC 389/80, *Dapei Zahav v. Broadcasting Authority* 35 (1) PD 421; HC 376/81, *Lugasi v. Minister of Communications* 36 (2) PD 449; HC 297/82, *Berger v. Minister of Interior* 37 (3) PD 29; HC 987/94, *Euronet Kavei Zahav v. Minister of Communication* 48 (5) PD 412; HC 6510/92, *Turkeman v. Minister of Defense* 42 (8) PD 217; HC 3477/95, *Beb-Atia v. Minister of Education* 45 (5) PD 1.

[10] See M. Mautner, *The Decline of Formalism and the Rise of Values in Israeli Law* (Tel Aviv, Dyonon, 1994) (Hebrew).

[11] HC 680/88, *Shnitzer v. The Military Censor et al.* 42 (4) PD 617 at 639–40. There, the Court quashed a decision not to allow the publication of criticism of the actions of the Head of the Mossad (the Security Service for Special Actions).

only when there is a real likelihood of serious harm to national security. The *Shnitzer* case and numerous other decisions reflect the tendency of the Court to expand its supervision over the field of national security.[12]

The willingness of the Israeli courts to supervise the actions of the military and the other security agencies extended also to the actions of these agencies in the occupied territories. Since the beginning of Israel's occupation of the West Bank and the Gaza Strip, the residents of these territories have been allowed to petition the Supreme Court in order to challenge the actions of the military government.[13] During the long period of military occupation, the Court issued some important decisions allowing protection of the basic liberties of the Palestinian population. For example, in its landmark decision in the *Elon Moreh* case, the Court ruled that the government is not allowed, under international law, to confiscate privately owned lands for the purpose of building new Jewish settlements, unless the seizure order can be justified on the basis of military needs.[14] The Court also restricted the ability of the military

[12] See e.g. HC 554/81, *Beransa v. Commander of Central Command* 36(4) PD 247; HC 448/85, *Dahar v. Minister of the Interior* 40(2) PD 701; HC 799/80, *Shlalam v. The Licensing Officer for Weapons* 36(1) PD 317; B. Bracha, 'Judicial Review of Security Powers in Israel: A New Policy of the Courts' (1991) 28 *Stanford Journal of International Law* 39; M. Hofnung, *Democracy, Law and National Security in Israel* (Aldershot, Dartmouth, 1996); I. Zamir, 'Rule of Law and the Control of Terrorism' (1998) 8 *Tel Aviv University Studies in Law* 81.
[13] HC 302 and 306/72, *Hilu et. al. v. Government of Israel* 27(2) PD 169; HC 393/82, *El Masulia v. Army Commander* 37(4) PD 785; M. Shamgar, 'The Observance of International Law in the Administrative Territories' (1971) 1 *Israeli Yearbook of Human Rights* 262. The legal standards applied by the Court to these actions derived from various sources: the local law in the territories, including both Jordanian law and orders of the military government itself; the principles of customary public international law (as integrated into Israeli law); and the general principles of judicial review derived from Israeli administrative law: see HC 393/82, *Gama't Asachan v. Regional Commander of Judea and Samaria* 37(4) PD 785; and HC 69 and 493/81, *Abu Ita et al. v. Regional Commander of Judea and Samaria* 37(2) PD 197.
[14] HC 390/79, *Dawikat v. Government of Israel* 34(1) PD 1. This decision forced the government to evacuate an already established settlement, and had – according to some observers – a wide impact on the ability of the Israeli Government to build new settlements subsequently. See M. Negbi, *Justice under Occupation* (Jerusalem, Kana, 1981) (Hebrew); M. Hofnung, *Democracy, Law*, pp. 246–51. Likewise, in another important case, the Court quashed the decision of the Interior Minister to refuse an application for a permit to publish a new newspaper in East Jerusalem on the ground that the petitioner was a subversive element: HC 2/79, *El-Asad v. Minister of Interior* 34(1) PD 505.

commander to make use of his powers under emergency regulations to take severe administrative action against persons involved in terrorist activities, such as deportation or house demolition. It did so by imposing procedural requirements on the authorities before any such action could be taken.[15] Despite the fact that the Court has been supervising, on an almost daily basis, every action of the Israeli forces and agencies in the occupied territories, the question of the effectiveness of its supervision on the human rights of the residents of the occupied territories remains subject to much debate. Thus, many critics contend that the Court's ability to effectively defend the human rights of Palestinians in the occupied territories was extremely limited, if not negligible, and that its supervision over the actions of the Israeli military legitimates the occupation regime rather than limits its harsh consequences for human rights.[16]

Judicial review and the institution of the High Court of Justice
Additional factors that influenced the rapid development of judicial activism are related to the institution of the High Court of Justice (HCJ). The HCJ is one of the functions of the Supreme Court, and is the primary jurisdiction for judicial review cases.[17] In this capacity, the Court is the first and last instance for most important judicial review cases in which decisions of the government, the actions of the

---

[15] HC 320/80, *Kawasme et al.* v. *Minister of Defense* 35(3) PD 113; HC 358/88, *Association for Civil Rights in Israel (ACRI)* v. *Commander of Central Command* 43 PD 529.

[16] See e.g. R. Shamir, 'Landmark Cases and the Reproduction of Legitimacy: The Case of Israel's High Court of Justice' (1990) 24 *Law and Society Review* 781; B. Kimerling, 'Bagatz Should Withdraw from the Occupied Territories', *Ha'aretz*, 29 January 1993, p. B-3; D. Kretzmer, 'Judicial Review of Demolition and Sealing of Houses in the Occupied Territories' in I. Zamir (ed.), *Klinghoffer Book on Public Law* (Jerusalem, Harry Sacher Institute, 1993) (Hebrew); J. Kuttab, 'Avenues Open for Defense of Human Rights in the Israeli Occupied Territories' in E. Playfair (ed.), *International Law and the Administration of Occupied Territories: Two Decades of Israeli Occupation of the West Bank and Gaza Strip* (Oxford, Clarendon Press, 1992), p. 489. But cf. Negbi, *Justice*; G. E. Bisharat, 'Courting Justice? Legitimization in Lawyering under Israeli Occupation' (1995) 20 *Law and Social Inquiry* 349; Y. Dotan, 'Judicial Rhetoric, Government Lawyers and Human Rights: The Case of the High Court of Justice During the Intifada' (1999) 33 *Law and Society Review* 319.

[17] The Supreme Court also serves as an appellate court for criminal or civil cases that were decided initially in the District Court and as a court of cassation for civil and criminal cases that were disposed initially in a magistrates' court and then appealed to the District Courts.

military and so forth are challenged. The fact that in its capacity as HCJ the Supreme Court (sitting normally in panels of three) functions in essence as a trial court has a profound impact on the nature of the process. The procedures in the HCJ are characterised by simplicity, brevity and expediency. Ease of access to the Court is assured by low court fees and by the lack of onerous formal requirements.[18] A petition to the HCJ can be written by a layman, and at no stage of the proceedings is representation by a lawyer required. Hearings are based on the parties' affidavits and on their oral arguments. Oral testimonies as well as cross-examination are usually not allowed. The Court is able to grant petitioners immediate relief and to issue orders and injunctions, either interim or permanent, at any stage. Petitions are usually brought for a preliminary hearing shortly after their submission and, in the vast majority of cases, are disposed of in full at this stage.[19]

These institutional characteristics contribute to the ability of the HCJ to extend its involvement and influence on the Israeli polity. In essence, the Court holds full discretion on whether to review any particular governmental decision, and there are no formal jurisdictional constraints precluding it from reviewing any such decision, should it decide to do so. Moreover, unlike most other high judicial institutions, judicial review by the HCJ takes place *in real time*, that is, immediately after the governmental action takes place, or even before it is completed.[20] Since the 1980s, the Court has also encouraged the involvement of many non-governmental organisations (NGOs) that specialise in litigation, to ensure that every potentially unlawful governmental decision finds its way into the Supreme Court's docket in the form of a petition to the HCJ.[21]

---

[18] The court fee for a petition to the HCJ is currently approximately equal to US$100.

[19] The vast majority of cases dealt with by the HCJ are disposed at the stage of the preliminary hearing without any order *nisi* (that is, an order by the Court to allow a full hearing of the case) being issued. For example, according to the data of the Central Bureau of Statistics of Israel, out of 4,266 cases disposed by the HCJ between 1985 and 1993, in only 886 cases was an order *nisi* issued.

[20] For example, in 1992, the Court halted, by an interim injunction, an attempt by the government to deport 415 members of the militant Islamic group *Hamas* to Lebanon, and its intervention seriously impaired the ability of the government to complete this controversial action. The deportees were eventually allowed to return to the occupied territories. See HC 5973/92, *Association for Civil Rights in Israel (ACRI)* v. *Minister of Defense* 47(1) PD 268.

[21] See Y. Dotan, 'Judicial Accountability in Israel: The High Court of Justice and the Phenomenon of Judicial Hyperactivism' (2002) 8 *Israel Studies* 87 at 97–101.

While it is common knowledge that the HCJ is a major player in
Israeli public life, the impact of its decisions on Israeli society has been
little subject to systematic academic research. Indeed, some previous
research focused on judicial behaviour in Israel, and in particular on
patterns of decision-making in the Supreme Court regarding human
rights issues.[22] In addition, some relatively recent research focused
on the practices of interest groups and political lawyers that use litigation as a strategy for social reform.[23] The question of whether and
to what extent litigation before the Supreme Court managed to bring
about reforms in governmental policies or other forms of social change
has scarcely been directly addressed in these studies. In this respect, the
current research differs from most previous works on the Court since it
aims to focus on the impact of judicial decisions on government practices rather than on the rhetoric of the Court or on patterns of judicial
behaviour.[24]

Terrorism and torture in Israel: a brief legal history

From its foundation Israel has been subject to the threat of terrorism.
Until 1967, most terrorist attacks directed against Israel came from
terrorist groups whose bases were located in the neighbouring Arab
countries. This situation changed when Israel took possession of the
West Bank and the Gaza Strip in 1967, which were populated by millions of Palestinians. During the first two decades after 1967, the scale
of hostile violent activity on behalf of the population in the occupied territories against the Israeli authorities was limited. Gradually,

---

[22] See e.g. Kretzmer, 'Judicial Review'; Shamir, 'Landmark Cases'; Dotan, 'Judicial
Rhetoric'.

[23] See e.g. L. Hajjar, 'Cause Lawyering in Transnational Perspective: National Conflict and Human Rights in Israel/Palestine' (1997) 31 Law and Society Review
473; Y. Dotan, 'Public Lawyers and Private Clients: An Empirical Observation
on the Relative Success Rates of Cause Lawyers' (1999) 21 Law and Policy 401;
Y. Dotan and M. Hofnung, 'Interest Groups in the High Court of Justice: Measuring Success in Litigation and in Out-of-Court Settlements' (2001) 23 Law and
Policy 1.

[24] For a recent case study analysis of the impact of Israeli court decisions in the field of
environmental law, see N. Morag-Levine, 'The Politics of Imported Rights: Transplantation and Transformation in an Israeli Environmental Cause-Lawyering Organization' in A. Sarat and R. S. Scheingold (eds.), Cause Lawyering and the State in a
Global Era (Oxford, Oxford University Press, 2001), p. 334.

however, armed organisations (such as the PLO and its affiliated organisations) whose headquarters remained outside the occupied territories widened their grip within the territories and intensified their attacks on Israeli military and civilians (both in the territories and in Israel itself). The level of violence against Israeli targets in the territories increased sharply when the (first) *intifada* broke out in December 1987.[25] The threat of hostile terrorist activity (HTA) did not end when the *intifada* finally ended towards the end of 1993, when the Middle East peace process started, and the Oslo Accords were signed between Israel and the PLO. Instead, most terrorist activities were conducted by Islamist groups who opposed the Oslo Accords on various grounds, and directed their attacks against civilian targets within Israel.[26] The number of terrorist attacks (and casualties) sharply increased after the collapse of the peace process and the eruption of the second *intifada* (this time with the active cooperation of and support by the forces of the Palestinian Authority).[27]

In order to combat terrorism and to maintain national security, Israel formed a number of security agencies. The largest agency, which is in charge of combating and preventing Palestinian HTA, is the General Security Service (GSS). Despite the fact that the GSS was formed as early as the establishment of the State of Israel, its powers were not defined in statute until very recently.[28] For many years, the very existence of the GSS was considered a national secret, and there was hardly any mention of the organisation in any formal legal document (let alone a court decision). Even when the existence of the agency became

---

[25] The *intifada* erupted in December 1987 and did not completely end until the breakthrough in the Middle East peace process, when Prime Minister Yitzhak Rabin and Yasser Arafat signed the first Oslo agreement at the end of 1993. In September 2000, after the collapse of the Oslo Accords, a second *intifada* began, this time with the active support of the armed forces of the Palestinian Authority. Unless otherwise stated, I shall use the term *intifada* to refer to the first uprising.

[26] Between September 1993 and September 2000, 253 Israeli military and civilians were killed in terrorist attacks by Palestinian militant groups (source: http://www.mfa.gov.il/mfa/go.asp?MFAH0don0).

[27] Between 29 September 2000 and 30 June 2003, 483 people were killed and 3585 severely injured in such terrorist attacks (source: http://www.mfa.gov.il/mfa/go.asp?MFAH0don0).

[28] Only in February 2002 did the Knesset legislate the General Security Service Act (2002) that defined the roles and powers of the GSS.

public and began to leave traces in courts' decisions (sometime in the late 1970s or early 1980s),[29] its legal status remained moot.[30]

Until 1967, the interrogation of HTA suspects (whose number was small) by the GSS staff was conducted in accordance with the general requirements of police procedures according to Israeli law.[31] Likewise, during the early years following the Six Day War in 1967 there was no evidence of improper or unusual procedures in that regard.[32]

During the 1970s, however, lawyers defending Palestinians accused of offences related to HTA began to resort to the courts while arguing that confessions – ostensibly made voluntarily – resulted from improper methods of interrogation used by the GSS interrogators. As a result, the courts began to summon GSS interrogators as witnesses in the course of these trials in order to attack the ingenuousness of the confessions. Until 1987, the GSS witnesses and the government flatly denied any use of torture during interrogations. Only in 1987, after the outbreak of two scandals that tarnished the GSS's reputation in the eyes of the Israeli public, was it revealed that the GSS staff, not only systematically used all sorts of measures of 'moderate physical pressure' in the course of their investigations, but also consistently perjured themselves

[29] In a search of electronic databases of court decisions (CD-ROM – DINIM), I found only one case, in 1983, referring to the GSS. All other (124) decisions that mentioned the agency were given after 1985. It may, however, be the case that the GSS was mentioned in some unpublished cases prior to 1985 (and therefore were not included in this database, or their public action was not allowed for security reasons).

[30] Presumably, since there was no specific statute authorising the GSS, it functioned on the basis of the 'general' (residual) powers of the government, as defined in section 40 of Basic Law: The Government. The section provides: 'The Government is authorized to perform in the name of the State, and subject to any law, all actions which are not incumbent on another authority.' According to the accepted reading of this section, it cannot, however, serve to empower the GSS to conduct interrogations and take other actions that infringe on basic human rights. See, e.g., HC 5128/94, *Federman v. Minister of Police* 48(5) PD 647; and see HC 5100/94, *The Public Committee Against Torture in Israel v. The State of Israel* 53(4) PD 817 (1999) (the GSS Case), at section 19.

[31] See 'The Report of the Commission of Inquiry into the Methods of Investigation of the General Security Service Regarding Hostile Terrorist Activities' (hereinafter the 'Landau Commission's report' or the 'Landau Report'), p. 20. The report was published in English in (1989) 23 *Israeli Law Review* 146. The references here are to page numbers of the original Hebrew version.

[32] See the Landau Report, *ibid.*

by denying the use of such measures in court.[33] These public scandals brought about the appointment of a special commission of inquiry into the investigatory methods of the GSS (the Landau Commission).[34]

The Landau Commission thoroughly investigated the GSS methods of interrogation, and publicly exposed in its report the use (and prevalence) of both torture and perjury by the GSS. While the commission was definite in its recommendation to outlaw perjury by GSS staff, it was much less definite in its attitude to the use of 'moderate physical pressure' by GSS interrogators. Instead of a complete ban on the use of such measures, the commission provided 'guidelines' for the service as to what measures could be used in its interrogations, and under what circumstances. These guidelines were included in a separate part of the commission's report that remained secret. It allowed the GSS – in situations of direct and immediate threat to human life or national security – to make use of 'moderate physical pressure' while detailing the restrictions under which such measures could be used.[35] The commission also maintained that the techniques it permitted stopped short of consisting of the actual torture that is banned under international law, and that they are less severe than the techniques authorised by other democratic states in similar situations.[36]

While the commission sought in essence to regulate the use of 'physical pressure' in the course of GSS interrogations, it did not

---

[33] *Ibid.*, pp. 21–33. The first scandal was that GSS officials had fabricated evidence to cover up an incident in 1984 in which agents beat to death two terrorists who hijacked a civilian bus, after they were taken into custody (an incident known as the 'Bus 300 Affair'). In the second incident, Lieutenant Izzat Nafsu, a member of Israel's Circassian (Turkic Muslim) minority, was released from prison after the Supreme Court ruled that he had been convicted of espionage on the basis of a false confession extracted under duress by GSS agents, who later lied in court when Nafsu challenged his confession.

[34] The commission was appointed under section 1 of the Commission of Inquiry Law, 1968. Its members were Justice Moshe Landau, a former President of the Supreme Court, Ya'akov Malz, the State Comptroller and a former Supreme Court judge, and Major General Yitzhak Hofi, a retired officer in the Israeli Defense Force who served as the head of the Mossad (the Israeli Secret Service).

[35] The techniques allowed by the commission included shackling the interogatee to a small chair, placing a hood over his head, playing loud music, putting him in a 'frug' position while the hands are tied over the head, and sleep deprivation. They are specified in HC 5100/94, *The Public Committee against Torture in Israel* v. *The State of Israel* 53(4) PD 817 (1999) (hereinafter the GSS *Case*) (translated in http://62.90.71.124/mishpat/html/en/system/index.html).

[36] See the Landau Report, pp. 66–71 and 78.

directly confront the questions concerning the *legality* of these measures. As noted earlier, from the point of view of the rule of law and the *ultra vires* doctrine, the whole basis for the activity of the GSS – let alone its power to exert such 'special' measures that seriously infringe on basic human rights – is moot (if not non-existent).[37] The commission, however, said hardly anything about the legal aspect. Instead, it concentrated on the legality of the behaviour of the GSS officials from the *criminal law* point of view. It examined at length the question of whether and under what circumstances the GSS staff, while using these measures, would be entitled to the defence of *necessity* – if criminal charges were to be issued against them as a result of their actions.[38]

While human rights NGOs strongly criticised the Landau Commission's recommendations as licensing torture, commentators questioned its internal logic, and lawyers questioned its legal rational,[39] the report remained (at least officially) the primary basis for the actions of the GSS. It was during the years following the publication of the report that the investigatory methods of the GSS began to be challenged in judicial review petitions in the HCJ (see below). This state of affairs was maintained until 1999, when the Supreme Court gave

---

[37] See note 30 above.

[38] The defence of necessity under section 22 of the Israeli Penal Code (as it stood at the time of the Landau Commission's report) exempted from criminal liability actions done in order to avoid consequences which could not otherwise be avoided and which would have inflicted grievous harm or injury on that person or on others he was bound to protect. See the Landau Report, section 3.11, pp. 54 *et seq.* See also e.g., S. Z. Feller, 'Not Actual "Necessity" But Possibly "Justification"; Not "Moderate" Pressure, But Either "Unlimited" or Not at All' (1989) 23 *Israeli Law Review* 201.

[39] See e.g. B'Tselem (the Israeli Information Center for Human Rights in the Occupied Territories), *The Interrogation of Palestinians During the Intifada: Ill-Treatment, 'Moderate Physical Pressure' or Torture: Comprehensive Report 1991* (Jerusalem, HCHROT, 1991); UN Human Rights Committee, General Comment No. 20 (44), Art. 7, UN GAOR Supp No. 40 (A/47/40), Annex VI (1994)); M. Kremnitzer, 'The Landau Commission Report – Was the Security Service Subordinated to the Law, or the Law to the "Needs" of the Security Service?' (1989) 23 *Israeli Law Review* 216; S. Kadish, 'Torture, the State and the Individual' (1989) 23 *Israeli Law Review* 343 at 356; A. Zuckerman, 'Coercion and the Individual: Ascertainment of the Truth' (1989) 23 *Israeli Law Review* 357 at 371; M. L. Clark, 'Note: Israel's High Court of Justice Ruling on the General Security Service Use of "Moderate Physical Pressure": An End to the Sanctioned Use of Torture?' (2000) 11 *Indiana International and Comparative Law Review* 145; M. Kremnitzer and R. Segev, 'Using Force During Investigations by the GSS – The Lesser Evil?' (1998) 4 *Mishpat Umimshal* 667 (Hebrew).

its landmark decision in *The GSS Case*.[40] In this case, the Court ruled that the interrogation techniques used by GSS officials in accordance with the guidelines established under the Landau Commission's report were illegal, since the GSS did not have the statutory legal authority to employ them.[41] Therefore, the use of such techniques was banned by the decision of the Court, at least until the Knesset could enact a statute authorising the use of 'moderate physical pressures' during interrogation.[42] The Court acknowledged the possibility that – under circumstances of severe and immediate danger to human life (the so-called 'ticking bomb' situation) – GSS officials who use extreme measures of interrogation may be exempted from criminal liability under the *necessity* rule. The Court maintained, however, that this fact could not serve as a valid legal source for authorising the GSS to adopt such measures *in advance* (i.e., as a basis for determining rules that constitute authority to enable the investigators to apply physical pressure).[43]

Following the publication of the Court's decision, there were suggestions both on behalf of Knesset members and on behalf of government officials to legislate a law specifically authorising the GSS to use moderate physical pressure in interrogations.[44] Those initiatives, however,

---

[40] See note 35 above.

[41] The Court did find that the GSS has the power, according to specific decrees issued by the Minister of Justice (issued under the Prevention of Terrorism Statute (1948) and other statutes) to conduct interrogations. Those powers, the Court said, only relate to the conduct of 'reasonable' investigation, and do not include the power to use the techniques at stake: see *ibid.*, sections 20–1.

[42] In fact, the powers of the Knesset to authorise the GSS to use such measures was also put into question since the Court specifically indicated that any such legislation should comply with the constitutional requirements entrenched in the Basic Law: Human Dignity and Freedom. See *ibid.*, section 18, p. 212.

[43] *Ibid.*, sections 34–7, pp. 222–5.

[44] See A. Beth, 'PM Barak Suggests: Senior Officials Would be Authorized to Approve "Special Interrogation Techniques" for the GSS in Cases of Immediate Danger', *Ha'aretz*, 9 September 1999, p. A-3; G. Alon, 'A Law to Overrule the HCJ GSS Decision to be Brought before the Knesset after the Holiday', *Ha'aretz*, 9 September 1999, p. A-3; and G. Alon, 'The Debate Concerning the Inclusion of GSS Interrogations in Statute Not Changed', *Ha'aretz*, 8 September 1999, p. A-3. For criticism of the efforts to legitimise torture by Knesset legislation after the GSS *Case*, see also M. G. St Amand, 'Note: Public Committee Against Torture v. The State of Israel: Landmark Human Rights Decision by the Israeli High Court of Justice or Status Quo Maintained?' (2000) 25 *North Carolina Journal of International and Commercial Regulation* 655 at 682–3.

failed, and, when the Knesset finally legislated the GSS Law of 2002, it was approved without any mention of such powers.[45]

Torture and judicial review: a conceptual analysis

What can a judicial system in a democracy do when faced with evidence (or with allegations that seem to be potentially supported by evidence) of the use of (any kind of) methods of investigating terrorists that involve torture? On the face of the matter, the answer may seem self-evident. The primary duty of courts in democracies is to protect human rights. Torture is a severe violation of basic human rights. Unlike other fundamental rights, the right not to be tortured is considered as absolute and is prohibited under international human rights conventions.[46] Therefore, there is no need for a 'balancing' of competing rights or interests (as in the case of limitations of other freedoms, such as the freedom of speech, etc.). The only possible reaction of a court, faced with an argument that interrogation techniques which involve physical pressure (of any kind) or other means of torture are being used (or may be used in the future), is to declare the illegality of such practices and to order *a complete ban* on their use.

In practice, however, courts in liberal democracies may often be rather slow to adopt the above response when faced with the issue. The savagery of terrorism, the difficulties of combating HTA with regular military means and the threat it poses to national security lead courts to adopt an alternative response, which is to choose the option of *avoidance*. A court in a democracy can hardly legitimise (or even countenance) the use of torture. However, for a court that operates within a society that is routinely victimised by terrorism and which lives under a constant threat of HTA, the alternative of avoidance is tempting. As the report of the Landau Commission indicates, the second way is that of hypocrites: '[T]hey declare that they abide by the rule of law, but turn a blind eye to what goes on beneath the surface.'[47]

---

[45] See note 28 above.

[46] Article 5 of the Universal Declaration of Human Rights (1948); Article 3(1)(a) of the Fourth General Convention Relative to the Protection of Civilian Persons in Time of War of 1949; Declaration on the Protection of All Persons from Being Subjected to Torture and Other Cruel, Inhuman or Degrading Treatment or Punishment of 1975. The same position is adopted in national legal systems: see e.g. W. Brugger, 'May Government Ever Use Torture? Two Responses from German Law' (2000) 48 *American Journal of Comparative Law* 661 at 662.

[47] Landau Report, section 4.4, pp. 77–8.

The avoidance alternative is tempting for a number of reasons. It releases the court from the need to directly confront the difficult dilemmas that are embedded in such situations, that is, to take responsibility for the human price that may be the result of adopting the (first) option of proclaiming a complete ban on extraordinary methods of investigation. On the other hand, it also saves the courts the need to bear the consequences should they explicitly legitimise, in any way, the use of torture. In the latter case, the court decision itself would seriously harm not only the image of the judiciary as the guardian of human rights but also the principle of the rule of law, the basis for the very existence of the court. As Justice Jackson once observed: 'A military commander may overstep the bounds of constitutionality, and it is an incident. But if we review and approve, that passing incident becomes the doctrine of the Constitution.'[48]

Therefore it is hardly surprising that the courts in democracies often resort to the alternative of avoidance rather than directly confront the questions that such cases raise.[49] In order to use this option, the judicial system must ensure that arguments concerning the use of torture by state authorities are kept out of the courtroom, so that the court would have no need to deal with them directly. This can be done by using techniques such as justiciability or by applying restrictions on the introduction of evidence as to the existence of torture.[50]

The Israeli Supreme Court, during the 1970s, when faced with this dilemma, adopted the alternative of avoidance. From the political

---

[48] *Koramatsu* v. *US*, 323 US 214 (1944) *per* Justice Jackson (dissenting).

[49] A. M. Dershowitz, 'Is It Necessary to Apply "Physical Pressure" to Terrorists and to Lie about It?' (1989) 23 *Israeli Law Review* 192; and J. Bishop, Jr, 'Control of Terrorism and Insurrection: The British Laboratory Experience' (1978) 42 *Law and Contemporary Problems* 140; and see the Landau Report, pp. 67–9 (discussing the case of Northern Ireland). See also Amnesty International Report 2001 (An Overview) (Amnesty International public document, AI Index Pol 10/008/2001, News Service No. 068 at http://web.amnesty.org/web/ar2001.nst/regEur/regEur? Open Document) indicating that in thirty-two European countries government authorities use methods of torture during interrogations.

[50] For the use of avoidance techniques by courts facing difficult political questions, see e.g. A. M. Bickel, *The Least Dangerous Branch – The Supreme Court and the Bar of Politics* (Indianapolis, Bobbs-Merrill, 1962); G. Gunther, 'The Subtle Vices of the "Passive Virtues" – A Comment on Principle and Expediency in Judicial Review' (1964) 64 *Columbia Law Review* 1; De Smith, *Judicial Review of Administrative Action* (4th edn, London, J. M. Evans, 1980), p. 290; P. Blair, *Federalism and Judicial Review in West Germany* (Oxford, Clarendon, 1981), pp. 28–31.

point of view, the unwillingness of the Court to look too hard at the methods of interrogation used by the GSS conformed with the general deference of the Court towards security agencies. It also conformed with the high respect given by the Israeli polity at large to the security apparatus. The Court was also well equipped to give effect to this choice by using the wide array of legal doctrines that were at its disposal for this purpose at the time (such as a wide conception of justiciability, and rules of evidence precluding the possibility of effectively questioning the veracity of GSS official testimony in court).[51]

While for the 'old Court' of the 1970s, the avoidance alternative was almost a 'natural' choice, it was virtually non-existent for the 'new Court' of the 1980s and beyond for a number of reasons. First, the Court, during the 1980s, systematically sought to diminish the access doctrines and therefore could hardly continue to use them as an excuse to avoid dealing with petitions regarding torture. In particular, the Court almost completely discarded the doctrine of justiciability as a bar to the judicial review of government actions.[52] Secondly, resorting to avoidance in cases regarding GSS interrogations would have threatened another major project initiated by the 'new Court', that is, to subject the security apparatus to close supervision by the judiciary. In fact, avoiding the torture issue could have been fatal to the fulfilment of the HCJ's judicial ambitions in this respect, because the scandals that brought the whole subject to the attention of the public (and subsequently led to the formation of the Landau Commission) dealt not only with torture by GSS officials but also with allegations of perjury.[53] Therefore, for the courts at this stage to turn a blind eye and continue their business as usual while knowing that the GSS officials had lied in court would have been to give up altogether their aspirations to ensure social control by the judiciary over the security apparatus. Finally, even if the

---

[51] Under section 44 of the Evidence Ordinance [New Version] 1971, the Prime Minister or the Minister of Defense can issue a privilege order to ban exposure in Court. While, since 1965 the privilege order has been subject to judicial review, the scope of such review is very limited. Therefore, GSS staff testimonies were usually heard behind closed doors before 1980 and, to large extent, also after 1980. See A. Rubinstein and B. Medina, *The Constitutional Law of the State of Israel* (5th edn, Tel Aviv, Schocken, 1996), pp. 797–800; Zamir, 'Rule of Law', pp. 398–401.

[52] See note 8 above and the accompanying text.

[53] Interestingly, the two public scandals that triggered the formation of the Landau Commission both involved allegations of perjury by GSS officials initiated to acquit or incriminate members of the Israel military (rather than Palestinian terrorists).

Supreme Court had wanted to resort to avoidance, it could not do so after the formation of the Landau Commission and the publication of its report.

On the other hand, for the 'new Court' of the 1980s and beyond, it was not at all easy to resort to the solution of a complete ban on the use of physical pressure in interrogations. This was not only because of the above-mentioned difficulties entailed by the terrorist–torture dilemma. Adopting a clear flat rule of complete ban on torture also conflicted with the general line of jurisprudence developed by the Court during the 1980s and 1990s. The judicial activism of the 'new Court' used the technique of *ad hoc balancing* as a central pillar of its reasoning. The use of *ad hoc* balancing was attuned to the wider and ambitious doctrine of justiciability.[54] The social message that the Court sought to send to all other players in the Israeli polity was: 'Bring *everything* [i.e. every social, moral, economic or political question] to *us* [since there are no limitations of access to judicial review] and *we* shall take *all considerations* into account [in the course of *ad hoc* balancing].' The combination of practically unlimited access to judicial review with the *ad hoc* balancing jurisprudence was aimed at fulfilling these judicial ambitions.[55] A clear-cut rule that sets a complete ban on physical pressure in interrogation, while clearly compatible with international norms of human rights and with a careful analysis of Israeli administrative law,[56] stood in contrast to the general philosophy of judicial review of the 'new Court'. Paradoxically, therefore, both alternatives – that of avoidance and that of a complete ban – stood in contrast with the jurisprudence of *inclusion* to which the court adhered.

As a result, following the publication of the Landau Commission's report, and when petitions regarding torture began flooding the Court's docket, the Court adopted a third way to deal with the issue: it fully adopted the recommendations of the Landau Commission. That is, instead of either avoiding the issue or banning torture altogether, it began to *regulate* the use of physical pressure in GSS interrogations. The regulatory process was founded on the combination of the internal guidelines adopted by the government following the Landau

[54] This was acknowledged also by the critics of the activist trend, such as Justice Elon: see HC 1635/90, *Zarzavski v. The Prime Minister* 45(1) PD 749.
[55] There were a number of other tools which the Court developed in order to ensure that major social, economic or political questions would make their way sooner or later (usually sooner) into the courts. See note 21 above and the accompanying text.
[56] See note 30 above and the accompanying text, and near note 37 above.

Commission's report on the one hand, with judicial supervision over their application, based on a *balancing* of the competing interests in each and every case on the other.[57] This was the legal situation until the landmark decision of the Supreme Court in 1999 (*The GSS Case*) when the Court re-assessed its prior position and resorted to the alternative of a complete ban on torture.

We can therefore summarize the legal development of the judicial attitude towards the issue of torture by the following table describing the legal regime that controlled the issue in each and every phase:

Years	Legal Regime Regarding Torture
1967 – 1987	Avoidance
1987 – 1999	Regulation
1999 – 2001	Complete Ban

In the next part of this paper I shall try to examine the impact of each of these three different legal regimes on the actual behavior of the GSS in its interrogation. Particularly, I shall try to analyse to what extent the judicial supervision during the second and third periods (i.e. regulation and complete ban) manages to assure the adherence of the GSS to the law in the books at the relevant period.

THE RESEARCH

Methodology
Studying the impact of judicial review on the behaviour of security agencies is a far from simple task. Apart from the difficulties accompanying impact research in general, the access to reliable information in the current case is complicated by the nature of the participants. The practices and actions of the Israeli GSS (like, I presume, any other secret service) are hidden behind a thick cover of secrecy. Any data (quantitative or otherwise) are either non-existent or highly confidential for security reasons. GSS personnel are normally not allowed to be

---

[57] Following the recommendations included in the second (and secret) part of the Landau Commission's report, the government developed a set of guidelines as to the types of measure which the GSS was allowed to use in its interrogations and the circumstances under which the interrogators were authorised to use them. The Court never *explicitly* endorsed the guidelines as a legally binding code (not even as a legitimate code of behaviour: see e.g. HC 2581/91, *Salachat* v. *The Government of Israel* 47(4) PD 837 at 844). In practice, however, the guidelines were presented to the Court during litigation several times, and judicial review was based on their existence (see below).

interviewed about their activities – and even if they had been allowed to be interviewed, it is doubtful whether they would have been keen to provide information about their practices. In order to overcome these difficulties, I used an array of methods, some of them quite untraditional. First, I studied systematically court files (as long as they were open to the public)[58] in which the GSS's practices of interrogation were challenged (see below). Secondly, I used public reports and media coverage provided by human rights organisations which followed the actions of the GSS and covered the issue of torture. This information was complemented through interviews with those who were involved in the judicial battles over torture on both sides.[59]

Studying the impact of judicial review in the 1990s (the 'regulation' regime)

The publication of the Landau Commission's report brought about the beginning of the era during which the Israeli legal system sought to regulate the use of torture by GSS officials. The regulation was founded on administrative guidelines developed by the GSS, under the supervision of the government and in accordance with the recommendations included in the second (and secret) part of the report.[60] The underlying assumption of the move to regulate the use of physical pressure during

---

[58] In general, I did not have a problem of access to files containing information about petitions challenging the practices of the GSS (see below). Still, experience shows that some files of the Supreme Court may have been kept back, due to their classification as pertaining to matters of national security.

[59] Interviews were conducted with lawyers who represented the government in petitions regarding torture and were involved in the process of regulating GSS procedures, as well as with some lawyers who represented detainees in petitions to the HCJ. Since I could not interview GSS personnel, I used for this purpose interviews conducted by a former student of mine in the course of seminar work she issued in 1998. Her access to the GSS staff was based on the fact that at the relevant time she served as an intern in the legal department of the GSS. I am well aware of the untraditional nature of the methodology of interviews, but I found no other way to interview directly any GSS staff.

[60] The government appointed a special committee of ministers that approved the guidelines and was authorised to issue 'permissions' to the GSS to apply physical pressure (of different degrees) during interrogations. The process also involved the active involvement of the Attorney General's Office, which was required to ensure the legality of these permissions. See e.g. G. Alon, 'The Ministers Committee Granted the GSS Permission to "Make Interrogation Methods More Efficient"', Ha'aretz, 14 November 1994; G. Alon, 'Permits for GSS to Apply "Intensified Physical Pressures" Renewed for Three More Months', Ha'aretz, 13 April 1995.

in interrogation was that the regulation could minimise the use of these measures, on the one hand, and ensure it would be carefully monitored by the legal regime apparatus (that is, by the Attorney General's Office and presumably by the courts) on the other.[61] The idea behind the legal supervision was to ensure that there would not be widespread and unauthorised use of torture, and that infringements on human rights would be minimised as far as possible under the exigencies of the fight against terrorism. The formation of this legal regime brought about the proliferation of petitions to the HCJ in which Palestinian detainees held by the GSS[62] petitioned the HCJ asking the Court to intervene in the process of their interrogation.

To what extent was the HCJ and the legal system at large successful in regulating torture? Did they manage to ensure that the use of torture was kept within the confines set by the Landau Commission's report? These questions will be examined in this section.

Petitions to the HCJ regarding torture

In order to study the impact of judicial supervision on the practices of interrogation by the GSS, I first examined HCJ files that existed, at the time of the research, in the Supreme Court's archives in the years 1990, 1992, 1994, 1996 and 1998, that is, during the period of the second phase of legal development (when the Court sought to regulate torture). This was done by systematically searching and locating any HCJ files in the archives in which there was a petition against the GSS (as sole or joint respondent) that raised the issue of interrogations.[63] The first findings refer to the number of petitions issued against the GSS that

---

[61] Interview with IZ 24 July 2002.

[62] It should be noted that, in principle, the mandate to use physical pressure was not limited to Palestinian detainees. Indeed, during the 1990s, there were some cases in which Jewish detainees arrested by the GSS on the basis of suspected terrorist activities complained about the methods of interrogation used against them by the GSS.

[63] This may seem a rather cumbersome and demanding procedure, but it is the only way to reach a full and accurate picture of the uses of litigation against torture. I could not limit the analysis to researching the Court's registers alone, since the Court's registers do not always contain full and accurate details of the parties involved and of the outcome of the case. I could not use only a sample of the files in each year either, since the number of relevant files is relatively small, and constitutes only a fraction of the general population of HCJ files for each year. Due to the time needed to search all the court files for one year, I only searched the archives for every second year during the 1990s and for six months (January–March and July–September) for each of those five years. Despite the fact that we searched virtually all the HCJ files in

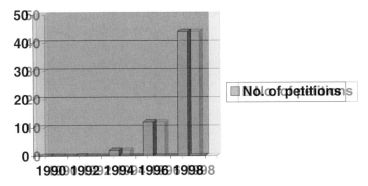

Figure 7.1 Petitions against torture 1990–1998
Source: HCJ files.
Note: n = 56. These numbers refer to files for six months in each of the relevant years. Therefore, it is estimated that the actual number of petitions for each year is double that shown.

raised allegations of torture during interrogations. The overall number of petitions dealing with the subject included in our database for these five years was fifty-six.[64] The relevant number per each year is presented in Figure 7.1.

As Figure 7.1 demonstrates, most petitions against the GSS regarding the practices of interrogation were issued during the second half of the 1990s. This seems surprising, due to the fact that the Landau Commission's report was published in 1987 and that there is no doubt that the practices of using physical pressure during interrogations was prevalent

those years, there may be some files that we missed due to administrative or security reasons (see note 58 above), or were skipped, since the issue of torture was not clearly indicated on the file.

[64] Taking into consideration that we checked only six months for each of these five years, the overall number for petitions in each year is expected to be double this number. Accordingly, the overall number of petitions involving the issue of torture during the 1990s is estimated at just above 200. It is important to note, though, that the GSS did not actually use physical pressure in all of these cases. The Emergency Legislation in the Territories authorises the security authorities to issue orders which preclude meetings between the detainees and their lawyers for up to thirty days from the day of the arrest. As a result, the standard practice of the lawyers representing these detainees has been to issue a petition that asks the court to enable them to meet with their clients and to refrain from using torture against them (without actually knowing what procedures are taken in the particular case of their clients). In reality, in many cases that were titled as 'petitions against torture', the State would appear in Court and declare that such measures were not being applied against the respective detainee. See note 68 below.

during the first half of the 1990s (at least as much as it was common during the second half of the 1990s).[65] Since the political fight against the practices of interrogation by the GSS was already ongoing during the first half of the 1990s, it seems, on the face of the matter, unexpected that it was not until 1994 (or 1993 at the earliest) that petitions against torture started making their way to the HCJ.[66]

The second and more important finding relates to the outcome of the petitions in our database. Out of fifty-six petitions, the Court allowed only one petition! That petition was, in fact, the well-known GSS *Case*.[67] Almost all other petitions in our database were either dismissed by the Court, or became moot after either party notified the Court that the issue of pressure during interrogation is no longer present.[68] A typical case belonging to this group was a case in which *at the time of the initial hearing* the representative of the State Attorney notified the court that either the petitioner's investigation was over, or that the GSS was *no longer* using any physical pressure in his interrogation, or that the State has no intention of using such measures in his interrogation in

---

[65] See e.g. B'Tselem, *1991 Report*; B'Tselem (the Israeli Information Center for Human Rights in the Occupied Territories), *Torture During Interrogations: Testimony of Palestinian Detainees, Testimony of Interrogators* (Jerusalem, IICHROT, 1994).

[66] Given that the same organisations (such as the Public Committee Against Torture and the Association of Civil Rights in Israel (ACRI)) that petitioned the court from 1994 onwards were already active in the early 1990s, and since there was no problem of access to judicial review, the lack of such petitions during 1990–2 seems puzzling. A possible explanation is that it took human rights organisations and activists a long time to identify the legal potential of the Landau Report and to translate it into a legal cause of action. As one lawyer-activist said: 'Nobody [at the beginning of the 1990s] thought we could make the Court intervene in an ongoing GSS interrogations by petitioning the HCJ' (interview with IL, 24 July 2002; see also interview with AL, 23 July 2002). An additional reason was that issuing a large number of petitions required organisation and funding on behalf of these NGOs (see interview with IL, 24 July 2002).

[67] See text near note 40 above. In fact, the case was decided in 1999, but it was included in our database since it was issued in 1994 (see below). In fact, the GSS Case included seven different petitions that were consolidated to one court file, and therefore constitute one petition in our database.

[68] In nine out of the fifty-six cases the petitions were dismissed by the court with neither writ nor interim injunction given. In forty-three cases (i.e. approximately 77 per cent of the total number of cases in our database) either the petitioner or the State notified the court that at the stage of the hearing (see below) the issue of torture was no longer present or the petition was dismissed as moot (in one additional case the litigation ended with a settlement while in the rest of the cases, the outcome could not be classified as success or failure or could not be verified from the files).

the future. In other words, it is clear from these files that the supervision by the court had almost no impact (at least not by the form of judicial orders) on the use of physical pressure, because, when the first court hearing was conducted, the GSS had already managed to complete the part of the interrogation that involved physical pressure. This point, regarding the timing of review, needs further explanation.

Normally, the judicial review process before the HCJ is relatively expedient.[69] In cases involving GSS interrogations, the initial hearing usually took place a few days after the arrest of the suspect. These few days, however, sufficed for the GSS to conduct the crucial part of the interrogation using whatever means they saw fit. On the face of the matter, there is a simple procedural solution to this quandary. The Court could issue an *interim injunction* immediately after the arrest, ordering the GSS not to use any measures until the hearing took place (a process that could be put into motion within a few hours in cases of urgency). In reality, only in six cases in our database (i.e., 11 per cent) did the Court issue an injunction. Therefore, in essence, the lack of willingness by the Court to use injunctions in these cases was the decisive factor in ensuring that the GSS was able to conduct its interrogation with minimal judicial intervention. Even in the few cases in which the Court did issue injunctions, this was not done immediately after the issuance of the petitions (in *ex parte* proceedings), but only after the State was invited to respond to the request, and after the interrogation was already ongoing (for at least a day or two). In such circumstances, the ability of human rights activists to effectively thwart the very use of physical pressure in GSS interrogations was extremely limited. Moreover, even in those few cases in which an injunction was issued, the GSS returned to the Court whenever it felt that the injunction inhibited the interrogation, and it was successful in achieving a revocation of the injunction. Thus, for example, in HC 7964/95, *Bilbeisi v. GSS* (1995), while the interim injunction was in effect, the petitioner confessed to taking part in a prior terrorist attack (suicide bombing) and that he was hiding more explosives ready for use by his fellow terrorists. After reviewing the evidence presented to it by the GSS representative,[70] the court

---

[69] See the text after note 17 above.

[70] The evidence presented by the GSS to the Court is usually secret, and is presented to the justices but not to the detainee or his lawyer. This is a voluntary procedure that can only take place with the consent of the detainee during the hearing (see also note 51 above).

accepted the GSS arguments stating that there is 'a clear and present danger of harm to human lives', and revoked the injunction.[71]

The overall picture that the study of the court files reveals points to the fact that judicial review of the implementation of the guidelines concerning GSS interrogation was hardly effective. Indeed, the HCJ played its part in the process of the bureaucratisation of torture (see below), but there is hardly any evidence that judicial involvement contributed to limiting the scope of use of physical pressure or to prevent violations of the guidelines. The review process usually took place only after the interrogation had been ongoing for several hours, and, therefore, there was no actual review of the initial decision to apply physical pressure, and even *ex post facto* the Court rarely intervened in the practices of the GSS.

I argued earlier that the 'new Court' of the 1980s and 1990s gave up the idea of using *avoidance techniques* in judicial review.[72] It seems however, that, in dealing with the torture issue, the HCJ, while giving up traditional avoidance techniques, developed alternative techniques. By declining interim injunctions and applying its review in *ex post facto* format (contrary to its normal practices), the Court in essence systematically used avoidance techniques to ensure that it would not face the need to directly interfere in GSS interrogations. Rather than using formal legal doctrines (such as justiciability) for avoidance, the Court systematically delayed the hearing in order to achieve a similar result.[73]

The most striking evidence for the use of avoidance strategy during the 1990s in regard to torture is probably the timing of the GSS *Case* itself. This landmark decision of the Court (that brought to an end the 'regulation' of torture) was given in September of 1999. The petition by the Public Committee Against Torture in Israel was, however, issued *five years* earlier (in September 1994). Why did the Court take so much time to decide the case? Given the fact that the use of physical pressure was illegal *per se* since the GSS lacked statutory powers to use such methods (as the Court itself finally declared), the Court should have been able to decide the case immediately. Instead, the Court conducted the first hearing of the parties only in May 1998 (i.e., over three years

---

[71] See also HC 8049/96, *Hamdan v. GSS* (1996); HC 3124/96, *Mubarak v. GSS* (1996); and Clark, 'Note', p.145 and n. 49.

[72] See the text near note 51 and note 54 above.

[73] See also Kremnitzer and Segev, 'Using Force'.

after the petition was issued). The only explanation for the delay is the unwillingness of the Court to deal with the case – i.e., the wish to avoid it.[74]

Studying the arena of interrogations during the 1990s
While the Landau Commission's report sought to regulate the use of physical pressure in GSS interrogations and thereby to minimise the infringement of human rights, various sources indicated that the legal apparatus formed after the publication of the report flatly failed to achieve this goal.

In 1991, B'Tselem (the Israeli Information Center for Human Rights in the Occupied Territories) published a comprehensive report on torture during GSS interrogations.[75] The report argued that the GSS routinely employed a variety of methods of physical pressure in its interrogations.[76] This was corroborated by numerous affidavits given by former detainees. While allegations made by human rights organisations could be rejected by the government as politicised and biased, the allegations regarding torture were supported by a variety of independent evidence. The most conclusive such evidence was a special report made by the State Comptroller that pointed to the fact that during the years 1988–92 there were 'severe flaws' in the mechanisms designed to monitor GSS practices. The report pointed to the fact that GSS officials made 'grave and systematic violations' of the guidelines set out in the Landau Commission's report. Moreover, the Comptroller indicated that not only did the GSS staff use unauthorized methods of interrogation, but also that they continued to lie about it as if the Landau Commission's Report had never been written.[77] Even more worrying was the Comptroller's statement that senior officials in the GSS were

---

[74] In fact, human rights activists made attempts to challenge the legality of the Landau Report guidelines as early as 1991. The petition was, however, dismissed by the Court on the ground that it was moot. See HC 2581/91, *Salachat v. The Government of Israel* 47(4) PD 837.

[75] See B'Tselem, *1991 Report*.

[76] See note 35 above. In addition, the report argued that GSS detainees are routinely beaten during interrogations.

[77] See the State Comptroller's Report on the issue of GSS interrogations in 1988–92. The report was issued during 1994 but was published only in 2000. Nevertheless, the issuance of the report was covered at the time by the media, which also pointed to its general findings and conclusions. The mounting evidence pointing to flagrant violations of the Landau Commission's guidelines also included some public scandals due to the death of some detainees during interrogations. See B'Tselem (the Israeli

well informed of these violations and in effect authorised them. The publication of the Comptroller's report was a shock for many senior government officials as well as for senior legal officials (including Landau himself[78]) and brought about tensions between the Attorney General and the government of the time.[79]

The aftermath of these scandals were some administrative reforms within the GSS and the governmental apparatus supervising the GSS. The guidelines were re-examined by the special Ministers' Committee, and some of the more severe measures were either taken out, or defined by the committee as referring only to exceptional situations of 'ticking bombs'. More importantly, the government took comprehensive action to ensure that the GSS reports to external supervisors would be accurate and complete. As a result, the GSS began documenting each and every step of its interrogations in detail. Thus, the process of bureaucratisation of torture reached its peak towards the second half of the 1990s. The GSS representatives in Court could present to the judges detailed documents describing the exact measures employed against the petitioner in each and every case, as well as the exact length of time and the dates in which they were employed.

The bureaucratisation of torture during the late 1990s contributed to the end of perjury by GSS staff, but hardly influenced the proliferation of the use of physical pressure.[80] In 1997, human rights organisations argued that almost any Palestinian detainee endures at least some sort of interrogation by illegitimate measures when arrested by the GSS.[81] This allegation was in fact corroborated by a senior legal advisor of the government, who said: 'The Landau Commission viewed physical

---

Information Center for Human Rights in the Occupied Territories), *The Death of Mustafa Barakat* (Jerusalem, IICHROT, 1992); O. Nir, 'Harizat Died from Torture – A Well-Known Method of the GSS', *Ha'aretz*, 30 April 1995.

[78] See G. Alon and E. Rabin, 'Justice Landau Says "He Feels Betrayed" by the Violations of the Rules of Conduct by the GSS', *Ha'aretz*, 9 January 1995.

[79] See e.g. 'Ben-Yair: Some Special Permits to GSS Investigators Are Illegal', *Ha'aretz*, 3 August 1995; 'Ministers to Discuss a Middle Course with Ben-Yair to Enable the Extension of Special Permission to the GSS', *Ha'aretz*, 6 August 1995.

[80] As one senior GSS member said: 'Currently, there is no case in which I . . . shall not be completely transparent *vis-à-vis* the prosecution and the Court. There is no situation in which someone [i.e. a GSS official] would take the stand and lie . . . We are not carrying this cross alone.' Interview with senior GSS official, 1998.

[81] B'Tselem (the Israeli Information Center for Human Rights in the Occupied Territories), *Legitimizing Torture* (Jerusalem, IICHROT, 1997); 'B'Tselem: GSS Torture 85% of Palestinian Detainees', *Ha'aretz*, 20 May 1998.

pressure as an exceptional measure. The GSS made it part of the "standard menu" in their interrogations.'[82] The legal guidelines, combined with routine judicial supervision, did affect the way in which the GSS conducted its business, but not the extent to which physical pressure was used. Instead of unruly interrogators violating basic norms of the rule of law, the GSS interrogators became bureaucrats of torture. Every step was carefully covered by legal permissions, documented, and presented to legal supervisors and judges. In the words of a lawyer who represented detainees:

> I prefer an interrogator who loses his temper and hits the interogatee to an interrogator that makes a request to his supervisor, who makes a request to his legal superior, who passes on the request to the Committee for Permissions [to use torture].[83]

While hardly influencing the practices of the GSS during the 1990s, the legal regime constituted by the Landau Commission and judicial supervision did have – eventually – an important impact on torture. It contributed to the end of the 'regulation' era. The mounting evidence on the practices of the GSS, coupled with the detailed documentation of torture that was exposed over and over again in each court case, brought increasing public criticism and international protest against these practices. And this, subsequently, brought about the decision in the GSS Case that put an end to this era.[84]

The impact of the HCJ decision in the GSS Case

In September 1999, five years after the case was begun, the Supreme Court finally gave judgment in the GSS Case. Unlike the complicated regime set up by the detailed guidelines in the Landau Commission's report, and the puzzling position expressed in judicial opinions throughout the 1990s, the Court was very decisive this time. It declared *all* the procedures of interrogation certified by the Landau Commission's report to be illegal,[85] and ordered them to be completely banned.

Unlike in the case of the 'regulation' regime, the impact of the decision in the GSS Case was immediate and comprehensive. The Israeli media reported an instant halt of all GSS interrogations the day the

---

[82] Interview with IZ, 23 July 2002.   [83] Interview AL, 22 July 2002.

[84] Interview with AL, 22 July 2002; interview with IZ, 23 July 2002; interview with IL, 24 July 2002.

[85] The Court stopped short, however, of identifying these procedures as 'torture': see the GSS Case, note 30 above, section 30, p. 20.

decision was given.[86] The impression that the use of physical pressure became rare as a direct result of the decision is shared by both lawyers representing Palestinian detainees and senior officials in the Ministry of Justice.[87] Even human rights organisations that previously argued that the GSS used torture as a standard measure reported 'a significant change' in the practices of the GSS as a result of the decision.[88]

The apparently immediate and far-reaching impact of the decision in the GSS Case on the practices of interrogation by the GSS may seem somewhat unexpected. Given the common knowledge regarding the limited ability of courts to bring about comprehensive reforms in social policy, and the dubious record of the GSS in abiding by legal constraints in the past, one may wonder whether, and to what extent, the Court ruling will be able to serve as an effective guarantee against the use of torture by the GSS in the future.[89] In any case, the above reported remarkable response of the GSS to the judicial order requires some explanation, even assuming that in the long run the GSS will withstand pressures to reinstate its previous practices.[90] It seems that the most probable explanation for the immediate and far-reaching impact of the

---

[86] See R. Shaked, 'New Model of Investigation', *Yeditoth Aharonot* 7 September 1999; A. Harel, 'Criticism by the GSS: We Were Left with Responsibility But No Power', *Ha'aretz*, 8 September 1999.

[87] Interview with AL, 22 July 2002; interview with IZ, 23 July 2002; interview with IL, 24 July 2002. See also Andrei Rosenthal, lawyer and human rights activist, cited in A. Regular, 'The Poetics of Shaking', *Kol Ha'ir*, 11 September 2001, p. 61. But cf. A. Harel, 'The GSS Used "Exceptional Methods of Interrogation" in 90 Cases Since the HCJ Ruling in 1999', *Ha'aretz*, 25 July 2002.

[88] B'Tselem, 'Torture' on B'Tselem website (21 July 2002); Public Committee Against Torture in Israel, *Flawed Defense: Torture and Ill-Treatment in GSS Interrogations Following the Supreme Court Ruling – 6 September 1999–6 September 2001* (Jerusalem, PCATI, 2001) (the latter report indicates 'significant change' in the practices of the GSS, but argues that the practices used by the GSS after the decision should also be banned). The GSS continues to make use of exceptional methods in 'rare and exceptional circumstances' identified as 'ticking bombs'. The number of such cases, as a senior Ministry of Justice official said, is 'a fraction of 1 per cent [relative to the general number of GSS investigations]' and normally can be counted 'on half the fingers of one hand' each year (interview with IZ, 23 July 2002).

[89] See G. N. Rosenberg, *The Hollow Hope: Can Courts Bring About Social Change* (Chicago, University of Chicago, 1991).

[90] It should be noted that the GSS Case was decided in 1999, about one year before the recent wave of violence in Israel and the occupied territories (known as the second *intifada*) erupted in September 2000. The era of the second *intifada* is not included in the research period of the current study. The account in the text refers to the impact of the GSS Case on practices of interrogation by the GSS during the period

decision on the GSS is the content of the judicial decision, on the one hand, and the political context within which the decision was made, on the other. It should be noted that the Israeli bureaucracy in general, and the Israeli military in particular, have a solid record of abiding by the decisions of the HCJ. As long as the judicial directives regarding torture were framed in the vague and complicated format of 'the balancing formula' (during the 'regulation era'), the GSS could proceed with its practices of interrogation, while using all kinds of procedural manoeuvres in order to evade effective supervision. This became virtually impossible once the Court ordered a complete and unconditional ban on torture. Likewise, during the 'regulation era' the politicians overseeing the GSS could turn a blind eye to the widespread use of torture, using the existence of judicial supervision as an excuse for their inaction. This was no longer true after the Court's ruling. The GSS staff understood that, ever since the decision was made, violations of the Court's ruling were relatively easy to detect, and that they would not enjoy the support of their superiors for committing them. Given the high profile of the issue of torture in the media and the extensive criticism of the GSS, the GSS could no longer bear the risk of ignoring the outright ban on the use of torture imposed by the Court.

CONCLUSION

The Israeli judicial system, presided over by the Supreme Court, made an extraordinary move during the 1990s. It sought to legalise a phenomenon that in a modern democratic state cannot be legalised – torture. This attempt was the result of ambitious conceptions as to the role of law and of courts in society. These conceptions were based on the belief that any activity of any government agency, as well as any other social phenomenon, can and should be defined, organised and regulated by legal principles and subjected to the supervision of the court system. It used the tool of interest balancing (by ambitious activist judges) as a solution to almost any political controversy or social dilemma.

The history of 'regulated torture' serves as a painful reminder of the limits of the jurisprudence of inclusion. In modern liberal democracies, the use of torture by secret service officials can, perhaps, be done in

immediately following the decision. The question of whether, or to what extent, recent military and political developments have worked to compromise this reported impact is beyond the scope of the current research.

the dark dungeons of the state's backyard, safely covered by practices of avoidance and ignorance, buttressed by over-zealous police officials, short-sighted politicians and public opinion terrified by terrorism. It cannot, however, be brought into the light of day, under the allures of legality – and survive the test of fundamental values of human rights and rule of law and of international public opinion.

It is therefore hardly surprising that the attempt by the Israeli judicial system to control the application of 'physical pressure' during interrogation by techniques of balancing flatly failed from the point of view of impact measuring, but, in the end, contributed to the complete collapse of the regime of regulating torture.

CHAPTER EIGHT

IMPLEMENTING COURT ORDERS IN THE UNITED STATES: JUDGES AS EXECUTIVES

MALCOLM M. FEELEY

INTRODUCTION

Since at least the publication of Richard Neustadt's book, *Presidential Power*, it has been commonplace to observe that few policies are self-executing, and that chief executives have only very limited abilities to accomplish their objectives. Indeed, a generation ago, a new field of research, implementation studies, emerged to address this issue. In their book, *Implementation*, that did much to establish this field, Jeffrey Pressman and Aaron Wildavsky proposed to stand a central question of public administration on its head. Rather than ask, 'Why do some policies fail?', they asked, 'Why do some policies occasionally succeed?'

Variations on this theme are now common in the American literature on public administration. In his classic book, *Street Level Bureaucracy*, Michael Lipsky attributes the routinisation of policy failure to two features of contemporary bureaucratic life: (1) the vast 'distance' between those who formulate formal policy – legislatures, chief executives, agency heads – and those who provide street level service; and (2) the vast discretion that these service providers exercise. In her study of federal policies to counter employment discrimination, Kirsten Bumiller argues that legal remedies are empty gestures, designed to give the appearance of doing something while reinforcing the *status quo*.[1] More generally, the late Murray Edelman elaborated a theory of policy

---

[1] K. Bumiller, *The Civil Rights Society* (Baltimore, Johns Hopkins University Press, 1984). Similarly, Alan Friedman has interpreted developments in anti-discrimination

failure, whose central thesis is captured in the titles of his books: *The Symbolic Uses of Politics, Words that Succeed But Policies that Fail* and *Constructing the Political Spectacle*.[2]

Studies of the impact of courts have not been exempted from such desultory conclusions. Donald Horowitz's 1973 book, *Courts and Social Policy*, maintained that courts cannot effect significant social policy because they lack the capacity to appraise policy issues, peruse alternatives, and select and implement the most appropriate choices. A short time later, in the *Politics of Rights*, Stuart Scheingold published a variation on this theme: rights foster myths that lead to political quiescence rather than change, though occasionally these myths might become catalysts in mobilising social movements. In his 1991 book, *The Hollow Hope*, whose title announces its theme, Gerald Rosenberg disputed even this modest role for courts. There is no evidence, he maintains, that litigation by itself can ever effect significant social change either directly or indirectly.[3] And most recently in *Rights at Work*, Michael McCann has challenged both Rosenberg's methods and conclusions, although his own findings are in fact not much different: at best litigation can sometimes be a catalyst in mobilising social movements.[4]

Thus the widespread conclusion of the implementation and impact literature is that policies fail because policy-makers are not powerful enough or are not sufficiently attentive to and involved with the drawn-out process of implementation. Judicial policy-making fails because courts lack the capacity to diagnose social problems and oversee the complex process of implementation.

law in much the same way; they are policies to appease liberal consciences, which were never intended to effect fundamental changes at all. See A. Friedman, 'Antidiscrimination Law: The View from 1989' in David Kairys (ed.), *The Politics of Law* (New York, Pantheon Books, 1990), pp. 121–50.

[2] There is of course a voluminous Marxist literature arguing that bourgeois liberal law reforms do little or nothing to ameliorate the issues they are ostensibly designed to address, and that their primary function is to legitimate the authority, which they mask. See e.g. D. Hay, 'Property, Authority, and Criminal Justice' in D. Hay (ed.), *Albion's Fatal Tree* (New York, Pantheon, 1973), pp. 17–64. For a more general survey of the functions of law according to various Marxist theories, see H. Collins, *Marxism and Law* (Oxford, Clarendon Press, 1982). For a reflective qualification by a long-standing Marxist, see E. P. Thompson, *Whigs and Hunters* (New York, Pantheon, 1977), pp. 254–60.

[3] G. N. Rosenberg, *The Hollow Hope: Can Courts Bring About Social Change?* (Chicago, University of Chicago, 1991).

[4] M. McCann, *Rights at Work* (Chicago, University of Chicago, 1994).

However, even as they diagnosed near-pervasive failure, Pressman and Wildavsky also identified what they believed was a prescription for success: 'Declaration of policies', they maintained, 'cannot be separated from implementation . . . Implementation is an extension of policy formulation, and thus has to be *factored into the design* of programs at the outset.'[5] Thus they argue that, if policies are to stand any chance of being successful, those who design them must also become involved with their implementation, and those who implement them must play a major part in designing them.

In our recent book, *Judicial Policy-making and the Modern State*, Edward Rubin and I examine a policy issue in which American federal courts seemed to have heeded Pressman and Wildavsky's advice. We found that at least in one arena, establishing policies for conditions within prisons, American trial courts have been relatively *successful* as policy-makers; their rulings have been widely accepted, and they have effected significant change in the nation's correctional institutions.[6] Our book focused on how judges in these cases overcame traditional doctrinal constraints in order to formulate bold new policies. In this chapter, I examine the steps the judges took to elaborate on and implement these policies, how they merged the process of policy-making with implementation in ways that fit Pressman and Wildavsky's prescription. In particular, this chapter explores how the judges expanded their capacities to develop expertise and engage in the process of reflexive policy-making and implementation in conjunction with correctional officials. Briefly, they did this by transforming themselves into something akin to administrative agencies or executives, complete with staff.

When first confronted with complaints about conditions by prisoners, American courts in the late 1960s and early 1970s responded in traditional legal terms. They characterised problems as violations of due process, failures to provide access to courts, violations of free speech or free exercise of religion, and the like, and expanded basic rights of expression to people in prisons. But when they confronted the Plantation Model that envisioned the prisoner as slave of the state and expected prisons to be run at no or low cost to the state, they abandoned this approach, transformed themselves into executive agencies, and set

[5] J. Pressman and A. Wildavsky, *Implementation* (Berkeley, University of California Press, 1975).

[6] M. M. Feeley and E. L. Rubin, *Judicial Policy-making and the Modern State: How the Courts Reformed America's Prisons* (New York, Cambridge University Press, 1998).

about to remake prisons, at times from the ground up. They viewed the Eighth Amendment's prohibition against cruel and unusual punishment not as doctrine to be interpreted, but as a grant of jurisdiction, a delegation of authority authorising them to make prison policy. They then set out to tackle the 'totality of the conditions' in these prisons by writing what amounted to an administrative code. Administrative agencies are distinctive because they not only adjudicate disputes, they also make, implement and enforce policy. They make mince meat of the separation of powers. In the prison conditions cases judges did the same thing: they embraced a multifaceted role. And, like administrative agencies, they were able to do this because they expanded not only their vision but also their capacities. They incorporated the defendant institutions into the policy-making process – working closely with them and requiring them to submit detailed plans for realising the court's general orders, and they acquired staffs in the form of special masters to help them in this process. Special masters not only extended the courts' capacities to manage their new and expanded responsibilities, they also aided hapless corrections officials who were often overwhelmed by the judicially initiated reform process.

IMPLEMENTATION AS POLICY-MAKING: A SPIRALLING AND SPRAWLING PROCESS

In these cases, policy was made in the process of implementation, and involved constant and continuous interaction and adjustment between the judges whose rulings outlined general policy goals and the defendant institutions that had to elaborate on and then implement them. The initial court opinions read like the findings of a legislative committee or an administrative agency; they identify a problem and point towards a solution, but leave the details to be worked out by corrections officials in consultation with the court. When officials were not forthcoming, judges became more insistent and detailed in their requests. And when officials were still unwilling or unable to comply, the courts turned to independent experts for help. As judges were drawn more deeply into the process of reform, their response was to become even more executive- like. Eventually, in many cases, they appointed special masters to assist them – and the parties – in this process. In so doing, they not only acquired staffs, they merged the process of policy-making and implementation in much the way that Pressman and Wildavsky prescribe.

Individual judges vary in temperament and personality and this affected the ways they embraced the conditions cases. In Arkansas, Judge E. Smith Henley, a courtly Southern gentleman, was at the outset content to quietly offer 'suggestions', in part because this style fitted his personality and in part because the commissioner of corrections not so secretly welcomed judicial intervention and had expressed a sincere interest in cooperating with the court. However when his successor, Judge Eisele experienced increased resistance, he appointed a special master and eventually developed an aggressive hands-on approach. In contrast, in Texas, a more rambunctious judge, William Wayne Justice, confronted a stone wall at the outset; initially and at every stage of the litigation his findings, his rulings and his orders were resisted by state officials. His first act after a long and bitterly contested trial was to appoint a special master, whom he came to rely on heavily throughout the long duration of the case. In contrast, in Georgia the judge presiding over the case and the governor, an old and close friend, quietly let it be known that they wanted the case settled amicably. Lawyers for the parties negotiated a settlement and oversaw implementation with a minimum of judicial oversight, no publicity, and no special master.[7]

Despite individual differences of temperament, philosophy and situation, the judges in all the cases approached their tasks cautiously. It was as if they entered a pool at the shallow end, but then were drawn step by step into the deeper parts. Although some were more adventuresome than others, certainly at the outset none was anxious to dive into the uncharted waters headfirst. But, once they were in deep water, they found they could swim. They developed both the confidence and the competence to manage structural reform. They issued increasingly detailed orders, specifying each step that officials – not only prison officials, but also at times the state legislature – needed to take to deal with the problems effectively. The state's continued unwillingness or inability to respond by correctional officials led the judges to conclude that problems were still more deeply embedded and resistance more firmly ensconced than they had originally thought. This drew them still deeper into the management of the institutions.

My question in this chapter is how, without sword or purse, did courts manage to formulate and implement such detailed policies? How were

[7] B. Chilton, *Prisons Under the Gavel: The Federal Court Takeover of Georgia Prisons* (Columbus, Ohio State University Press, 1991).

they able to become successful policy-makers and administrators? How were they able to master the details of prison administration? Press hard enough to produce extra resources? Oversee the details of implementation? Assess the effects of their orders? A partial answer, suggested above, is that at some point early on in the process, they abandoned the task of trying to 'interpret' the law, embraced policy-making, and transformed themselves into administrators. Another is that they developed their executive capacities. In particular, they acquired staff assistants, special masters.[8] Although nominally appointed by the court to monitor compliance with its orders, special masters performed a variety of roles. Invariably judges granted them total access to the prisons, allowed them to report directly to the court, encouraged them to make their own recommendations, and let it be known to the parties that they were agents of the court. The duties of these special assistants varied widely – from judge to judge and case to case and over time – but everywhere they expanded the capacities of judges to understand problems, formulate solutions, and monitor implementation.

JUDGE & CO.

A comprehensive study of the history and authority of special masters in American law has yet to be written,[9] but it is clear that judges had the authority to appoint them. Since at least the fifteenth century, English

---

[8] This is the term used in the Federal Rules of Civil Procedure, although in these cases, courts assigned different names to them. Sensitive to the term 'master' in the South, especially when substantial numbers of prisoners are African-American, judges often preferred other labels, such as monitor and compliance coordinator. I use these terms interchangeably in this chapter.

[9] There are a number of studies, almost all of which are not so much scholarly treatments as they are justifications for the use of masters in areas of interest to the authors. A perfunctory review of the ancient lineage of the institution is often contained in the first part of the article, which seeks to impart legitimacy for the institution through reference to its long lineage. See e.g. V. Nathan, 'The Use of Special Masters in Institutional Reform Litigation' (1979) 10 *Toledo Law Review* 464. The most careful work to date on the authority to appoint special masters under Rule 53(b) and Rule 70 of the Federal Rules of Civil Procedure is D. I. Levine, 'The Authority for the Appointment of Remedial Special Masters in Federal Institutional Reform Litigation: The History Reconsidered' (1984) 17 *University of California Davis Law Review* 753. For brief histories of the origins of the office of master of chancery, see D. Bryant, 'The Office of Master of Chancery: Early English Development' (1954) 40 *American Bar Association Journal* 498; and D. Bryant, 'The Office of Master in Chancery: Colonial

judges, and later American judges, have appointed experts to act in their behalf, advise them on special matters, and perform other sorts of duties for the court.[10]

Special masters began to be used regularly in the United States in the late nineteenth century. Beginning in the 1870s, special masters were appointed by federal judges in bankruptcy cases to serve as receivers and manage insolvent businesses – often railroads – protecting them against creditors, disavowing or renegotiating contracts, preventing the piecemeal sale of property to satisfy creditors' judgments, and when possible helping businesses regain their footing as viable institutions. In the 1960s and 1970s in the United States, special masters began to be used widely in school desegregation cases.[11] When school boards would not or could not design bold enough desegregation plans, federal judges often appointed educational experts as special masters to do the job. They designed their own desegregation plans, reviewed plans submitted by the parties, and negotiated with the parties to jointly design plans. At times a judge might place an especially recalcitrant school district in receivership and ask a special master to manage both the district

Development' (1954) 40 *American Bar Association Journal* 595. In making appointments in remedial institutional reform cases, federal judges often specify that their authority to do so derives both from Rule 53(b) and from their inherent powers (as per Justice Brandeis' observation (see note 10 below)). Although commentators observe that Rule 70 also provides a strong source of authority (perhaps stronger than Rule 53(b)), few if any judges have specifically tied their appointments to this specific provision. See e.g. Levine, *ibid.*

[10] As Justice Brandeis observed in 1920:

Courts have (at least in the absence of legislation to the contrary) inherent power to provide themselves with appropriate instruments required for the performance of their duties . . . this power included authority to appoint persons unconnected with the court to aid judges in the performance of specific judicial duties, as they may arise in the progress of a cause. From the commencement of our Government, it has been exercised by the federal courts, when sitting in equity, by appointing either with or without the consent of the parties, special masters, auditors, examiners and commissioners.

Justice Brandeis, in *Ex parte Peterson*, 253 US 300 (1920) at 312–13, quoted in Nathan, 'The Use of Special Masters', p. 423. Rule 53(b) of the Federal Rules of Civil Procedure also grants federal judges the power to appoint special masters, but it is widely considered that the Rule simply restates the traditional inherent power of the judiciary.

[11] Levine, 'The Authority'.

and the process of desegregation.[12] Since the late 1970s, judges have regularly appointed special masters in prison conditions cases, ostensibly to monitor compliance with agreed-upon plans. But typically this has meant working closely with prison officials to translate the courts' general statements of goals into detailed action plans and to cope with the new problems revealed in the process of implementation. Thus the process of monitoring implementation has involved them in the process of developing still more detailed and new plans, and in so doing the process of implementation has been blurred with the process of policy-making. More generally special masters have been appointed to aid judges in any complex cases.

Clearly Chief Justice Rehnquist is correct when he asserts that judges in prison conditions cases have abandoned their traditional role as adjudicators and become managers. Indeed, this is the key to their success in these cases. In these cases, judges were transformed – or rather, transformed themselves – into executives, and in so doing acquired some of the accoutrements of executives – special assistants – in order to develop the capacities to effect their orders.

Everywhere in large-scale organisations, special assistants aid busy executives in formulating and implementing policies. And everywhere a difficult policy has been implemented successfully, it is likely that a special assistant acting on behalf of a chief executive has played an important role in this process. Special assistants are energetic people appointed to a specific set of tasks, have the confidence of the executive, are (or quickly can become) experts about the issues, and are able to devote full time to their well-focused responsibilities. Thus they are indispensable to overburdened and overextended executives. Special assistants have not been examined carefully in public administration, but they are ubiquitous, and widely acknowledged to be important. They provide a direct link between a chief executive on the one hand and those charged with implementing and administering policies on the other, a link that bypasses formal chains of command, and one that is staffed by a person who has the full confidence of the executive. As bureaucratic structures have grown and chains of command lengthened, so too has the importance and value of special assistants. And in the

---

[12] For a description of the many functions special masters have served in the school desegregation cases, see D. L. Kirp and G. Babcock, 'Judge and Company: Court-Appointed Masters, School Desegregation, and Institutional Reform' (1981) 32 *Alabama Law Review* 313.

United States as litigation against large-scale institutions has increased, so too has the use of special masters.

The role of the special assistant is both powerful and ambiguous, and is powerful because it is ambiguous. Special assistants are distinctive types of appointments. Although they must have support and respect from those with whom they deal, they are personal emissaries of and stand in a privileged relationship to the executive, whom they serve in ways that permanent staff do not. Job descriptions of special assistants are rarely well defined, and, even when they are, they are not likely to fully capture the range of their responsibilities. Although they may be appointed to deal with a selected issue or problem, they have few set responsibilities, and, within broad parameters, are free to orient their concerns as they see fit, so long as they retain the confidence of their boss. Within their spheres of responsibility, their 'suggestions' can carry the weight of 'orders from the chief'. It is of course not unlimited author-ity, and if it becomes known that they have exceeded it – if for instance their boss publicly undercuts them – their authority and usefulness can disappear instantly. They are easily dispensed with.

SPECIAL MASTERS IN THE PRISON CONDITIONS CASES

In the prison conditions cases, special masters served the role of special assistants. Below I briefly describe the activities of special masters in three well-known institutional conditions cases in the United States.[13] There probably is no 'typical' set of duties for a special master, but the types of activities described below are representative of what special masters have done in a great many institutional conditions cases in the United States over the past three decades.

Arkansas
In Arkansas's *Holt v. Sarver*,[14] the nation's first major and long-running systems-wide conditions case, Judge E. Smith Henley initially con-fronted a receptive department of corrections. Indeed, at the time there were rumours that the commissioner of corrections had helped the pris-oners' attorneys draft their complaint against him. The trial in this

[13] The discussion that follows draws on the discussion in Feeley and Rubin, *Judicial Policy-Making*.
[14] 300 F Supp 825 (ED Ark., 1969).

case revealed the state's prisons to be horrible 'places of evil', rampant with torture and brutality. Organised on the Plantation Model, the prison was run as a slave plantation, as a self-sufficient enterprise expected to return a profit to the state. The regime was brutal. It had no free world guards, and instead co-opted the most brutal inmates to run the prison. It provided virtually no services for inmates. Corruption, torture and sadism were a way of life. Its Tucker Prison Farm was famous for the 'Tucker telephone', an apparatus used to administer electric shocks to prisoners' genitals. No doubt emboldened by a continuing scandal initiated by a report prepared by the Governor's special police, the judge after trial found conditions in the Arkansas prisons to be unconstitutional and in need of root and branch reform. The newly appointed top leadership in the state's corrections department agreed, and began to proceed in good faith. However, eventually, they proved both unable and unwilling to effect all the agreed-upon plans. When they turned their attention to solve one issue, they let other problems slide. Resources devoted to solving one problem meant that there were fewer resources to remedy others. The good will of the top leadership was quietly subverted by resentful subordinates. And inevitably close investigation of one problem revealed still more and more deeply embedded problems. The department simply lacked the capacity to address so many issues all at once, and eventually officials were worn out by the effort. Although they had begun the reform process in relative good faith, at each step they had to be prodded by the court. Eventually, they grew tired of this never-ending process and came to resent – and resist – the court's efforts.

As these issues were mounting, the judge handling the case received a promotion to the court of appeals and was replaced by a new judge, Thomas Eisele. The mounting resistance by corrections officials led the new judge to take a new tack. At the outset of his assignment to the case, he announced that he would assume active oversight in the case and to this end appointed a special master, whom he termed a compliance coordinator, to assist him and the department in developing more aggressive and detailed plans for rooting out problems and implementing the consent agreement. With the approval of all the parties, the judge, appointed Stephen La Plante, a well-regarded correctional expert from San Francisco, to serve in this capacity.

These moves had the desired effect. Over the course of the next three years, La Plante issued a series of reports responding to the department's plans to comply with the consent decree, and specifying what steps they had to take to implement them. Many of these plans had been written with his help, in part because the department welcomed his expertise and in part because it was assured that the court would approve plans he had drafted. As a correctional expert, unconstrained by the rules and procedures governing judicial fact-finding, and able to devote a substantial part of his time to the prisons, he was able to probe at greater depth than had either the judge or the magistrate who presided over occasional hearings, or the prisoners' attorneys. His reports were insightful, and they were also more detailed and more critical than the earlier self-monitoring reports that had been prepared by the department's own staff before his appointment. Although La Plante approved of some of the department's practices and procedures, more often than not he was critical of both its efforts and its results. As he probed the department's activities and worked with officials to implement the consent decree, lists of problems grew longer not shorter. Department officials began to see him as the sorcerer's apprentice; the harder they worked the more their problems multiplied. And, when they complained to the court, the judge unreservedly supported the special master and urged the department to follow his 'suggestions'.

Although the special master and the judge took great pains to link his reports to provisions in the original consent decree, critics in the department complained that the master's reports constituted a general plan for restructuring the entire prison system that went well beyond what had originally been contemplated in the consent decree. To some extent this was true. As they delved more deeply into the problems of the correctional system, the judges and the compliance coordinator uncovered a host of problems that had not been evident at the outset of the remedial process. They believed that changes originally ordered by the court could not be sustained without more and deeper structural changes within the department. Not surprisingly, corrections officials, especially those at the lower levels, took issue with this claim.

As the compliance coordinator's list of concerns grew, his conflict with the department increased. The problem was exacerbated by his willingness to 'go public' with his criticisms rather than work quietly with the department and the court to resolve problems. In the spring of 1981, this conflict reached a crisis when without the court's authorization or the department's knowledge, the compliance coordinator invited federal authorities to investigate allegations that the corrections commissioner was corrupt. The department claimed that this 'vendetta' was cause for his dismissal. Although the judge had always staunchly supported the compliance coordinator, he seemed to agree with the critics on this point. He agreed to the dismissal of the compliance coordinator, but conditioned it upon the department's commitment to make one last heroic effort to implement the outstanding items on the compliance coordinator's latest reports. After securing this agreement, the judge publicly announced that since the case was winding down there was no longer any need for a compliance coordinator, and that he would assume direct authority for monitoring the department in the final stages of the consent decree. He profusely complimented the department for all that it had done, but also quietly extended the compliance coordinator's appointment for another few months in order to allow him to complete his final reports. However, the judge was true to his word; even when these reports revealed major additional problems, he allowed the appointment to lapse and assumed active oversight of the department's compliance efforts. He continued to use the special master's reports as guides, and insisted that the department submit detailed periodic reports that addressed the problems he claimed were still not fixed.

This was a masterful move. The judge appeared to give ground by agreeing to the dismissal of the compliance coordinator, but at the same time expanded the scope of the case and his involvement in it. He went beyond the special master's recommendations and directed the department to develop and follow even more aggressive plans to reduce the prison population, to confine inmates in administrative segregation, and the like, and to file detailed compliance statements with the court. Over the next two years, the judge received a series of detailed reports from the department and held frequent hearings to determine if the department was in compliance with them.

Whether consciously or not the judge shaped the dynamics of this last stage of litigation. With the loss of the special master, the department itself had to produce compliance reports and present them directly to the court. And, by investing the time to immerse himself in the day-to-day operations of the department, the judge assumed an important leadership role in the continuing reform process. This involvement created a sense of urgency among corrections officials, and heightened their belief that closure of the case was within reach. This produced a burst of energy that finally did convince the judge that the department was in compliance with the consent decree. On 20 August 1982, seventeen years after the first handwritten note from an inmate at the Cummins Prison Farm had been received by Judge Smith, the case came to an unceremonious conclusion.

At the outset, the prison system had been a feudal-like institution replete with instruments of torture and overseen by a handful of politically appointed officials who were expected to run the prison farms with prison labour at no cost to the state, and who relied upon prisoner trustees to guard the inmates. Seventeen years later, the state department of corrections possessed a recognisable bureaucratic structure with its own budget, had new facilities with safer cells, and was staffed by trained leaders and free world guards who provided at least a modicum of services to inmates. Although the general directions of these reforms had been dictated by the court, the detailed arrangements required by the reforms had been fashioned – often with reluctance – by corrections officials themselves. One of the important mechanisms that facilitated this process was the compliance coordinator, whose expertise allowed the court to be specific in its expectations and persistent in its oversight.

Texas

In the Texas prison conditions case, *Ruiz* v. *Estelle*,[15] Judge William Wayne Justice presided over a contentious trial that lasted 180 days, after which the court found that conditions in the state's prisons violated a host of constitutional standards. Rather than allow the court to draft its own remedial order, the Texas Department of Corrections (TDC) agreed to negotiate a consent decree with the attorneys for the prisoners. Unlike Arkansas officials, however, the TDC leadership bitterly resented the court's ruling and continued to oppose the litigation in the remedial phase. Indeed, they steadfastly continued to deny the findings made at trial, and agreed to negotiate a consent order only because they believed that the judge was so hostile that a negotiated agreement was the lesser evil. After three months of arm-twisting, Judge Justice finally got the parties to agree to a brief document that outlined the steps to be taken to remedy most of the violations found at trial. The agreement contained a list of improvements that had been made since the trial – in the areas of healthcare, provisions for special-needs prisoners (retarded, physically handicapped, developmentally disabled or mentally ill), work safety and hygiene, the use of chemical agents, the terms and conditions of solitary confinement, and the terms and conditions in administrative segregation – but specified that the TDC must prepare additional plans to address continuing

[15] *Ruiz* v. *Estelle*, 503 F Supp 1265 (SD Tex., 1980).

problems in these areas. This document remained conspicuously silent on the most vexing issue in the case, the claim that TDC used armed inmates to guard other inmates. The agreement was probably reached only because it was brief and couched in very general language and because it avoided this explosive issue. This approach of generality and issue-avoidance was successful in the short run, but guaranteed that the intense conflict that had characterised the trial would eventually re-emerge.

The agreement was submitted to Judge Justice in the spring of 1981 and immediately received his blessing. At this time, the judge also persuaded the parties to agree to the appointment of a special master to monitor the preparation and implementation of the detailed plans that were anticipated under the agreement. A short time later, with the approval of the parties, he selected Vincent Nathan as the special master. Nathan, a former law professor, had served as a special master in several previous cases. By the time he was appointed in *Ruiz*, he had a reputation for being knowledgeable, businesslike and well organised, but even his most ardent admirers described him as arrogant. Justice's order gave Nathan sweeping powers. Although it emphasised that he could not 'intervene in the administrative management of the Texas Department of Corrections', or 'direct the defendants or any of their subordinates to take or to refrain from taking any specific action to achieve compliance', the order also provided that he could appoint assistants as needed, and that they could

> observe, monitor, find facts, report or testify as to his findings, and make recommendations to the court concerning steps which should be taken to achieve compliance. The special master may and should assist the defendants in every possible way, and to this end he may and should confer informally with the defendants and their subordinates on matters affecting compliance.[16]

The court also granted the office of the special master access to TDC files and the authority to conduct confidential interviews with staff and inmates, to attend all formal meetings of TDC officials, to require written reports from any TDC staff member, and to 'order and conduct hearings with respect to the defendants' compliance with this court's orders'. In short, it granted him nearly unlimited access to the entire prison system in Texas.

[16] Order of the court, quoted in Feeley and Rubin, *Judicial Policy-making*, p. 86.

Almost immediately, TDC officials came to regret their support for Nathan's appointment. Their worst fears came to be borne out. Nathan and his associates were aggressive in holding hearings, conducting their own investigations and issuing recommendations to the court. In doing so they challenged TDC's factual accounts on virtually every facet of the case, reported that TDC's compliance plans were woefully inadequate, and catalogued long lists of new problems. TDC officials responded by acknowledging some minor violations, but categorically denied the more serious ones. Where TDC proposed modest, incremental reforms, Nathan saw the need for sweeping structural changes. When such disagreements occurred, as they regularly did, the special master would ask the TDC to revise its plans in light of his findings and offer 'suggestions' about what would be required to make the new plans satisfactory. At the outset, the issues would be appealed to Judge Justice, who invariably supported his special master. Eventually, the TDC grudgingly came to work with Nathan and his staff, and a pattern developed. The master would order a report, the TDC would eventually submit it, only to be told that it was inadequate and had to be revised and expanded. The special master's office would then sketch out what an acceptable plan would look like. This pattern occurred so frequently that the sequence – submission of plans followed by the master's review and revision and resubmission – became confused, and perhaps even reversed. Nathan gradually came to be perceived as the director of TDC's planning process, rather than simply the assessor of its plans.

From Nathan's perspective it was the recalcitrance of the defendants that forced him to be so aggressive and detailed in specifying the steps TDC needed to take in order to meet the requirements of the consent decree. From the defendants' perspective, Nathan was revelling in his power to 'run the institution', and nothing they did could ever satisfy him. Of course, final authority to resolve disputes remained with Judge Justice, but when they arose he continued to support his appointee and often upbraided the TDC for its continued recalcitrance. Indeed, as TDC's complaints continued, Justice's confidence in the special master seemed to grow, and the size and resolve of the master's office grew apace. At its apogee, the office had three monitors, a staff of thirteen, and an annual budget of well over one million dollars. It also had the collective determination to compel the TDC to abide by both the letter and the spirit of the consent decree, by persuasion if possible but by force if necessary.

As difficult as it was, Nathan was slowly able to pry out of the TDC a series of increasingly detailed plans that covered virtually every facet of prison life – delivery of health services, inmate access to law libraries, vocational training programmes, space requirements, exercise, diets, heating and ventilation, inmate classification systems, plans to deal with inmate gangs, correctional officer hiring, promotion policies, early release options, architectural plans for new construction in the face of the mushrooming prison population. Each of the plans, together with the special master's reports on them, could run into hundreds or even thousands of pages, and involve extraordinary levels of detail. Many of the recommended actions depended on vast funding increases for hiring and training new correctional officers, renovating large, old facilities, building still larger new ones, and expanding health, education and other services. The court routinely approved these recommendations and ordered TDC officials to comply with them. The not-so-hidden audience for many of these recommendations and court orders, of course, were the governor and state legislature. Most required vast increases in expenditures. All told, Judge Justice ordered new programmes that cost the state well over one billion dollars. The master's findings and recommendations also emboldened plaintiffs' attorneys, who continued to expand their own inquiries and unearth new issues. For a period, it seemed that the more actions TDC took to alleviate these criticisms, the more new problems were revealed and the more the court's concerns expanded.

The most divisive issue in the entire case, and the one that best reveals the deep hostility between plaintiffs and defendants, involved the building tenders, inmates who were assigned to guard other prisoners. At trial, the TDC had categorically denied the existence of inmate guards. But their use was later confirmed by one of the special master's earliest reports, and subsequently substantiated by a whistleblower within the TDC. This revelation was momentous. Up till then, both the governor and the state Attorney General, who had gubernatorial ambitions that were shortly to be realised, had staunchly defended the TDC and vigorously condemned Judge Justice and his meddlesome orders. However, the revelation of the inmate guards and the fact that TDC officials were caught in a bald-faced lie, sowed the seeds of doubt among Texas officials. As time went on, the extent of the TDC's prevarications became increasingly apparent; state officials began to place more credence in the court's findings, began to conduct investigations of their own, uncovered still more abuses, and eventually took steps to restructure the TDC and replace its top leadership. It is likely that none of this would have occurred without the persistence of the judge and his special master.

By the late 1980s, the old order in TDC's top leadership had resigned or been removed, and a new leadership, guided by modern views of prison management, had been installed. During the period of nearly twenty years of continuous court oversight, the prison system had been transformed. Due to rising crime rates and the war on crime, the prison population in Texas had more than quadrupled TDC's housing capacity and its budget had grown accordingly. Texas prisons were certainly not ideal places or even model prisons. But on balance they were far different and far better places than they had been when the *Ruiz* case had first been filed. Virtually all of the improvements had required vast expenditures that had been appropriated by the state legislature, but the leadership that had forced these increases, and the detailed plans that had made the case for them, were largely due to the efforts of Judge Justice and Vincent Nathan, and his staff of monitors, who both independently and by working with resistant and reluctant corrections officials had successfully made the case for changes and then implemented them.

Santa Clara County

The Santa Clara (San José, California) County jail case, *Branson v. Winter*,[17] began in 1982, when an inmate serving a short jail term for a petty offence submitted a brief handwritten note to a county court judge complaining of the conditions in the local jail. Like the two cases described above, it eventually grew into a class action, although because an earlier suit had been filed in federal court on behalf of women inmates, it was aimed only at the jail facilities for men. After a bitterly contested trial, the parties agreed to hammer out a settlement agreement specifying what remedial steps the county would take to bring its jails into compliance with the court's ruling.

Each step of this process was also contested, although, with prodding from the judge, a settlement was reached. It called for the construction of a new 850-bed jail and provided a timetable for its construction. It also provided for funds to renovate the existing jail and to upgrade various temporary units. The agreement did not address the administrative competence of the sheriff's jail staff, although at the time the

---

[17] *Branson v. Winter*, Case No. 78807, Santa Clara County, Superior Court, Order 10, Court Record, 19 March, 1982.

judge viewed this as a problem and it was understood that it would be upgraded. The agreement did, however, call for the appointment of a special master, termed a compliance officer in the document, to oversee implementation of the court order, and anticipated that this person would be someone with extensive experience in jail administration.

With the approval of the parties, the judge subsequently selected Thomas Lonergan, a former deputy sheriff and jail commander in Los Angeles, to serve as the compliance officer. Lonergan was granted sweeping access to the whole of the jail and all its staff, authority to call meetings with jail officials and issue recommendations necessary to enforce agreed-upon plans, and the right to petition the court for orders to enforce, supplement or modify the agreement. All the parties were enthusiastic about this appointment. The prisoners' attorney welcomed the appointment of an experienced, reform-minded jail administrator to help guide the process. And the county Board of Supervisors welcomed his appointment since it removed the court from day-to-day involvement with the jail. Sheriff Winter, the named defendant in the suit, did not object, and quickly came to admire and depend upon Lonergan's expertise. This unanimous enthusiasm augured well for Lonergan's work since in fact there were deep divisions between the Board of Supervisors and the sheriff. As an independently elected official – and the only Republican to hold county-wide elective office – the sheriff had a long history of antagonism with the five-member Board of Supervisors, all Democrats. Throughout the trial, the sheriff blamed the Board for his problems, claiming it did not provide his agency with sufficient funds. The Board in turn defended its level of funding, and claimed that the sheriff was an incompetent administrator. Indeed, the animosity was so great that, during the trial, the sheriff, the first-named defendant in the suit, was often found sitting at the table of the counsel for the prisoners, helping her marshal evidence of the consequences of inadequate funding against the other defendants in the case, the Board of Supervisors. Such finger-pointing and odd alliances among the parties continued throughout the duration of the long case, although Sheriff Winter eventually obtained separate counsel. Nevertheless, for different reasons, everyone seemed to agree, at least at the outset, that Lonergan was the right person for the job as special master.

With everyone looking to him for leadership in resolving the litigation, Lonergan got off to a quick start. The day after the settlement agreement was signed, he presented detailed plans for reducing the jail's population so that it would be under the cap established in the settlement agreement. He recommended early release of some inmates and redistribution of others so that there would be vacant beds in each facility. But he realised that these measures were temporary, and that the more deep-seated problems could not be resolved so readily. The jail had no real inmate classification system. Nor did it even have a functioning chain of command for the staff; simple orders for repair and maintenance work were ignored or at times did not even reach their intended recipient. Lack of funds was part of the problem, but lack of administrative capacity was an even larger part of the problem. Although lack of funding was an issue, the basic responsibility for these failures, in Lonergan's view, belonged largely to the sheriff, who Lonergan felt was an ineffective and indifferent administrator.

As indicated above, Lonergan's response to this disarray was to take charge, and neither the sheriff nor any of the other parties objected. Whether they were weary of the responsibility, or felt that the court's appointment of Lonergan had deprived the sheriff of his autonomy, they were clearly willing to let Lonergan take charge, and were pleased that he was doing so. Under these conditions, Lonergan was able to act decisively and institute a number of important administrative changes; he moved middle-level management from the Sheriff's Department into the main jail, and improved the jail's systems of command and control. He asked the court to grant him authority to meet with any of the parties or the court *ex parte*, to design a permanent classification and population management system, to order as many releases as necessary to keep the population within the limits established by the court, and to exercise the full authority of the court unless his action was appealed to it within three days. He even asked for and was granted authority to hire his own experts at county expense. Once again, the defendants' reaction to this far-reaching expansion of Lonergan's powers was relieved acquiescence.

During this period, which lasted for most of 1984 and 1985, the court held few hearings. Instead, the judge acted informally, allowing the compliance coordinator to continue to reform the jail and resolving occasional issues through negotiation. In his view, the two basic challenges were the need for more cell space and the need for better management, and he felt that under Lonergan's leadership both issues were being addressed. With respect to crowding, the county was moving swiftly to renovate the old jail and to build a new one. And with respect to administrative competence, Lonergan had asked for and received more administrative positions, reorganised the staff, and instituted a new command and control structure for the jail staff. He continued to refine his system for early releases, expand the use of non-custodial alternative sentences, and expand pre-trial release and diversion pro-grammes. He developed a schedule of regular inspection and mainte-nance of facilities, instituted procedures for disciplining inmates, and developed plans for improved medical care, exercise and mental health treatment for inmates. Finally, he instituted training programmes for new staff members, and instituted new security plans that reduced escapes. For all practical purposes, Lonergan ran the county jail for two years. He issued countless directives to jail staff and filed forty-two formal statements of findings of fact, notices of non-compliance, and lists of recommendations with the court. Most of these required jail administrators to make important changes or the Board of Supervisors to increase appropriations for the jail. And for the most part Lonergan obtained what he sought.

In retrospect, this two-year period was the calm before the storm. That storm finally broke in June 1985, when Lonergan and the Board reached an impasse. Shortly after he had assumed his duties, the county had agreed to his recommendation that another of the new facilities should consist entirely of single cell units. However, as the Board con-fronted the cost of jail construction and the burgeoning arrest rate in the county, it decided to modify the plans and construct dormitory-style housing. This would both reduce construction costs and add much-needed bed space. In spring 1985, the Board adopted new plans without consulting Lonergan or informing the court. When he learned of the decision the next day, Lonergan was furious. It was, he believed, not only unwise jail policy, it was a direct violation of the court's order. He immediately asked the judge to rescind the decision and to hold the entire Board in contempt. In response, Board members asserted that the settlement agreement only committed the county to build a new facility for at least 200 inmates, and that the design specifications in it were non-binding details that it had the authority to alter. They were free, they felt, to make changes in light of additional information about space needs and rising construction costs. Like Lonergan, the judge was amazed at the Board's claims, and reinstated the original plans. He also held Board members in contempt and sentenced them to five days in their own inadequate jail, but stayed execution pending the inevitable appeal.

The judge ended his ruling with a dramatic announcement: he was 'withdrawing' from the case which was to be assigned to another judge.

However, after his withdrawal, every other judge in the county refused to accept the assignment. Their ostensible reason was conflict of interest, since the costs of the court-ordered new jail might affect funding for a long-planned new courthouse (some members of the Board had hinted that, if the judges wanted a fancy jail so much, they might just have to pay for it themselves, from funds earmarked for the new courthouse). This fear was fuelled by the fact that the judge presiding over the case had been passed over for an appellate court position, although he had long been widely regarded as the frontrunner for the position.

Eventually, this impasse was resolved when the state judicial counsel appointed a judge from neighbouring Alameda County to handle the case. The new judge, the council reasoned, could not be beholden in any way to Santa Clara County officials, and thus would have a free hand. Once appointed, the new judge immediately began meetings with the parties in an effort to negotiate a resolution to the problem. He proposed a compromise: some space in the new facility would be devoted to single cells and the balance to a dormitory. However, he too met resistance from a Board which was continuing to assert its newfound confidence. In short-order, he reactivated the contempt order, imposed a jail sentence of five days for each supervisor, and 'tentatively' fined the county nearly ten million dollars. But again, the order was stayed, and between March and June 1987 as the appeal was pending, he continued to press the county to agree to the original single cell plan or devise a suitable alternative.

He also continued to offer Lonergan his full support, and Lonergan in turn continued to develop and implement a host of plans to expand the numbers of early releases and non-custodial sentencing alternatives, and still more types of pre-trial release alternatives. The Board cooperated with him on these proposals; it funded virtually everything he asked for. However, it remained adamant about plans for the new facilities, feeling that it was both the right plan and that it and not the court had the authority to decide the matter. Despite progress on many fronts, in June 1987, this judge too announced his withdrawal from the case, citing his frustration with county officials whom he felt were engaged in endless, purposeful delays over plans for the new jail. His decision to withdraw resulted in the appointment of a second out-of-county judge, and eventually his contempt order was reversed by an appellate court.

This decision by the appellate court was a watershed. Although limited in scope and silent on the issue of whether the county was required to construct a new jail with single cells, the decision further energised the Board and irreparably damaged its relations with the compliance officer who had staked his authority upon having his way with the Board. And it further alienated the Board from the sheriff, who had openly supported Lonergan in the controversy. The Board's response was in effect to fire the sheriff. Since he was independently elected, the Board could not remove him. However, it was successful in taking the jail away from him. In a series of swift moves, it created a new county department of corrections, vested it with full responsibility for managing the jails, and appointed an experienced corrections administrator to run them. As soon as the proposal was first broached, the sheriff sought a court injunction to block the Board's move, arguing that authority over the jail was an 'inherent' part of the sheriff's constitutional duties. However, California law does not explicitly mandate this, and at least one other California county had a separate department of corrections. After months of legal wrangling, the courts ruled in the county's favour and the issue was effectively ended. And in the interim the county had moved ahead in implementing its plans.

All this added to the Board's growing tension with the compliance officer, and when the new director of corrections took office, Lonergan withdrew from active involvement with the case. The new commissioner was an experienced and aggressive hands-on manager, who neither wanted nor welcomed Lonergan's continued involvement with the jail. A short time later, seizing upon these developments and the by-now nearly completed new jail, a weary judge – the fourth to preside over the case – agreed to terminate the court's jurisdiction. Although many people, including the compliance officer, were concerned that a new and effective system had not yet been firmly set into place, they did acknowledge that a great many positive steps had been taken. A new jail was in the final stages of construction. Older facilities had been improved and expanded. The county's jail capacity had grown from 1,635 beds in 1981 to 3,848 beds in 1988, and more spaces were scheduled to be added in the near future. A new and effective inmate classification system was up and running. A host of non-custodial sentencing alternatives had been added. New and more effective provision for social services, healthcare, dining, education and exercise had been developed. And a new Department of Correction, headed by an experienced corrections administrator, had been established. In light of all this and coupled with exhaustion, a weary judge finally terminated jurisdiction.

THE ROLES OF SPECIAL MASTERS

The discussion above highlighted the role of the special masters in three institutional conditions cases. My purpose here was to show how courts have adapted themselves to complex cases. In traditional litigation, the judicial remedies are self-executing. In complex structural reform cases, courts have had to develop executive-like capabilities. By so doing, they have expanded their ability to gather information, manage complexity, and through the appointment of special masters devote sufficient time to these types of case. Although people are likely to assess these activities quite differently and certainly some judges are more successful in these efforts than others, by now such adaptation is routine. What is remarkable about the activities of the special masters is just how unremarkable they are. Although at first blush they may appear to be a strange set of responsibilities to be overseen by a court, seen in the context of any basic understanding of executive activity, they are unremarkable. Mayors, governors, agency heads of all sorts employ the sort of assistance that the judges have employed in these cases. Everywhere special assistants are appointed by executives to focus intensively on certain objectives that are high on the executive's agenda. This is precisely what the special masters in these prison conditions cases did. Their duties were multifaceted, and contingent upon the particular situation and setting. Activities were determined by the nature of the problem, the degree of resistance to reform, the abilities of the parties, their personalities and the chemistry between them. So, just as there is no recipe to determine factors that distinguish successful from unsuccessful executive actions, so too there is no recipe to distinguish successful from unsuccessful managerial oversight by judges and their special assistants. Still, it is possible to identify a range of roles that special masters assumed in their relationship to their appointing judges. They served as the eyes and ears of the court in order to expand its capacity to gather information and assess the consequences of particular actions. They provided much needed expertise, both for the court and for the agency being reformed. Finally, they floated trial balloons and took the heat for their bosses, thus at least partially insulating them from criticism. I explore each of these roles below.

Eyes and ears of the court

The literature on implementation describes a journey filled with zigs and zags, dead ends, unanticipated obstacles, and a lack of sustained focus. One result is that policy-makers often lose control if not sight of their objectives as they move on to other issues. New policy directives or reforms are all too often rudderless ships, launched with much fanfare but left to drift aimlessly. Occasionally, if the issue is pressing enough, a chief executive will make it a high priority and provide sustained leadership. But other issues always compete for the limited attention of the leader. Realising that their time is limited, effective executives must search for ways to sustain momentum on a particular reform even as they must direct their attentions elsewhere. Delegating a special assistant to take charge of the problem and to act in their behalf is one such solution. Special masters often serve this function for judges. When appointed to monitor implementation of court orders, special masters greatly enhance the court's capacity to keep abreast of issues and to shape their development. Like many types of policy pronouncements, court orders provide only broad outlines. The all-important details are to be filled in later, and the challenge is to acquire information and to influence future developments. In litigation in complex cases, the plaintiff's attorneys are ill-equipped to do this and defendant institutions usually unwilling or unable to do so. And judges must move on to other cases. Furthermore, even if any of these people had the time and skills, formal proceedings are slow and cumbersome. In contrast, special masters can move about and communicate informally, with the judge, the parties and other actors. In doing so, they can quickly assimilate a great deal of information to be passed on to the court and act decisively on behalf of the court. In the case studies above, we saw that one of the most important jobs of the special master was to help the parties (and the court) translate broad pronouncements of goals or aspirations into concrete plans, and found that this was a process that repeated itself again and again as each seeming solution generated still more problems or experienced unanticipated new challenges in ways that reshaped the nature of the courts' concerns in fundamental ways. However, the special masters were able to keep on top of this process, and inform both the court and others involved in the process of reform. As corrections experts, they were alert to the myriad of impediments that could and did arise to frustrate the aims of the court's orders. As agents of the court, they provided the court with continuous updates of developments.

Corrections experts
Reform-minded governors, legislators and agency heads are generalists, not experts in the issues they implement. They compensate for this lack

of expertise by appointing special assistants who are, or quickly become, experts. Judges, at least successful judges, in complex cases are no different. As we saw, when confronted with policy issues beyond their capacity, they too turned to experts. But, instead of relying entirely on experts invited by the parties to present evidence in formal hearings, they appointed their own experts whose first loyalty was to them alone. In so doing, they greatly expanded their ability to make and effect informed choices.

In the cases described above, the special masters helped their judges assess the often exaggerated and at times ill-informed claims of the parties, and helped their appointing judges develop their own sense of the situation. In each of the cases, these masters were experienced corrections experts who had the confidence and the capacity to offer independent diagnoses of problems and to present them and their proposals for solutions to the court. In two of the cases, Arkansas and Texas, corrections officials tended to identify lack of resources as the source of the problems, and were either unwilling or unable to acknowledge other types of deep-seated problems in the structures of their institutions. The special masters expanded the diagnosis to include organisational structure and administrative competence. In Texas, the special master's investigation revealed continued and widespread use of inmate 'trustees' who served as guards, and more generally exposed the intransigence of top correctional officials. One result was that the judge kept pressing officials to make changes and in so doing forced a number of them to resign and be replaced with administrators whose views were more compatible with the court's. In Arkansas, the special master served as a knowledgeable consultant. He confidently and competently identified areas where improvements had been made, and what else had to be done – and how – to overcome continuing problems. In Santa Clara County, this problem of administrative weakness was painfully obvious, and for two years the sheriff in effect relinquished his authority and allowed the special master to run the jail. Thus, in Texas, when confronted with a recalcitrant leadership, the judge used his special master as a battering ram who eventually prevailed over the entrenched leadership. In Arkansas, the special master served as a correctional consultant, helping corrections officials take steps to improve their prisons and informing the court what these steps should be. In California, the court – with no protest from the parties – allowed the special master the freedom to in effect run the jail in order to implement his ideas on what a modern jail should be. It may sound strange for a court to foster all this, but such activities are standard fare for executive-based reformers.

Floating trial balloons and taking heat for the boss

In a wonderfully frank account of his life as a special master in a Coney Island school desegregation case, Columbia University Law Professor Curtis Burger reports how he approached his assignment with zeal.[18] Appointed by Judge Jack Weinstein, of the federal district court of the Eastern District of New York, an old friend and colleague at Columbia, to help the parties formulate a remedy for school desegregation, Burger assumed (probably correctly) that he was appointed because of his expertise in land use planning and as an old friend of the judge. According to his account of events, he quickly came to the conclusion that the finding of segregation was due to pervasive discrimination in the city's housing practices and policies. In light of this, he presented his 'solution' to the court: change the city's housing policies. To this end, he set about to enlist support from the parties, various public officials and the Ford Foundation. His goal was for the court to order a massive urban renewal project whose core objective was more stable integrated housing. In pursuing his objective, he demonstrated immense enterprise and indeed was on the verge of realising his ambition when Judge Weinstein rejected it summarily and instead imposed a simple solution that transformed one highly segregated school into a special magnate school and then terminated the court's jurisdiction. The special master was stunned and wondered why the judge had approved his quixotic quest for such a wide-ranging solution. Several years later, the judge acknowledged to this author that he had been interested in understanding his options, and thus encouraged the special master to explore a wide range of alternatives. Far from being a waste of time, as Burger viewed his effort, Judge Weinstein thought it invaluable. As a judge, he could not easily have embarked on such a wide-ranging inquiry without attracting a great deal of attention and criticism. But he was able to do this indirectly through his special master. Through the special master, Judge Weinstein was able to explore an expansive alternative, and when he saw that it would be too cumbersome, reject it. It was the special master and not the judge who was charged with outrageous

[18] C. Burger, 'Away from the Courthouse and into the Field: The Odyssey of a Special Master' (1978) 78 *Colorado Law Review* 707.

over-reaching. When the case ended, the court was celebrated for its wisdom and foresight, and the special master discredited for his outlandish suggestions. Such is the fate of special assistants generally. They receive the criticism while their bosses receive the glory.

A similar process occurred in the prison conditions cases described above. In Texas, over the course of a decade, the special master and his staff repeatedly clashed with Texas corrections officials, at times publicly contradicting and challenging them. His aggressive stance eventually wore corrections officials down and they resigned and were replaced with others more in tune with the court's concerns. Although the judge was widely attacked for his actions, to some extent he was able to remain above the fray. Criticism of him paled in comparison to the vitriolic attacks heaped upon the special master. On a smaller scale in Arkansas, the special master also took much of the heat for his judge. When enthusiasm for continued reform waned, the court appointed a special master to badger unenthusiastic corrections officials, and later he agreed to fire the special master if they would redouble their efforts to improve the jails. Here the special master was something of a sacrificial lamb. In Santa Clara County, the special master was aggressive and some of his recommendations were the source of great controversy – it was he who proposed, and insisted upon, single-cell construction in the new jail. However, this did not insulate the court from criticism. It was the judges who took the drubbing from the Board of Supervisors and not the special master.

CONCLUSION

Students of public policy want to know 'what difference does it make?' How are things different after than they were before the introduction of a new policy? Such questions imply a set of criteria for judgment and a capacity to make a clear before and after comparison. And as students of implementation reveal, the process of making policy is intimately connected with the process of implementation in ways that make it difficult if not impossible to distinguish cause from effect. For these and still other reasons, we cannot assert with confidence precisely what impact court orders in the prison conditions cases had. There are no singularly identifiable goals, and certainly no clear metric by which to assess all the changes. Furthermore, the courts' jurisdiction last so long – over twenty years in Texas – that issues originally identified by the court were intermingled with so many other issues – most notably the population explosion – that it is impossible to factor out the influence of various factors and policy makers.

In light of this complexity, the question is less, what impact did the courts by themselves have, as it is, were the courts significant players in an ongoing process? Did they have the capacity and resources to make them so? The answer to this question for the prison conditions cases is yes, undoubtedly the judges were major players. This is in part because they relied on techniques used by successful administrators everywhere to impose reforms. The judges drew corrections officials into the process, required them to supply seemingly endless planning documents and compliance reports, and kept them focused on the long term. In order to do this, they had to create and then rely upon staff assistants. If one considers the activities of the judges in these cases in light of what students of implementation have identified as the conditions necessary for successful implementation, the courts, at least in these cases, possessed them. In particular, they were able to sustain the focus on the issues because they delegated the task to special assistants who had both the time and expertise to be effective. Indeed, judges appear to be remarkably effective managers.

The traditional legal process school holds that the form of adjudication severely restricts its functions. The prison conditions cases reveal this claim to be false. Form does not inevitably dictate function; rather function determines form. In the prison conditions cases examined here, and in a host of structural reform cases in other areas, American judges adapted to the challenge and developed structural arrangements long employed by successful executives. Although reasonable people might assess the results differently and make various judgments about the success of the courts, what is not so disputable is that the courts dramatically expanded their repertoire in dealing with complex structural reform cases and that this expansion is now well institutionalised in the judicial process. As a consequence, we must no longer assess the impact of a court's orders, we must access the process of change overseen by Judge & Co.

PART THREE

THE FUTURE OF JUDICIAL
REVIEW AND BUREAUCRATIC
IMPACT

JUDICIAL REVIEW AND BUREAUCRATIC IMPACT: THE FUTURE OF EUROPEAN UNION ADMINISTRATIVE LAW

MARTIN SHAPIRO

In the last decade a number of words and phrases have become central to thinking about public policy making and implementation. They are 'transparency', 'participation', 'governance', 'deliberation', 'network', 'epistemic community' and 'the new public management'. Taken together, what they represent is an erosion of the boundaries between the governors and the governed and a commitment to the belief that everyone and anyone with sufficient interest or knowledge should be incorporated into those public decision-making processes that result in decisions that affect them. These words and phrases are both empirical or positive and normative. They are believed both to describe what is happening in post-industrial democratic polities and to prescribe what should be happening. If they correctly describe either what is happening or our aspirations, they ought to have fairly clear implications for administrative law.

Beginning in the 1960s, there came to be a severe disjunction between both the actual administrative law and the scholarship about it in the United States and Europe. Earlier, on both sides of the Atlantic, administrative law had been essentially procedural and oriented to the individual. It dealt almost exclusively with the rules for how government officials must behave when either supplying or refusing to supply a benefit to or levying a sanction upon an individual. In the US, the law school course was often labelled administrative procedure, echoing the course in civil procedure and concentrating on what procedural rights individuals did or should enjoy in trial-type administrative hearings. In the Germanic tradition, this same focus was enshrined in the jurisdictional principle that an administrative court might quash only the particular application of a legal norm to the particular individual who had been injured by and who had complained of the application, not the norm itself.

Beginning in the 1960s, a radical transformation occurred in US administrative law. The focus of both judicial and academic attention moved from the individual application of rules to the rules themselves. As the regulatory tasks of government expanded, legislatures everywhere, including the US Congress, markedly increased their delegations of law-making authority to administrators. The American name for such delegated legislation is 'rule'. US courts developed an extraordinarily demanding judicial review of rule-making and merrily struck down administrative rules themselves, not merely their individual applications, on both procedural and substantive grounds.[1]

The aim of this new administrative law was that everyone and anyone whose interests might somehow be affected should have full knowledge of, and the right to actively participate in, every step in the process by which government officials exercised their delegated power to make rules. And the everyone and anyone typically consisted of interest groups who went to court to challenge rules even before they had been applied to any particular person or enterprise. Indeed, much of the current talk of governance, etc., has arisen out of this new American administrative law which demanded so much incorporation of interest groups into the process of delegated law-making itself that the boundary between government and governed, public regulator and private regulatee, disappeared. The courts declared both that the public rule-makers must engage in 'dialogue' with all interested private groups and that the reviewing courts would become partners with the administrators in rule-making, partners who would be particularly concerned with ensuring maximum participation of interest groups in the rule-making process. Given the strength and influence over executive agencies of Congressional committees, American rule-making became quadrangular, the joint product of the relevant Congressional committees, administrative agencies, interest groups and reviewing courts. American rule-making became the world's most transparent, participatory law-making process, one in which everyone inside and outside government got to speak and everyone was compelled to listen.

---

[1] R. Stewart, 'The Reformation of American Administrative Law' (1975) 88 *Harvard Law Review* 1667–813.

The new American administrative law was a major component of the hyper-pluralism that came to be thought of as dominating American political and legal culture. A multitude of interest groups constantly manoeuvred, making and breaking alliances and suing everybody in sight. Rousseau's problem of the will of all versus the general will came to be acutely felt. The pluralist process of interest aggregation came to be seen as more likely to favour the most powerful special interests than to achieve the public interest. Just as our talk of governance largely arises out of American pluralism, our current infatuation with 'deliberation' is a response to American hyper-pluralism. Deliberation, somehow, magically, is to keep the transparency, the participation and the groups but transform the group struggle for selfish advantage into a rational, collaborative search for the public good.

By the end of the century, the governance etc., etc., etc., discourse was trans-Atlantic, and rested as much in European intellectualising as in American experience, but American administrators and administrative law scholars were heavily focused on the legal problems of rule-making and European administrative law scholars were not.

We have already noted that in the Germanic tradition administrative courts could invalidate only the application of rules, not the rules themselves. It is true that even a Northern European administrative court could hold an application to an individual unlawful because the rule being applied was unlawful, but even when such a court was bold enough to do so, the finding of the rule's unlawfulness was merely an element in the court's reasoning. Its actual holding only concerned the unlawfulness of the application. And in civil law cultures, with their formal rejection of *stare decisis*, a finding of unlawfulness of a rule by one court might have little influence on other courts or on the rule-makers.

In the UK, courts could hold rules themselves unlawful as exceeding the authority granted to the rule-maker by the delegating statute,[2] but they rarely did so, at least when the delegatee was an officer or organ of the central government. Given a (roughly) two-party system and strong party discipline, the UK parliament is the humble servant of the government. Should a British court find a piece of administrative, that is government, delegated rule-making unlawful because it was in conflict with the delegating parliamentary statute, it is not the statute but the rule that will often win the conflict. That is, the government can

---

[2] H. W. R. Wade and C. F. Forsyth, *Administrative Law* (8th edn, Oxford, Oxford University Press, 2000), p. 855.

simply order the Parliament to amend the statute to bring the statute into accord with the conflicting rule. Not particularly fond of exercises of futility, British judges are not anxious to declare administrative rules of the central government unlawful, thus saving the government the trouble of having to resuscitate judicially quashed rules by changing the statutes. (In the oft-proclaimed new age of British judicial activism, the courts have managed one such instance of striking down a major rule of the central government.)[3]

Things should have been different in France and the southern European tier with its Council of State tradition. In that tradition, administrative courts can strike down administratively made rules as unlawful, and may do so on substantive as well as procedural grounds. But, as in the UK, although the norms enacted by local institutions may sometimes be struck down, norms enacted by central administration rarely are. In the Fifth Republic of course, the constitution invests much rule-making authority directly in the Executive. Such rules are not, therefore, delegated legislation and cannot be unlawful in the sense of being in conflict with delegating parliamentary legislation. Even when the French Parliament enacts legislation delegating rule-making authority to an administrative body, typically it provides that such rules shall be made 'in council', that is with the participation of the Council of State. While we, or at least I, have no idea how much the Council actually intervenes to ensure conformity of the rule to the delegating statute, it is obvious that the judicial section of the Council is not going to subsequently declare unlawful a rule of the central government that the Council itself has approved at the drafting stage. Thus there is no substantial body of Council jurisprudence on central government rule-making, although in fact the Council may have intervened effectively at the drafting stage to ensure conformity of the rule to the statute.

Quite apart from these narrow jurisprudential matters, Europe has not participated in the American explosion of the administrative law of rule-making for broader reasons of regulatory politics. The American administrative law developments were concomitant with an American explosion of environmental, safety, health and consumer protection regulation. Government regulators and private sector regulatees fell into a highly adversarial stance towards one another. Part of that

---

[3] R. v. Secretary of State for Social Security, ex parte Joint Council for the Welfare of Immigrants, [1997] 1 WLR 23.

adversarial stance played out in enforcement litigation. But the regulated soon learned that it was better to legally challenge the rule as such before it was enforced rather than wait to be cast as an offender in enforcement litigation. The new regulatory legislation typically delegated vast rule-making authority to administrative agencies, but did so in vague terms and with many statutorily defined limitations. And typically these statutes provided for pre-enforcement judicial review of such rules and granted very generous standing to seek such review. Thus a fertile ground was prepared for rule-challenging litigation. As the courts responded actively, striking down many rules, more litigation by the regulated was encouraged. When regulatory agencies themselves seemed to some to be overcautious, pro-regulatory forces learned to litigate to spur more vigorous regulation. Eventually, legal challenges to nearly every rule became a part of the American political culture.[4]

It is, of course, something of a commonplace that European regulatory style has been different from American, non-adversarial, cooperative and cooptive, semi-corporatist or syndicalist. Regulatory rules serve as the basis for negotiated compliance rather than as occasions for litigation. In such a culture there is little impetus to challenge the lawfulness of rules before they are enforced and little enforcement litigation, quite apart from the jurisprudential situation. Precisely because the regulated are 'insiders' in the process of regulatory implementation, they do not push for participation and transparency for 'outsiders'. Such participation and transparency would only complicate their negotiations with the regulators by bringing more voices to the table, most of which would be demanding stricter enforcement.[5]

This situation has been altered by the rise of the EU as a regulatory authority. Most implementation of EU regulations will be done by member state bureaucracies. Many of the detailed rules for implementing EU legislation will also be made by member state administrative organs. So the corporatist regulatory style is not going to suddenly disappear. Nevertheless, the regulated face a new set of problems. Given the single market, regulatory rules themselves become more important. The regulated can be less sure that what they lose at the rule-making stage can be won back or at least substantially ameliorated at the implementation stage. First of all, to the extent that their competitors in other

---

[4] R. Kagan, *Adversarial Legalism: The American Way of Law* (Cambridge, MA, Harvard University Press, 2001).
[5] See S. R. Ackerman, *Controlling Environmental Policy: The Limits of Public Law in Germany and the United States* (New Haven, Yale University Press, 1995).

member states are more successful than they at softening regulatory implementation, those competitors will gain a competitive advantage. So the regulated will actually come to have an interest in reducing the corporatist quality of implementation, at least in states other than their own. Moreover, multinationals will face a situation in which their own corporatist efforts in individual states' implementation will be more and differently successful in softening regulatory outcomes in some states than in others, resulting in different final regulatory demands in some states than in others. Quite often, a multinational would prefer to confront uniform regulatory demands in all states in which it operates rather than differing demands in each, even when differences would result from implementation concessions in some states. Finally, the EU Commission and the EU courts will necessarily put pressure on member state bureaucracies' corporatist concessions to the regulated that result in non-uniform regulatory enforcements.

If the regulated are less willing and/or less able to rely on concessions at the national implementation stage to soften the impact of EU regulatory rules, they must become more interested in softening the rules themselves. Moreover, to the extent that pro-regulatory forces confront corporatist national implementation of EU rules, they will be inclined to head off soft national implementation by seeking tougher EU rules. The regulated who opposed transparency and participation in national implementation, will come to demand such transparency and participation in transnational rule-making where they are far less assured of insider status. And, in making those demands, the regulated will find themselves in a *de facto* alliance with the very pro-regulatory forces they have tried to keep out of their national regulatory corporatist enforcement. This alliance should find a sympathetic ear for those demands in EU organs bent on strengthening the rules themselves and weakening corporatist member state implementation which not only weakens regulation but tends to make it non-uniform from state to state.[6]

I have argued elsewhere at length that the political theory of one period allows us to predict the administrative law of the next. The orthodox pluralist democratic theory of the 1950s became the

---

[6] M. Shapiro and A. Stone Sweet, *On Law, Politics and Judicialization* (Oxford, Oxford University Press, 2002), pp. 228–57; M. Shapiro, 'The Institutionalization of European Administrative Space' in A. Stone Sweet, W. Sandholtz and N. Fligstein (eds.), *The Institutionalization of Europe* (Oxford, Oxford University Press, 2002); H. P. Nehl, *Principles of Administrative Procedure in EC Law* (Oxford, Hart, 1999).

American administrative law of rule-making in the 1960s and there-after.[7] If the European theory of today is built on concepts of gover-nance and deliberation, then can we reasonably expect the growth of a European administrative law of rule-making that incorporates those concepts?

As a regulatory regime, the EU depends centrally on delegation. That is, EU directives depend upon member state legislative and administra-tive enactment of detailed implementing rules. Over time, however, the dangers to the single market of the state-to-state non-uniformity that necessarily results from member state construction of implement-ing rules has led the EU Council to delegate more and more rule-making power not to member states but to the comitology process and the inde-pendent agencies, or, if you prefer, to the EU Commission which, in the-ory at least, controls these organs. If the regulated and pro-regulatory forces want to be 'insiders' in rule-making, then it is to these organs that they must turn their efforts to build a new administrative law guaran-teeing them insider status. If current political theory of governance and deliberation are to enter administrative law, they are likely to enter a newly created administrative law of EU rule-making more easily than into established bodies of member state administrative law. Those who see themselves as 'outsiders' to EU regulatory rule-making and who wish to become insiders are likely to push forward ideas of governance and deliberation as a way of building an administrative law that grants them insider status.

This prospect is complicated by a dynamic of democracy versus tech-nocracy currently being played out in the politics of EU-building. The issue is participation, transparency, governance and deliberation for whom? One answer involves what, from a perhaps prejudiced view, amounts to a hijacking of deliberation. Suppose we prescribe EU rule-making by 'networks' within 'epistemic communities' which grant transparency and participation in a deliberative process to all those inside and outside government *who share the technical knowledge relevant* to the rule being made. In this way, all the new theoretical parapher-nalia can be used to exclude the non-expert, the *demos*, the voters, from the rule-making process. This move can be bolstered or camou-flaged by the claim that, while the *demos* necessarily engages in politics, defined as the pursuit of naked self-interest, an epistemic community or

---

[7] Martin Shapiro, *Who Guards the Guardians* (Athens, GA, University of Georgia Press, 1988).

network of experts can engage not in interest group, pluralist politics, the American hyper-pluralism, but in informed deliberation or rational decision-making. The epistemically anointed can achieve deliberative truth. Networks of experts will talk to themselves until they achieve the right answer where the *demos* divided into groups can only aggregate interests. And such aggregation can only reflect the relative strengths of the various groups, an aggregation that will never, or only accidentally, correspond to the right answer. In short, while the people can only do interest group politics, the experts can truly deliberate.[8] Precisely this approach is to be found in recent Community initiatives.[9]

Because most regulation today is high-tech, there is enormous appeal to this approach. Surely the people who do understand nuclear power generation or internet communication ought to regulate those things, not people who don't understand them. And the democracy problems that seem to arise from rule-by-experts can be evaded by asserting that experts are better deliberators than the rest of us. Somehow, the PhD washes away all those selfish interests that make true deliberation so difficult in politics. If the EU suffers from a democratic deficit, then democratic legitimacy may be replaced by technocratic legitimacy.[10] Or, ultimately, regulatory policy should be made by expert deliberation resulting in rational, correct decisions; the rest of public policy may be left to politics. Particular interests that perceive themselves harmed by rational regulation may seek compensation in the political process.

The technocratic version of deliberation thus demands participation and transparency for all those with the relevant expertise but the opposite for everyone else. With all the experts and only the experts in, those who are not in the expert network, not members of the appropriate epistemic community, will be shut out and shut out in the most effective way possible. They will not speak or even understand the language in which the deliberation is carried on.

---

[8] See C. Joerges and J. Neyer, 'From Intergovernmental Bargaining to Deliberative Political Processes: The Constitutionalization of Comitology' (1997) 3 *European Law Journal* 273–99.

[9] Cf. K. Lenaerts and A. Verhoeven, 'Toward a Legal Framework for Executive Rule-Making in the EU? The Contribution of the New Comitology Decision' (2000) 37 *Common Market Law Review* 645–86 with 'Taking Governance Seriously: Response to the Commission White Paper on European Governance by the LSE Study Group on European Administrative Law' (2002).

[10] G. Majone, 'Two Logics of Delegation: Agency and Fiduciary Relations in EU Governance' (2001) 2 *European Union Politics* 103–37.

The democratic version of deliberation would provide transparency and broad participation in the rule-making process for all interested persons. It too stresses full factual information, but the experts are to provide translations for the laymen. The gravest difficulty with the lay model of deliberation is the difficulty of distinguishing it from pluralism and thus from the risk of American hyper-pluralism. Both pluralism and democratic deliberation call for maximum participation for the interested and thus for interest groups. Both call for maximum information to be made available to all participants. Indeed, maximum participation guarantees maximum information as rival groups each bring their own versions of the relevant facts to the table. So most administrative law rules designed to ensure maximum transparency and participation will be the same for both democratic pluralists and democratic deliberators. The difference between the two is that, once all parties with full information are at the table, pluralists expect the various interests present to bargain to an aggregation of their rival interests while the deliberators want them to suppress their selfish interests in favour of seeking that outcome which best satisfies the public good. But, so far at least, deliberators have been unable to suggest procedural rules for the discourse at the table that would ensure deliberative as opposed to interest aggregative outcomes.

Thus the administrative law rules that deliberators can propose, being the same as pluralist rules, raise the same danger, that of strategic behaviour. And judicial review to back those rules further increases the potential for strategic behaviour. All of this has already been played out in the US, which has pushed participation- and transparency-enforcing administrative law rules and judicial activism in enforcement of those rules to the extreme.

The US rules require repeated public notification by the rule-making agency of what rule it proposes to make, first of the general area in which it is contemplating a rule, then of a draft rule, and then of its revised version. The agency must provide for full public comment at each of these stages and engage in exhaustive dialogue responding to every relevant comment made and even to significant points not raised in the comments. The agency must compile a 'rule-making record' that documents that it has granted maximum transparency and participation to everybody interested, and has taken reasonable account of all this input in arriving at its final rule. This rule-making record enables a reviewing court to fully enforce the transparency and participation requirements. And, in spite of recent Supreme Court efforts to cut back on the extremes of standing, a very, very wide range of individuals and organisations are able to trigger such judicial review.

One result is that anyone who wishes to delay or block the enactment of a rule will raise every imaginable argument and alleged fact during the rule-making process compelling the rule-making agency to make exhaustive and exhausting replies. Every point raised in the rule-making proceedings creates an opportunity for later reversal of the rule by a reviewing court on the grounds that the agency did not take sufficient account of it. Lawyer lobbyists become increasingly adept at manufacturing things to talk about. More and more time and resources are devoted to building a longer and longer rule-making record. The longer and more elaborate the rule-making record, the potentially more searching the judicial review. Today in the US it is sometimes quicker and easier to get Congress to change the statute than it is to get the agency to write a new rule under the rule-making authority delegated to it by the statute.

Of course, if the participants were true deliberators rather than entrenched interest pursuers, this strategic behaviour would not occur. But we do not know what the magic incantation is that turns interest pursuers into deliberators.

In spite of this problem of strategic behaviour, I am about to assert that, in the name of deliberation, the EU will shortly move to an administrative law of participation and transparency akin to American-style pluralism. In doing so, I am *not* arguing that US administrative law is somehow better or more advanced than European law or that Europe is emulating or should emulate the US. And I am not arguing that the administrative law of the member states will be or should be harmonised.

Let me take this last negative point first. While an administrative law for EU rule-making, that is rule-making by comitology and/or independent agencies, will necessarily reflect the administrative law experience of the member states, it does not require any change in the administrative law of any of the member states. It can be a *sui generis* procedural law for rule-making by organs of the EU alone without requiring changes in the procedural law or degree of judicial review of national rule-making.

As to 'Americanisation', I am not arguing that the EU must, can or should emulate the US, but rather that like causes have like effects. If American pluralist theory of the 1950s generated a new, subsequent, pluralist, US, administrative law of participation and transparency, so a European deliberative governance theory is likely to generate a new EU administrative law of participation and transparency. And in both places a wave of heightened, arm's-length regulation spurs litigators to push courts towards demanding heightened participation and transparency and courts to respond. But one cause is not alike. The EU situation occurs after the culmination of the US experience so that the US experience is known to the EU. As EU courts move towards an administrative law of transparency and participation, they will be more aware of the dangers of strategic behaviour or hyper-pluralism than were American courts.

I have argued elsewhere at length that the EU courts have already taken the first steps towards an administrative law of heightened participation and transparency and a more active judicial review to ensure obedience to that law. And I also argued there that the European Court of Justice is also signalling to litigators that it will be hostile to strategic behaviour, which will lead to the manufacture of endless arguments and issues designed to delay rule-making, and will increase the chances for judicial reversal. I will not repeat my argument here.[11]

I have also said elsewhere that I think the technocratic hijack will fail. It may be worth saying a bit more on this point. The basic force behind the technocratic version of deliberation is the substitution of technocratic for democratic legitimacy. If the EU suffers from a democratic deficit, then one can substitute a different basis of legitimacy, namely expertise. This attempted substitution seems to me unworkable for three reasons. First, there are strong anti-expertise movements present in most post-industrial societies including those of Europe. Much of the animosity expressed towards bureaucracy in general and the Eurocracy or 'Brussels' in particular is really anti-technocratic sentiment. Indeed, one of the most popular of the deliberation themes is that deliberation must be local and based on local senses of community. That localism is in part an expression of distrust for far distant experts. Experts, almost by definition, are cosmopolitans not locals. Popular love of the technical expert is far too weak and fickle to serve as a reliable substitute for democratic legitimacy.

Secondly, whatever democracy there is in the EU quickly recognises technocracy as its enemy. It has been the European Parliament that has been the principal source of pressure for more transparency in the technocratic comitology process. While the Council may be happy to

---

[11] See note 6 above.

exclude lay participation from the comitology process, the Parliament is not happy to exclude such participation, particularly its own.

Thirdly, the myth that technical experts are less self-interested and thus better deliberators than laymen is not likely to survive very long in the crucible of real politics. The first to learn the truth are the regulated who quickly come to see that who is on the committee determines the content of regulatory rules. The regulated themselves typically employ experts in their own R & D, testing and production units. They also typically have the money to hire outside experts and create their own scientific foundations or other fronts for their versions of science. They will learn to challenge comitology decisions on the basis that the committee's membership was stacked against them, and themselves insert numbers of their own experts in the networks or epistemic communities that staff the committees. As committee and agency memberships themselves become subjects of contention, the legitimacy of expertise is undermined. People learn that everyone with money can hire experts to be on their side. And the more transparency is demanded of expert deliberation the more it is revealed as yet another, if disguised, form of interest group bargaining. The public will grant legitimacy to experts for non-contentious public policy issues, but, when an issue becomes hot, public faith in experts rapidly declines as the conflicts among experts are highlighted and the interest basis of those conflicts revealed.

The technocratic version of deliberation is actually an attempt to limit transparency and participation. Those experts in the network get to know and participate fully. Those outside the epistemic community are not to know what is going on and couldn't understand it even if they did. Thus regulation is to be saved from politics. Technocracy is claimed to equal deliberation. Democracy is claimed to equal the discredited interest group pluralism. For believers in technocratic deliberation, full transparency and participation would open the floodgates through which nasty self-interest would pour into a regulatory process which can remain rationally deliberative only if it is reserved to experts. This form of deliberation reflects the movement from government to governance in the sense that the boundary between government and non-government experts is eroded, but it seeks to establish a new, even more impervious boundary between the governors and the governed.

If, however, we address ourselves to a more general, and non-technocratic, version of deliberation, and look at its potential impact on administrative law, both an opportunity and a set of problems emerge. Initially at least, pluralists and democratic deliberators would opt for roughly the same rules governing the rule-making or delegated legislation process. For both pluralists and deliberators opt for maximum transparency, participation and information. The three are, of course, interconnected. Non-governmental actors can only participate if they know what the government actors are considering and what information they have. Maximum participation requires maximum transparency. The best way to know what the government actors are considering is to participate in their decision-making. Maximum participation ensures maximum transparency. And the more interested parties participate and the more transparency, the more information will ultimately be available to decision-makers, not only about the decision-making process itself but also about the real world that the decision is being designed to alter in some way.

Thus rules that approximate those of American, 'notice and comment' rule-making are going to be pushed by both pluralists and deliberators for EU delegated legislation processes. First, we must know at the very beginning of the game who the initially chosen decision-makers are going to be and in general the subject matter of the proposed rule-making. Secondly, we must know at each succeeding step in the rule-making who has been added to the decision-makers and, in progressively greater detail, what rule is being contemplated. Thirdly, all interested outsiders must be granted access to participation in the process and their contributions responded to. All outsiders who want to be inside must be allowed inside.

A brief additional word about the American 'dialogue' requirement, which in the EU is potentially lodged in the treaty language of 'giving reasons' and the ECJ-constructed duty of good administration and now also acknowledged in the new Charter of Rights. While in the US the dialogue requirement may have taken on an independent life of its own, it began as a derivation of participation and transparency requirements. Unless the insiders respond to the points raised by the outsiders, there is no real transparency or participation. Without responses, outsiders cannot know what to say next and so cannot become real participants. Only through dialogue can outsiders become insiders. Moreover, only through a dialogue requirement can we force insiders to really take account of what those initially outside have to say. If they need not respond, insiders can simply register their receipt of outsider comments and then ignore them thus denying outsiders real participation.

On all these matters, pluralists and deliberators will be in agreement, and both will insist on repeated rounds of 'notice' and 'comment' and dialogue. And concrete rules ensuring such notice and comment are not difficult to write or agree upon, at least for those really committed to maximum transparency and participation.

The great problem for deliberators is how, once access to the process is maximised, to ensure that the process is one of true deliberation rather than interest group bargaining or mere interest aggregation. I for one do not have the slightest idea what concrete procedural rules will move people who come to the table precisely because they have interests to see beyond those interests to the general good and act to achieve it. Pluralists could write the EU rules right now. Deliberators could, right now, join them in agreeing to all those rules, but what additional rules can they suggest to ensure deliberation?

The technocratic hijack is attractive precisely because it promises a solution to this problem. Maximise transparency, participation and information for experts only and shut everyone else out. Being disinterested, these experts will then deliberate, not bargain. This solution, however, depends on a premise that I believe to be false, namely that experts are disinterested.

Finally, the pluralists and the deliberators share the problem of judicial review. Although it is true that, in the US, the courts constructed a whole new administrative law of rule-making without any significant modification of the governing statute (the Administrative Procedures Act, or APA), the courts did not usurp Congressional authority. Congress is in the habit of writing particular procedural requirements into each piece of legislation delegating rule-making authority. The APA acts only as a residual or fallback law when Congress does not do so or does so only incompletely. During the period in which the courts built up a new case law of rule-making procedures, Congress echoed and supported, and sometimes went even further than, that case law in numerous procedural provisions in its new health, safety and consumer-protection statutes. And Congress consistently opted for maximum judicial review.

Nevertheless, the extremely intrusive and aggressive American style of judicial review, amounting to a self-declared judicial 'partnership' in the rule-making process, has been the subject of much criticism, in the US. There has probably been some judicial retreat, although such retreat is extremely hard to prove or measure. Rules maximising participation and 'dialogue', when combined with aggressive judicial review, generate much strategic behaviour. Some parties to the rule-making offer endless comments both to delay the final rule and to maximise their chances that a reviewing court will find inadequate response to some comment they have made and quash the rule. Even parties who want a prompt and effective rule will tend to expand, inflate and exaggerate their claims in anticipation of the adversarial stance they must necessarily take in review litigation. The tendency of parties to conduct the rule-making with an eye towards subsequent litigational advantage obviously reduces the chance that real deliberation will occur. Even from pluralist perspectives, however, this infection of the rule-making process with 'adversarial legalism' tends to greatly increase the costs in both time and effort of reaching a 'satisficing', pluralist aggregation of interests.

US rule-making is characterised by maximum transparency, participation and information. There is little doubt that its rules are better for having become the product of governance rather than of government regulators acting in isolation from the subjects and proposed beneficiaries of the regulations. But rule-making in the US is an extremely slow and expensive process and may result in rules that are less good than those that would result from a less participatory process.

Clearly, Americans do not believe that administrative regulators will provide sufficient transparency and participation or pay sufficient attention to outsiders without judicial review. Is it possible to write procedural rules for rule-making that inspire sufficient judicial review to enforce adequate participation and transparency without setting off a cycle of more and more strategic behaviour by those participating and more and more judicial intrusion which in turn encourages even more strategic behaviour and judicial intrusion?

I believe that it is precisely this goal that the ECJ is signalling that it is seeking in its convoluted *Sytraval II* decision.[12] Clearly, it is troubled by what it sees as a danger that the Court of First Instance will turn 'giving reasons' into a full-scale judicially enforced dialogue requirement that will generate strategic behaviour and start the EU down the road to American hyper-pluralism. Yet the ECJ itself is clearly feeling the intellectual currents of the times. Its ultimate holding that courts must ensure that the Commission responds to 'not secondary' outside comments exhibits its yearning for a 'three bears' solution – not too much judicial review leading to 'too hot' American hyper-pluralism,

---

[12] Case 367/95, *Sytraval II* [1998] ECR I-1719.

nor too little review leading to 'too cold' barriers between governors and governed, but 'just right' review that leads at least to 'just right' pluralism or even deliberation.[13]

In my own mind there is little doubt that, given the current state of political theory, the EU courts will sooner or later seek to ensure that the comitology process and whatever rule-making authority is granted to the independent agencies exhibit governance, transparency, participation, etc. If the courts can be persuaded to accept the technocratic hijack of deliberation, they will speak much of judicial deference to 'expertise', and engage in minimal real review, trusting the experts to deliberate and demanding only that the full range of experts has been consulted. If not, EU administrative law will centre on the creation of procedural rules for and levels of judicial review of rule-making that move the EU partway but not too far down the American path.

For those concerned with empirical studies of the impact of review on bureaucratic behaviour, a comparison of past US and potential EU experience with judicial review of administrative rule-making signals some paradoxes and difficulties. The transformation of US administrative law was massive, relatively quick and generated enormous amounts of litigation. To meet the dialogue and partnership requirements, agencies had to fully document every step and stage in their decision-making processes and lay out in a 'rule-making record' not only all the procedural steps they had taken but virtual proof that the rule they had chosen was the best possible rule. Given that nearly every major rule was litigated, and the supporting documentation was a matter of public record, there was really no need of subtle empirical studies of change in bureaucratic behaviour. At least in terms of receiving, recording and responding to outside influences, changes in bureaucratic behaviour were obviously and observably massive and obviously and observably responses to judicial demands. Moreover, the elaborate notice requirement the courts came to impose meant that the rule-makers had to set out detailed draft rules. In most instances, differences between draft and final rules were substantial so that it was clear that the massive changes in record-making administrative behaviour were resulting in substantial policy results. Bureaucrats were not simply going through the motions of listening. Thus there were no general empirical studies of the impact of review precisely because that impact was so obvious, massive and

[13] For a CFI attempt at such a 'just right' review, see Case T-206/99, *Metropole Television SA v. Commission* [2001] ECR II-1057.

documented in public records. There were a family of studies of particular policies, tracking their legislative, administrative and judicial
histories, all of which showed the substantial impact of actual judicial
review and the even more substantial impact of seeking to make proposed rules review-proof.[14] On the other hand, Supreme Court attempts
to rein in what it apparently saw as excessively active review by the US
courts of appeal, which are the principal reviewing courts for delegated
legislation, have generated seemingly insoluble problems for the mea-
surement of impact. Because the Supreme Court itself actually hears
only a handful of rule-review cases, it must seek to rein in the courts of
appeal by general doctrinal pronouncements in the cases it does take.
Because the Supreme Court has really generally agreed with the courts
of appeal on heightened review, its doctrinal pronouncements in such
famous cases as *Vermont Yankee*[15] and *Chevron*[16] have not been clear-
cut 'no' but rather 'yes, but a little bit less'. It is hard to figure out how to
measure the impact of such decisions even on the courts to which they
are directed, let alone on the agencies subject to review.[17] Agency batting averages may or may not have gone up, although all sorts of causes
other than Supreme Court calls for restraint determine those averages.
As to the agencies themselves, they still face the necessity of creating
a full-scale rule-making record for review. They still face a substantial
risk of adverse judicial review. And such adverse review would trigger
a new round of large investment of agency resources to generate a new
rule-making record to support a new rule. Even batters with high averages spend a lot of time and energy at batting practice. It is unlikely
that the agencies have much reduced their rule-making preparations
just because they now hope to win more often than in the past. So

[14] See, e.g., R. Katzmann, *Institutional Disability: The Saga of Transportation Policy for the Handicapped* (Washington, DC, Brookings Institution, 1986); J. Mashaw and D. Harfst, *The Struggle for Auto Safety* (Cambridge, MA, Harvard University Press, 1990); S. Mezey, *No Longer Disabled: The Federal Courts and the Politics of Social Security Disability* (New York, Greenwood Press, 1988); R. Shep Melnick, *Regulation and the Courts: The Case of the Clean Air Act* (Washington, DC, Brookings Institu-tion, 1983); R. Shep Melnick, *Between the Lines Interpreting Welfare Rights* (Brookings Institution, Washington, DC, 1994).
[15] *Vermont Yankee Nuclear Power Corp. v. Natural Resources Defense Council*, 435 US 519 (1978).
[16] *Chevron v. Natural Resources Defense Council*, 467 US 837 (1984).
[17] See J. Mashaw, 'Small Things Like Reasons Are Put in a Jar: Reason and Legitimacy in the Administrative State' (2001) 70 *Fordham Law Review* 17–35; T. Merrill and K. Hickman, 'Chevron's Domain' (2001) 89 *Georgetown Law Journal* 833–87.

there is little incentive to invest in elaborate empirical inquiries into their responses to a somewhat more favourable review climate.[18]

So US scholarship is not likely to help students of EU review of delegated legislation much. Moreover, even if I am correct and the EU courts broaden and deepen their review of rule-making, it is not going to be easy to distinguish changes in Commission, comitology and independent agency behaviour in the direction of transparency and participation that are due to heightened judicial review from those that result from heightened pressure from the European Parliament, the Council or the Commission's own desire to reduce its democratic deficit. What is clear, to me at least, is that both empirical and doctrinal administrative law scholarship in Europe will be shifting some of its attention from administrative adjudication to administrative law-making.

---

[18] One exception is J. L. Smith and E. Tiller, 'The Strategy of Judging: Evidence from Administrative Law' (2002) 31 *Journal of Legal Studies* 61, who find that agency reversal rates have actually gone up since *Chevron*.

CHAPTER TEN

JUDICIAL REVIEW AND BUREAUCRATIC IMPACT IN FUTURE RESEARCH

MARC HERTOGH AND SIMON HALLIDAY

INTRODUCTION: TOWARDS A GENERAL THEORY OF IMPACT?

The field of judicial impact studies really started flourishing in the 1970s. After an initial period of descriptive studies – registering the reactions and the behaviour of public offices and the general public – researchers began to develop explanatory hypotheses and theoretical approaches. At this point in the endeavour, many scholars shared a feeling of great optimism that a 'general theory of impact' had finally come within reach. This is also reflected in *The Impact of Supreme Court Decisions*,[1] one of the earliest collections of impact research at the time. The most important difference between the first (1969) and second (1973) edition of the book was the introduction of an entirely new section called 'Toward a Theory of Impact'. According to the editors, the articles included therein 'demonstrate that interest in impact has matured'.[2] In his chapter, Stephen Wasby lists a total of 135 hypotheses that were derived from the existing impact literature.[3]

At present, more than three decades of judicial impact studies later, there is still no general theory of impact. Moreover, for most scholars working in the field, the early optimism of the 1970s has been traded

---

[1] T. L. Becker and M. M. Feeley (eds.), *The Impact of Supreme Court Decisions: Empirical Studies* (2nd edn, New York, Oxford University Press, 1973).

[2] *Ibid.*, p. v.

[3] S. L. Wasby, 'Toward Impact Theory: An Inventory of Hypotheses' in Becker and Feeley, *The Impact*, pp. 214–17.

in for a sense of realism that the present body of literature is still a long way from any type of theoretical synthesis. Canon and Johnson[4] in their survey of the present literature retrieve not *one* but as many as *nine* competing theories of impact, ranging from psychological and utility theories to approaches from communications and organisational theory. This divergence of opinions is also illustrated in the extensive debate surrounding Gerald Rosenberg's important book, *The Hollow Hope: Can Courts Bring About Social Change?*.[5] In fact, the theoretical and methodological discussion with regard to Rosenberg's book is remarkably similar to the concerns that were raised in the 1970s by those critical of the ambition for a general theory of impact. Many of Feeley's early concerns in 1973 – the relation between power and impact; the problem of causal analysis and 'spurious correlation'; and the significance of anticipated reactions in response to court decisions – are also at the heart of the debate about *The Hollow Hope*. Confronted with such a (seemingly) small amount of development within the field, some commentators have adopted a sceptical approach to the research about judicial impact.

Impact agnosticism

Peter Cane opened this volume of essays by injecting a sense of caution into the enterprise of investigating the impact of judicial review on bureaucracies. Cane's scepticism about our ability to ever collect sufficient data to be able to talk comprehensively in terms of the impact of judicial review – a kind of 'impact agnosticism' – raises a fundamental question: should we, as law and society scholars, continue with the enterprise? Not surprisingly, perhaps, our answer to this question is 'yes'.

Scepticism like Cane's about the scale and the difficulty of the impact question certainly increases the attractiveness and comfort of focusing on the 'expressive' functions of judicial review (where the terrain is normative and policy choices have at least some chance of being dictated by a level of consensus). But the fact that notions such as the rule of law are powerful normative claims in democratic states sets up an agenda for empirical research. Judicial mandates for bureaucratic behaviour have an authoritative and prescriptive quality which unavoidably invites

---

[4] B. C. Canon and C. A. Johnson, *Judicial Policies: Implementation and Impact* (2nd edn, Washington, DC, CQ Press, 1999).
[5] G. N. Rosenberg, *The Hollow Hope: Can Courts Bring About Social Change?* (Chicago, Chicago University Press, 1991).

social enquiry. If the courts set out some level of guidance about how government should go about its business, or about some other kind of behavioural change which should take place in society, it is difficult to resist the temptation to at least try to find out if and how law matters – regardless of how difficult the task is, or how elusive the answers might be. Of course, as McCann has pointed out,[6] a focus on compliance with court rulings is only a small (though, it is suggested, indispensable) part of the overall judicial impact project. Further, we should be cautious in not exaggerating the potential of the courts to produce social change.[7] Nevertheless, given that the courts are important constitutional actors, it is important to investigate their influence on the bureaucracies which are (in part at least) the target audience of their rulings. If our aim, at its most basic level, is to understand social action and the role of law in society, then the significance of law and court judgments to bureau-cratic behaviour is an unavoidable question. It is clearly only *one* of a number of possible socio-legal questions. But it is an important one which is worthy of our attention and our continued research efforts.

Of course, to be fair to Cane, asserting the unavoidable imperative to enquire into the impact of judicial review does not address the more specific point about whether informed policy choices can be made on the back of the relatively little empirical data that currently exists. But this, we suspect, is a generic problem for policy-making, and is not con-fined to the field of judicial impact studies.

The focus of this chapter

One of the attributes of this volume of essays is that it illustrates the great diversity of the ways in which the bureaucratic impact of judicial review might be analysed. However, we do not consider this a weak-ness, but rather one of the greatest strengths of the field. In this con-cluding chapter, we move our focus away from questions of impact as such towards more general questions of law and society. We will use the essays in this volume to help us set up an agenda for future research. We will identify three major challenges for future judicial impact studies. First, the essays in this collection suggest that future empirical research

---

[6] M. W. McCann, '"Reform Litigation on Trial": Review of *The Hollow Hope*' (1992) 17 *Law and Social Inquiry* 715–43; M. W. McCann, *Rights at Work: Pay Equity Reform and the Politics of Legal Mobilization* (Chicago, University of Chicago Press, 1994).

[7] M. M. Feeley, '"Hollow Hopes, Flypaper, and Metaphors": Review of *The Hollow Hope*' (1992) 17 *Law and Social Inquiry* 745–60.

should be inspired by an interdisciplinary perspective and by method-ological pluralism. Secondly, we argue for a more contextual approach that recognises the highly dynamic relations between law, bureaucracy and impact and that appreciates the fact that law often has to compete with other values. Finally, the international case studies make it clear that the empirical study of the bureaucratic impact of court decisions should be more integrated with the general field of law and society.

INTERDISCIPLINARITY AND METHODOLOGICAL PLURALISM

A collection of this kind invites some reflection on method. The ques-tion of methodological approach in judicial impact studies has, of course, been canvassed extensively in the wake of Rosenberg's book, *The Hollow Hope*.[8] Indeed, the specific debate between Rosenberg and McCann has been rehearsed on a number of occasions.[9] We certainly do not aim to continue that debate here. Nor is our aim here to offer a substantive discussion of social science research methods in relation to judicial review's bureaucratic impact. Our (much more modest) aim is simply to draw some of the methodological material of this volume together, to give it a central focus and to argue for interdisciplinarity and methodological pluralism in researching judicial review and bureau-cratic impact.

Political science and socio-legal studies

Cane has argued that we should be sensitive to the constitutional set-ting of judicial review, and notes that judicial review is ascribed differ-ent functions in various constitutional contexts. Our contention here is that, to an extent, different constitutional contexts have histori-cally invited different intellectual disciplines in the research of judicial

---

[8] Rosenberg, *The Hollow Hope*.
[9] McCann, 'Reform Litigation'; M. W. McCann, 'Causal Versus Constitutive Expla-nations (or, On the Difficulty of Being So Positive . . .)' (1996) 21 *Law and Social Inquiry* 457–82; M. W. McCann, 'Law and Political Struggles for Social Change: Puz-zles, Paradoxes, and Promises in Future Research' in D. A. Schultz (ed.), *Leveraging the Law: Using the Courts to Achieve Social Change* (New York, Peter Lang, 1998), pp. 319–49; G. N. Rosenberg, 'Hollow Hopes and Other Aspirations: A Reply to Feeley and McCann' (1992) 17 *Law and Social Inquiry* 761–78; G. N. Rosenberg, '"Positivism, Interpretivism, and the Study of Law": Review of *Rights at Work*' (1996) 21 *Law and Social Inquiry* 435–55; G. N. Rosenberg, 'Knowledge and Desire: Thinking About Courts and Social Change' in Schultz, *Leveraging the Law*, pp. 251–91.

impact. In other words, the research histories of different countries can be explained (at least in part) by the different constitutional roles of judicial review. For example, it is perhaps not surprising that judicial impact studies in the United States have been dominated by political science where, as we noted in our introduction, the concern has been to explore the broad dynamics of power in society. By way of contrast, in the United Kingdom, for example, judicial impact studies have been dominated by socio-legal scholars of administrative law where the concern has more narrowly been to test the ability of the law to guide or control government agencies. This is in keeping with the different constitutional roles of judicial review in the two countries. As Cane described in his chapter, judicial review has been at the heart of the American constitution, whereas the UK's constitution has rested on the doctrine of parliamentary sovereignty, and the courts, accordingly, have traditionally had a much more limited role.

This point, of course, should not be taken too far. The characterisations of the interests of US political science and UK socio-legal studies are painted with a broad brush and miss some of the detail of these research traditions, as the chapters by Canon and by Richardson show. More importantly, there is more to the explanation of respective research traditions than the constitutional setting of judicial review. The research process is, after all, a social process like everything else, and our understanding of it, then, cannot be reduced to a focus on a single context. However, it seems to us that the constitutional positioning of judicial review has something important to say in explaining the different disciplines which have addressed judicial impact. Further, this suggestion serves to focus our attention on the importance of interdisciplinary work. With the rise of human rights[10] and the incorporation of international norms into domestic law, and the consequent shifts in constitutional dynamics, legal scholars have much to learn from the political scientists. To return to our example of the US and the UK, the enactment of the Human Rights Act 1998 in the UK has altered the UK's constitution, and permits the court both to interpret primary legislation in the light of the European Convention on Human Rights(ECHR), and to issue declarations of incompatibility in relation to Acts of Parliament which conflict with the demands of the ECHR. The courts, therefore, now enjoy an increased constitutional status, and

---

[10] B. Edgeworth, *Law, Modernity, Postmodernity: Legal Change in the Contracting State* (Aldershot, Ashgate, 2003).

much of the domestic UK debate about the merits of the Human Rights Act can be seen as one of how much we should trust the judges.[11] Nevertheless, our point here is that UK socio-legal scholars have much to gain from the rich history of empirical US political science research which has explored the power of the courts in society and their significance to social change. Conversely, of course, political science scholars of judicial impact in the US have much to gain from socio-legal administrative law research which has uncovered comparable complex dynamics of power writ small within a single bureaucracy. Traditionally, political science and socio-legal studies have focused on different questions of impact and engaged in different levels of analysis. The contention of this section, and the rationale underpinning the book as a whole, is that the two disciplines have shared interests and much to gain from each other.

Positivism and interpretivism
As Canon describes in his essay, the enterprise of investigating the role of courts in relation to social action has been largely described as 'judicial impact studies'. The more specific exploration of judicial review and bureaucratic impact in this volume can easily be understood as falling within this tradition. However, it should be noted that for some scholars who investigate the relationship between judicial review and bureaucratic behaviour (including those in this volume) the notion of 'impact' sits in some tension with their underlying methodological approach.

Sunkin has already noted the methodological divide between interpretive and positivist approaches to the social sciences in general and judicial impact studies in particular. Both approaches seek to explain social action. However, their framing of research questions and their approach to inquiry are quite different. Positivism may be characterised as a process of research which *observes* social change from the outside, whereas interpretivism may be characterised as a process which seeks to *understand* social action from the inside. Positivists seek out patterns of behaviour and aim to establish correlative or causal relationships between sets of factors and observable social action. Interpretivists hold the individual or sets of individuals as the focus of study and seek to penetrate and understand the ways in which they make sense of their social worlds. It is clear that the concept of 'impact'

---

[11] T. Campell, K. D. Ewing and A. Tomkins, *Sceptical Essays on Human Rights* (Oxford, Oxford University Press, 2001).

sits more comfortably within a positivist approach. From a positivist vantage point, the research task is to focus first on a court judgment and to observe and document the behavioural changes (if any) in its wake. Where behavioural change is observed and a causal or correlative relationship can be traced to the court decision, then 'impact' can be concluded. For interpretivists, however, the task is not to observe from the outside but to understand it from the inside. The enquiry, then, inevitably starts with those whose perceptions and actions one is interested in understanding. The core of the research endeavour is the body of research subjects who are generating meaning and engaging in social action. This, rather than judicial impact *per se*, is the primary focus and aim of the research. So, for example, McCann's[12] study of pay equity reform sought to understand the legal consciousnesses of those involved in the struggle for social change. Part of this enquiry clearly relates to the significance of court decisions in the consciousnesses of the social actors. But this is not the same as having the 'impact' of court decisions as the core of one's enquiry. For interpretivist scholars, the concept of 'impact' betrays their research ambitions. The notion of 'impact' invites a more precise assessment of the consequences of court judgments than interpretive approaches permit. If one's aim is to explore the complex ways in which meaning is achieved and the overlapping contexts in which social action is performed, then the 'impact' of judicial review simply cannot be captured. In short, it is too clinical a question to ask.

Top-down and bottom-up approaches

Allied to the interpretivism–positivism divide is another distinction in the literature – that of 'court-centred' or 'top-down' approaches to studying judicial impact, versus 'de-centred' or 'bottom-up' approaches. It is important to note that these two sets of categories do not match perfectly and are capable of obscuring rather than enlightening. As Sunkin describes, an interpretivist approach can be used to conduct court-centred studies. The fact that this volume of essays seeks to explore the impact of judicial review on bureaucracies will no doubt destine it to fall within the 'court-centred' camp. However, a number of the case studies in this book adopt an explicitly interpretivist approach to their research (and other similar studies are cited) – in other words, they take a 'bottom-up' approach to a 'court-centred' research question. This kind of work is important because it demonstrates the distinctly subtle

---

[12] McCann, *Rights at Work*.

analyses of the significance of judicial review to bureaucratic behaviour which bottom-up approaches produce. It also undermines the alliance between interpretivism and de-centred studies, demonstrating that the approach of one can be useful in pursuing the primary research focus of the other. A de-centred focus has clear and obvious affinities for interpretive approaches to socio-legal studies, but it is not inevitable.

There is still the question, of course, of whether court-centred research can be defended. One of the main criticisms of court-centred studies is that they ask too limited a question about the role of law in society. McCann,[13] for example, argues that a focus on court rulings and compliance obscures the other indirect and constitutive effects of law in society. This warning is important and has much merit. It is resonant of the criticism by legal consciousness scholars of 'law-first' socio-legal scholarship – that it 'exclude[s] from observation that which needs to be explored and explained: how, where and with what effect law is produced in and through commonplace social interactions within neighbourhoods, workplaces, families, schools, community organisations and the like'.[14] Such criticisms, it is suggested, simply demonstrate the breadth of the socio-legal research agenda. It would be a mistake in our view to see de-centred and court-centred studies as mutually exclusive enterprises. Instead, they should be seen as complementary. Both have much to offer our understanding of law and society. The conviction which underlies this volume of essays is that studies which focus on court rulings and their influence on bureaucracies have important things to say about the role of law in society. This is simply because bureaucratic behaviour is an important aspect of society (though it is clearly not the only one). The contribution of scholarship like the essays in this volume is undoubtedly limited (as all research is). But the broad research question remains important, we have much to learn from the data, and such research is to be encouraged (though it is clearly not for all).

Future research
A number of the case studies make the important point that all research methods have their limitations. It is important, it is suggested, to be modest about the social scientific claims one makes. Most social science

[13] *Ibid.*; McCann, 'Reform Litigation'.
[14] P. Ewick and S. Silbey, *The Common Place of Law: Stories from Everyday Life* (Chicago, University of Chicago Press, 1998), p. 20.

projects are (or at least should be) in the business of offering cautious conclusions. Some questions of impact, as Sunkin has noted and as the international case studies demonstrate, lend themselves to particular kinds of research technique, and exclude themselves from other techniques. For example, an interest in the responses of government agencies to judicial review litigation in relation to the plight of the citizen who litigated invites a survey questionnaire,[15] though such a technique is less illuminating if one seeks to understand the competition between legal and non-legal values in routine decision-making.[16] Hence, an alliance of such approaches is necessary in order to build up a more comprehensive picture of judicial review's impact on bureaucracies.

As a collection of case studies, this book manifests the basic methodological point for future research that interdisciplinarity, a combination of approaches and some level of methodological pluralism, is required to undertake a comprehensive enquiry about judicial review and its impact on bureaucracies. The range of questions which are asked in judicial impact studies must be matched by a complementary range of research techniques. Further, given that the case studies also address different aspects of the question of judicial review's impact on bureaucracies, the international case studies in this volume illustrate how a more comprehensive picture of impact might begin to be built up.

THE AWKWARD POSITION OF JUDICIAL REVIEW

In many countries judicial review has become immensely popular as a treatment for the pains of modern governance. A heightened expectation about the practical significance of judicial review to administrative practice precedes or accompanies the use of judicial review as a remedy. However, much of the research on judicial impact, including many of the essays in this volume, illustrates the considerable barriers which lie between judicial rulings and practical administrative action. As a result, judicial review often finds itself in a difficult and extremely awkward position. This volume of essays provides an illustration of some of the circumstances which give rise to this awkwardness and some of its consequences. In this section, we draw attention to three important and interrelated themes which emerge clearly from the essays: the changing nature of government, the role of legal values in the 'administrative soup' of influences, and the role of communication processes.

---

[15] See Chapter 6 above.   [16] See Chapter 4 above.

The changing nature of government

In some of the judicial impact literature the issue of 'impact' is conceived of in terms of straightforward cause–effect relationships. In this model, judicial review is thought of as having a fixed effect on bureaucratic decision-making. In most empirical studies in this volume, however, impact does not have a fixed, but rather a more dynamic, organic and changing character.[17] Sunkin found, for instance, in his study of the British Independent Review Service (IRS) of the Social Fund, that the level of impact on judicial review on this agency changed dramatically over the first decade of its existence. Whereas, at first, all court decisions were taken very seriously, in later years the influence of judicial review on administrative action was far less obvious. Sossin has found a similar level of dynamics in his analysis of the impact of judicial review in government bureaucracies in Canada:

> Cycles of litigation, policy development and administrative renewal overlap and become intertwined. Only a framework of analysis which sheds light on this dynamic set of institutional and individual relationships has the capacity to illuminate the impact of judicial decisions on bureaucratic action.

The bureaucratic impact of judicial review is constantly changing because bureaucracies are constantly changing. In much of the early judicial impact literature, the impact of court decisions was analysed *ceteris paribus* – all other things were considered to remain equal. By contrast, the international case studies in this volume suggest that we can only properly understand the impact of court rulings if we understand the dynamic relationship between law and government. Careful empirical analysis of the bureaucratic impact of judicial review points our attention to several important changes in the nature of contemporary government.

The first development, echoed in many of the case studies, is the recent proliferation of independent regulatory agencies in Europe, Britain, Canada, Australia and elsewhere. These 'governments in miniature'[18] have had a profound effect on the nature of government and on the ability of courts to control administrative action through

[17] S. Halliday, 'Researching the Impact of Judicial Review on Routine Administrative Decision-Making' in D. Cowan (ed.), *Housing, Participation and Exclusion* (Aldershot, Ashgate, 1998), pp. 189–212.
[18] See Chapter 1 above.

judicial review. The second signifigant development is the fact that government policy is increasingly the result of intense consultations and negotiations with interest groups, businesses and private citizens in processes of 'negotiated decision-making'[19] or other forms of 'modern governance'.[20] According to Shapiro, this development, witnessed in the US from the 1960s onwards, will soon be followed by a similar move in the EU towards more 'horizontal' policy-making, only now with a stronger emphasis on the involvement of experts. Finally, a third major change in government is that in some cases government policy is no longer created and implemented in close cooperation with non-governmental actors, but by private actors only. With this process of 'contracting out', large areas of government policy now are no longer within reach of the traditional system of checks and balances (including judicial review). As a result of these three developments, 'government' has become a highly complex and dynamic concept. All three images of government have significant implications for the position and the impact of judicial review.

Law and competing values
One major consequence of these changes in the nature of contemporary government, is that law finds itself increasingly competing with other values. In modern governance, the full implementation of court rulings usually does not enjoy the highest priority. In her discussion of the existing judicial impact research in the UK, Richardson argues for instance that, despite their many differences, there is one central conclusion that all these studies have in common. In her view, they suggest that the instrumental potential of judicial review should not be over-estimated, particularly in the context of routine bureaucratic decision-making. '[T]here is nothing particularly significant about judicial review, it is simply one of a number of factors.'[21] This was also reflected in her study of the impact of judicial review on the Mental Health Review Tribunal (MHRT). Requirements of fairness and other legal values often did not manage to penetrate the way the medical members on the tribunal see things.

---

[19] B. De Waard (ed.), *Negotiated Decision-Making* (The Hague, Boom Juridische Uitgevers, 2000).

[20] J. Kooiman (ed.), *Modern Governance: New Government–Society Interactions* (London, Sage Publications, 1993).

[21] See Chapter 4 above.

In everyday bureaucratic decision-making, legal values become part of one big 'administrative soup' of influences.[22] Here elements of judicial review might simply dissolve or become reconstituted, in which case they are no longer recognised as such by the administrators. Agencies have their own internal dynamics to consider when meeting external demands. They need to maintain employee morale by instilling a sense of mission and accomplishment, to develop logical and efficient routines, and to acquire and preserve resources. As a result, court decisions requiring changes in existing administrative practice are often seen as the 'new kid on the block' and are met with similar hostile reactions.[23] Given these and similar considerations, an agency's reaction to a court decision may ultimately be affected less by the substance of a judicial policy, and more by a decision's 'liveabililty' – how inconvenient it is for the agency to implement the decision.[24]

Communication matters

This situation, in which law finds itself competing with a host of other values in administrative practice, increases the significance of adequate communication in judicial review. First, of course, there is the communication between the courts and government bureaucracies. An agency's normal first step in the process of implementing a court's decision is to interpret what the decision means and how it applies to its own actions. In some situations, as Shapiro indicates, this is a fairly straightforward business. More often, however, this is more easily said than done. Or, as Canon put it, 'what the court proclaims is not always what the agency understands'.

In interpreting the potential consequences of a court's decision, there is also an important need for adequate communication within the agency itself. How does an agency learn about a decision? Important information on recent court rulings are disseminated to front-line workers through different types of 'soft law', including informal guidelines, circulars, operational memoranda, directives, codes and oral instructions.[25] It turns out that the dissemination of court decisions needs special attention. Creyke and McMillan[26] have found, for instance,

[22] See Chapter 2 above.   [23] See Chapter 3 above.   [24] *Ibid.*
[25] See Chapter 5 above.
[26] R. Creyke and J. McMillan, 'Executive Perceptions of Administrative Law – An Empirical Study' (2002) 9 *Australian Journal of Administrative Law* 163–90.

that public officials are generally satisfied with the existing methods of disseminating information through the organisation, but there were also complaints that some important information was not distributed rapidly enough, or that information was given to some but not to others.

Facing the increased need for more adequate communication, some courts and administrative agencies have launched several important initiatives that may be of significance outside their own jurisdictions as well. US courts, for instance, working to promote prison reforms, have turned to the use of special masters to help bridge the gap between courts and administrators.[27] Among other things, these special masters are used to gather information, to organise hearings and to meet informally with the bureaucracies involved. This approach has made a substantial contribution to the successful implementation of many of these court decisions. With regard to the dissemination and communication of court decisions within the government bureaucracy itself, it has been established that an agency's own mechanism for communicating policy changes is not always most suited for communicating court decisions as well. To overcome some of these difficulties, the Canadian Ministry of Immigration – following the important *Baker* ruling of the Supreme Court of Canada – has recently decided to move away from an approach focusing exclusively on guidelines, memoranda and other written material and to organise a day of workshops and lectures instead.[28] During this day ('Baker and Beyond'), some 100 front-line workers from the immigration services in the Toronto region heard from academics, lawyers and ministry staff on the significance of the court decision.

Future research

Future judicial impact studies may benefit from putting more emphasis on the highly dynamic relations between law, public administration and bureaucratic impact. How do changes in modern governance affect the position of (public) law and *vice versa*? Moreover, researchers should work towards a more contextual approach to judicial review that reveals the many different ways in which law and legal values have to compete with other influences within a bureaucracy. One

---

[27] See Chapter 8 above.   [28] See Chapter 5 above.

way to address this issue is by putting more emphasis on the many communication processes surrounding the bureaucratic implementation of court decisions.

BRINGING LAW AND SOCIETY BACK INTO JUDICIAL IMPACT STUDIES

In this chapter, we have put forward several elements for an agenda for future impact studies. In some respects, this agenda follows some of the main elements of the research programme of the 1970s, yet in other and more important respects it suggests an alternative course.

One important element of the general theory programme of the 1970s was its leading scientific ideal to keep a mind open to as many different approaches to the study of judicial impact as possible. Moreover, its central aim to construct a general theory required a high level of specification and clarity of all basic concepts and theoretical frames that were being used. Both elements should also be retained in a future research agenda. Like some of the early studies of the 1970s, future studies of judicial impact should not be limited to a single theoretical approach and will benefit greatly from conceptual explicitness and clarity.

In one crucial respect, however, the future study of the (bureaucratic) impact of judicial review should divert from the research tradition of the 1970s and make a fresh start. The central aim of this tradition was a high level of *specialisation*. Many studies in this field were explicitly aimed at producing one single theory of impact. Moreover, scholars involved in these projects worked hard to establish the study of judicial impact as a new and independent field of study. Although this aim was perhaps understandable at the time, this central ambition of specialisation did in fact result in a high level of isolation. While many judicial impact scholars were busy creating their own highly specialised field of study, it became increasingly difficult to stay sufficiently in touch with different – yet related – developments in the study of the role of courts and government bureaucracies in law and society as well. As a result, many judicial impact studies include hardly any references at all to contemporary empirical findings and theoretical innovations. This leads some to characterise this area of research as 'lying in a "no man's land" between the studies of public administration and judicial politics' (Canon). In our opinion, any future research agenda should therefore no longer be aimed at specialisation, but at *integration* with the general field of law and society instead.

Many of the empirical, conceptual and theoretical puzzles that have surfaced in this volume are closely related to wider issues of law and society, and will thus benefit greatly from such a new integrative approach. To name only a few:

- To understand the position of law in competing with other values, the field of legal pluralism is highly relevant.[29] The position of legal rulings within a pluralist normative environment is not unique for the field of judicial review, but is very similar to wider issues relating to the relationship between 'state law' and 'living law'.[30]
- We can only fully understand the position of court rulings in a government bureaucracy in relation to the bigger picture of bureaucracies and other formal organisations in general. Moreover, in studying bureaucratic impact, we should also draw upon all that is already known about law and discretion in general and regulation in particular.[31]
- The way a bureaucracy handles a court decision may also be understood more fully, once we tap into the extensive body of socio-legal literature related to modes of bureaucratic rule-application,[32] street-level bureaucracy,[33] and the changing nature of the legal consciousness of those working in these agencies and their attitudes towards the law in general.[34] In addition, the way that public officials react

[29] See e.g. J. Griffiths, 'What is Legal Pluralism?' (1986) 24 *Journal of Legal Pluralism* 1–55; B. Z. Tamanaha, 'The Folly of the "Social Scientific" Concept of Legal Pluralism' (1993) 20 *Journal of Law and Society* 192–217.

[30] E. Ehrlich, *Fundamental Principles of the Sociology of Law* (New Brunswick, NJ, and London, Transaction Publishers, 2002).

[31] See Chapter 4 above; S. Halliday, *Judicial Review and Compliance with Administrative Law* (Oxford, Hart, 2004).

[32] R. A. Kagan, *Regulatory Justice: Implementing a Wage-Price Freeze* (New York, Russell Sage, 1978); J. Mashaw, *Bureaucratic Justice: Managing Social Security Disability Claims* (New Haven, Yale University Press, 1983).

[33] M. Lipsky, *Street-Level Bureaucracy: Dilemmas of the Individual in Public Services* (New York, Russell Sage, 1980).

[34] P. Ewick and S. Silbey, *The Common Place of Law: Stories from Everyday Life* (Chicago, University of Chicago Press, 1998); M. Hertogh, 'The Living *Rechtsstaat*: A Bottom-Up Approach to Legal Ideals and Social Reality' in W. van der Burg and S. Taekema (eds.), *The Importance of Ideals: Debating Their Relevance in Law, Morality, and Politics* (New York, Peter Lang, 2004).

to court rulings may also be linked to the complex phenomenon of juridification.[35]

- Finally, the role of communication in explaining the bureaucratic impact of judicial review may be regarded as an aspect of a much wider field of study that looks at law in terms of communication processes.[36]

The early pioneers in the field of judicial impact studies deserve credit for their ground-breaking studies on the role of law in public bureaucracies. Although they were forced to start from scratch, they managed to disclose much of the often sobering reality of the ability of courts to effectively control administrative action. However, their quest for a general theory of impact has proved less successful than many of them no doubt had anticipated. One way to overcome the most important limitations of this early project is by substituting their original ambition of specialisation by a new ambition of integrating the study of bureaucratic responses to court decisions with wider issues. The biggest challenge in future studies of judicial review and bureaucratic impact is therefore to bring law and society back into judicial impact research.

---

[35] G. Teubner, *Law as an Autopoietic System* (Oxford, Blackwell Publishers, 1993); D. Cooper, 'Local Government Legal Consciousness in the Shadow of Juridification' (1995) 4 *Journal of Law and Society* 506–26.

[36] Teubner, *Law*; N. Luhmann, *Social Systems* (Stanford, Stanford University Press, 1995; originally published in German, 1984).

BIBLIOGRAPHY

Ackerman, S. R., *Controlling Environmental Policy: The Limits of Public Law in Germany and the United States* (New Haven, Yale University Press, 1995)

Alon, G., 'The Ministers Committee Granted the GSS Permission to "Make Interrogation Methods More Efficient" ', *Ha'aretz*, 14 November 1994

'Permits for GSS to Apply "Intensified Physical Pressures" Renewed for Three More Months', *Ha'aretz*, 13 April 1995

'The Debate Concerning the Inclusion of GSS Interrogations in Statute Not Changed', *Ha'aretz*, 8 September 1999, p. A-3

'A Law to Overrule the HCJ GSS Decision to be Brought before the Knesset after the Holiday', *Ha'aretz*, 9 September 1999, p. A-3

Alon, G. and E. Rabin, 'Justice Landau Says "He Feels Betrayed" by the Violations of the Rules of Conduct by the GSS', *Ha'aretz*, 9 January 1995

Ayres, I. and J. Braithwaite, *Responsive Regulation: Transcending the Deregulation Debate* (Oxford, Oxford University Press, 1992)

Baldwin, R. and M. Cave, *Understanding Regulation: Theory, Strategy, and Practice* (Oxford, Oxford University Press, 1999)

Baldwin, R. and K. Hawkins, 'Discretionary Justice: Davis Reconsidered' [1984] *Public Law* 570

Baldwin, R., and J. Houghton, 'Circular Arguments: The Status and Legitimacy of Administrative Rules' [1985] *Public Law* 239

Barak-Erez, D., 'Judicial Review of Politics: The Israeli Case' (2002) 29 *Journal of Law and Society* 611–31

'From an Unwritten Constitution to a Written Constitution: The Israeli Challenge in American Perspective' (1995) 26 *Columbia Human Rights Law Review* 309

Bartlett, P. and R. Sandland, *Mental Health Law: Policy and Practice* (London, Blackstone, 2000)

Baum, L. A., 'Implementation of Judicial Decisions: An Organizational Analysis' (1976) 4 *American Politics Quarterly* 86

Becker, H. and B. Geer, 'Participant Observation and Interviewing: A Comparison' (1957) 16 *Human Organisation* 28

Becker, T. L. (ed.), *The Impact of Supreme Court Decisions: Empirical Studies* (New York, Oxford University Press, 1969)

Becker, T. L. and M. M. Feeley (eds.), *The Impact of Supreme Court Decisions: Empirical Studies* (2nd edn, New York, Oxford University Press, 1973)

Beetham, D., *Bureaucracy* (2nd edn, Buckingham, Open University Press, 1996)

Ben, A., 'PM Barak Suggests: Senior Officials Would Be Authorized to Approve "Special Interrogation Techniques" for the GSS in Cases of Immediate Danger', *Ha'aretz*, 9 September 1999, p. A-3

'Ben-Yair: Some Special Permits to GSS Investigators are Illegal', *Ha'aretz*, 3 August 1995

Bennion, F., *Statutory Interpretation* (2nd edn, London, Butterworths, 1992)

Bickel, A. M., *The Least Dangerous Branch – The Supreme Court and the Bar of Politics* (Indianapolis, Bobbs-Merrill, 1962)

Bisharat, G. E., 'Courting Justice? Legitimization in Lawyering under Israeli Occupation' (1995) 20 *Law and Social Inquiry* 349

Bishop, J. Jr, 'Control of Terrorism and Insurrection: The British Laboratory Experience' (1978) 42 *Law and Contemporary Problems* 140

Black, J., 'Constitutionalising Self-Regulation' (1996) 59 *Modern Law Review* 24

    Rules and Regulators (Oxford, Clarendon, 1997)

    'Reviewing Regulatory Rules' in J. Black, P. Muchlinski and P. Walker (eds.), *Commercial Regulation and Judicial Review* (Oxford, Hart, 1998)

    'Regulatory Conversations' (2002) 29 *Journal of Law and Society* 163

Blair, P., *Federalism and Judicial Review in West Germany* (Oxford, Clarendon, 1981)

Bracha, B., 'The Protection of Human Rights in Israel' (1982) 12 *Israel Yearbook of Human Rights* 110

    'Judicial Review of Security Powers in Israel: A New Policy of the Courts' (1991) 28 *Stanford Journal of International Law* 39

Brewaer, P., *Ethnography* (Open University Press, Buckingham, 2000)

Breyer, S., 'Judicial Review of Questions of Law and Policy' (1986) 38 *Administrative Law Review* 363

Breyer, S., R. B. Stewart, C. R. Sunstein and M. L. Spitzer, *Administrative Law and Regulatory Policy: Problems, Texts, and Cases,* (4th edn, New York, Aspen Publishers, 1999)

Bridges, L., C. Game, J. McBridge, O. Lomas and S. Ranson, *Legality and Local Politics* (Aldershot, Gower, 1987)

Bridges, L., G. Meszaros and M. Sunkin, *Judicial Review in Perspective* (London, Cavendish, 1995)

'Regulating Judicial Review' [2000] *Public Law* 651

Brugger, W., 'May Government Ever Use Torture? Two Responses from German Law' (2000) 48 *American Journal of Comparative Law* 661

Bryant, D., 'The Office of Master in Chancery: Colonial Development' (1954) 40 *American Bar Association Journal* 595

'The Office of Master of Chancery: Early English Development' (1954) 40 *American Bar Association Journal* 498

B'Tselem (the Israeli Information Center for Human Rights in the Occupied Territories), *The Interrogation of Palestinians During the Intifada: Ill-Treatment, 'Moderate Physical Pressure' or Torture: Comprehensive Report 1991* (Jerusalem, IICHROT, 1991)

The Death of Mustafa Barakat (Jerusalem, IICHROT, 1992)

Torture During Interrogations: Testimony of Palestinian Detainees, Testimony of Interrogators (Jerusalem, IICHROT, 1994)

Legitimizing Torture (Jerusalem, IICHROT, 1997)

Buck, T., 'Judicial Review and the Discretionary Social Fund' in T. Buck (ed.), *Judicial Review and Social Welfare* (London, Pinter, 1998)

The Social Fund (2nd edn, London, Sweet & Maxwell, 2000)

Bulmer, M., 'Facts, Concepts, Theories and Problems' in M. Bulmer (ed.), *Social Research Methods* (London, Macmillan, 1984)

Bumiller, K., *The Civil Rights Society* (Baltimore, Johns Hopkins University Press, 1984)

Burger, C., 'Away from the Courthouse and into the Field: The Odyssey of a Special Master' (1978) 78 *Colorado Law Review* 707

Campbell, A., and K. C. Glass, 'The Legal Status of Clinical and Ethics Policies, Codes, and Guidelines in Medical Practice and Research' (2001) 46 *McGill Law Journal* 473

Campbell, T., K. D. Ewing and A. Tomkins, *Sceptical Essays on Human Rights* (Oxford, Oxford University Press, 2001)

Cane, P., 'Merits Review and Judicial Review: The AAT as Trojan Horse' (2000) 28 *Federal Law Review* 213

Canes-Wrone, B., 'Bureaucratic Decisions and the Composition of Lower Courts' (2003) 47 *American Journal of Political Science* 205

Canon, B. C., 'Is the Exclusionary Rule in Failing Health? Some New Data and a Plea Against a Precipitous Conclusion' (1974) 62 *Kentucky Law Journal* 651

'Courts and Policy: Compliance, Implementation and Impact' in J. B. Gates and C. A. Johnson (eds.), *The American Courts: A Critical Assessment* (Washington, DC, CQ Press, 1991)

Canon, B. C. and C. A. Johnson, *Judicial Policies: Implementation and Impact* (2nd edn, Washington, DC, CQ Press, 1999)

Cassels, J., 'Judicial Activism and Public Interest Litigation in India: Attempting the Impossible?' (1989) 37 *American Journal of Comparative Law* 495

Chilton, B., *Prisons Under the Gavel: The Federal Court Takeover of Georgia Prisons* (Columbus, Ohio State University Press, 1991)

Clark, M. L., 'Note: Israel's High Court of Justice Ruling on the General Security Service Use of "Moderate Physical Pressure": An End to the Sanctioned Use of Torture?' (2000) 11 *Indiana International and Comparative Law Review* 145

Collins, H., *Marxism and Law* (Oxford, Clarendon Press, 1982)

Cooper, D., 'Local Government Legal Consciousness in the Shadow of Juridification' (1995) 4 *Journal of Law and Society* 506

Cotterrell, R., 'Judicial Review and Legal Theory' in Richardson and H. G. Genn (eds.), *Administrative Law and Government Action* (Oxford, Oxford University Press, 1994)

Craig, P., *Administrative Law* (4th edn, London, Sweet & Maxwell, 1998)

Cranston, R., 'Reviewing Judicial Review' in G. Richardson and H. Genn (eds.), *Administrative Law and Government Action* (Oxford, Clarendon Press, 1994)

Creyke, R. and J. McMillan (eds.), *The Kerr Vision of Australian Administrative Law – At the Twenty-Five Year Mark* (Canberra, ANU Centre for International and Public Law, 1998)

'Executive Perceptions of Administrative Law – An Empirical Study' (2002) 9 *Australian Journal of Administrative Law* 163

Creyke, R., J. McMillan and D. Pearce, 'Success at Court – Does the Client Win?' in J. McMillan (ed.), *Administrative Law under the Coalition Government* (Canberra, Australian Institute of Administrative Law, 1997)

Crouch, B. W. and J. Marquart, 'Ruiz: Intervention and Emergent Order in Texas Prisons' in J. J. DiIulio (ed.), *Courts, Corrections and the Constitution: The Impact of Judicial Intervention in Prisons and Jails* (New York, Oxford University Press, 1990)

Curtis, L., 'The Vision Splendid: A Time for Re-appraisal' in R. Creyke and J. McMillan (eds.), *The Kerr Vision of Australian Administrative Law – At the Twenty-Five Year Mark* (Canberra, ANU Centre for International and Public Law, 1998)

Daintith, T. and A. Page, *The Executive in the Constitution* (Oxford, Oxford University Press 1999)

Davis, K. C., *Discretionary Justice: A Preliminary Inquiry* (Baton Rouge, Louisiana State University Press, 1969)

De Smith, S. A., *Judicial Review of Administrative Action* (4th edn, London, J. M. Evans, 1980)

De Smith, S. A., H. Woolf and J. A. Jowell, *Judicial Review of Administrative Action* (5th edn, London, Sweet & Maxwell, 1995)

De Waard, B. (ed.), *Negotiated Decision-Making* (The Hague, Boom Juridische Uitgevers, 2000)

Denscombe, M., *The Good Research Guide* (Buckingham, Open University Press, 1998)

Dershowitz, A. M., 'Is It Necessary to Apply "Physical Pressure" to Terrorists and to Lie about It?' (1989) 23 *Israeli Law Review* 192

des Rosier, N. and B. Feldthussen, 'Discretion in Social Assistance Legislation' (1992) 8 *Journal of Law and Social Policy* 204

Desai, A. H. and S. Muralidhar, 'Public Interest Litigation: Potential and Problems' in B. N. Kirpal (ed.), *Supreme But Not Infallible: Essays in Honour of the Supreme Court of India* (Oxford, Oxford University Press, 2000)

Dewees, D., D. Duff and M. Trebilcock, *Exploring the Domain of Accident Law: Taking the Facts Seriously* (New York, Oxford University Press, 1996)

Dicey, A. V., *An Introduction to the Study of the Law of the Constitution* (10th edn, New York, St Martin's Press, 1959)

Dolbeare, K. M. and P. E. Hammond, *The School Prayer Decisions: From Court Policy to Local Practice* (Chicago, University of Chicago Press, 1971)

Dotan, Y., 'Judicial Rhetoric, Government Lawyers and Human Rights: The Case of the High Court of Justice During the Intifada' (1999) 33 *Law and Society Review* 319

'Public Lawyers and Private Clients: An Empirical Observation on the Relative Success Rates of Cause Lawyers' (1999) 21 *Law and Policy* 401

'Judicial Accountability in Israel: The High Court of Justice and the Phenomenon of Judicial Hyperactivism' (2002) 8 *Israel Studies* 87

Dotan Y. and M. Hofnung, 'Interest Groups in the High Court of Justice: Measuring Success in Litigation and in Out-of-Court Settlements' (2001) 23 *Law and Policy* 1

Dyzenhaus, D., 'Constituting the Rule of Law: Fundamental Values in Administrative Law' (2002) 27 *Queen's Law Journal* 445

Dyzenhaus, D., M. Hunt and M. Taggart, 'The Principle of Legality in Administrative Law: Internationalization as Constitutionalization' (2001) 1 *Oxford University Commonwealth Law Journal* 5

Eastman, N. and J. Peay, *Law Without Enforcement: Integrating Mental Health and Justice* (Oxford, Hart, 1999)

Edelman, L. B., 'Legal Ambiguity and Symbolic Structures: Organizational Mediation of Civil Rights Law' (1992) 95 *American Journal of Sociology* 1401

Edgeworth, B., *Law, Modernity, Postmodernity: Legal Change in the Contracting State* (Aldershot, Ashgate, 2003)

Ehrlich, E., *Fundamental Principles of the Sociology of Law* (New Brunswick, NJ, and London, Transaction Publishers, 2002)

Ekland-Olson, S. and S. J. Martin, 'Organizational Compliance with Court-Ordered Reform' (1988) 22 *Law and Society Review* 359

Estreicher, S. and R. L. Revesz, 'Nonacquiescence by Federal Administrative Agencies' (1989) 98 *Yale Law Journal* 679

Ewick, P. and S. Silbey, *The Common Place of Law: Stories from Everyday Life* (Chicago, University of Chicago Press, 1998)

Feeley, M. M., '"Hollow Hopes, Flypaper, and Metaphors": Review of *The Hollow Hope*' (1992) 17 *Law and Social Inquiry* 745

Feeley, M. M. and E. L. Rubin, *Judicial Policy Making and the Modern State: How the Courts Reformed America's Prisons* (New York, Cambridge University Press, 1998)

Feldman, D., 'Judicial Review: A Way of Controlling Government?' (1988) 66 *Public Administration* 21

Feller, S. Z., 'Not Actual "Necessity" But Possibly "Justification"; Not "Moderate" Pressure, But Either "Unlimited" or Not at All' (1989) 23 *Israeli Law Review* 201

Forsyth, C. F. (ed.), *Judicial Review and the Constitution* (Hart, Oxford, 2000)

Francis, J. G., *The Politics of Regulation: A Comparative Perspective* (Oxford, Blackwell, 1993)

Fredman, S., 'Scepticism Under Scrutiny: Labour Law and Human Rights' in T. Campbell, K. D. Ewing and A. Tomkins (eds.), *Sceptical Essays on Human Rights* (Oxford, Oxford University Press, 2001)

Freedman, J. O., *Crisis and Legitimacy: The Administrative Process and American Government* (Cambridge, Cambridge University Press, 1978)

Friedman, A., 'Antidiscrimination Law: The View from 1989' in David Kairys (ed.), *The Politics of Law* (New York, Pantheon Books, 1990)

Gageler, S., 'The Underpinnings of Judicial Review of Administrative Action: Common Law or Constitution' (2000) 28 *Federal Law Review* 303

Galanter, M., 'The Radiating Effects of Courts' in K. O. Boyum and L. Mather (eds.), *Empirical Theories about Courts* (New York, Longman, 1983)

Galligan, D., *Discretionary Powers: A Legal Study of Official Discretion* (Oxford, Clarendon Press, 1986)

Due Process and Fair Procedures (Oxford, Oxford University Press, 1996)

Gambitta, R., 'Litigation, Judicial Deference and Policy Change' in R. Gambitta, M. May and J. Foster (eds.), *Governing Through Courts* (New York, Sage, 1981)

Ganz, G., *Quasi-Legislation: Recent Developments in Secondary Legislation* (London, Sweet & Maxwell, 1987)

Goldsmith (Lord), 'New Constitutional Boundaries' (paper delivered by the Attorney General to a Government Legal Service Conference on Current Developments in Administrative Law, London, 22 March 2002)

Gordon, L., *Pitied But Not Entitled: Single Mothers and the History of Welfare* (Toronto, The Free Press, 1994)

Griffith, J., 'The Political Constitution' (1979) 42 *Modern Law Review* 1

Griffiths, J., 'What is Legal Pluralism?' (1986) 24 *Journal of Legal Pluralism* 1–55

Gunther, G., 'The Subtle Vices of the "Passive Virtues" – A Comment on Principle and Expediency in Judicial Review' (1964) 64 *Columbia Law Review* 1

Hadfield, B. and E. Weaver, 'Trends in Judicial Review in Northern Ireland' [1993] *Public Law* 12

Hajjar, L., 'Cause Lawyering in Transnational Perspective: National Conflict and Human Rights in Israel/Palestine' (1997) 31 *Law and Society Review* 473

Halliday, S., 'Researching the Impact of Judicial Review on Routine Administrative Decision-Making' in D. Cowan (ed.), *Housing, Participation and Exclusion* (Aldershot, Ashgate, 1998)

'The Influence of Judicial Review on Bureaucratic Decision-Making' [2000] *Public Law* 110

'Internal Review and Administrative Justice' (2001) 23 *Journal of Social Welfare and Family Law* 473

Judicial Review and Compliance with Administrative Law (Oxford, Hart, 2004)

Hammersley, M. and P. Atkinson, *Ethnography: Principles in Practice* (2nd edn, London, Routledge, 1995)

Hammond, A., 'Judicial Review: The Continuing Interplay Between Law and Policy' [1998] *Public Law* 34

Handler, J., *The Conditions of Discretion: Autonomy, Community Bureaucracy* (New York, Russell Sage, 1986)

'Dependent People, the State and the Modern/Postmodern Search for the Dialogic Community' (1988) 35 *UCLA Law Review* 999

Harel, A., 'Criticism by the GSS: We Were Left with Responsibility But No Power', *Ha'aretz*, 8 September 1999

'The GSS Used "Exceptional Methods of Interrogation" in 90 Cases since the HCJ Ruling in 1999', *Ha'aretz*, 25 July 2002

Harlow, C., 'Administrative Reaction to Judicial Review' [1976] *Public Law* 116

Harlow, C. and R. Rawlings, *Pressure Through Law* (London, Routledge, 1992)

Law and Administration (2nd edn, London, Butterworths, 1997)

Hawkins, K., *Environment and Enforcement* (Oxford, Oxford University Press, 1984)

'The Uses of Legal Discretion: Perspectives from Law and Social Science' in K. Hawkins (ed.), *The Uses of Discretion* (Oxford, Clarendon, 1992)

Law as a Last Resort: Prosecution Decision-Making in a Regulatory Agency (Oxford, Oxford University Press, 2002)

Hawkins, K. and J. Thomas, *Enforcing Regulation* (Boston, Kluwer-Nijhoff, 1984)

Hay, D., 'Property, Authority, and Criminal Justice' in D. Hay (ed.), *Albion's Fatal Tree* (New York, Pantheon, 1973)

Hennesey, P., *Whitehall* (2nd edn, London, Fontana, 1990)

Hertogh, M., 'Coercion, Cooperation, and Control: Understanding the Policy Impact of Administrative Courts and the Ombudsman in the Netherlands' (2001) 23 *Law and Policy* 47

'The Living *Rechtsstaat*: A Bottom-Up Approach to Legal Ideals and Social Reality' in W. van der Burg and S. Taekema (eds.), *The Importance of Ideals: Debating Their Relevance in Law, Morality, and Politics* (New York, Peter Lang, forthcoming 2004)

Hiebert, J., 'Determining the Limits of Charter Rights: How Much Discretion Do Governments Retain?' (Toronto University, PhD Dissertation, 1991)

Hofnung, M., *Democracy, Law and National Security in Israel* (Aldershot, Dartmouth, 1996)

Hogg, P. and A. Bushell, 'The Charter Dialogue Between Courts and Legislatures (Or Perhaps the Charter of Rights Isn't Such a Bad Thing After All)' (1997) 35 *Osgoode Hall Law Journal* 75

Hood, C., C. Scott, O. James, G. Jones and T. Travers, *Regulation Inside Government: Waste-Watchers, Quality Police and Sleaze-Busters* (Oxford, Oxford University Press, 1999)

Houle, F., "La zone fictive de l'infra-droit: l'integration des regles administratives dans la categorie des textes reglementaires" (2001) 47 *McGill Law Journal* 161

Hunter, S. and R. W. Waterman, *Enforcing the Law: The Case of the Clean Water Acts* (Armonk, NY, M. E. Sharpe, 1996)

Hutter, B., *Compliance: Regulation and Environment* (Oxford, Clarendon, 1997)

James, S., 'The Political and Administrative Consequences of Judicial Review' (1996) 74 *Public Administration* 613

Janisch, H., 'The Choice of Decision-Making Method: Adjudication, Policies and Rule-Making' in *Administrative Law: Principles, Practices and Pluralism* (Scarborough, Ont., Carswell, 1992)

Joerges, C. and J. Neyer, 'From Intergovernmental Bargaining to Deliberative Political Processes: The Constitutionalization of Comitology' (1997) 3 *European Law Journal* 273

Johnson, C. A., 'Judicial Decisions and Organizational Change' (1979) 11 *Administration and Society* 27

Johnson, R., *The Dynamics of Compliance* (Evanston IL, Northwestern University Press, 1967)

Jowell, J., 'The Rule of Law Today' in J. Jowell and D. Oliver (eds.), *The Changing Constitution* (4th edn, Oxford, Oxford University Press, 2000)

'Judge Over Your Shoulder: Judicial Review: Balancing the Scales' (Cabinet Office, London, 1994)

Kadish, S., 'Torture, the State and the Individual' (1989) 23 *Israeli Law Review* 343

Kagan, R. A., *Regulatory Justice: Implementing a Wage-Price Freeze* (New York, Russell Sage, 1978)

'Adversarial Legalism and American Government' in M. Landy and M. A. Levin (eds.), *The New Politics of Public Policy* (Baltimore, Johns Hopkins University Press, 1995)

Adversarial Legalism: The American Way of Law (Cambridge, MA, Harvard University Press, 2001)

Katzmann, R., *Institutional Disability: The Saga of Transportation Policy for the Handicapped* (Washington, DC, Brookings Institution, 1986)

Kelly, J., 'Bureaucratic Activism and the Charter of Rights: The Department of Justice and Its Entry into the Centre of Government' (1999) 42 *Canadian Public Administration* 478

Kerr, J. R., *Commonwealth Administrative Review Committee Report August 1971*, Parliamentary Paper No. 144 of 1972 (Canberra, Government Press, 1971)

Kerry, M., 'Administrative Law and Judicial Review' (1986) 64 *Public Administration* 163

Kimerling, B., 'Bagatz Should Withdraw from the Occupied Territories', *Ha'aretz*, 29 January 1993, p. B-3

King, M., 'The "Truth" about Autopoiesis' (1993) 20 *Journal of Law and Society* 218

Kirp, D. L. and G. Babcock, 'Judge and Company: Court-Appointed Masters, School Desegregation, and Institutional Reform' (1981) 32 *Alabama Law Review* 313

Kooiman, J. (ed.), *Modern Governance: New Government–Society Interactions* (London, Sage Publications, 1993)

Kremnitzer, M., 'The Landau Commission Report – Was the Security Service Subordinated to the Law, or the Law to the "Needs" of the Security Service?' (1989) 23 *Israeli Law Review* 216

Kremnitzer, M. and R. Segev, 'Using Force During Investigations by the GSS – The Lesser Evil?' (1998) 4 *Mishpat Umimshal* 667 (Hebrew)

Kretzmer, D., 'Judicial Review of Demolition and Sealing of Houses in the Occupied Territories' in I. Zamir (ed.), *Klinghoffer Book on Public Law* (Jerusalem, Harry Sacher Institute, 1993) (Hebrew)

Kuttab, J., 'Avenues Open for Defence of Human Rights in the Israeli Occupied Territories' in E. Playfair (ed.), *International Law and the Administration of Occupied Territories: Two Decades of Israeli Occupation of the West Bank and Gaza Strip* (Oxford, Clarendon Press, 1992)

'Leading Cases' (2001) 115 *Harvard Law Review* 518

Lempert, R., 'Strategies of Research Design in the Legal Impact Study: The Control of Plausible Rival Hypotheses' (1966) 1 *Law and Society Review* 111

Lenaerts, K. and A. Verhoeven, 'Toward a Legal Framework for Executive Rule-Making in the EU? The Contribution of the New Comitology Decision' (2000) 37 *Common Market Law Review* 645

Leo, R. A., 'Miranda's Revenge: Police Interrogation as a Confidence Game' (1996) 30 *Law and Society Review* 259

Levine, D. I., 'The Authority for the Appointment of Remedial Special Masters in Federal Institutional Reform Litigation: The History Reconsidered' (1984) 17 *University of California Davis Law Review* 753

Lipsky, M., *Street Level Bureaucracy: Dilemmas of the Individual in Public Services* (New York, Russell Sage, 1980)

Little, M., *No Car, No Radio, No Liquor Permit: The Moral Regulation of Single Mothers in Ontario, 1920–1997* (Toronto, Oxford University Press, 1998)

Little, M. and I. Morrison, 'The Pecker Detectors are Back' (1999) 34 *Journal of Canadian Studies* 110

Livingstone, S., 'The Changing Face of Prison Discipline' in E. Player and M. Jenkins (eds.), *Prisons After Woolf: Reform Through Riot* (London, Routledge, 1994)

  'The Impact of Judicial Review on Prisons' in B. Hadfield (ed.), *Judicial Review: A Thematic Approach* (Dublin, Gill and Macmillan, 1995)

Livingstone, S. and T. Owen, *Prison Law* (2nd edn, Oxford, Oxford University Press, 1999)

Loughlin, M., *Public Law and Political Theory* (Oxford, Clarendon, 1992)

  'The Underside of the Law: Judicial Review and the Prison Disciplinary System' (1993) 46 *Current Legal Problems* 43

  Legality and Locality: The Role of Law in Central–Local Government Relations (Oxford, Oxford University Press, 1996)

Loughlin, M. and P. M. Quinn, 'Prisons, Rules and Courts: A Study in Administrative Law' (1993) 56 *Modern Law Review* 497

Loveland, I. D., *Housing Homeless Persons: Administrative Law and the Administrative Process* (Oxford, Clarendon Press, 1995)

Luhmann, N., *Social Systems* (Stanford, Stanford University Press, 1995; originally published in German, 1984)

Majone, G., 'Two Logics of Delegation: Agency and Fiduciary Relations in EU Governance' (2001) 2 *European Union Politics* 103

Maranville, D., 'Nonacquiescence: Outlaw Agencies, Imperial Courts and the Perils of Pluralism' (1986) 39 *Vanderbilt Law Review* 471

Mashaw, J., *Bureaucratic Justice: Managing Social Security Disability Claims* (New Haven, Yale University Press, 1983)

  Due Process in the Administrative State (New Haven, Yale University Press, 1985)

  Greed, Chaos and Governance: Using Public Choice to Improve Public Law (New Haven, Yale University Press, 1997)

  'Small Things Like Reasons Are Put in a Jar: Reason and Legitimacy in the Administrative State' (2001) 70 *Fordham Law Review* 17–35

Mashaw, J. and D. Harfst, *The Struggle for Auto Safety* (Cambridge, MA, Harvard University Press, 1990)

Mason, A., 'Administrative Law Reform: The Vision and the Reality' (2001) 8 *Australian Journal of Administrative Law* 135

Mautner, M., *The Decline of Formalism and the Rise of Values in Israeli Law* (Tel Aviv, Dyonon, 1994) (Hebrew)

McBarnet, D. and C. Whelan, 'The Elusive Spirit of the Law: Formalism and the Struggle for Legal Control' (1991) 54 *Modern Law Review* 848–73

McCann, M. W., '"Reform Litigation on Trial": Review of *The Hollow Hope*' (1992) 17 *Law and Social Inquiry* 715

  Rights at Work: Pay Equity Reform and the Politics of Legal Mobilization (Chicago, University of Chicago, 1994)

  'Causal Versus Constitutive Explanations (or, On the Difficulty of Being So Positive . . .)' (1996) 21 *Law and Social Inquiry* 457

  'Law and Political Struggles for Social Change: Puzzles, Paradoxes, and Promises in Future Research' in D. A. Schultz (ed.), *Leveraging the Law: Using the Courts to Achieve Social Change* (New York, Peter Lang, 1998)

McCubbins, M. D. and T. Schwartz, 'Congressional Oversight Overlooked: Police Patrols Versus Fire Alarms' (1984) 28 *American Journal of Political Science* 165

Medalie, R., L. Zeitz and P. Alexander, 'Custodial Interrogation in Our Nation's Capital: The Attempt to Implement *Miranda*' (1968) 66 *Michigan Law Review* 1347

Melnick, R. Shep, *Regulation and the Courts: The Case of the Clean Air Act* (Washington, DC, Brookings Institution, 1983)

  Between the Lines Interpreting Welfare Rights (Washington, DC, Brookings Institution, 1994)

Merrill, T. and K. Hickman, 'Chevrons Domain' (2001) 89 *Georgetown Law Journal* 833

Mezey, S., *No Longer Disabled: The Federal Courts and the Politics of Social Security Disability* (New York, Greenwood Press, 1988)

  Pitiful Plaintiffs: Child Welfare Litigation and the Federal Courts (Pittsburgh, University of Pittsburgh Press, 2000)

'Ministers to Discuss a Middle Course with Ben-Yair to Enable the Extension of Special Permission to the GSS', *Ha'aretz*, 6 August 1995

Moe, T., 'The New Economics of Organization' (1984) 28 *American Journal of Economics* 739

Morag-Levine, N., 'The Politics of Imported Rights: Transplantation and Transformation in an Israeli Environmental Cause-Lawyering Organization' in A. Sarat and R. S. Scheingold (eds.), *Cause Lawyering and the State in a Global Era* (Oxford, Oxford University Press, 2001)

Muir, W. K., Jr, *Prayer in Public Schools: Law and Attitude Change* (Chicago, University of Chicago Press, 1967)

Mullan, D., *Administrative Law* (Toronto, Irwin, 2001)

Mullen, T., K. Pick and T. Prosser, *Judicial Review in Scotland* (Chichester, Wiley, 1996)

Murphy, W., 'Lower Court Checks on Supreme Court Power' (1959) 53 *American Political Science Review* 1017

Nathan, V., 'The Use of Special Masters in Institutional Reform Litigation' (1979) 10 *Toledo Law Review* 464

Negbi, M., *Justice under Occupation* (Jerusalem, Kana, 1981) (Hebrew)

Nehl, H. P., *Principles of Administrative Procedure in EC Law* (Oxford, Hart, 1999)

Nir, O., 'Harizat Died from Torture – A Well-Known Method of the GSS', *Ha'aretz*, 30 April 1995

Obadina, D., 'Judicial Review and Gypsy Site Provision' in T. Buck (ed.), *Judicial Review and Social Welfare* (London, Pinter, 1998)

Ogus, A. I., *Regulation: Legal Form and Economic Theory* (Oxford, Clarendon Press, 1994)

O'Leary, R., 'The Impact of Federal Court Decisions on the Policies and Administration of the US Environmental Protection Agency' (1989) 41 *Administrative Law Review* 569

Patric, G., 'The Impact of a Court Decision: Aftermath of the McCullom Case' (1957) 6 *Journal of Public Law* 455

Peay, J., *Decisions and Dilemmas: Working with Mental Health Law* (Oxford, Hart, 2003)

Pressman, J. and A. Wildavsky, *Implementation* (Berkeley, University of California Press, 1975)

Prosser, T., 'Politics and Judicial Review: The Atkinson Case and its Aftermath' [1979] *Public Law* 59

    Test Cases for the Poor: Legal Techniques in the Politics of Social Welfare (London, Child Poverty Action Group, 1983)

Public Law Project, *The Impact of the Human Rights Act on Judicial Review: An Empirical Research Study* (Oxford, Nuffield Foundation, 2003)

Rawlings, R., 'Litigation as Political Action' in I. Loveland (ed.), *A Special Relationship? American Influences on Public Law in the UK* (Oxford, Clarendon Press, 1996)

Regular, A., 'The Poetics of Shaking', *Kol Ha'ir*, 11 September 2001

Reinfeld, M., Y. Melman and M. Nesher, 'Mordechei Kedar, "Mr X", Petitioned the HCJ Demanding a Re-trial', *Ha'aretz*, 5 January 1996

Richardson, G., *Law, Process and Custody: Prisoners and Patients* (London, Weidenfeld and Nicolson, 1993)

Richardson, G. and D. Machin, 'A Clash of Values? Mental Health Review Tribunals and Judicial Review' (1999) 1 *Journal of Mental Health Law* 3

    'Doctors on Tribunals: A Confusion of Roles' (2000) 176 *British Journal of Psychiatry* 110

'Judicial Review and Tribunal Decision Making: A Study of the Mental Health Review Tribunal' [2000] *Public Law* 494

Richardson, G. and M. Sunkin, 'Judicial Review: Questions of Impact' [1996] *Public Law* 79

Richardson, U. H., 'Administrative Policy-Making: Rule of Law or Bureaucracy?' in D. Dyzenhaus (ed.), *Recrafting the Rule of Law* (London, Oxford University Press, 1999)

Ringquist, E. J. and C. E. Emmert, 'Judicial Policy-Making in Published and Unpublished Decisions: The Case of Environmental Civil Litigation' (1999) 52 *Political Research Quarterly* 7

Roach, K., 'Constitutional and Common Law Dialogues Between the Supreme Court and Canadian Legislatures' (2001) 80 *Canadian Bar Review* 481

Robson, P., 'Judicial Review and Social Security' in T. Buck (ed.), *Judicial Review and Social Welfare* (London, Pinter, 1998)

Rodgers, H. R. Jr, and C. S. Bullock, *Law and Social Change: Civil Rights Laws and Their Consequences* (New York, McGraw-Hill, 1972)

Rosenberg, G. N., *The Hollow Hope: Can Courts Bring About Social Change?* (Chicago, Chicago University, 1991)

'Hollow Hopes and Other Aspirations: A Reply to Feeley and McCann' (1992) 17 *Law and Social Inquiry* 761

'"Positivism, Interpretivism, and the Study of Law": Review of *Rights at Work*' (1996) 21 *Law and Social Inquiry* 435

'Knowledge and Desire: Thinking About Courts and Social Change' in D. A. Schultz (ed.), *Leveraging the Law: Using the Courts to Achieve Social Change* (New York, Peter Lang, 1998)

Rubinstein, A. and B. Medina, *The Constitutional Law of the State of Israel* (5th edn, Tel Aviv, Schocken, 1996)

Ryder, B., 'Case Comment on Little Sisters' (2001) 39 *Osgoode Hall Law Journal* 207

Sadurski, W., 'Rights-Based Constitutional Review in Central and Eastern Europe' in T. Campbell, K. D. Ewing and A. Tomkins (eds.), *Sceptical Essays on Human Rights* (Oxford, Oxford University Press, 2001)

'Judicial Review and the Protection of Constitutional Rights' (2002) 22 *Oxford Journal of Legal Studies* 275

Sainsbury, W., 'Social Security Decision-Making and Appeals: Chequered History, Uncertain Future?' in N. Harris (ed.), *Social Security Law in Context* (Oxford, Oxford University Press, 2000)

Sathe, S. P., *Judicial Activism in India: Transgressing Borders and Enforcing Limits* (Oxford, Oxford University Press, 2002)

Schuck, P. H., *Suing Government: Citizen Remedies for Official Wrongs* (New Haven, Yale University Press, 1983)

Schuck, P. H. and E. D. Elliott, 'Studying Administrative Law: A Methodology for, and Report on, New Empirical Research' (1990) 40 *Administrative Law Review* 519

'To the Chevron Station: An Empirical Study of Federal Administrative Law' (1990) *Duke Law Journal* 984

Schultz, D. A. (ed.), *Leveraging the Law: Using the Courts to Achieve Social Change* (New York, Peter Lang, 1998)

Schultz, D. A. and S. E. Gottlieb, 'Legal Functionalism and Social Change: A Reassessment of Rosenberg's *The Hollow Hope*' in D. A. Schultz (ed.), *Leveraging the Law: Using the Courts to Achieve Social Change* (New York, Peter Lang, 1998)

Scott, C., 'Accountability in the Regulatory State' (2000) 27 *Journal of Law and Society* 38

Shaked, R., 'New Model of Investigation', *Yeditoth Aharonot*, 7 September 1999

Shamgar, M., 'The Observance of International Law in the Administrative Territories' (1971) 1 *Israeli Yearbook of Human Rights* 262

Shamir, R., '"Landmark Cases" and the Reproduction of Legitimacy: The Case of Israel's High Court of Justice' (1990) 24 *Law and Society Review* 781

Shapiro, M., *The Supreme Court and Administrative Agencies* (New York, Macmillan, 1968)

Who Guards the Guardians? Judicial Control of Administration (Athens, GA, University of Georgia Press, 1988)

'The European Court of Justice' in P. Craig and G. de Búrca (eds.), *The Evolution of EU Law* (Oxford, Oxford University Press, 1999)

'The Institutionalization of European Administrative Space' in A. Stone Sweet, W. Sandholtz and N. Fligstein, *The Institutionalization of Europe* (Oxford, Oxford University Press, 2002)

Shapiro, M. and A. Stone Sweet, *On Law, Politics and Judicialization* (Oxford, Oxford University Press, 2002)

Simon, W., 'Legality, Bureaucracy and Class in the Welfare System' (1983) 92 *Yale Law Journal* 1198

Skolnick, J., *Justice Without Trial* (New York, Wiley, 1966)

Slotnick, E. and J. A. Segal, *Television News and the Supreme Court: All the News That's Fit to Air?* (Cambridge, Cambridge University Press, 1998)

Smith, J. L. and E. Tiller, 'The Strategy of Judging: Evidence from Administrative Law' (2002) 31 *Journal of Legal Studies* 61

'So What Have Our Judges Got Against Britain?', *Daily Mail*, 20 February 2003

Songer, D. R., J. A. Segal and C. M. Cameron, 'The Hierarchy of Justice: Testing a Principal–Agent Model of Supreme Court–Circuit Court Interactions' (1994) 38 *American Journal of Political Science* 673

Sorauf, F., 'Zorach v. Clauson: The Impact of a Supreme Court Decision' (1959) 53 *American Political Science Review* 777

Sossin, L., 'The Politics of Discretion: Toward a Critical Theory of Public Administration' (1992) 36 *Canadian Public Administration* 364

'Redistributing Democracy: Authority, Discretion and the Possibility of Engagement in the Welfare State' (1994) 26 *Ottawa Law Review* 1

Boundaries of Judicial Review (Toronto, Carswell, 1999)

'Regulating Virtue: A Purposive Approach to the Administration of Charities in Canada' in J. Phillips, B. Chapman and D. Stevens (eds.), *Charities: Between State and Market* (Kingston, Ont., McGill-Queen's Press, 2001)

'An Intimate Approach to Fairness, Impartiality and Reasonableness in Administrative Law' (2002) 28 *Queen's Law Journal* 809

'Discretion Unbound: Reconciling the Charter and Soft Law' (2002) 45 *Canadian Public Administration* 465

'Law and Intimacy in the Bureaucrat–Citizen Relationship' in N. des Rosiers (ed.), *No Person is an Island: Personal Relationships of Dependence and Independence* (Vancouver, University of British Columbia Press, 2002)

'Le juridique et l'intime dans le rapport entre fonctionnaires et citoyens' in N. des Rosiers (ed.), *Les rapports de dependance et d'interdependance* (Quebec City, Les Presses de l'Universite Laval, 2002)

'The Rule of Policy: *Baker* and the Impact of Judicial Review on Administrative Discretion' in D. Dyzehaus *et al.* (eds.), *The Unity of Public Law* (London, Hart, 2003)

Sossin, L. and C. Smith, 'Hard Choices and Soft Law: Ethical Codes, Policy Guidelines and the Role of the Courts in Regulating Government' (2003) 40 *Alberta Law Review* 867

St Amand, M. G., 'Note: Public Committee Against Torture v. The State of Israel: Landmark Human Rights Decision by the Israeli High Court of Justice or Status Quo Maintained?' (2000) 25 *North Carolina Journal of International and Commercial Regulation* 655

Sterett, S. M., *Creating Constitutionalism? The Politics of Legal Expertise and Administrative Law in England and Wales* (Ann Arbor, University of Michigan Press, 1997)

Stewart, R., 'The Reformation of American Administrative Law' (1975) 88 *Harvard Law Review* 1667

'Vermont Yankee and the Evolution of Administrative Procedure' (1978) 91 *Harvard Law Review* 1805

Stover, R. and D. Brown, 'Understanding Compliance and Noncompliance with the Law: The Contributions of Utility Theory' (1975) 56 *Social Science Quarterly* 363

Sunkin, M., 'Judicial Review's Liveability' (1989) *Legal Action* 10

'Withdrawing: A Problem in Judicial Review?' in P. Leyland and T. Woods (eds.), *Administrative Law Facing the Future: Old Constraints and New Horizons* (London, Blackstone Press, 1997)

Sunkin, M. and A. Le Sueur, 'Can Government Control Judicial Review' (1991) 44 *Current Legal Problems* 161

Sunkin, M. and K. Pick, 'The Changing Impact of Judicial Review: The Independent Review Service of the Social Fund' [2001] *Public Law* 753

Taggart, M. (ed.), *The Province of Administrative Law* (Oxford, Hart, 1997)

Tamanaha, B. Z., 'The Folly of the "Social Scientific" Concept of Legal Pluralism' (1993) 20 *Journal of Law and Society* 192

Teubner, G., 'Substantive and Reflexive Elements in Modern Law' (1983) 17 *Law and Society Review* 239

  Enterprise Corporatism: New Industrial Policy and the 'Essence' of the Legal System (Florence, European University Institute, 1987)

  'Juridification: Concepts, Aspects, Limits, Solutions' in G. Teubner (ed.), *Juridification of Social Spheres: A Comparative Analysis in the Areas of Labor, Corporate, Antitrust and Social Welfare Law* (Berlin, de Gruyter, 1987)

  Law as an Autopoietic System (Oxford, Blackwell Publishers, 1993)

Teubner, G., A. Bankowska, R. Adler and Z. Bankowski, *Law as an Autopoietic System* (Oxford, Blackwell, 1993)

Thompson, E. P., *Whigs and Hunters* (New York, Pantheon, 1977)

Tribe, L. H., *American Constitutional Law* (3rd edn, New York, Foundation Press, 2000)

Tushnet, M., *Taking the Constitution Away from the Courts* (Princeton, Princeton University Press, 1999)

  'Scepticism about Judicial Review: A Perspective from the United States' in T. Campbell, K. D. Ewing and A. Tomkins (eds.), *Sceptical Essays on Human Rights* (Oxford, Oxford University Press, 2001)

Vining, J., *The Authoritative and the Authoritarian* (Chicago, University of Chicago, 1986)

Von Hirsch, A., A. Ashworth and M. Wasik, *Fundamentals of Sentencing Theory: Essays in Honour of Andrew Von Hirsch* (Oxford, Clarendon Press, 1998)

Wade, H. W. R. and C. F. Forsyth, *Administrative Law* (8th edn, Oxford, Oxford University Press, 2000)

Wald, M. S., R. Ayers, R. Hess, M. Schanz and C. Whitebread, 'Interrogations in New Haven: The Impact of *Miranda*' (1967) 76 *Yale Law Journal* 1519

Walker, S. and L. Fridel, 'The Forces of Change in Police Policy: The Impact of *Tennessee v. Garner* on Deadly Force Policy' (1993) 11 *American Journal of Police* 97

Wasby, S. L., *The Impact of the United States Supreme Court: Some Perspectives* (Homewood, IL, Dorsey Press, 1970)

  'Toward Impact Theory: An Inventory of Hypotheses' in T. L. Becker and M. M. Feeley (eds.), *The Impact of Supreme Court Decisions: Empirical Studies* (2nd edn, New York, Oxford University Press, 1973)

Small Town Police and the Supreme Court: Hearing the Word (Lexington, MA, D. C. Heath, 1976)

Waterman, R. W. and A. Rouse, 'The Determinants of the Perceptions of Political Control of the Bureaucracy and Venues of Influence' (1999) 9 *Journal of Public Administration Research and Theory* 527

Way, F. H., Jr, 'Survey Research on Judicial Decisions: The Prayer and Bible Reading Cases' (1968) 21 *Western Political Quarterly* 189

Weber, M., *The Theory of Social and Economic Organization* (New York, Free Press, 1947)

Wexler D. B. and B. W. Winick (eds.), *Law as a Therapeutic Key: Developments in Therapeutic Jurisprudence* (Durham, NC, Carolina Academic Press, 1996)

Zamir, I., 'Rule of Law and the Control of Terrorism' (1998) 8 *Tel Aviv University Studies in Law* 81

Zuckerman, A., 'Coercion and the Individual Ascertainment of the Truth' (1989) 23 *Israeli Law Review* 357

Zysblat, A., 'Protecting Fundamental Human Rights in Israel without a Written Constitution' in I. Zamir and A. Zysblat (eds.), *Public Law in Israel* (Oxford, Oxford University Press, 1996)

INDEX

Coventry University